THE WORLD SPORT PSYCHOLOGY SOURCEBOOK

Second Edition

John H. Salmela, PhD
University of Ottawa

Human Kinetics Books
Champaign, Illinois

Library of Congress Cataloging-in-Publication Data

Salmela, John H.
    The world sport psychology sourcebook / by John H. Salmela. -- 2nd
ed.
        p.   cm.
    Includes bibliography and index.
    ISBN 0-87322-315-2 (pbk.)
    1. Sports--Psychological aspects.   2. Sports--Psychological
aspects--Directories.   I. Title.
    GV706.4.S25 1991   71456
    796'.01--dc20

90-49043
CIP

ISBN: 0-87322-315-2

This book is endorsed by the International Society of Sport Psychology.

Development Editor: Kathy Kane
Managing Editors: John Robert King and Julia Anderson
Assistant Editor: Elizabeth Bridgett
Copyeditor: Laurie McGee
Proofreader: Karin Leszczynski

Typesetter: Kathy Fuoss, Julie Overholt, Sandra Meier, Angie Snyder
Text Design: Keith Blomberg
Text Layout: Tara Welsch, Denise Lowry, Denise Peters
Cover Design: Jack Davis
Printer: Versa Press

Printed in the United States of America

10 9 8 7 6 5 4 3 2 1

Human Kinetics Books
A Division of Human Kinetics Publishers, Inc.
Box 5076, Champaign, IL 61825-5076
1-800-747-4457

Canada Office:
Human Kinetics Publishers, Inc.
P.O. Box 2503, Windsor, ON N8Y 4S2
1-800-465-7301 (in Canada only)

UK Office:
Human Kinetics Publishers (UK) Ltd.
P.O. Box 18
Rawdon, Leeds LS19 6TG
England
(0532) 504211

Contents

Preface

The World Sport Psychology Sourcebook has been written for sport psychologists, defined as the term is used internationally—namely, professionals in motor behavior (motor learning, motor performance, motor development, and motor control); sport social and educational psychologists, researchers, practitioners, counselors; and others interested in developmental, experimental, and social psychological approaches to sport.

The purpose of this work is to help these individuals and other professionals gain a greater understanding of the international status of sport psychology and to encourage readers to exchange ideas, to network, and to improve the research, clinical, and educational practices of the field.

This new edition of The World Sport Psychology Sourcebook is significantly different from the 1981 edition in a number of ways. The first edition came about because in 1978 Miroslav Vanek, then president of the International Society of Sport Psychology, wanted to know how "sport psychologists" were academically prepared —and he charged me with the task of finding out.

I undertook a worldwide survey of the academic and professional backgrounds of the people active in the field. The responses formed the backbone of the first edition and were published as its first part. This survey has not been updated since 1981, and that section does not appear in the new edition. But some of the same content of that international overview still appears in each of the national contributions.

The process for creating Part I, "International Programs in Sport Psychology," also changed markedly between editions. In 1981 I was a youngish, energetic professor, eager to travel by car to visit institutions, interview hundreds of individuals, and study programs at night as I camped in a tent. All the information in Part I of the first edition resulted from my impressions and interpretations of this firsthand data.

By the time of the preparation of the second edition, I was a fortyish professor not so keen anymore on all those car miles and even less on roughing it in a tent. So I requested the collaboration of colleagues in various countries to help me with the update, which then allowed me to write more accurately about changes in each national program. Though considerably more democratic, this process was logistically more vexing.

The final product reflects a much more balanced global viewpoint. New countries were added, with the most significant increase being from the Middle East, Africa, Asia, and, to a lesser extent, South America. In some cases, particularly when a correspondent could not be coerced to write, information was updated only through the use of secondary sources such as national reports. Contributing colleagues, whose efforts are highly appreciated, are named in the national chapters.

Another significant addition is the insight into the dramatic changes relative to sport psychology that have occurred in Eastern Europe with the advent of perestroika and the democratization of the former Soviet bloc countries. Collaborators from that region have provided new information and fresh perspectives on the developments reforming their countries.

Part II of the new edition, "International Figures in Sport Psychology," was also approached completely differently. The new Who's Who lists all those who completed surveys for the first edition, but adds sport psychologists who found the entry form in various journals or newsletters or at academic and professional meetings. This resulted in expanding the original list from 856 to over 1600 entries. In addition, Human Kinetics contacted everyone on the list just before publication allowing each to update his or her information. The number of countries represented has grown from 39 to 61, reflecting the important gains made in the field of sport psychology.

The present edition has made important advances in quantity and quality. The increased number of sport psychology specialists offers optimism about the seriousness of this burgeoning field. And the fact that greater intellects than my own contributed to the second edition makes it more faceted and more accurate than the first.

The changes in The World Sport Psychology Sourcebook please me. I was fortunate to be able to undertake this project while the field was still small enough to be described comprehensively, and I have been able to watch it evolve into a serious academic and professional concern.

Acknowledgments

Many people helped prepare this second edition of the *Sourcebook*. In many ways this edition was more difficult to prepare than the first because the responsibility was spread among more people. I especially appreciate the efforts of the collaborators for each national chapter because they had to express their own unbiased perceptions of sport psychology in their country while knowing that I would be writing the final version of each chapter. The final product is much improved over the first edition.

I would also like to acknowledge the support of Dr. François Péronnet, director of the physical education department at the Université de Montréal for providing me with support and freedom for the administration, mailing, and compilation required for the Who's Who section. Pierre Beauchamp and his able secretaries Rachel Elmoznino, Chantal Lalande, Lucie Senneville, Ginette Handfield, and Francine Major also provided top-quality word processing and other finicky things that I required over the last four years. The constant computer support of Gérard Ouellet of our laboratory is also very much appreciated. I must also mention the friendship and support that Dr. Bruce Abernethy and Dr. Ian Jobling and his staff gave me on my sabbatical stay at the University of Queensland in Australia. Rainer Martens, developmental editors Kathy Kane, Rob King, and Julia Anderson, and acquisitions editor Rick Frey of Human Kinetics were also a great source of strength and support.

Finally, I would like to give my heartfelt thanks and love to my wife Storm and the recently arrived Maxim Henry for their belief in what I think is a worthy project. This book is dedicated to them.

Part I

INTERNATIONAL PROGRAMS IN SPORT PSYCHOLOGY

Chapter 1

WORLD SPORT PSYCHOLOGY PROFILES

When I wrote the first edition of this book, I found it somewhat ironic and amusing to attempt to describe and explain the evolution of the discipline of sport psychology, a relatively new academic and professional area, when the parent field (or rather one of the parents), psychology, was also in a state of disarray.

At the time, I cited Cohen's (1957) book in humanistic psychology, which described psychology as "the most undisciplined of all disciplines, the nursery and romping ground for every extravaganza, a Tower of Babel for every known and unknown tongue, a mint for counterfeit and spurious coins, a market place for every peddler of far-fetched and unlikely theories" (p. 1). In a more serious vein, Melzack (1989) recently stated that psychology is still in a state of crisis: "We are no closer now to understanding the most fundamental problems in psychology than we were when psychology became a science a hundred years ago" (p. 1). Melzack goes on to say that Descartes's 17th-century concept of the "mind," Locke's and Kant's 17th- and 18th-century ideas on "reality," and William James's 19th-century view of cognition have been only minimally improved upon by modern psychological theory. Rather than new theoretical insights, we now have myriad isolated facts accruing daily in an increasing number of journals.

Melzack's lament brings to mind Koch's (1969) earlier reflections on the difficulty of maintaining coherence in the area of psychology: "Psychology was stipulated into life. At the time of its inception, psychology was unique in the extent to which its institutionalization preceded its content, and its methods preceded its problems" (p. 64). The Victorian rationalism that was the source of psychology's academic raison d'être appeared to leave the theoretical constructs in the 19th century while psychology's development as a profession moved constantly and confidently into the 20th century, although not without encountering a number of pitfalls. What then is the evolutionary status of the academic and professional aspects of sport psychology, an equally "undisciplined subdiscipline" (Martens, 1974), whose roots can be traced back only 25 years? As was the case in psychology, sport psychology was also stipulated into existence in many areas of the world—that is, its professional developments often preceded its academic ones. The actual professional profile of sport psychology is quite vibrant, considering its short history.

This chapter focuses on the evolution of sport psychology around the world, especially over the last 10 years. I will borrow from Wilensky's (1964) conceptual model of the evolution of various work groups as a framework for the demographic profiles of the professional and academic activities in sport psychology.

A Chronological Life History of Work Groups

Wilensky outlines five steps through which any work group must sequentially pass in evolving from an occupation to a profession. First, the group must demonstrate a substantial number of full-time workers in an activity that needs doing. Second, a training school must be established to prepare these people academically and professionally. Next, a professional association must be created that directs the activity of the group. Then the group must engage in political agitation to secure its place among the other professions. Finally, the group must develop and live by a functional code of ethics.

How does the field of sport psychology in the 1990s measure up professionally to Wilensky's model?

Substantial Full-Time Activity in Sport Psychology. Three critical features must be demonstrated to successfully realize the initial phase of the life history of work groups: the involvement of a "substantial number of people," the evolution of this involvement to "full-time status," and the achievement of "demonstrated importance" of the activity. Because they are measurable, it is somewhat easier to make a case for numbers and level of involvement than for importance.

Substantial Sport Psychology Activity. Sport psychology programs exist in every highly industrialized country of the world. In fact, the earliest programs of study can be traced to the 1920s to Coleman Griffith in the United States, A.T. Puni in the Soviet Union, and M. Matsui in Japan. In 1981, there were more than 800 entries in the *Who's Who of Sport Psychology* from an estimated population of 1,320 individuals active in the field in 39 countries (Salmela, 1981). At the time of the 1981 survey, it was believed that the 1970s was sport psychology's most rapid period of growth, with the initial impulse being the inaugural meeeting of the International Society of Sport Psychology (ISSP) in Rome in 1965.

But less than 10 years later (in 1990), we can see that the number of Who's Who entries has more than doubled, while the countries claiming some form of sport psychology have increased from 39 to 61. By regrouping these countries along convenient geopolitical lines we can see a dramatic 48.8% worldwide increase since 1981 in the number of sport psychologists, as well as a 56.4% increase in the number of countries having new levels of activity (see Table 1.1).

The greatest number of individuals active in sport psychology live in North America (43.1%), with the second-largest group in Europe (21.4%). Latin America,

Table 1.1 Demographic Analysis of Continental and Regional Breakdown of Individuals/Countries Active in Sport Psychology in 1981 and 1989

Continent region	Number of individuals/ countries		% increase of individuals/ countries
	1981	1989	
Africa and Middle East	22/5	51/11	132/120
Asia	27/3	838/10	207/233
Oceania	48/2	64/2	33/0
Europe			
Eastern Europe	136/8	172/8	22/0
Western Europe	189/12	440/16	133/33
Scandinavia	30/4	53/4	77/0
Americas			
Latin America	6/3	84/8	1580/167
North America	400/2	116/2	79/0
Totals	858/39	1663/61	

Asia, and Africa have shown the fastest rates of growth in terms of the number of newly active individuals as well as the quantity of emerging national programs. We can estimate the total number of individuals active in some capacity worldwide by multiplying the number of Who's Who entries by 1.6, as was done in 1981, bringing the population of individuals active in sport psychology to around 2,700.

To put this figure into perspective, consider that the 1988 American Psychological Association (APA) Membership Register (APA, 1988) reported a total of 66,996 registered psychologists, mainly from the United States and Canada. The total sport psychology population seems in comparison only a small fraction of the North American psychologist population. However, closer inspection of APA divisional membership statistics reveals that the greatest numbers of APA specialists are in general psychology (6,324), clinical psychology (5,765), and independent practice (5,413). Thus the emerging field of sport psychology is at least in the same order of magnitude as these major parent disciplines. In fact, the newest APA division—47, "exercise and sport psychology"—reported 458 members, similar to the numbers for consumer psychology (449), population and environment psychology (426), and the psychology for the study of ethnic minority issues (453). From another perspective, these measures of sport psychology define it as a fairly substantial sport science if measured by the yardstick of the almost 12,000 members of the American College of Sports Medicine, which is made up mainly of exercise physiologists and sports medicine physicians (45%). In terms of the quantity of active individuals,

sport psychology appears to be a relatively small, yet still emerging area of sport science.

Full-Time Sport Psychology Activity. For the field of sport psychology to evolve into a respected academic and professional field of concern, it must go beyond merely demonstrating the involvement of sufficient numbers of individuals. These individuals must also be engaged in full-time activity, covering the fundamental tasks of teaching, conducting research, and counseling.

In 1981 I showed that sport psychologists from all the industrialized countries divided their time between undergraduate and graduate teaching, planning and doing research, writing and publishing, intervention, consultation, and administration. The percentage of time spent on each area depended on the geopolitical nature of the country concerned, its level of industrialization, and the specific background of the researcher in question.

To assume that most existing professionals in the industrialized world are involved with sport psychology on a full-time basis would be erroneous. Data from the 1981 world sport psychology survey, which was the basis for the first edition, indicate that Eastern Europe has the highest number of full-time professionals; 78% of individuals considered sport psychology their primary means of employment. Only 56% of North Americans considered sport psychology their main vocation, and in Western Europe the percentage of full-time academics fell to 36%.

It appears relatively clear that though we might like to see much higher levels of professional involvement applied to sport psychology, this has not yet happened. If levels of professional involvement remain modest within the industrialized world, how can we expect more in developing countries?

In North America, Eastern Europe, and Oceania there are substantial numbers of positions at major educational or sport institutions. Full-time sport psychology specialists can be found in 83% and 75% of the countries in Western Europe and Scandinavia, respectively. This percentage falls as we consider Africa and the Middle East (64%), Asia (50%), and Latin America (38%). Until full-time positions are created in these developing countries, sport psychology will be vulnerable to dilettantism and will remain of only secondary interest to people in medicine, coaching, or general psychology who are mildly interested in the subject but who have not yet committed themselves to sport psychology as a profession.

The Necessity of Sport Psychology. At the 1965 ISSP Congress in Rome, sport psychology became a discipline with a professional society well before textbooks, institutionalized positions, and training programs were created. This organizational impetus was provided by Ferruccio Antonelli, the "father of international sport psychology" (Cei & Salmela, 1988). The Congress showed belief in sport psychology that propelled the discipline from the late 1960s all the way to the present. In Europe and

North America in the 1970s, many programs, publications, and graduate students became the first generation of this new discipline. The boom in sport psychology came about partly because university physical education training institutions began to recognize that sport science knowledge can provide valuable support to sport practice as well as a sound academic field of study within institutes of higher learning. In addition, sport associations recognized that training procedures could be better rationalized using the latest knowledge from exercise physiology, biomechanics, sport psychology, and sports medicine.

Perhaps because sport psychology was the newest kid on the block, the technical directors of Canadian sport federations reported in 1979 that sport psychology was the sport science that could best enhance sport practice (Gowan, Botterill, & Blimkie, 1979). More recently, Partington and Orlick (1986) reported that the psychological readiness of Canadian Olympians at the Los Angeles Games was the only factor that predicted final rankings, whereas physical and technical readiness appeared unrelated to performance at this level. It is significant that the Canadian governmental body, Sport Canada, has funded more than 20 sport psychology consultants accompanying national sport teams to world championship and Olympic games in 1984. At the 1988 Seoul Olympics, a greater number of industrialized countries sent sport psychology consultants, including Canada, the United States, Japan, Australia, and Sweden, as did developing nations such as Nigeria, Colombia, and Algeria.

Such liberalized use of sport psychology is only amplified when the lot of developing nations that are not moving in this direction is considered. Ba (1982) of Senegal wrote about the lack of a sufficient ''scientific and technological environment'' that could potentially widen the gap in sport between developing nations and industrialized countries that use sport science and sport psychology in training and competition.

Establishment of a Training School.   Phase 2 of the professionalization process in the sport sciences is establishing appropriate institutions that can house sport psychology research activities and, perhaps more importantly, educate the next generation of students, researchers, and scholars. If we in sport psychology can learn one thing from the North American situation, it is that each succeeding generation becomes increasingly more skilled, more sophisticated, and more populous than its predecessors.

From what I have observed in a number of industrialized countries, a great amount can be accomplished in sport psychology with quite limited physical resources and technology. Basic requirements are a small, specialized library; a microcomputer; and a photocopy machine. More essential than fancy equipment are trained, scientifically competent leaders and supporting personnel to direct eager graduate students. To borrow from computer terminology, appropriate training schools are not a function of hardware (buildings and equipment) but rather of software (personnel, planning, and training).

A decade ago, a number of industrialized countries dealt with similar academic training decisions that some developing nations now face. In most cases, the countries sent candidates to study abroad and return with the most appropriate elements for their own country. For example, in the late 1960s, many Canadians went south for postgraduate study in the United States and returned to establish graduate programs back home. These programs then welcomed graduate students from the United Kingdom, Australia, and Asia who did the same. Eastern Europeans and some developing nations in Asia and Africa sent students to the Soviet Union; likewise they returned home and created similar programs.

The universal imposition of university status to all programs of physical education in the Western European countries that are part of the European Common Market (EEC) will be of primary importance in the 1990s. Beginning in 1992, all analogous institutions of physical education and sport science must provide for transfer students. This ensures that physical education will become a university program in all EEC countries. The spin-off will be that sport psychology will be an institutionalized subject in post-secondary education. This will provide a short cut to academic responsibility for this discipline in those countries where traditional structures in the university have been slow to adjust to those programs.

Selecting the most appropriate training ground is often tied to a country's privileged political affiliations with other industrialized nations. The curricula of North America and Western and Eastern Europe differ markedly in available technology, selected subject matter skills taught, and methods advanced in the field of sport psychology. For this reason, Sachs and Burke (1989) have collated a directory of graduate programs, primarily in North America. This directory lists programs, resource personnel, specialized equipment, potential funding, and possibilities for supervised internships in North America and abroad.

Because these training institutions not only transmit knowledge to undergraduate students but also create a knowledge base through the dissertation work of their graduate students, an increasingly large quantity of data has been generated over the last 2 decades. This has resulted in a proliferation of first multidisciplinary and then sport psychology–specific journals at both the international and national levels.

In 1970 the *International Journal of Sport Psychology*, published and edited by Ferruccio Antonelli in Rome, was the only available publication vehicle for sport psychology research in the world. The *Journal of Sport Behavior* was then published in 1978, followed by the *Journal of Sport and Exercise Psychology* in 1979, both in the United States. Around the world, *Sportpsychologie* began publication in Germany in 1987, in 1984 *Movimento* was created as a specialized Italian review, and the *Japanese Journal of Sport Psychology* goes back to 1974. In 1986 and 1989, even further specialization occurred in the field with the publication in North America of two applied sport psychology journals, respectively, *The Sport Psychologist* and the *Journal of Applied Sport Psychology*.

According to Pavalko (1972), because of sport psychology's abstract and esoteric knowledge base, its relevance to basic social values, and the specialized nature of its lengthy academic preparation, it now has all the trappings of what could be termed a "profession in progress," along with nursing, optometry, and pharmacy, but below "established professions" such as medicine, law, and engineering. However, in the major industrialized countries, sport psychology would be considered higher on the professionalization scale than so-called "new professions" (city management, engineering) or "doubtful professions" (funeral direction, advertising).

The analysis of the present world data bank on the availability of training institutions that have curricula within the specialized field of sport psychology and that provide postgraduate training requiring a research project again points out the global disparity in the availability of academic preparation opportunities.

In North America, Oceania, and Eastern Europe there are a large number of postgraduate opportunities at a number of centers within each country. Sachs and Burke (1989) reported that the United States has 68 centers for postgraduate study whereas Canada has 13 and Australia 7. Denmark is the only Scandinavian country with no postgraduate possibilities, and only 50% of Western European centers have this potential. The percentages decline in the other geographic spheres with only a few postgraduate programs in Africa and the Middle East (Egypt, Nigeria), Asia (China, India, Japan), and South America (Brazil), even though these areas have extremely large population bases.

Foundation of Professional Associations. The third phase marking the professional advancement of a work group is the creation of a professional association. It is somewhat ironic that the ISSP was formed well before the buildup of a sufficient number of people involved in sport psychology and the creation of specialized training schools. The reversal of Wilensky's chronology, however, was fortuitous in this case because it resulted directly in stimulating the creation of continental societies in Europe [Fédération Européan de Psychologie du Sport et Activité Corporelle (FEPSAC)] and North America [North American Society for the Psychology of Sport and Physical Activity (NASPSPA)]. In addition, as a result of this Rome meeting a number of national societies were founded whose membership numbers have been escalating in recent years to the point that 59% of the surveyed countries now have national societies and 48% can claim the existence of training institutions. This reversal of Wilensky's orderly progress of a profession is not in itself undesirable if the creation of an association results in the mobilization of a population, the stimulation of specific disciplinary interest, and the emergence of training schools.

The most impressive professional developments have occurred in certain countries that have evolved rapidly as the result of dynamic leadership. For example, the Sport Psychology Association of Nigeria (SPAN) has run five congresses in the last 4 years and has made radical inroads into the country's sport structure. In a similar manner, the Japanese Society of Sport Psychology (JSSP) has held annual research meetings since 1972 and has run practical workshops for top athletes. Arbeitsgemeinschaft für Sportpsychologie in der Bundesrepublik Deutschland (ASP) is the dynamic force in German sport

psychology behind much of the interaction and publication coming out of that country, whereas NASPSPA in North America and Societé Canadienne d'Apprentissage Psychomoteur et Psychologie du Sport (SCAPPS) in Canada have more than 20 years of activity. All of the groups are formally recognized by their governments, the sport federations, and the psychological profession as prime academic players in their respective countries. Most recently, at the seventh ISSP Congress held in Singapore in 1989, the Asiatic South Pacific Association of Sport Psychology (ASPASP) was created. This body will act as a continental association for this area of the world much as FEPSAC does for Europe and NASPSPA for North America.

A number of interesting developments have recently occurred that have somewhat modified the global face of sport psychology. The first has been the creation of sport-related sections within existing psychological societies to complement societies dedicated to sport psychology. This phenomenon has existed for a number of years in Czechoslovakia, the German Democratic Republic, and China. In 1986, a special division (47) on exercise and sport psychology was created in the APA as well as in the Canadian Psychological Association (CPA). This development has introduced the area of sport psychology to a new population of individuals whose primary interest is not sport as such, but psychology as applied to physical activity.

The second development of note was the creation of applied sport psychology societies, in North America [Association for the Advancement of Applied Sport Psychology (AAASP)] and in Australia [Australian Applied Sport Psychology Association (AASPA)], that were separate from those dedicated to purely academic pursuits. Though the AAASP boasts more than 500 members as well as its own newsletter and journal, the Australian association is much more modest in scope and restrictive in its membership. Both, however, are concerned mainly with issues related to professional practice rather than the generation of knowledge as such, and in their own way they provide elements of a solution to the next step in Wilensky's model.

Engagement in Political Agitation. Harrison and Feltz (1980) documented examples of how active lobbying had to occur between the field of psychology and the medical profession for psychology to win the legal right to defend its territorial domain. The medical profession once claimed that clinical services such as counseling and psychotherapy should exist only within its own jurisdiction. The first licensing laws for psychology in the United States were only established in 1945. Since then, similar struggles for territorial rights have been carried on with other specialty areas such as guidance, social psychology, and rehabilitation.

In both Europe and North America, various forms of lobbying and political agitation have been necessary to enable the various sport sciences to evolve into their present professional status. For example, it was necessary for exercise physiology practitioners to justify the need to perform certain professional acts, such as exercise stress testing, against protests from the medical profession. The same occurred in psychology regarding counseling and relaxation training. In certain European countries, such as France, these discussions are still controversial, whereas in North America they have been settled for a number of years.

Based on what has occurred elsewhere in the world, it is likely that some sort of political lobbying must take place with at least two different professional groups. The first discussions would probably occur with sport-related bodies, such as the various Olympic committees or the sport federations. These organizations would have to be convinced that sport psychology is not an academic frill but is central to coherent progress in sport. Compromises would have to be made, because implementing sport psychology would necessarily incur some costs that would have to come from existing budgets. All of those negotiations are normal and expected.

It is hoped that the mistakes of some industrialized countries are not repeated in the developing nations. In fact, a unique situation requiring no agitation occurred in Nigeria, where the Sports Council created a permanent sport psychologist position on the Olympic committee. At present countries such as the United States, Canada, Australia, Sweden, and Germany have had a longer history of such involvement.

The second area that might require some form of political lobbying occurs outside of sport-related groups—discussions between sport psychology and its parent discipline, psychology. For example, during the early years of sport psychology in North America, there was some discussion as to whether physical education graduate students could take courses in the psychology department. Now it is common for undergraduates and graduate students to take, and to do well in, extra-departmental courses. In fact, some departments have welcomed these students because they can offer new applications of their field to sport, and at times further insights into mainstream psychological theory. Although academic mobility is not as common in Europe and elsewhere as it is in North America, this opportunity for academic cross-fertilization is, in my opinion, the desired state.

One difficult and contentious issue for sport psychology has been the definition of its field of application in relation to the acquired territory of psychology. The Canadian group SCAPPS has worked professionally in collaboration with Canada's national sport and psychology associations to create a three-tiered registry for sport behavioral professionals. In this system, national licensing laws stipulate that only clinically trained psychologists can be called sport psychologists. This provision of leveled areas of intervention, along with the suggestion of academic and professional experiences that allow an individual to upgrade his or her professional status, has kept territorial bickering to a minimum by providing all the players with a forum for dialogue. The applied American-based group AAASP has decided to opt for the title of "Consultant, Association for the Advancement of Applied Sport Psychology," and by doing so hopes to avoid any direct confrontation with state licensing boards. Groups in Australia and Great Britain have suggested the attainment of dual qualifications in both the sport sciences and psychology, thus making the process somewhat more cumbersome. As the levels of interaction between sport psychology and psychology increase, a greater streamlining of training programs appears to be emerging, along with more cross-disciplinary cooperation and fewer adversarial exchanges at the professional level.

Development of a Code of Ethics. According to Pavalko (1972), the significant feature that distinguishes an occupation from a profession is the degree to which the work group adheres to the ideal of public service rather than self-interest. This is made explicit in the group's code of ethics. The code of ethics must be carefully designed so that the claims of public interest and altruistic service are indeed justified. Again Pavalko points out that these codes do not control and shape the group's behavior through threat or fear of punishment. They are, rather, an explicit statement of the group's goals and expectations that provide the individual members with a measuring stick for their own behavior. The modification of an individual's own behavior to fit the code is compatible within the principle of individual autonomy.

In 1984 the Canadian sport psychology group published, through Sport Canada, ethical guidelines that outlined the types of services, service contracts, and expectancies a sport consumer should expect from a sport psychologist or sport consultant (SCAPPS, 1984). In the United States, Great Britain, and Australia, the sport psychology groups have simply adopted the ethical codes of the psychological association of their respective countries. Without being required to do so, a number of sport psychology associations have completed Wilensky's final step toward professionalization. It would be expected that this degree of professional sophistication will continue in other countries over the next decade.

Concluding Remarks

In 1981 it appeared that the field of sport psychology was in full bloom, and so it was. Yet since that time still further advances, reflecting the maturity of the field, have been signaled from all over the world. Events that then occurred for the first time in North America and Europe are now beginning to occur in parts of Asia, Africa, and South America. Pavalko's road map, however, has already been drawn and followed, because the field of sport psychology has now nearly completed its first cycle of full professional development.

Sport psychology, one of the last sport sciences to appear in the industrialized nations, appears to be a pioneering discipline among those that are still developing. Within the societies, preliminary research questions about sport may be best answered using knowledge and methodologies from the humanities rather than the hardware of the biological or medical sciences. This process, no matter what direction the discipline takes in the future, will be interesting for all to observe. The professional evolution of the field of sport psychology, as was the case with mainstream psychology, will evolve at a faster pace than the academic state of the field. The fundamental issues of science that were raised by Melzack (1989) in the parent field of psychology have also been raised by Martens (1974) in the field of sport psychology. The evolution of the profession continues even if the academic side falters. A Russian proverb sums it up: "When dancing with a bear and the music stops, keep on dancing."

References

American Psychological Association. (1988). *APA membership register*. Washington, DC: American Psychological Association.

Ba, A.L. (1982). Why a new strategy for the development of sport in Africa? *Review of the International Council of Sport Science and Physical Education, 1*, 8-13.

Cei, A., & Salmela, J.H. (1988). Ferruccio Antonelli: The father of international sport psychology. *The Sport Psychologist, 2*, 351-356.

Cohen, J. (1957). *Humanistic psychology*. London: Unwin and Allen.

Gowan, G.R., Botterill, C.B., & Blimkie, C.J.R. (1979). Bridging the gap between sport science and sport practice. In P. Klavora & J.V. Daniel (Eds.), *Coach, athlete and the sport psychologist*. Toronto: University of Toronto.

Harrison, R.P., & Feltz, D.L. (1980). The professionalization of sport psychology: Legal considerations. In C.H. Nadeau, W.R. Halliwell, K. Newell, & G.C. Roberts (Eds.), *Psychology of motor behavior and sport—1979*. Champaign, IL: Human Kinetics.

Koch, S. (1969, September). Psychology cannot be a coherent science. *Psychology Today*, pp. 14, 64-68.

Martens, R. (1974). *Psychological kinesiology: An undisciplined subdiscipline*. Paper presented at the North American Society of Psychology of Sport and Physical Activity 1974 Annual Conference, Anaheim, CA.

Melzack, R. (1989). Phantom limbs, the self and the brain. *Canadian Psychology, 30*, 1-16.

Partington, J.T., & Orlick, T. (1986). *Documenting athlete readiness for the 1984 Olympics and evaluating sport consulting. Final report* (Government report for Sport Canada). Ottawa: Coaching Association of Canada.

Pavalko, R.M. (1972). *Sociology of professions and occupations*. Isthasca, IL: F.E. Peacock.

Sachs, M.L., & Burke, K.L. (1989). *Directory of graduate programs in applied sport psychology* (2nd ed.). Timonium, MD: Association for the Advancement of Applied Sport Psychology.

Salmela, J.H. (1981). *The world sport psychology sourcebook*. Ithaca, NY: Mouvement.

Societé Canadienne d'Apprentissage Psychomoteur et Psychologie du Sport (1984). *Sport and psychology: Ethics and practice*. Ottawa: Coaching Association of Canada.

Wilensky, H.L. (1964). The professionalization of everyone? *American Journal of Sociology, 10*, 137-158.

Chapter 2

OCEANIA
Australia

in collaboration with

Bruce Abernethy
University of Queensland

Jeffrey Bond
Australian Institute of Sport

Denis J. Glencross
Curtin University of Technology

J. Robert Grove
University of Western Australia

Australian Sport Psychology Résumé

Sport psychology in Australia is now well established as an integral part of most programs in human movement studies. Traditionally, the main emphasis has been on research in the area of skill acquisition or motor control, but recently there has been increasing interest in areas such as cognition, attention, expert-novice differences, and coaching behaviors. Applied sport psychology is practiced throughout the country at the institutes of sport and in private practice. Though both research and applied sport psychology are on the upswing, there appears to be a need for better communication and cooperation between these two components.

Estimated Number of Sport Psychologists. 120

Prominent Institutions. Australian Institute of Sport, Canberra College of Advanced Education, Curtin University of Technology, Footscray Institute of Technology, University of Queensland, University of Western Australia, University of Wollongong

Orientation. Skill acquisition and applied sport psychology

Privileged Topics. Motor processes, applied sport psychology

Publication Vehicles. *Australian Journal of Science and Medicine in Sport, Sports Coach, Excel*

Societies. Australian Applied Sport Psychology Association; Special Interest Group of Australian Council of Health, Physical Education and Recreation (ACHPER); Australasian Society for Motor Control; Australian Psychological Society Sport Psychology Network

During its golden era of the 1950s and 1960s Australia, along with Finland, was one of the finest sporting nations in the world, based on the percentage of the population that participated in sports. British-based traditions of club sport coupled with favorable weather provided an effective base for sport excellence. Other countries have surpassed Australia's record in recent years, however. Australian sporting standards now appear to be falling short of international standards set by the likes of the Eastern Europeans. However, a visitor cannot fail to see, hear, and breathe the sport climate while in Australia. Journalist Keith Dunstan writes in a cynical vein: "Sport is the ultimate Australian super-religion, the one thing every Australian believes in passionately. Sport is wholesome. It can do no wrong. It builds stronger Australian men and women, and, best of all, is spreads the fame of Australians overseas. It helps to unify Australia as a nation" (Dunstan, 1973, p. 1).

In Australia's short history, sport has played an important role, mainly as a form of diversion from mainstream work activities. With the increased interest in professional sport, mass sport participation has turned to mass sport entertainment. Sport studies have become an integral part of the programs in universities and colleges of advanced education (CAEs). Sport psychologists have been appointed to state and national institutes of sport, and the locus of sport administration is being coordinated by state and nationally supported administrative agencies.

Training in Sport Psychology

Many CAEs include sport psychology as a topic within human movement, sport science, or physical education programs. It is possible to study up until the doctoral level at four Australian universities and more recently at the CAEs.

Australia's educational system was influenced during its earliest years by the British, who brought with them their traditional values in education and sport. These forces are still evident in the structure of the university system due to the large-scale importation of British citizens to fill professorial and management positions. A second influence in the Australian sport psychology picture came from North America. A large number of now-influential individuals studied in the United States and Canada and returned to set up similar programs.

Before World War II, the only available training in physical education was a 2-year diploma course at the University of Melbourne. After the war, five universities established programs to develop the national fitness level and included sections in their curricula on skill acquisition. With the return of new Ph.D.s from North America in the late 60s and early 70s sport science and sport psychology began to take on a look of academic respectability. The programs at the universities of Queensland, Western Australia, and, more recently, Wollongong were given degree status within the academic area of human movement studies. These programs were unique compared to the British-based curricula because they did not lead to a teaching degree for physical education. These science-based programs exist also in CAEs such as Footscray, Ballarat, and the Phillip Institute of Technology. The program at Footscray has a professional staff of 32, more than 500 specialist students, and facilities that exceed those of many universities.

Students take an additional year for a teaching diploma in some cases, whereas an integrated 4-year degree existed at Queensland. After 1989, the Queensland degrees moved to the science faculty, with a 3-year bachelor of science and a 4-year bachelor of applied science program. At all these universities is the possibility of graduate work at the master's and doctoral levels in sport science generally, and in sport psychology specifically.

Students who graduate with a passing or honors degree from a sport sciences program can obtain a graduate degree. The absence or presence of an honors degree determines the length of an individual's master's program. Master's degrees typically involve 2 years of full-time study. The first year is considered a ''master's preliminary'' and consists almost entirely of course work. The second year is designated as the ''degree year'' and may involve course work or thesis research, depending on which track the student has selected and institutional offerings. Good students with an undergraduate major in human movement studies or physical education are usually admitted directly into the preliminary year, but those with poor undergraduate marks or majors in other areas must augment their course work. It is rare for a student with only a degree in psychology to be admitted without some human movement science course work.

A student with an honors degree in human movement studies can be admitted directly to the degree year—normally only an additional year for graduates from the same university—and an outstanding student can even enroll as a Ph.D. candidate. Acceptance into a Ph.D. program is handled at the central university, with consultation at the departmental level regarding the assignment of a supervisor.

Often students who choose to specialize in one area of sport psychology have also picked up the undergraduate units from the psychology department. There is, however, a unique joint honors program between human movement studies and psychology at the University of Queensland. This program provides an avenue through which students with a sport science specialization can take sufficient mainstream psychology subjects to gain registration with the Australian Psychological Society as a psychologist. To gain entry into the joint 4th year of study, students must take approximately the equivalent of an undergraduate double major in psychology. This gives students exposure to the subject areas of developmental, physiological, organizational, social, and experimental psychology as well as courses in learning and cognition, perception, personality and motivation, and experimental design and analysis to go along with specific offerings on skill acquisition and sport psychology in the department of human movement studies.

The final honors year consists of compulsory course work in multivariate design and analysis, optional course work in neuropsychology and behavior modification, some counseling and clinical psychology experience, and a research thesis jointly supervised by members from both departments. Similar programs are also available at the University of Wollongong, Footscray CAE, and Canberra CAE/Australian National University. Because these joint requirements have been recognized by the Australian Applied Sport Psychology Association as necessary for membership as a professional sport psychologist, these programs indeed serve a unique function.

A double major at the University of Western Australia also allows for an emphasis in exercise and sport psychology. This is a standard bachelor of science program rather than an honors-level program.

The CAEs also offer specialized sport psychology courses to undergraduates and, more recently, to graduate students. Whereas these programs used to be taught by physical education generalists, now specialists with tertiary university qualifications are actively recruited. In the program at Footscray, five discrete sport psychology subjects are taught, and students have opportunities for further directed studies and research project in the area. Rusden CAE also has an undergraduate specialized option in sport psychology that was one of Australia's first developed programs in the discipline.

Serious economic restrictions confront the tertiary education sector in Australia, presenting the likelihood of amalgamation of institutions and making it necessary to rationalize all courses and programs. This is unfortunate for the general field of physical education because some academics have questioned its legitimacy as a university-level area of study. It is even more unfortunate for the field of sport psychology, however, because the physical science tradition often creates an atmosphere in which ''soft'' social sciences specialties are considered expendable.

There will be limited opportunity for new programs or expansion of existing departments or faculties. We can only wait and see what impact this will have on courses in sport psychology and on sport science in general.

Topics of Study. Historically, there has been a distinct tendency for the area of skill acquisition to flourish in Australia. This results from the specific academic training of the country's leading figures in sport psychology. For example, Denis Glencross was a student of A.T. Welford, the prominent scholar who worked at Cambridge with Craik and Bartlett before moving to Flinders University. Welford wrote *Fundamentals of Skill* (1968) just before he arrived in Australia. Similarly, Gerry Jones, now retired from Western Australia, benefited from the information-processing approach to motor skills of Bob Wilberg in Canada, whereas David Russell, formerly at Queensland and now in New Zealand, studied under the guidance of Ron Marteniuk in Canada and Dick Schmidt in the United

States. Subsequently, each has turned out his own graduates who have also carried out work in skill acquisition, the most notable of whom is Bruce Abernethy working at Queensland. John Gross, now of the Canberra CAE; Mark Anshel of the University of Wollongong; and Bob Grove at Western Australia were all trained abroad, Gross with Diane Gill at Iowa and Anshel and Grove at Florida State with David Pargman and Bob Singer.

Work in the social and differential aspects of sport psychology has been a great deal less voluminous, but it has gained momentum in recent years. In Western Australia, the late Geoff Watson was doing pioneer research in a number of theoretical dimensions of play and leisure. In Victoria, the work of Brian Nettleton at the University of Melbourne with communication processes during sport performance has also been influential, as was the research of Colin Davey that focused on substantial personality testing of elite Australian athletes. More recently, contributions in the social area have increased substantially and include research on the attributional processes in sport (Bob Grove, University of Western Australia; Kevin Spink, Footscray Institute of Technology, since returned to Canada) and coaching behaviors (Phil Davis, Ballarat CAE; Sandy Gordon, University of Western Australia; John Gross, Canberra CAE). Other active researchers in the colleges include Patsy Tremayne (MacArthur Institute of Higher Education, New South Wales), Sue Napier (Tasmanian Institute of Technology), Neil Barras (Phillip Institute of Technology, Victoria), and Nigel Sherlock (Footscray Institute of Technology). Neville Owen (University of Adelaide) and Christina Lee (University of Newcastle) have written prolifically in the area of health psychology, and the latter has also written about self-efficacy in sport. Finally, Ian Robertson in the South Australian CAE has been writing a long time on youth sport in Australia.

Apart from the lead given in universities and colleges, opportunities for applied research have now been opened up at the national and state headquarters of the Australian Institute of Sport (AIS). In the early 1980s, applied work at the AIS consisted almost entirely of counseling top-level athletes and coaches. This first occurred at the national AIS at Canberra (Jeff Bond, John Crampton, Chris Horsley, and Brian Miller, since returned to England), and later in the state branches in Queensland (Ian Lynagh, Bradley Johnson, and John Dillon), and at the South Australia Institute of Sport (Kathy Martin and Graham Winter). In recent years, through the Australian Coaching Council's courses, seminars, and applied internships, teaching and applied research has increased within these institutes. This has given sport psychology far greater contact with and input at all levels of Australian sport.

Publications

The appearance of physical education Ph.D.s in Australia in the 1970s caused a bit of culture shock in postsecondary institutions. Up to this point, physical education was basically teacher training–oriented, and those well placed within the existing programs were not academically prepared to do research. Initially the newly trained academics could be housed comfortably only within the two departments of human movement studies in Queensland and Western Australia, which were not created specifically for teacher training. In the mid-1980s, a third program at Wollongong in New South Wales was also created, as well as science-based programs in some CAEs.

This lack of an appropriate niche for sport psychology shows up in the publication process. The only academic journal that publishes sport psychology articles on a regular basis is the *Australian Journal of Science and Medicine in Sport*, a combination of the *Australian Journal of Sports Medicine* and the short-lived *Australian Journal of Sport Sciences*. Under the direction of editors Frank Pyke and Bruce Abernethy, this journal has become a useful, high-quality publication by all standards. The applied arena has also been well served with some applied sport psychology articles published in the *Sports Coach*, a journal that was published in Western Australia and is now published by the Australian Coaching Council in Canberra. This publication has had a number of timely articles on general sport science issues of interest to coaches. Applied sport psychology articles also appear in the AIS publication *Excel*, usually simple "how-to" articles on teaching athletes mental skills. With the support of the Australian Sports Commission, John Gross and Jeff Bond have published an edited book of papers of the Inaugural National Sport Psychology Conference. Brian Nettleton has also written a number of useful applied sport psychology chapters that were adopted by the National Coaching Accreditation Scheme.

A growing number of Australian researchers have published articles within the area of motor performance in North American academic journals. Judith Laszlo (motor development and control) and Denis Glencross (motor behavior) are perhaps the best known. Others who have published abroad are Bruce Abernethy, John Gross, Bob Grove, Christina Lee, Tony Sparrow, Kevin Spink, Jeff Bond, John Crampton, Brian Miller, and Jeff Summers.

It is noteworthy that though sport psychology does not have a specialized publication vehicle in Australia, a number of Australians contribute to overseas editorial boards. Examples here are Denis Glencross, consulting editor of the *Journal of Motor Behavior*, a member of the advisory board of the *Journal of Sport Sciences*, and regional editor of *Sports Training, Medicine and Rehabilitation*; and Bruce Abernethy, member of the revamped editorial board of the *International Journal of Sport Psychology*.

Denis Glencross has also edited and contributed to the only Australian sport psychology textbook, *Psychology and Sport* (1978). The publisher initially asked A.T. Welford to do this book, but he graciously referred them to Glencross, who years earlier was one of his doctoral students. More recently, a number of notable monographs have been published by Australians. Examples are Geoff Watson's three monographs (published posthumously), *Approach Avoidance Behaviour in Team Sports*; *Sport, Socialisation and Education*; and *Childhood Socialisation and Competitive Swimming*; Neville Owen and Christina

Lee's *Why People Do and Do Not Exercise*; and Wes Snyder and Bruce Abernethy's *Understanding Human Action Through Experimentation*.

The Role of Sport Psychology in Australia

Institutions. Sport psychology finds its home within the universities, institutes of technology, and CAEs. A recent survey revealed that about 15 tertiary institutions offered a substantial number of courses in sport psychology, with the majority of these courses taught by staff members holding Ph.D.s. During the early 1970s, the universities of Queensland and Western Australia were permitted to establish degree programs as well as postgraduate study up to the doctoral level. This in itself initially established these centers as the most important ones in Australia. In 1984, however, the University of Wollongong upgraded its education degree to a bachelor of applied science, and with this came the introduction of a graduate program.

Western Australia has maintained a balanced program with Dick Lockwood and Helen Parker working in the area of skill acquisition, Bob Grove and Sandy Gordon working as sport psychology specialists, and Neal McLean working in clinical sport psychology within the psychology department.

The University of Queensland has had some bad luck, losing both Warren Walsh in motor performance and Kent Pearson in the social domain in the early 1980s. The program that Dave Russell began in motor control and skill acquisition was continued by Walsh until his untimely death in 1982 and has since been maintained by Bruce Abernethy. Abernethy has taken up very active research in motor performance, examining skill differences in experts as compared to novices. Social and clinical aspects of sport have received less attention, although a framework has been constructed through the joint honors program that appears well suited to the development of a sport psychology training option. Collaboration with the psychology department in this program at Queensland may be closer than in similar programs in the country. The lack of adequate staffing seems to be the limiting factor in the Queensland program at this moment, although the appointment in the social/clinical area of Stephanie Hanrahan has recently improved the situation. The course at the University of Wollongong began with promise due to the work of John Gross, who has since moved to Canberra CAE and was replaced by Canadian sport psychologist Mark Anshel. The effect of career changes on various institutions can be precarious because all the responsibility for many Australian programs rests on the shoulders of only a few individuals. If these people leave the program, the program's future is in doubt.

Though these centers are well equipped for sophisticated research and enjoy good collaboration with their psychology departments, in all cases, perhaps with the exception of Western Australia, the lack of adequate staffing has severely limited research output. Heavy teaching loads and the necessity of directing energy to establishing new programs have also attenuated the impact of sport psychology on the international level. Western Australia is, however, Australia's exception to these constraints, with numerous qualified personnel and good working conditions.

Denis Glencross has moved from his established position at Flinders University in Adelaide to chair the psychology department at the new Curtin University of Technology in Perth. Glencross has published extensively in motor performance and sport psychology journals at home and abroad and has also been active in professional matters of sport and sport psychology. He now plays an important role as a member of the managing council of the ISSP.

The Curtin University program offers graduate courses in sport psychology along with industrial and counseling psychology. The exact nature of Glencross's impact as the chair of this program remains to be seen. There is no doubt, however, that the west coast of Australia will become the undisputed center of sport psychology, with proven resources at both Western Australia and Curtin universities.

Jeff Summers at the University of Melbourne, working in motor control and timing, and Neville Owen at the multidisciplinary center at the University of Adelaide are rare exceptions in Australia of individuals working on sport psychology projects from within mainstream psychology departments.

A number of the CAEs, mainly in the eastern states, have initiated programs in sport psychology with varying degrees of success. These programs were initially limited by the existence of few postgraduate opportunities for study. Now their departments are in some cases better equipped than those of the more established universities but still suffer from a shortage of personnel. Colin Davey has provided a unique emphasis in the area of mainstream sport psychology at the Victorian College of Education, Rusden, where an opportunity for undergraduate specialization in sport psychology exists. Footscray Institute of Technology imported Canadian Kevin Spink to set up a program of research in Melbourne, but he has since returned to Canada. His replacement, Tony Morris from West Sussex in England, did postdoctoral research work in motor skills with John Annett, before moving full time into sport psychology and motor skills work. He has been involved in National Coaching Foundation funded research on cue-utilization and perception in table tennis and was funded by the Sports Council of England to act as sport psychology consultant to the English Table Tennis squad for more than 4 years. Morris has immediately commenced supervising sport psychology doctoral work and intends to expand further the contribution of sport psychology at undergraduate levels at Footscray. He will also develop research and consultancy interests within sport psychology in Melbourne.

The University of Melbourne has maintained contact with real and varied sport psychology problems through the efforts of Brian Nettleton, especially in the coaching accreditation schemes. Sport psychology has been integrated into the coaching accreditation program that was implemented in the 1980s and was patterned after the Canadian coaching certification program.

Sport psychology has also been institutionalized within nonuniversity institutes of sport, both federally and in the states. The first, the Western Australian Institute of Sport (WAIS), was established in 1980 with the tasks of coordinating coach training, planning, promotion, analysis, and research for this state, and it still maintains an ongoing consultation arrangement with practitioners in Perth. Soon after, the South Australian Institute of Sport (SAIS) was modeled after its western counterpart, and two full-time staff members, Graham Winter and Kathy Martin, provide services for its coaches and athletes.

At the federal level, the AIS national training center was established for the long- and short-term preparation of international athletes and teams. Full-time personnel in sport psychology have been involved with elite athletes since early 1982. The head sport psychologist, Jeff Bond, has made an important contribution to the field both nationally and internationally. Three other specialists have been associated with Bond—John Crampton, Chris Horsley, and Brian Miller. It has always been an accepted practice for sport psychologists to travel nationally and overseas with national teams and athletes to practice psychological skills monitoring, stress management, and crisis intervention.

In Queensland, two decentralized units of the federal AIS are situated in Brisbane. These units are serviced by Ian Lynagh, a clinical psychologist, and more recently by John Dillon, a product of the Queensland joint honors program in sport psychology.

Societies.   In 1975, the Australian Council for Health, Physical Education and Recreation (ACHPER) decided at its meeting in Perth to form special interest groups. These ad hoc groups represented both disciplinary interests (e.g., sport psychology, philosophy) and professional thematic areas. The sport psychology interest group was headed initially by Bob Paddick and subsequently by Gerry Jones. Though the formation of the group was in itself laudable, its functioning was fraught with pitfalls that the analogous Canadian group, the special interest group of the Canadian Association of Health, Physical Education and Recreation (CAHPER), also experienced—namely, a lack of academic freedom within the professional association, no clear group guidelines or constitution, and little or no status as a professional association outside of the structure of the main group and thus the exclusion of those coming from psychology rather than physical education. In the situation it faced, the special interest group of CAHPER in 1977 formed a legally constituted sport psychology society.

As early as 1977, in a report on Australian sport psychology developments, Glencross urgently recommended the creation of a sport psychology group or organization whose prime concern would be the area of sport, games, and recreation. In spite of this admonition, the Australians took no such action until 1990. Despite the special interest group's early inactivity, sport

psychology has still been represented within ACHPER, with 15 formal papers presented at the 1988 biennial conference as well as a number of poster presentations.

In late 1990 Denis Glencross began the negotiation process with all of the professional associations involved in sport psychology in Australia to create an umbrella group of professional and academic nature. In addition, Glencross, as an elected member of the managing council of the ISSP, has taken a leadership role in initiating action with about 120 people in Australia and New Zealand through a newsletter. He has also encouraged sport psychology in Fiji, Samoa, and New Guinea through visits and lectures. In collaboration with Atsushi Fujita of Japan, he began work on creating the Asian and South Pacific Association for Sport Psychology (ASPASP) in 1988 at the Seoul Olympic Scientific Congress. This project will give Australia and other countries in Oceania an accessible international forum for scientific and professional exchange, much like NASPSPA does in North America. Given the potential of Australia's human resources in sport psychology, a leadership role for Australia has already been exercised in this hemisphere, and the inaugural ASPASP congress will be held in 1991 in Melbourne under the direction of Australian representative Colin Davey.

Perhaps the most controversial development in Australian sport psychology resulted from the formation of the Australian Applied Sport Psychology Association (AASPA) in 1986. This group, based at the Canberra AIS, with a 1989 mailing list of 75 and a growing membership numbering in 1988 between 15 and 20 members, was created with the express aim of providing a professional association for the guidance and development of the practice of applied sport psychology in Australia. AASPA is specifically targeted at those working in the area of providing psychological services to coaches and athletes at all levels on a regular basis. Membership is available to those working in sport who are eligible for legal registration by the various state psychology boards and for membership in the Australian Psychological Society (APS), and who also may have additional training and experience in sport, such as postgraduate sport psychology courses, supervised internships, or experience as a coach or an athlete. These membership criteria represent an attempt by AASPA to encourage those who wish to pursue careers in applied sport psychology to seek out the most relevant training experiences, and to provide end users with some means of identifying those who might best be able to provide sport psychology services.

AASPA has been endorsed by a number of significant groups including the the APS, the Australian Sports Commission, and the Australian Olympic Federation. The organization is seen to be complementary to the other professional groups interested in physical education and sport sciences, though with a narrower focus. AASPA was formed to assist in the professional development of the discipline in such a way as to eliminate earlier problems of unqualified and at times unscrupulous self-proclaimed "sport psychologists" in Australian sport.

The controversy arose initially because of the perceived nature of AASPA's defined scope of activity and its restrictive and closed membership. The APS membership requirement eliminated other sport psychology specialists interested in education and research in sport psychology, many of whom were productive, internationally recognized Australians who had worked in basic and applied sport psychology research and teaching in the universities for close to 2 decades. This initial tension was recently tempered somewhat with the creation of the Sport Psychology Association of Australia and New Zealand (SPAANZ) at the ISSP 1989 Singapore Congress. This umbrella group brings together the interests of AASPA, the sport science group, and ACHPER around the same table. For the first time, an opportunity for dialogue now exists.

At the 1990 APS meeting in Melbourne, delegates from SPAANZ, APS, and AASPA found strong support for the amalgamation of these groups within a division or board of APS. This step would enable Australia to become a world leader in sport psychology by having such an integrated program.

Another specialized group interested in research and improving communication on motor control issues was formed in 1988 in the aftermath of the 1987 Australasian International Conference on Brain Research in Queenstown, New Zealand. This group, currently convened by Greg Anson of the University of Otago and Graham Kerr in Western Australia, called itself the Australasian Society for Motor Control. The future of this small group will be of interest.

Sport Psychology and Top Sport.   Australia's use of sport psychology for top sport is unique in the world. What makes things different in Australia is the respective ways that sport and sport psychology are organized.

Sport in Australia finds its basic organization at the club level. The great stars of Australian tennis (Hoad, Laver, Goolagong), swimming (Fraser, Gould, Wickham), and track (Cuthbert, Elliot) all developed within small sport ecosystems based on individual efforts of volunteers and a limited number of professionals, rather than through any coordinated effort on the national level. In fact, powerful voices have criticized the Australian government because far less governmental money is spent per capita on sport promotion, organization, and coaching than in the majority of other countries in the Western world (Bloomfield, 1973). Bloomfield has argued, ''The federal government is currently spending 20 times more money on the arts than it spends on the development of sport, yet it is doubtful that the average taxpayer would consider the arts to be more important than sport'' (p. 1).

This situation has improved considerably with increased public funding over the last 8 years given to the AIS, the state institutions, and the other Australian Sports Commission programs. In 1989, the Australian government pledged an additional $40 million to Australian sport at all levels, with funding guaranteed for the remainder of the 1992 Olympiad.

The second factor that contributes to the special blend of sport psychology and top sport in Australia is the way that sport psychology is organized, or, more accurately, not organized. As mentioned earlier, a significant but now reduced number of people are not psychologists but are writing in sport psychology, teaching accreditation and university courses in sport psychology, and advancing research in sport psychology. During the 1970s a minor state of chaos was created when a number of individuals who called themselves ''sport psychologists'' were paid by and associated with Australian rules football and rugby teams. These individuals were trained in a number of different areas, including physical education, general psychology, and medicine, and had no formal sport psychology background. Their activity was a source of great professional concern and public misconception about the field of sport psychology. This situation has been brought under control through better education of coaches and athletes, increased exposure of athletes to applied sport psychology at the institutes, and the work of the AASPA.

This lack of professional standards and control in sport psychology has prompted leading academic voices to call for increased government involvement. As long ago as 1977, Denis Glencross reported to the ISSP concerning sport psychology and top sport in Australia that ''the time would appear ripe to consider some formal group or organization . . . because of urgent ethical and moral issues already raised, including the use of 'restricted' psychological assessment procedures, the confidentiality of information, and the potential invasion of individual freedom'' (Glencross, 1977, p. 14).

Against this unsettled background, controlled use of sport psychology procedures have been introduced into top sport in Australia through governmental agencies. A number of state and federal agencies have begun to introduce sport psychology into coaching accreditation programs in which thousands of amateur athletes now participate.

Western Australia led the way in 1980 with the development of institutionalized top sport by creating WAIS to coordinate sport programs in an attempt to end the ''kitchen table era'' of sport administration (Bloomfield, 1973).

In Canberra, the national capital, the AIS was inaugurated early in 1981 as an attempt to centralize the widely dispersed elements of Australian sport. Today, top Australian athletes from the states are brought to AIS where they are housed, schooled, and provided with financial and training support in multimillion-dollar facilities. To accommodate the maximum number of sports in the most economically efficient manner, satellite units have been created in other parts of the country using existing facilities. Thus, whereas athletes in sports such as basketball, gymnastics, swimming, tennis, netball, track and field, rowing, water polo, and soccer still use the Canberra facilities, field hockey was decentralized to Perth, cricket and cycling to Adelaide, volleyball to Sydney, and diving, canoeing, and squash to Brisbane.

The full- and part-time sport psychologists who work at the national and state centers are assigned primary responsibilities for a limited number of sports, and often travel with the team. These AIS specialists also provide group-oriented workshops for national youth squads that visit the institute on a regular basis for training camps.

Finally, another new dimension has been added to top sport performance: the attribution of about $60,000 to $100,000 annually to the Applied Sports Research Program, with the aim of assisting sport in finding solutions to practical, researchable problems that are considered relevant and have immediate or long-term value. Important here is the collaboration between national sporting bodies and researchers within institutes of higher education. This program is directed by Julie Draper, National Sports Research Coordinator of the Australian Sports Commission. This program is important for both sport and research because funds for basic sport psychology research from other sources have been diminishing. Some concern, however, has been expressed about the continued availability of these sources of funds, given the variation in the total annual funding accorded.

Examples of research funded through this program to date include studies on team cohesion and coaching behaviors in basketball (John Gross), vision and cricket batting (Neil Barras), talent identification in field hockey (Denis Glencross), anticipation in squash (Bruce Abernethy), motivation in youth sport (Ian Robertson), and psychological factors in shooting (Jeff Bond).

Perspectives for Sport Psychology in Australia

It was noted in the first edition of this book that Australia had by far the greatest potential for rapid advancement in sport psychology, but it also had structural barriers to overcome before this potential could be realized. The sources for this potential were the formal educational structures that permitted advanced study in the field and the presence of qualified academics to direct such study. The barriers were underdeveloped professional networks and a resultant pulling apart rather than a bonding together of individuals in the fields.

In many ways the situation changed significantly at the end of the 1980s. The number of qualified academics has increased in recent years. Fortunately for the future of Australian sport psychology and Australian sport, the framework now exists for considerable cooperative effort between academic sport psychologists, professional sport psychology organizations, applied sport psychology practitioners, various sport institutes, and coaches and athletes. Australian athletes and coaches have a very high level of acceptance of sport psychology services, but there still remains a shortage of well-qualified and experienced individuals to meet this need. An important development in the future of Australian sport psychology lies in the area of appropriate learning experiences in theory, practice, and research at the tertiary institutions. The gradual advent of opportunities for internships will be a significant contribution to the training requirements of future Australian sport psychologists.

The increased funding now directed toward sports research and a discussed streamlining of the publication vehicles for this research will improve what has been a problem facing Australian sport psychology researchers for many years.

The further expansion of the sports institute concept through the increased development of the institutes at Melbourne, Sydney, and Brisbane will increase the explosure of applied sport psychology to athletes and coaches at all levels, along with the employment opportunities for sport psychologists.

It is probably accurate to say that sport psychology is the current sport science/sports medicine area of greatest public interest in Australia, and the ball is in sport psychology's court. Sport psychology has begun to organize itself and develop the infrastructure necessary for the next phase in its development. It will be interesting to see how the Australian sport psychology community deals with their future development and what the outcome will be. Many lessons can be learned from past developments in North America. It is clear that in the future the contribution sport psychology has to make in Australia will extend beyond the sport field and into the areas of health, personal management, and lifestyle change in general. However, this surge of interest must make a genuine contribution to education, research, and practice and to the broader field of Australian sport and sport psychology.

New Zealand

in collaboration with

L.R.T. Williams
University of Otago

New Zealand Sport Psychology Résumé

Sport psychology in New Zealand is beginning to move out of its former stage of infancy. Most activity is still located at the University of Otago on the South Island. Research and intervention in applied sport psychology has now been added to the existing research in perceptual motor behavior.

Estimated Number of Sport Psychologists.   30

Prominent Institution.   University of Otago, Faculty of Physical Education, Dunedin

Orientation.   Skill acquisition

Privileged Topic.   Motor control

Publication Vehicles.   *New Zealand Journal of Health, Physical Education, and Recreation; New Zealand Journal of Sports Medicine; New Zealand Psychological Society Bulletin*

Society.   New Zealand Sports Psychology Interest Group

New Zealand is another special hybrid of British traditions and indigenous elements in sport and other aspects of life. The British influence in sport is reflected in the choice of sports (rugby, rowing, field hockey) as well as the means of organization (amateur, club systems). It is surprising that this country that is slightly larger than the United Kingdom but has only 1/20th of its population does as well as it has in sport. Like Australia, it has the climate and the isolation that have produced the likes of Peter Snell and John Walker.

The infrastructure of the club system has also produced the fiercely competitive "All Black" rugby team that allows this country of 3.5 million people to have a top international reputation. It has also produced several world champions in other areas, including men's and women's squash, rowing, canoeing, and yachting.

Like several other Commonwealth countries, New Zealand is often criticized for its sporting contacts with South Africa; and though the government has recently taken a firm stance against such relations, some unofficial meetings remain. The political flavor is not welcomed by the average New Zealander, who simply prefers to ignore politics and be free to "get on with the game."

One other remarkable feature of the New Zealand sport tradition has been the export of an excellent group of its own sport scientists abroad to Australia, Canada, and the United States, where they have taken on positions of authority in biomechanics, sport psychology, exercise physiology, and sport history. The lack of appropriate positions within institutionalized structures forced New Zealand's product abroad.

Training in Sport Psychology

Training in sport psychology is now possible through the doctoral level at the University of Otago, and the program's first graduate, Bruce Abernethy, has taken on a position in Queensland, Australia. More graduates have not been rapidly churned through because of a lack of trained personnel.

The training profile is similar to Australia's but is less developed. A number of teacher education colleges train people in a practical manner in physical education and other specialist areas of teaching. In a 3-year program, a student receives an emphasis on pedagogy in physical education and little other specialized disciplinary training in sport psychology or the other sciences.

The University of Otago offers a 4-year specialized degree in physical education. Before 1983, students received a compulsory course, "Psychology of Physical Activity," which had a motor learning and sport psychology component, for 4 hours each week. Associated with this was an obligatory course in motor development. Les Williams offered sport psychology course work along with an advanced course in psychomotor behavior. Since then, degree restructuring has shifted the sport psychology component to be included in the sport sociology course taught by Rex Thomson.

This shift was a temporary one representing the university's preparation for developing specific sport psychology courses at both introductory and advanced levels under the control of a new appointment. This appointment has recently been confirmed, and it is expected that sport psychology will receive full attention.

The postgraduate program encompasses master's and doctoral levels and is progressing well. However, apart from the motor behavior area where some students are working at the interface of sport and motor learning/control, little mainstream sport psychology work is being conducted.

Topics of Study.   The original work in sport psychology began in 1971 when Les Williams continued the efforts of Jim Hay with the rowing federation. Psychological data of the personality type was added to anthropometric and physiological measures to create "psychobiological profiles" of these athletes. These data were then used by the coaches for diagnostic purposes. This multidisciplinary aspect was to become a distinguishing feature of early New Zealand research. As in many other countries, this work was a "sideline" to research within the psychomotor behavior area.

After completing doctoral studies with Franklin Henry in 1970, Williams began and has continued research centering on certain basic movement phenomena, but has also crossed disciplines into the areas of measurement and exercise physiology. David Russell's appointment as dean in 1981 led to considerable restructuring and expansion of the faculty at Otago; it is only a matter of time before sport psychology reaches maturity in New Zealand.

Publications

Two potential sources of published information on sport psychology exist in New Zealand: the *New Zealand Journal of Health, Physical Education and Recreation* and the *New Zealand Journal of Sports Medicine*. A review of the former journal revealed more than 300 articles indexed and cross-referenced in a number of areas, including those that make up sport psychology. Of this number, about 30 dealt with sport psychology topics that touched on practice effects, cognitive structures, timing, and personality. More recently, greater sophistication appears to be present, in the titles at least. In the sports medicine journal sport psychology topics occasionally surface, although the appropriateness of such a vehicle for experimental sport psychology can be questioned. A few articles on sport have begun to appear in the *New Zealand Psychological Society Bulletin*.

A few timely events that took place in the area of perception and skill acquisition resulted in publications in the form of collected papers. In 1982, the Otago Symposium in Motor and Memory Control resulted in the publication of *Motor Memory and Control* (Russell & Abernethy, 1985). A second series of books, *Imagery I* (Marks & Russell, 1985) and *Imagery II* (Russell, Marks, & Richardson, 1986), were the result of two congresses of the International Imagery Association held in New Zealand and England, respectively.

At present, the low frequency of sport psychology publications does not warrant a separate national publication. It is highly probable that New Zealanders could play important roles within the proposed *Australian Journal of Science and Medicine in Sport*. No books on sport psychology have yet been published by native Kiwis; however, Williams, Russell, and their students have managed to publish their research in a number of prestigious North American journals.

The Role of Sport Psychology in New Zealand

Institutions. Sport psychology is beginning to gain recognition in other New Zealand universities, and some sport-related theses have been conducted in other psychology departments.

In 1978, a national conference for coaches and university people was convened, and a national association for coaches was formed as the result. Coach certification and related programs created in Canada and Australia have been tailored to New Zealand's needs, including some sport psychology components. Plans for a number of national sport institutes for the different disciplines have been slow to evolve.

New Zealand Sport Psychology Interest Group. In 1984, a sport psychology interest group was formed when a small group of psychologists gathered to discuss sport psychology at the annual conference of the New Zealand Psychological Society at Massey University. This group is now centered at the University of Canterbury under the leadership of Graeme Clarke. The group so far has about 30-plus members with clinical and research interests. Their specific interests are the promotion of healthy perspectives of sport with children and adolescents and assisting the performance of elite athletes by means of a variety of psychological interventions. Still, the fundamental New Zealand problem is a severe shortage of suitably qualified people. This has been the limiting factor in the development of any academic activity on a broad scale.

The New Zealand Physical Education Association does not yet have special sections for interest groups such as sport psychology, as has occurred in Australia, Canada, and the United States. It is expected that the New Zealand and Australian psychological societies will ulti-

mately provide the structure to allow the efficient organization of both academic and professional activity in sport psychology and associated areas.

Sport Psychology and Top Sport. It is often heard in New Zealand that this is the last bastion of truly amateur sport in the world, although there are signs that this is beginning to change.

One example in particular exemplifies the nature of top sport and sport science support. Prior to the Munich Olympics, Fritz Hagerman and Jim Hay were involved in sport science evaluations for the national rowing team. In 1971, Les Williams took over this work and added data on the rowers' personality profiles. The eight-man crew won the gold at Munich, and this momentum was maintained for more than a decade. Despite severe difficulties in funding international competition, the team's success rate has been high. More recently, Williams was closely associated with preparing the New Zealand team for the America's Cup in 12-meter yachting. A major development in this association was the attraction of large corporate sponsorship.

Though New Zealand's waiting for the developing of appropriate institutionalized mechanisms for the support of top sport can give it advantages in borrowing the best from systems in other countries, there is also a critical delay period in their adoption. With the exception of rugby, which has an extremely broad support system and perhaps can remain amateur, New Zealand sports have taken the first firm steps toward increased professionalization.

Perspectives for Sport Psychology in New Zealand

The direction that the broad area of sport psychology has taken in New Zealand in the past has been one of a "non-direction," according to Les Williams. This non-direction has been the result of the lack of human resources who are in tune with contemporary directions in the fields of sport psychology, sport science, and physical education.

Though the academic structure shows medium-term promise, a major risk will be the integration of sport psychology's resources with political, economic, and other forces that influence sport in New Zealand.

References

Bloomfield, J. (1973). *The role, scope and development of recreation in Australia*. Canberra: Commonwealth of Australia.

Dunstan, K. (1973). *Sports*. North Melbourne: Cassell.

Glencross, D. (1977). The development of sports psychology in Australia. In K. Feige (Ed.), *The development of sport psychology*. Kiel: Bundesinstitut für Sportwissenschaft.

Chapter 3

ASIA

China

in collaboration with

Ma Qi-Wei
Beijing Institute of Physical Education

Qiu Yijun
Wuhan Institute of Physical Education

Ye Ping
Chengdu Institute of Physical Education

Chinese Sport Psychology Résumé

Sport psychology in China plays an active role in education, research, and coaching, mixing traditional methods from the East with the newest information from the West.

Estimated Number of Sport Psychologists. 200

Prominent Institutions. Beijing, Shanghai, Wuhan, Shangyang, Xian, and Chengdu Institutes of Physical Education

Orientation. Assistance of top athletes

Privileged Topics. Psychological training and consultation, personality psychograms

Publication Vehicle. *Information on Sport Psychology*

Societies. National Society of Sport Psychology–Branch of the China Society of Sport Sciences; Physical Education and Sport Psychology–Branch of the China Society of Psychology

Sport was one of few activities spared during the 1966 to 1976 Cultural Revolution in China. Athletes selected from the many specialized sports schools and spare-time sports schools, at which children practice selected sports after school, were sent to the national team centers in Beijing. These schools do basic sport training and select athletes to train at the larger, more sophisticated centers when they attain a higher level of proficiency in sport. By the ninth Asian Games in 1980, China was highly ranked and continued to win world and Olympic championships in a variety of sports including table tennis, diving, and gymnastics. Sport psychology, on the other hand, did not escape the wrath of the Gang of Four. Although it was taught since the 1950s as a compulsory course in the institutes of physical education and physical culture, it was considered a bourgeois pseudoscience and was banished from all programs until 1976. Ever since the rebuilding process began for psychology in 1976 as China began its period of modernization, psychology and sport psychology have both undergone a transformation so that previous influences of the Soviet Union have been tempered with knowledge and methods from the West.

Training in Sport Psychology

Generally speaking, before 1937 psychology or educational psychology, child psychology, and psychohygiene were offered as courses in the pedagogy and the physical education specialties in higher education, but no sport psychology courses were offered at that time. Beginning in 1933, the physical education department of Beijing Normal University, which was the earliest department of its kind in the country, started to offer many additional courses, including physical education theory, biomechanics of sports, biochemistry, and exercise physiology, but none in sport psychology.

With the smashing of the Gang of Four in October 1976 came the resurgence of interest in science, and the research institute of psychology was restored in June 1977. To meet the needs of the "four modernizations" of China, seven specialized commissions were set up in the China Society of Psychology, one of which was devoted to physical education and sport psychology. Through this commission psychologists are trained to teach and then do research in the 140 universities and institutes that teach physical education and train coaches for the masses, and the 17 institutes of physical culture for elite athletes.

Since 1984, at the Beijing and Wuhan Institutes of Physical Education, a limited number of sport psychology courses have been given to three different populations of students in China, including those working in departments of physical education, teachers' universities for physical education, and research institutes of sport science. The psychologists and researchers in sport psychology work in close collaboration with teachers and coaches, thus increasing their own practical knowledge in sport and the theoretical sophistication of the practitioners.

The resulting collection of research results was compiled in two volumes in 1978 to be used as the reference book for training teachers and coaches. This was followed by the appearance of a number of other collections from the institutes of Tianjin, Chengdu, Wuhan, and Shanghai. Finally, the Sport Psychology Commission decided in 1980 to standardize these texts, and after a lengthy period of study, a single textbook, *Psychology*, was published and used for all undergraduate training of coaches and athletes.

Since 1984 at the Wuhan Institute of Physical Education and at other major research institutes of physical culture, a limited number of master's programs were initiated in sport psychology, and there are now plans for a doctoral program in this area. In 1988 at the Wuhan Institute, a sport psychology research division was created, and Qiu Yijun was appointed dean. The graduates from this program have since gone to work as assistants in Beijing University, Southwest Normal University, and the Yunan Institute of Advanced Studies for Administrators of Physical Culture.

China now has produced 10 professors, 20 associate professors, 40 lecturers, and more than 150 assistants specializing in sport psychology.

Topics of Study. In the 1950s, Chinese psychologists were greatly influenced by the classical Russian school of psychology. To learn psychology from the Soviet Union, the then Central Ministry of Education invited Soviet psychologists to give lectures in China during the period from 1952 to 1956. The study and discussion of Pavlov's theory was established in the academic circles of psychology, medicine, and physiology, and some exploratory research projects were completed in this theoretical area.

At that time, only a few lectures given by foreign scholars dealt with sport psychology. It was not until 1957 that the book *Psychology*, written by Peter Rudik, a Soviet scholar, and translated by Sun Jinghao, came off the press. The book contained a great deal of material on physical education and was a major reference book for sport psychology workers in China. *Questions on Sports Psychology*, written by Chernikewa of the Soviet Union and translated by Wang Bing in 1958, became the main reference in teaching sport psychology at physical education institutions.

The early 1960s saw the gratifying development of scientific research in sport. Initial research was conducted on the following topics: the objectives and contents of sport psychology, the participation motives of sports enthusiasts, the effect of verbal instructions on sport performance, and the presence of psychological barriers during competition. However, owing to the lack of a unified and clear research orientation at that time, the topics studied did not focus clearly on important subject areas. Not until the establishment of the Physical Education and Sports Psychology Commission in 1978 did research really begin in sport psychology.

The annual meeting of the National Society of Sport Psychology provides a representative sample of the main topics of interest in this country. From 1979 to 1985 about 200 sport psychology papers were presented in the following areas: sport task demands (21%), personality (15.8%), psychological training (12.3%), psychological theory (9.7%), teaching (8.8%), psychological abilities (7.9%), competition (7.9%), psychometrics (7%), social psychology (5.3%), and talent identification (4.4%). Examples of applied research presented at these meetings include "The Effect of Training in Thinking on the Teaching of Hurdles," "An Experimental Research of the Effect of Strengthening the Motion Perception Control on Shooting in Basketball," and "Psychological

Preparation of Gymnasts in Learning New and Difficult Elements and the Initial Study of Its Teaching Methods."

One interesting incentive for doing research in China relates to the award system attached to all projects. For example, for the period 1980 to 1982, the Wuhan Institute for Physical Education won a first-class award, the Scientific Technology Progress prize, from the Sports Commission for the project "Research on Scientific Selection of Elite Athletes."

Publications

The earliest sport psychology publications in China were translations of Russian books by Rudik and Chernikewa and appeared during the 1950s. Since the formulation of the Sport Psychology Commission in 1978, national collections of Chinese research have been compiled and used as textbooks. For example, the Wuhan Institute of Physical Education has been particularly active in putting together two compilations of research, *Readings in Sport Psychology* and *Information on Sport Psychology*. The Beijing Institute of Physical Education also published the abstracts of all sport psychology theses from 1978 to 1984 and has since updated it.

Some research in sport psychology has also been published in these mainstream psychology journals: *Journal of Psychology, Newsletter of Psychology,* and *Acta Psychologica Sinica*.

The Role of Sport Psychology in China

Institutions. The institutions in China are based on the Soviet structure of institutes of physical education and culture that are directed at training coaches and physical educators for the sports schools and spare-time sports schools.

The research institutes for physical culture are centered more on providing research and support services for top-level athletes. Six of these large centers are generously funded by the All China Sport Federation.

National Society of Sport Psychology. The Research Institute of Psychology in 1979 created a section on physical education and sport psychology as one of its founding commissions. The commission became fully functional in the same year, and members presented more than 30 papers at the annual meeting of the psychology society in Tianjin.

In December 1980, the annual meeting of the China Sports Science Society met in Beijing, at which time the China Society of Sport Psychology was created and Ma Qi-wei elected President. This new society thus became a subcommittee of both the sport science and psychology committees, with 20 provincial academic subgroups. The society meets at the annual conference and more frequently on the provincial level. In total, there are about 200 members actively involved in sport psychology in China.

Sport Psychology and Top Sport. All research done at the research institutes is directed toward enhancing the performance of top-level athletes. Sport psychologists work in close contact with coaches to help them improve athletes' self-control during competition. Little is written, however, about the exact methods used in clinical settings.

Perspectives for Sport Psychology in China

After a long and stormy history, psychology and sport psychology appear to be coming into a new age of development and stability. After living through the influence of Soviet perspectives in the 1950s and the Cultural Revolution in the 1960s and 1970s, Chinese sport psychology has taken a new road during the 1980s and 1990s that balances traditional Oriental approaches with those from abroad. Sport psychology is certainly in a position of strength because it plays a central role in the mainstream of both psychology and sport science. It remains to be seen what impact this interesting new force will have on the rest of the world.

Hong Kong

in collaboration with

Roy C. Chan
The Chinese University of Hong Kong

Hong Kong Sport Psychology Résumé

Sport psychology in Hong Kong is in its early developmental stage. With the formation of the Sports Medicine and Sports Science Association and the support of the Chinese University of Hong Kong, its future appears encouraging.

Estimated Number of Sport Psychologists. 3

Prominent Institutions. The Chinese University of Hong Kong, Jubilee Sports Center

Orientation. Educational and experimental

Privileged Topics. Transactional analysis in sports, psychological profiles of handicapped athletes

Publication Vehicle. *The Proceedings of the Sports Medicine and Sports Science Conference*

Society. The Sports Medicine and Sports Science Association

The former British colony of Hong Kong is a small seaport that shares many of the values of mainland China as well as those of the industrialized world. The contrast between the traditional shops of Hong Kong and the electronics-based skyscrapers on the Kowloon side is startling. Sport is also a blend of traditional martial arts contrasted with private-school sports such as cricket and rugby. Only in very recent times has the area of sport psychology begun to take hold in this unique area.

Training in Sport Psychology

Hong Kong, because of its lack of a higher institution degree program in physical education, has not yet offered any opportunities for teaching or doing research in sport psychology. At present, the first individuals who have gone abroad to receive advanced training in postgraduate physical education institutes have returned to Hong Kong.

The situation is starting to look brighter for the near future. In September 1989, the Chinese University of Hong Kong began to offer the first degree program in physical education in the country. This program is accessible to on-the-job physical education teachers who have at least 4 years of experience. Classes are offered in the evening, and sport psychology is one of the required courses.

Topics of Study. Frank H. Fu and Lena Fung of the Chinese University have contributed their efforts in several survey research projects in the area of transactional analysis in sport. With the addition of Roy Chan, who specializes in sport psychology at the same institution, the development of sport psychology in Hong Kong should begin to take shape soon.

Publications

At this early stage of development of the sport sciences in Hong Kong and with such a small number of people involved, there does not appear to be a need for sport science publications. However, both Roy Chan and Frank Fu have published their research in international journals.

The Role of Sport Psychology in Hong Kong

Institutions. The dominant sports institute is the Jubilee Sports Center, which provides training for most of the national sports teams. Currently, its development and research are mainly concentrated on the physiological aspects of performance. It is hoped that more sport psychology development can be coordinated in the future with the leading academic institutions in Hong Kong, especially the new physical education program at the Chinese University of Hong Kong.

Sport Psychology and Top Sport. Recently, the two major sports associations expressed their interest in sport psychology by inviting Roy Chan to lecture on goal setting in the Advanced Coaching Course sponsored by the Asian Olympic Committee and the Hong Kong Basketball Association. There was also a lecture in the Coaching Program sponsored by the Hong Kong Football Association on the psychological development of athletes in different age groups. This recent attention from major sports associations signifies the recognition

and respect that sport psychology is beginning to command on the national sport scene.

Perspectives for Sport Psychology in Hong Kong

With more than 6 million people crowded into such a small place, Hong Kong needs a special blend of sport psychology that is more educational and motivational than elitist. It is foreseeable that there will be a greater demand for sport psychology in the future, because the emotional and physical needs of this dense but prosperous mass of people must be channeled in a proper direction in physical activity and sports.

India

in collaboration with

M.L. Kamlesh
Lakshmibai National College of Physical Education

Indian Sport Psychology Résumé

Sport psychology has developed in India at one of the fastest rates of any country in the world. Within a very short time, sport psychology has created new institutional and organizational structures directed by highly enthusiastic leaders. Growth of the discipline is still limited by the country's financial difficulties.

Estimated Number of Sport Psychologists.   30

Prominent Institutions. Netaji Subhas National Institute of Sport, Lakshmibai National College of Physical Education

Orientation.   Experimental research and coach education

Privileged Topics.   Personality and anxiety

Publication Vehicle.   *National Institute of Sports (NIS) Scientific Journal*

Society.   Sports Psychology Association of India

It is somewhat ironic that the country that spawned the idea of the benefits of a harmonious mind-body relationship through yoga many centuries ago is just now embarking on its introduction to sport psychology. Some of the pressure to create this field of study has arisen from sportspersons who recognize the importance of adding mental training to physical and technical conditioning. Where once India dominated the world in field hockey and cricket, it has found that countries with more

integrated training and sport science support are now beating them.

This late start in the development of sport psychology can be understood considering that the field of sports medicine came into existence only in 1970. From this group the Sports Psychology Association of India was founded in Hyderabad in 1977 but quickly became defunct. In 1985, M.L. Kamlesh reignited the enthusiasm for the discipline, and progress in the field has been astonishing.

Training in Sport Psychology

In the northwest corner of India in the province of Punjab is one of Asia's premier sport institutes, the Netaji Subhas National Institute of Sport (NIS). The NIS has been located since 1961 in the old Moti palace of a former maharaja, an impressive physical plant of fields, gymnasiums, swimming pools, residences, laboratories, and classrooms providing many services for top sport in India. Since 1980, sport psychology has been taught at the NIS through different levels of courses to develop and upgrade elite coaches and to prepare teams for international competitions. Until recently, the NIS course was the only available center teaching information on sport psychology. As will be discussed later, this situation has changed radically, with further development of institutionalized programs in university departments.

Within the NIS regular 10-month coaches' course as well as in the 22-month long master's course, there are specialized courses in sport psychology. This course was first offered in 1979 and makes up 50 hours, or 3.5%, of a total program of 1,450 hours. Agyajit Singh was the first part-time person in sport psychology hired by the NIS in 1980.

Since the opening of the YMCA College of Physical Education at Madras in 1920, there always has been some form of psychology in the curriculum, usually educational. Presently, there are now established courses in sport psychology for those students attempting the bachelor of physical education degree in elementary school physical education or recreation, or secondary school education. These courses are offered in training colleges in each of India's 31 states. For each degree students are required to take one educational psychology "paper," or course, and now a paper in sport psychology as well. Each paper is about 4 hours per week over a full year. The candidates for the different courses are academically screened and must have national experience in top-level sport. There is also a compulsory sport psychology course for students who do postgraduate study in physical education. Half a dozen individuals in India have completed their doctorates in physical education with theses in sport psychology and are now teaching the subject as the first qualified generation of Indian sport psychologists. The curriculum for these individuals now teaching in the sport institutes or training colleges includes postgraduate study and a love of sport. A large number of this first generation were self-trained, using only North American sport psychology textbooks and personal initiative.

Most recently, sport psychology has been introduced as an option for study within the psychology departments of Punjab University, Chandigarh University, Patiala, Varanasi, and Kashi Vidya Peeth. There is now some discussion about creating a postgraduate diploma specifically in sport psychology at the Lakshmibai National College of Physical Education of Alagappa University (LNCPE) in the southern states and at the Indira Gandhi Institute of Physical Education and Sport Science in New Delhi.

There is also a tendency for NIS specialists to study abroad where there is a greater emphasis on sport psychology. For example, at least 12 staff members at NIS and LNCPE have completed various level courses in the German Democratic Republic, the Soviet Union, or Germany.

Topics of Study.   Because a formal sport psychology program was established so recently, it is normal that there are a limited number of areas of concern. As often occurs in countries beginning programs in sport psychology, the first step is in psychometrics, or the study of the sport personality. Personality assessment tended to dominate Indian publications in the early 1980s with much effort directed to determining the differences between athletes and nonathletes. The recently felt presence of Indian sport psychologists at international meetings, as well as the visits of foreign scientists, has opened the horizon to more contemporary areas of study.

At the newly established laboratory in sport psychology at the NIS and at the LNCPE, there has been a strong interest in conducting research in motor learning, with special emphasis on reaction time of athletes.

It is clear that when more centers are established in the different parts of India, as is planned, research will become even more diverse.

Publications

At the moment, no specialized publication in sport psychology exists in India, although there is some ongoing lobbying to initiate this project. Actually, one issue of the *Journal of Sports Psychology* did appear in 1977, but it never was published again.

In Patiala, the NIS Publication Unit provides low-priced books that are either discipline-specific or cover general training methods. Of the 12 books that have been published to date, one is on sport psychology—the notable English translation of the Soviet writer A.T. Puni's *Outlines of Sports Psychology*. This book is a valuable contribution to the sport psychology literature because Puni, considered the father of Soviet sport psychology, was one of the first individuals active in sport psychology, with publications dating back to the 1920s.

The only sport psychology book written in Hindi by an Indian was Kreeda Manovignan's 1983 work *Psychology of Physical Education and Sports*, which was notable in that it won a national award as an outstanding publication in the sport and leisure field.

Other journal publications accept sport psychology contributions, such as the *National Institute of Sports Scientific Journal*, the *Journal of Physical Education*, and the *Research Biannual for Movement*. There are also a number of conference proceedings in sport science and physical education.

The Role of Sport Psychology in India

Institutions.   The NIS was created in 1961 and was the first institution to offer a formal sport psychology course and to hire a part-time staff member in the area (Agyajit Singh). In addition, the NIS serves as a documentation, publication, and conference center for India as well as for specialists from other Afro-Asian countries. Two other regional institutes exist at similar but smaller centers in India—the NIS South Center in Bangalore and the NIS East Center in Calcutta. Both the NIS and the LNCPE are now under the direction of the Sports Authority of India, thus giving them more national coherence in programming.

Aside from the NIS, sport psychology subjects can be studied in postgraduate university programs offered by a small number of active individuals at the Lakshmibai National College of Physical Education in Gwalior (Avinash Sidhu and Rajender Singh), the LNCPE, Trivandrum (M.L. Kamlesh), Punjab Univeristy in Patiala (Agyajit Singh), Punjab University in Chandigarh (Jitendra Mohan), Kashi Vidya Peeth (G.P. Thakur and Anand Kumar), NIS Patiala (H.A. Khan), Post Graduate Degree College of Physical Education in Amravati (V.D. Bapat), the University of Kalyani (S.R. Ghosh), and the University of Calcutta (Sukumar Bose). No sport psychologists are believed to work in private practice in India.

Sports Psychology Association of India. After a failed attempt to begin a sport psychology society in 1977 in Hyderabad, little was done in this area until February 23, 1985, when the Sports Psychology Association of India (SPAI) was formed, mainly through the energies of M.L. Kamlesh of Trivandrum. Jitendra Mohan, an eminent psychologist from Punjab University at Chandigarh, was elected the first association president.

Approximately 120 physical educators, coaches, sport scientists, and sport psychologists actively support the activities of SPAI, especially through its annual conferences. At the first conference in Gwalior, 40 attendees listened to 30 papers on the theme of psychology and athletic excellence. Since then the number of participants has steadily risen, the quality of papers has improved, and a number of foreign speakers from the United States, East Germany, and Great Britain have addressed the conference.

SPAI members have also begun to venture into the international arena by associating themselves with the ISSP as well as becoming founding executive members of the umbrella group, the Asian–South Pacific Society of Sport Psychology, which was formed on September 12, 1988, in Seoul, South Korea.

Sport Psychology and Top Sport. In 1979 the NIS began integrating input of a psychological nature into all its various coaching courses. Interestingly enough, the initiative for creating a sport psychology unit came from specialists in exercise physiology who recognized that the study of human behavior was omitted from the preparation of top athletes. This realization occurred at the same time as decreasing international performances by Indian athletes in sports they once dominated. Because the students at NIS for the most part have international sport experience, they were already aware of the limitations in training only the physical components, and these initiatives were well received.

In the earliest years of the NIS, sport psychology was taught in a purely educational manner; that is, students received information in theory courses in the lecture hall, with no assurance that this information was actually being applied. The staging of clinics, workshops, and counseling sessions with coaches and athletes is anticipated but must await further development of adequate staffing and competence in these areas.

Initially, the only sport science support personnel who accompanied Indian teams at international games were medical doctors. However, at the Seoul Olympics, Shri H.A. Khan, who had been working with the Indian field hockey team for some time, was brought in at the last minute to be with the team. Since that time, the Sports Authority of India has indicated that about five sport psychologists will be selected, on an experimental basis, to work with national teams during training camps as well as participate in the Asian Games in September 1990.

Perspectives for Sport Psychology in India

India has seen remarkable improvements in its sport psychology situation over the last 10 years. The nucleus of activity that once took place only at the NIS has now spread across the country. Sport psychology is beginning to take a bigger place in postsecondary institutions as well as at the postgraduate level. The activity of SPAI members has energized the programs, an unenviable task considering there are so few members and a population of 600 million.

These efforts at giving such an impetus to sport psychology in the face of such a formidable challenge are admirable. However, judging from what has occurred in the last decade, there is no reason to believe that the future should not be as bright.

Japan

in collaboration with

Atsushi H. Fujita
Nihon University

Japanese Sport Psychology Résumé

Sport psychology in Japan is deeply rooted in the physical education tradition of research and teaching. Sound direction in the area maintains high standards in research and publication, and applied work with top sport has been increasing over the last 10 years.

Estimated Number of Sport Psychologists. 250

Prominent Institutions. Tskuba University, Ibaragi Prefecture

Orientation. Experimental and educational research

Privileged Topics. Psychophysiological research, personality adjustment

Publication Vehicle. *Japanese Journal of Sport Psychology*

Society. The Japanese Society of Physical Education

Sport in Japan is an intriguing mixture of change-resistant ancient traditions, attitudes, and activities that still pervade the training and competition process combined with the most up-to-date electronic gadgets and devices that evolve at a frightening pace.

Nowhere was the confrontation between the age-old and the modern more striking than at a Tokyo sumo wrestling tournament at the Kokugikan Stadium in 1981. The elephantine athletes who take part in this sport engage in a ritualistic behavior that includes tossing salt into the corners to ward off evil spirits, squatting down in a four-point starting position and giving steely eyes to the opponent, and general strutting around in traditional scanty garb that dates back almost 1,800 years. This prematch ceremony that builds up the athlete's psychological and spiritual state is captured by cameras from every angle using the most advanced technology in the world and beamed live, with instant replays, to the 65% of the nation's television sets that are tuned to this final match. The interest was particularly high on this occasion because a young wrestler named Chiyonofuji had just defeated the grand champion, Kitanoumi. The reason for this special coverage was that Chiyonofuji was brash rather than reserved, charismatic rather than lumbering, and by sumo standards skinny, at 115 kg, rather than fat.

But it was not biomechanics that designed this new efficient body, nor was it sport psychology that counseled this new sumo competitive attitude; both were anomalies that successfully combined through chance. Most of the traditional sport pastimes in Japan, such as judo, kendo, kyudo archery, and sumo wrestling, are outside the realm of application for sport psychology and the other sport sciences. They remain more within cultural rather than athletic circles.

Sport psychology in Japan was traditionally concerned with the psychological aspects of physical education but since the 1980s a greater focus has been on top-level sport. The Japanese tradition in physical education research was based in earlier years on work coming out of Europe and the United States. The attention given to the psychological aspects of physical education was mostly due to Mitsuo Matsui, the father of sport psychology in Japan, who majored in aviation psychology and started research in 1924, when the National Institute of Physical Education was established in Tokyo. This date is particularly noteworthy because at about the same time sport psychology laboratories were started in Germany (Carl Diem in Berlin, 1920) and in the United States (Coleman Griffith at the University of Illinois, 1925). Matsui prepared the present generation of scholars in sport psychology in Japan at the Tokyo University of Education. Though still based somewhat on American practice, sport psychology in Japan combines the old and the new into a unique and emerging entity. When Matsui retired in 1954, Iwao Matsuda replaced him as sport psychology professor at the Tokyo University of Education.

Training in Sport Psychology

Following the war, in accordance with directives of the American authorities of the occupying forces, Japanese physical education turned away from gymnastics and the martial arts and put a greater emphasis on sport and games. In the ensuing reforms that took place after the restoration of independence in 1951, physical education was modeled after the American elementary, junior high, and high school systems, right through the curricula of all universities and colleges.

With the creation of the Japanese Society of Physical Education, now Tskuba University, in 1950, it became possible to present and publish research results. This forum stimulated the growth of individual sport science disciplines to flourish, and in 1960 a special psychological section was created. At the same time, a number of specialized courses in sport psychology were developed in the universities.

These courses, however, were called "The Psychology of Physical Education" rather than "The Psychology of Sport," indicating the particular emphasis within Japan. Rather than generating information that had specialized application, the universities adopted a somewhat broader approach that aimed at developing mental and physical abilities, skill acquisition, socialization processes, and principles in health and safety. This global approach to learning is not specific to sport psychology, but applies to much of the Japanese learning in other aspects of life.

There are presently 30 universities and five colleges in Japan where it is possible to study physical education at the undergraduate level. Sport psychology is a compulsory subject in these programs. Fourteen universities and one college offer postgraduate study for a master's degree in either physical education or education. Those who major in sport psychology can obtain both a master's and a doctorate degree in sport psychology, although not many individuals do either. However, students within these programs have carried out quite specific research projects, especially in the broad areas of motor learning and personality adjustment.

Study in a specialized physical education program used to be most often within education departments, but now a number of universities have separate physical education faculties. During this course of study general developmental, differential, and social psychology are taught, along with motor learning. At the moment, a few courses directed to top-level sport exist in Japan.

The master's degree is 2 years of study whereas the Ph.D. degree is specialized into 5 years of research and course work in either history, sport psychology, social psychology, physiology, or coaching.

Good research students can be hired at the university as assistants to work at a certain level under the direction of the professor. Loyalty to the "family," or the institution, is high, as in Japanese industrial institutions. A "team feeling" that I have not often experienced elsewhere exists within these educational programs.

Topics of Study. Nowhere in the world was it easier than in Japan to accurately assess both the relative importance of sport psychology as compared to the other sport sciences and the most frequently considered areas of study within sport psychology. Hiroshi Suetoshi published a content analysis of physical activity research from 1950 to 1974, broken down into 5-year segments within each sport science discipline.

Of the 10,705 research reports published, 1,756 or 16.4%

were in the subareas that make up the broad field of sport psychology. Only exercise physiology had a greater number—2,270, or 21.2% of the total publications.

The subject of personality adjustment made up the greatest share (36.8%) of the sport psychology papers and included work in personality, attitudes, adjustment and adaptation, and mental hygiene, in decreasing order of frequency. Motor learning and practice followed in second place (22.9%), encompassing areas of response timing, motor learning, perception and recognition, and aspects of learning and educability.

Cross-cultural comparisons with other countries having similar data would be instructive. Since the early 1980s, greater emphasis has been given to narrower areas of specialization, including top sport.

Publications

The earliest Japanese publication in sport psychology was Mitsuo Matsui's 1952 book *Psychology of Physical Education*, which he based on work completed at that time in Japan, Germany, and the United States. Matsui's successors, especially Iwao Matsuda and Atsushi Fujita, have since dominated the area of sport psychology in Japan and have continued in his footsteps.

Because many large publishing houses are interested in sport psychology, original Japanese publications are abundant, as are translations of sport psychology books from the American (Cratty, Gaylord, Lawther, Singer, Tutko), the English (Kane, Whiting), and the Russian (Puni) literature.

Matsuda has been the most active individual in publication, and his text, also titled *Psychology of Physical Education*, includes chapters on research, psychophysiology, psychoeducation, psychological characteristics of physical education, motor development, motor learning, personality, group dynamics, and mental hygiene.

Individual sport psychology research can be published either in the *Japanese Journal of Physical Education* if it has broad application, or in the *Japanese Journal of Sport Psychology* if the research is more specific. This journal is an exact replica in its format of the *International Journal of Sport Psychology* but in Japanese with English abstracts. This journal began publication in 1974 and is believed to be the oldest national publication devoted to sport psychology in the world.

The Role of Sport Psychology in Japan

Institutions. A large number of universities in Japan offer courses in the psychology of physical education, the most important being Tskuba University, where the oldest and biggest faculty of physical education in Japan exists. Tskuba was formerly the Tokyo University of Education, and most of the active individuals throughout Japan were trained here, by either Matsui or Matsuda.

Nihon University in Tokyo has recently made a name for itself in the area of training effects, especially the effects of training on decision making, under the direc-

tion of Atsushi Fujita. There are many signs, however, that increasing levels of activity will develop in centers outside of the Tokyo area or the east, especially in the Osaka-Nara-Kyoto region as well as the Hiroshima and Kyushyu region in the south.

Japanese Society of Sport Psychology (JSSP). The JSSP was founded in 1973 with Iwao Matsuda elected as president and Atsushi Fujita as secretary general. This group holds its annual scientific meetings at different places in Japan.

These annual two-day meetings provide more than 100 people a forum for discussion. The 12-member managing council, directed by the president, decides the theme of the congress. Each congress results in the publication of the annual edition of the *Japanese Journal of Sport Psychology*. In 1979, the JSSP included a special international symposium in its annual congress, at which time the ISSP managing council also met. The Japan Amateur Sports Association directs amateur sport for all of Japan. Within this association, some sport psychology information is available to coaches. Most JSSP members are physical education teachers with an interest in psychology, and the remainder are either university professors, assistants, or researchers, only a few of whom are trained psychologists.

One very interesting force that will have a considerable impact on Asia's future is the initiative by Fujita to create an Asiatic and South Pacific Association of Sport Psychology (ASPASP). This regrouping of specialists from this part of the world would have a structure and function parallel to those of NASPSPA in North America and FEPSAC in Europe. A greater opportunity for more frequent meetings that deal with local and regional issues would be the most obvious benefit of the creation of this group.

Sport Psychology and Top Sport. One of the major causes of the growth of interest in sport science in general and sport psychology in particular was the awarding of the 1964 Olympic Games to Tokyo. A committee of distinguished professors was formed in 1960 as a part of the Japan Amateur Sports Association to apply sport science knowledge to elite athletes. This committee thoroughly analyzed the physiological characteristics of the entire Japanese contingent participating in the 1964 Olympic Games. (In an impressive long-term project, Iaso Hirata has carried out these types of analyses at each subsequent Olympiad.) Applied sport psychology was introduced to some athletes at that time in terms of counseling, relaxation, and autogenic training.

However, most individuals trained in sport psychology have been trained within an experimental rather than intervention-based framework. It is also important to realize that most top-level coaches have backgrounds in sport practice itself, not the university physical education system. They are therefore not sensitized to some of the academic areas of sport psychology that could potentially benefit their sport training. But perhaps most important are the cultural differences inherent in the Japanese psyche that are not present in Westerners.

Japanese athletes train in a disciplined manner, motivated from within. In Western cultures, athletes may require external pressures to show up, practice hard, and compete well. Western coaches wonder what they can do to motivate athletes. As a contrast, Japanese gymnasts very often train by themselves, without the coach's supervision. This dedication, however, may be changing, as young Japanese appear less willing to dedicate themselves to extensive sport training, choosing instead to devote more time to studies.

In our Western culture, we try to train athletes to be tough-minded, and we hope that they will respect their coach and teammates. In Japan, it is part of athletes' psyche to endure long, torturous training, as is evidenced by films of 5-hour training sessions of the victorious women's volleyball team at the Tokyo Olympics, or by Shun Fujimoto competing with a broken leg at the Montreal Olympic gymnastic competition. In Japan, respect and honor for oneself and for the coach is assumed, and it remains the cornerstone of the Japanese culture.

Perhaps the types of interventions that occur in Western sport psychology are not essential to success in Japan's top-level sport. Still, the Japan Amateur Sports Association has been requesting more frequently information from sport psychologists that could enhance sport performance at the top levels. As an indication of these changes, during the period of 1986 to 1988, the government sponsored a research project with an annual budget of 20 million yen ($125,000) entitled "Mental Management for Athletes."

Perspectives for Sport Psychology in Japan

In recent years sport psychology activity in Japan has increased in intensity and has also been decentralized so that its effects are felt across the country, initially with the common citizen, but lately more with top-level athletes. As might be expected in a country that is both geographically and culturally isolated, Japan has developed its own brand of sport psychology. Many of the themes for research have been borrowed from North American textbooks and adapted to the Japanese manner. However, there is recent evidence of research developments in behavioral aspects of sport, using electrophysiological measurements and complex data transformations and analyses. These possibilities are by-products of Japan's advanced state of technology. Recent changes in orientation will give a new slant to the work in sport psychology directed toward the elite athlete. The increased contact between coaches and researchers is a starting point. At present, it is essential that all coaches take courses in the sport sciences and specifically in sport psychology through the seminar sponsored by the Japan Amateur Sports Association.

The potential interaction of sport psychology with the traditional areas of sport that seem to be directed by cultural rather than scientific forces will be of great interest. If the traditional sports such as sumo open their doors to sport science, one or both entities might change. Chiyonofuji's transformation of sumo from survival of the fattest to survival of the fastest may be the harbinger of change in this country.

Singapore

in collaboration with

Quek Jin-Jong
College of Physical Education

Singapore Sport Psychology Résumé

Although the importance of sport psychology for the acquisition and performance of skills was recognized in the mid-1970s, only a few coaches included it as part of their training. The first step toward the introduction of sport psychology for learning and performance was made only in the mid-1980s, and progress since then has been constant.

Estimated Number of Sport Psychologists. 8

Prominent Institutions. College of Physical Education, Singapore Sports Council

Orientation. Applied sport psychology

Privileged Topics. None

Publication Vehicles. None

Society. None

Singapore is a pragmatic society that gears practically every facet of its life to its economic survival. Education is oriented toward preparing individuals for the industrial and commercial needs of the nation. The emphasis has been on academic achievements to bring about this national objective. As a result, the desire to excel in one's studies and professional career has left little room for the pursuit of leisure activities and sports.

The Singapore Sports Council (SSC), an organization responsible for the construction and maintenance of all public sports facilities, embarked on a "Sport for All" program in the 1970s. Mass participation in swimming, cycling, and jogging have thus been encouraged. In recent years, however, the focus has been on producing higher levels of sport performance at international competitions.

The government's recent emphasis on excellence, including sports, initiated the formation of the Advisory Council on Sports and Recreation. The Council was formed in April 1988, and it seeks, among other objectives, "to help talented Singaporeans strive for excellence in sports." This thrust by the government should pave the way for greater changes toward more efficient administration of sports organizations, better training of coaches, and the establishment of more effective training programs. In this context, sport psychology will definitely play a more prominent role in the effort toward excellence in sport.

Training in Sport Psychology

The increased awareness of the importance of physical education and sport science resulted in the establishment of the College of Physical Education (CPE) in mid-1984. Though this move may appear insignificant compared to the development in many other countries, it still marks a milestone in the history of physical education in Singapore.

Singapore does not offer a formal course in the specialized area of sport psychology. However, the CPE has a 60-hour unit on sport psychology, which is one of the compulsory components of professional teacher training. This course is designed to familiarize teacher trainees with the subject and help them be aware of the psychological aspects related to teaching and coaching games and other sporting activities.

In July 1991 CPE will be elevated to a school of Human Movement Studies (HMS) in the Nanyang Technical University (NTU).

Topics of Study. The sport psychology component in CPE and the school of HMS has emphasized the applied principles of teaching. The unit covers a wide range of topics like motivation, arousal, information processing, personality, and relaxation techniques, with the focus on pedagogy. This survey course is meant to help teacher trainees be aware of the multiple effects of the environment and the learner/performer on the performance of skills.

Also in the mid-1980s, the SSC introduced sport psychology as one of the many components of sports training for coaches. Medical doctors of the SSC Sports Medicine and Research Centre and visiting sport psychologists have conducted clinics and lectures introducing coaches to the principles of applied sport psychology since 1985. It is also believed that Singapore's hosting of the Seventh ISSP World Sport Psychology Congress in 1989 heightened interest in this area and provided the impetus for new fields of study.

Publications

Sport psychology is a relatively new area of study in Singapore. As a result, at this time no journal on sport psychology or the sport sciences has been published. However, sport psychology articles can appear in *CPE Forum*, the journal of the CPE.

The Role of Sport Psychology in Singapore

Institutions. As the sports associations become more receptive to the use of sport psychology to train and prepare athletes for performance, more sport psychologists will be needed. Although the school of HMS could offer a specialized program in the future, doing so may not be cost-effective because of the limited needs of such a small population. It would be more prudent to identify suitable candidates with the necessary prerequisites and send them abroad for training. This practical approach will satisfy the immediate need for sport psychologists, and the students will have the opportunity to work with and learn from the best in the world during theirx training.

Society. Although about half a dozen persons have received training in various aspects of sport psychology, no move has been made to form a sport psychology society. The potential once again lies with the CPE, which has the highest number of trained lecturers in the area of sport psychology. Perhaps it is premature to have an association at this stage of development, but possibly a committee will be formed in the near future.

Sport Psychology and Top Sport. Not many national coaches formally use sport psychology, probably because most, if not all, of the sports associations and clubs are managed by volunteers and untrained personnel. As a result, any psychologically and physiologically based approaches that were adopted by individual coaches were sporadic and not sustained. To quote from a retrospective report, "Some aspects of sport psychology have been employed by a few coaches of a few associations for a few periods" in the mid-70s and early 80s. So far, no national team representing Singapore in international competition has included a sport psychologist in its contingent, except for team doctors playing a dual role.

In 1988 the chairman of the Football Association of Singapore announced through local newspapers that psychologists interested in sport will be recruited to help soccer players prepare for competition. A similar call has been made for the training of the nation's swimmers. These moves could herald the turning point for more widespread use of sport psychology in Singapore. It is hoped that as the national associations, together with support institutions like CPE and SSC, include sport psychology as part of athlete training, major strides will be made in the areas of training and athlete performance. Such development could lead to the inclusion of a full complement of trained staff, including professional coaches and sport psychologists, for all future national teams.

Perspectives for Sport Psychology in Singapore

The teaching and application of sport psychology is at an embryonic stage in Singapore. All attempts made over the years have been modest. So far, there has been little appreciable effort toward including sport psychology as part of the training regimen, except in a few sports. However, top administrators of national associations are generally aware that it takes more than just physiological fitness and conditioning to bring about top perfor-mances. These administrators are also looking to sport psychologists for answers to bring about better perfor-mances in athletes. They are hopeful that with sport psychologists' help, athletes will experience greater success in international competition. During this interim period, however, the administrators will carefully moni-tor the doctors and psychologists. The responsibilities of these pioneers will be great, because they are expected to provide the ultimate answers to the lackluster perfor-mances of Singapore's athletes at various national and regional competitions. Until steps are taken to train sport psychologists, either locally or abroad, the attempts of the previously mentioned personnel to double as sport psychologists are like fitting a square peg into a round hole.

Chapter 4

MIDDLE EAST AND AFRICA
Algeria

in collaboration with

Ammar Bachir-Cherif
Institut des Sciences de la Technologie du Sport, Alger

Algerian Sport Psychology Résumé

Sport psychology is perhaps as well developed in Algeria as it is anywhere else in North Africa. Algeria has institutionalized programs for physical education and sport and is now embarking on a program of graduate study and intervention for top sport.

Estimated Number of Sport Psychologists. 3

Prominent Institutions. Institut des Sciences de la Technologie du Sport; Institut de Technologie du Sport

Orientation. General education

Privileged Topics. Self-regulation and social psychology

Publication Vehicle. *Sciences et Technologie du Sport*

Society. Centre d'Etude et de Recherche en Sport

Algeria geographically dominates the north of Africa and is now in the midst of a fundamental transition from a French-controlled physical education system to one that is evolving using self-generated models as well as those from the Soviet Union. The arabization process that has dominated the Maghreb, or the Arabic countries of North Africa, is also in effect in Algeria, and thus many parallels exist between the institutional structures of Algeria and those of its neighbors. At present, the principles of sport psychology are beginning to influence basic athlete preparation in sports such as swimming, football, and track and field.

Training in Sport Psychology

Sport psychology has begun to assume a place of importance in a number of structures that relate to both physical education and sport in Algeria. Coaches and athletes are beginning to perceive the important role that psychology plays in everyday training, and this interest is spreading to teachers and administrators in sport.

At this time, limitations to the widespread implementation of sport psychology exist because there are an insufficient number of individuals trained in the discipline. At the moment, it is impossible to pursue the study of sport psychology in the classic Algerian universities, so individuals who want this training must study abroad. In 1978, the Institut des Sciences de la Technologie du Sport (ISTS) introduced three basic units relating to psychology in its 5-year program for coach training, which leads to a diploma in advanced studies (D.E.S.). The first 60-hour unit is in general psychology, which gives an overview of the field, and 30 hours are spent in developmental psychology. There is also a 60-hour unit in sport psychology that comprehensively presents the areas of research methods, motor learning, mental preparation, and psychoregulation.

Teaching is carried out by Algerian *maîtres de conférence*, or conference masters, as well as Algerian teaching assistants. Near the end of the program, students with a special interest in sport psychology can become integrated into a special scientific circle with the opportunity for concentrated study leading toward a graduating thesis. Since 1983, a modest number of D.E.S. theses in sport psychology have been produced.

A postgraduate program of study leads to a magister, or master's degree, and the first group of graduates finished in 1988. There is also a course in sport psychology at the Institute of Physical Education and Sport (IEPS) that prepares students to teach in secondary and university programs. Its 4-year program leads to a license in physical education. There is also a 3-year program at the Technological Institute of Sport (ITS) in Alger, Oran, and Constantine, as well as 3-year programs of study for sport coaches. Further, during the residency program in sports medicine there is an 8-hour unit devoted to sport psychology.

Topics of Study. In 1988 and 1989 the Olympic Academy established a number of research priorities for the betterment of sport practice. The main concerns for the present regard the prediction of sport ability in children and the organization of school sport for children. There is also a strong preoccupation with evaluating and monitoring the psychological dimensions of training.

Publications

Since 1988 the ISTS has published *Sciences et Technologie du Sport*, a quarterly journal dedicated to the sport sciences and open to research in sport psychology. This journal is believed to be the first of its kind in Africa, and it promises to be an interesting initiative in the field.

The Role of Sport Psychology in Algeria

Institutions. Sport psychology is being taught to coaches and teachers at different levels at three post-secondary institutions in programs that last from 3 to 5 years. All programs have similar units in sport psychology that give an overview of the field.

In 1988, the Algerian Olympic Committee created a Center of Study and Research in Sport (CERS) targeted at aiding the advancement of sport practice by means of multidisciplinary research. The first major project of this group was to organize a national seminar on systems of preparation and evaluation of high-level athletes. Members of this group have also presented research at various international meetings such as those of FEPSAC and the ISSP.

Sport Psychology and Top Sport. For the moment, all coaches who go through the institutes of sport receive course work in sport psychology. Ammar Bachir-Cherif has been the only person to intervene directly with top-level athletes, assisting athletes in track and field and swimming in preparing for the Seoul Olympics. It is believed that this type of intervention will increase as the sport institutes begin to function more efficiently.

Perspectives for Sport Psychology in Algeria

The field of sport psychology is still in the embryonic stage in Algeria but things are changing rapidly. In the last 5 years postgraduate programs, research theses, and a new journal have been initiated. In addition, there is increasing pressure from the field to bring sport psychology out of the laboratories and lecture halls into the applied areas of sport.

Egypt

in collaboration with

Mohamed Allawy
Helwan University

Egyptian Sport Psychology Résumé

Sport psychology in Egypt is relatively well developed within limited aspects of the field, and Egypt has become the leader in the field among Arabic countries. Certain unique achievements have already taken place, but the base of support for the programs is rather narrow.

Estimated Number of Sport Psychologists. 27

Prominent Institutions. Helwan Universities, Cairo and Alexandria

Orientation. Arabic test validations

Privileged Topic. Anxiety in sports

Publication Vehicles. Variety of Egyptian textbooks

Society. Egyptian Society of Sport Psychology

Sport in Egypt has a special form of organization, with the central focus being private sports clubs. These clubs are scattered across the major cities, taking up huge acreages for soccer fields, outdoor volleyball and basketball courts, and field hockey pitches. They are veritable oases of tranquility amid the honking, frenetic traffic that is particular to Egypt. Clubs are private in nature and are throwbacks to the period of British occupation; the most famous of the Cairo clubs are the Zamalak and the National. A large club can have from 20,000 to 30,000 members. All ages can participate in activities ranging from polo to croquet. In Cairo's Shooting Club, a modification of North American skeet shooting uses live pigeons, which are later sold as food.

Though most recently Egypt has been regaining some of its former prosperity, there are still chronic shortages in the area of education. Schools are overcrowded, due partially to the direction of a large portion of the national budget to the military. Some schools have three shifts of students a day, and consequently physical education is neglected or reduced to a program of calisthenics rather than sport. Most schools do not have attached playing fields. In 1966 the Supreme Council for Youth and Sports tried to implement an exercise program via the sports clubs, but this stopped after 2 years of effort.

Training in Sport Psychology

Many old Islamic traditions prevent the rapid implementation of innovations from the Western world. For example, much duplication occurs in teaching physical education in universities because men and women have separate faculties. Most other university faculties in Egypt are coeducational.

In Egypt sport psychology holds a unique position among the sport sciences as compared to most countries in the world. Here, sport psychology is the most important of the sport sciences for the simple reason that initially, Egypt did not have the laboratories necessary for studying the other areas in the biological sciences. Sport psychology research in Egypt is based solely on the use of translated pencil-and-paper psychological inventories coming mainly from North America.

Psychology has always played an integral role in training physical education teachers in Egypt. Since 1937, a psychology course has been in the curriculum at Helwan University. In 1964, Mohamed Allawy, the founder of Egyptian sport psychology, completed his doctorate in sport psychology at the Deutsche Hochschule für Körperkultur (DHfK) in Leipzig. In 1965, upon his return to Helwan University in Cairo, three special courses in sport psychology were offered in the final 3 years of the physical education program. They touch on the topics of general psychology and physical education, developmental psychology, motor learning, personality, mental health, application, and guidance. No laboratories yet exist, so much of this information was transmitted through conventional lectures.

There are two physical education faculties of Helwan University, with identical programs in Cairo and in Alexandria. Each has a men's and a women's faculty. Traditionally, Cairo has been the major center, and the men's program in sport psychology there has been far superior to the others under Allawy's guidance. However, two major changes in direction have occurred in recent years.

The first direction shift has been at the men's faculty in Alexandria, where a unique laboratory has been constructed for both biomechanics and sport psychology, using up-to-date electronic and audiovisual equipment along with many homemade contraptions. This rapid development was due to the strong guiding hand of Professor Shalaby, Dean of the Alexandria campus.

The second change has been within Cairo itself, where the women's faculty has equipped itself with modern laboratory apparatus and is showing great potential for growth. However, due to the initiatives of Allawy and his many students, the main sport psychology center is still in Cairo. Allawy introduced both a master's degree (1965) and a Ph.D. degree (1973) in Cairo in which men and women study together, with a specialization in sport psychology.

The master's degree takes 3 years to complete, and the main emphasis is on motor skills based on communication theory and information processing. A thesis on a specific research problem is required. The doctoral course, which finishes with a Ph.D. degree, takes from 3 to 4 years, includes a thesis, and is made up of four concentrations: two courses in the psychology of motor skills and two courses in sport psychology in sport training. Normally, there are 3 to 6 doctoral students each year and about 20 master's candidates. Once these students complete their studies, they are able to teach at universities, either in Egypt or in neighboring countries. The graduates from Egypt have had a profound effect on other sport psychology programs in the Middle East because of Allawy's many disciples.

Top-level coaches also receive sport psychology input in the form of 30 hours of specific lectures pertaining to their sport. For the moment, however, no practical clinics or workshops have been organized to develop psychoregulation skills.

Topics of Study. Due to the high cost of laboratory technology, until most recently all research in the field has used paper-and-pencil tests for different psychological factors with Egyptian samples of athletes. Spielberger's tests of state and trait anxiety and Marten's Sport Competitive Anxiety Test have been translated into Arabic, validated, and applied to different sport groups in Egypt. Cattel's 16PF and Eysenck's personality test have received similar treatment. Finally, Kenyon's test of attitudes toward physical activity has also been translated into Arabic. Some studies in motor skill acquisition have been carried out using field tests and factor analysis techniques.

Publications

Because Egypt has the most advanced university system of all the Arabic nations in the Middle East, it is logical that it would produce most of the scientific literature in sport psychology. Allawy has integrated the research findings of his many doctoral students and innumerable master's students into his five books, which are used across Saudi Arabia, Kuwait, Iran, Iraq, Sudan, and Jordan in their small colleges. Many of Allawy's Egyptian students were attracted to these other lands to work for abundant petrodollars.

The popularity of Allawy's books is indicated by the number of editions of each: *Psychological Factors of Sport Activity*, 4th edition (1966); *Sport Psychology*, 4th edition (1971); *Psychology and Physical Education*, 8th edition (1974); *Psychology of Training and Conditioning*, 4th edition (1976); and *Measurement in Physical Education and Sport Psychology* (1980). Researchers can also publish their sport psychology findings in a university journal entitled *Research at Helwan University* with English abstracts.

The Role of Sport Psychology in Egypt

Institutions. Helwan University's four campuses all offer sport psychology with opportunities for studying at the doctoral level. Because women came on the scene later than men, the men's programs have been traditionally stronger than the women's. But this appears to be changing, at least in Cairo where the greatest concentration of sport psychologists are working. So far only limited contact has been made with the university psychology department, perhaps because interdisciplinary study in physical education is not the rule outside of North America.

The Supreme Council for Youth and Sports has also authorized sport psychology courses for top sport coaches, but so far this has been purely an academic transmission of information rather than a practical application.

Helwan University is a key center not only for the Middle East countries but also for some Arabic countries in North Aftica. Egyptian specialists academically prepare foreign students, set up research programs, and provide all the sport-related literature.

Egyptian Society of Sport Psychology. This group was founded by Mohamed Allawy in 1975 and has about 27 members, 22 of whom work in Cairo. The main activity of this society is the symposium held in April each year that is part of a larger physical education conference. In 1983 and 1984, the Egyptian society hosted two international congresses in sport psychology that attracted a large contingent of foreign scholars from Europe and North America.

In 1981, the Egyptian group was the only organized sport psychology society in the Arab world, but since then similar developments have occurred in Jordan and Iraq. Most important of all, in 1987 the Arabic Federation of Sport Psychology was formed. This group has representation from 22 Arabic countries in Africa and the Middle East and now boasts more than 400 members. The activity of this continental society will be watched with great interest to see if it can sustain the same interest as FEPSAC has in Europe, NASPSPA in North America, and the newly formed ASPASP in Asia.

Sport Psychology and Top Sport. Top-level coaches receive sport psychology information in the form of 30 hours of academic lectures. But it is inaccurate to say that sport psychology is totally integrated into the training and competition phases of top sport as it is in Eastern Europe and parts of North America. No special sessions of an applied nature have yet been attempted with coaches or athletes in practical settings. To date, a sport psychologist has not accompanied an Egyptian sport team to an international competition, unless one counts Mohamed Allawy, who accompanied the 1988 team to Seoul as Egyptian Olympic Committee General Secretary.

Perspectives for Sport Psychology in Egypt

Egypt has the potential to do much more in sport psychology than it is presently. Because the educational levels in sport science in the bordering Arab countries are very low, Egypt is not stimulated by these countries to improve. It is still the big frog in the small pond in this part of the world.

A number of centers have made encouraging attempts to upgrade research by establishing laboratories at an advanced technological level. Perhaps this will stimulate others to follow suit.

Finally, the intended implementation of applied workshops and the assigning of sport psychology people to practical sport situations would increase the impact of sport psychology, provide needed experience for these individuals, and reduce the demands on the few who are now shouldering the load.

Israel

in collaboration with

Shulamit Raviv
Wingate Institute for Physical Education and Sport

Israeli Sport Psychology Résumé

Sport psychology in Israel mirrors the nature of the country itself. Though small in stature, it is bold in design. All the necessary elements for a successful sport psychology program are in place from the technical, methodological, and personnel standpoints.

Estimated Number of Sport Psychologists. 50

Prominent Institutions. The Wingate Institute for Physical Education and Sport, Beer-Sheeba and Ohalo Colleges

Orientation. Applied, theoretical, and interdisciplinary research in youth sport and coach education

Privileged Topic. Psychodiagnostics

Publication Vehicle. Wingate conference publications

Society. Israeli Association of Sport Psychology

The photos in the Wingate brochure tell the story. In the first, taken in 1955, a smiling Israeli is standing in the middle of a virtual desert. Isolated tufts of some form of arid plant life are scattered about. In the background are two modern sport facilities under construction. The second photo is dated 1975. The solitary smiling Israeli has been replaced by three chatting contemporary university Israelis, such as might appear on a brochure from a large American college. The two buildings have been completed, and the surroundings have been magically transformed. The ground is now covered with lush green grass and healthy shrubs. Large trees line the modern pathways to the two original buildings and the many others that have since been built. The scene is the Wingate Institute for Physical Education and Sport in Netanya, but it is representative of the dynamic activity that has taken place across Israel in almost every aspect of life. Since the attainment of statehood in 1948, this small country (a shade larger than the state of New Jersey) with a small population of 4 million has also achieved rapid development in sport and inevitably in sport psychology.

The newness of sport psychology in Israel goes back to the late 1960s, when Shalom Hermon proposed that dimensions of a psychological nature should complement the areas of sport physiology and biomechanics. Sport pedagogy at the Institute was the first step toward the development of sport psychology in Israel. Two key people joined the Wingate staff in the early 1970s. Gilad Weingarten arrived in 1970 and was followed by Ema Geron, already an established author and researcher in sport psychology, who emigrated from her native Bulgaria. As the area has evolved, others have joined the sport psychology team: Gershon Tenenbaum, Shulamit Raviv, Michael Bar-Eli, Yakov Gal-Or, Shraga Sade, Raya Yuval, Rubi Friedman, and Dubi Lufi.

Training in Sport Psychology

Though Israel's earliest sport psychologists were trained abroad, it is now possible to receive doctoral certification in Israel through the faculties of psychology or medicine (public health) of the universities of Tel Aviv and Jerusalem, using sport as a research focus. Some Israelis are presently following this route with the disadvantage being the lack of sport-specific course content. This deficiency is being compensated for by the introduction of a master's level course in sport psychology at the Zinman College of Physical Education at the Wingate Institute. Though the college does not yet grant a master of arts degree, the master's level courses are recognized toward that degree by several universities in Israel (Tel Aviv, Jerusalem, and Haifa) and in the United States (Adelphi and Boston universities).

The Wingate Institute is located on 110 acres of verdant terrain that house a variety of modern sports facilities. The institute's Zinman College is the only Jewish academic institution devoted to physical education, sports, dance, movement, and recreation. The college has close to 2,000 students and is directed by 200 half- and full-time staff. Besides this college, there are also schools for physiotherapy; the Nat Holman School for Coaches and Instructors, which offers diplomas for short courses in coaching; and the sport department. The sport department has four emphases: research, sports medicine, elite sport, and the development of young talent. The objective of this department is the continuous promotion of higher standards of the professional and scientific services provided for all who study and train at the Institute. The practical results achieved by the research and sports medicine divisions are disseminated through national and international publications, and by consultative and advisory services involving coaches, sport organizations, and athletes.

Israelis can study for a number of undergraduate degrees and diplomas that have sport psychology components: a 3-year program leading to a senior certified teachers' diploma; a 4- or a 5-year program of combined studies at Zinman College and at the universities in Tel Aviv or Haifa, leading to a bachelor of arts or a bachelor of science degree; or a 4-year bachelor of education degree that emphasizes a well-rounded program in educational science and skills in dance, movement, and sport. Students must specialize in one of a broad spectrum of areas ranging from posture cultivation, nautical education, outdoor education, dance, sports medicine, and cardiopulmonary rehabilitation.

The Zinman College offers specific compulsory and optional courses in sport psychology, motor learning, and development, including perceptual and cognitive aspects in motor development; mental health, illness, and physical education; personality and psychomotor tests in physical education and sport; sensorimotor and cerebral organization and intellectual processes; sport psychology; information processing and its implications on motor skill learning; relaxation techniques and biofeedback; and verbal and movement communication.

Sport psychology is also taught in secondary schools. Thirty schools in Israel have courses at the high school level in physical education. These courses consist of 150 hours during the 3 years, 90 of which are academic and 60 practical. Students who select this option receive 30 hours of philosophy, 30 hours of sociology and psychology, and 60 hours of the biological aspects of physical education and sport. The idea that guided the initiators of this program was teaching high school students the subjects that are relevant, interesting, and important to them. In addition, this is the age when students develop positive attitudes toward physical activity and attain proper control of the body. It appears that this structure may be unique in the world.

Topics of Study. Sport psychology in Israel is an independent scientific discipline in which two distinct thrusts can be identified: the theoretical and the pragmatic. The theoretical area deals primarily with identifying the psychological methods and other causal elements that influence learning and development in sport. The influence of sport in children's intellectual, social, and ethical development is studied. Investigations in the theoretical areas view sport as a natural laboratory and an ideal environment for the measurement of emotional reactions, personal characteristics, and social relationships.

The pragmatic aspects center on the solution of three problems in physical education and sport: psychodiagnostic problems, psychological guidance for coaches and athletes, and professional psychotherapy. Empirical studies are carried out in both laboratory and field settings in the sport department and at the college. Within the behavioral sciences section of the research unit, three measurement tools were developed and validated: a motoric achievement motivation test (MMT) for the evaluation of levels of aspiration and reactions to success and failure during a competitive laboratory motor activity (tapping); a kinesthetic measurement technique based on the reproduction of real gross body movements; and a test to measure the ability to learn motor reactions to signals from different spatial positions.

A number of specific projects in a variety of areas are also underway in both fundamental and psychodiagnostic areas. Varied studies are also underway on self-control strategies with learning-disabled individuals, participants in exercise programs, and the highly anxious. A number of projects also relate to the psychometric evaluation of top athletes, especially regarding anxiety and personality measures. There are also several studies regarding the use of cognitive strategies in game situations and in crisis resolution.

Publications

Many general scientific publications and a great deal of applied and sport-specific literature has been enhanced in the last few years. Israelis have published research in North American and international journals that are specific to sport psychology or sport science in general. Publication is also encouraged in a variety of European and North American proceedings in sport psychology as well as in the applied psychology congresses.

Because it is costly and often impossible for Israelis to travel freely in the world, Wingate yearly hosts one or two international symposia or seminars. To date, the proceedings from two psychologically related seminars have been published by the publications department at Wingate: *Motor Learning in Physical Education and Sport* (1976) and *Psychological Assessment in Sport* (1977); and the first and second *Proceedings of the National Conference of Psychology and Sociology of Sports and Physical Education* (1982, 1986).

In addition to these four collections of conference papers, Ema Geron's *Physical Preparation of Athletes* (1976) was translated from Bulgarian into Hebrew, and her *Children in Sport* (1981) and *An Introduction to Sport Psychology* (1982) were published in English. Other general volumes have also been published in Hebrew, such as *A Handbook of Sport Psychology* (1984) by Gilad Weingarten, and *Motor Learning* by Fuchs, Ben-Sira, and Zikovsky.

The Role of Sport Psychology in Israel

Institutions. For the moment, Wingate plays the central role in spreading the sport psychology word to upcoming teachers and coaches and in coordinating and carrying out research. The people of Israel have a strong, positive perception of this institute. This image results from the careful but aggressive guidance given by the directors of Wingate that makes it one of the premier sport institutes in the world.

However, to provide a broader base for research and advanced study of sport psychology, the institute must enter into a graduate program. The judicious use of graduate students as the cutting edge of research will improve the capacity for dialogue regarding research and

thus upgrade its quality. This will also dramatically increase the number of people working in sport psychology to perhaps the highest per capita in the world.

An individual's impression of an institution and a country is directly related to how that person is treated during a visit. One special feature that anyone visiting Wingate for a conference remembers is the warm, personalized reception, the quality of the organization before, during, and after the conference (i.e., publications), and the unforgettable tours to both historic and modern sites.

The close connections between Wingate and Israel's small satellite colleges and its relationship with the Ministry of Education give sport psychology a broad base that is in close contact with the grass-roots needs of the country—something that is universally desirable but more difficult to attain in larger, more populous, and less conceptually unified countries.

Israeli Association of Sport Psychology. In 1974 Ema Geron initiated the formation of a sport psychology society that aims to participate in research, promotion, teaching, and dissemination of sport psychological science. Presently there are about 50 members, including individuals with degrees in physical education, psychology, and medicine. The chair of the group rotates periodically, and the position has been held by eminent scholars such as Ema Geron, Gilad Weingarten, and Gershon Tenenbaum. The current chair of the group is Michael Bar-Eli.

Approximately 12 to 15 members of the group meet bimonthly, and guest lectures, group research reports, or discussions in sport psychology are held. This association also organized the International Symposium on Psychological Assessment in Sport in 1977 as well as the two conferences on psychology and sociology of sport in 1982 and 1986. In 1989 the society held a successful international conference in association with the Maccabiah Games that attracted more than 600 participants in sport psychology and other sport sciences. Membership to this association is voluntary and open to anyone interested in the field regardless of specialized training.

Judging by the publications that have come out of Israel, Israeli research is better than average by international standards. However, the isolation of this small Jewish state is startling: It is surrounded almost entirely by unfriendly countries, is not an accepted part of Asian sport events for reasons obviously political, has been trying to become a member of the European sport federations and has been accepted by only six Western European nations, and finally has not been accepted as a member of the "nonpolitical" European Sport Psychology Federation (FEPSAC) for reasons that were obviously nonpolitical. This isolation has to affect both the quality of research and the disposition to engage in free discussion based on purely academic and professional grounds.

Sport Psychology and Top Sport. The main input into elite sport has occurred through the courses at the Nat Holman School for Coaches' one-year program. Candidates who study at this school often have a physical education degree already, and having this certification earns them extra salary. However, the sport psychology information is delivered in the form of 20 hours of course work and discussion of problem areas in coaching; there are few attempts at clinics, workshops, or other practical sessions to assure that coaches master the various techniques of psychoregulation.

More recently, the top athletes who are participating as candidates for the Olympic teams have undergone intensive training in psychoregulation under the direction of Shraga Sade and Raya Yuval of the Israeli Sport Psychology Association with a great deal of appreciated enthusiasm from the athletes.

Perspectives for Sport Psychology in Israel

Sport and recreation in Israel are rapidly emerging as more than simple leisure activities. With the possible advent of the 5-day work week, they will take on greater importance. Along with this interest in sport and recreation, the interest in sport psychology will increase at a similar rate. Although budgetary concerns limit the immediate overall development of the discipline, there are indications that a marked growth in the area of sport psychology are imminent.

Ivory Coast

in collaboration with

Ernest Dagrou
Institut National de la Jeunesse et des Sports, Abidjan

Ivory Coast Sport Psychology Résumé

Sport psychology at an institutionalized level has just begun in the Ivory Coast, with formalized courses being given at the national sports institute. Professors have been trained abroad, and now some examples of research have given an impetus to what has become one of the first such initiatives in black Africa.

Estimated Number of Sport Psychologists. 2

Prominent Institution. Institut National de la Jeunesse et des Sports, Abidjan

Privileged Topic. Applied research

Publication Vehicle. None

Society. None

The Ivory Coast is a former French colony on the underside of the western coast of Africa. The French colonizers had a very dominant influence in the Ivory Coast, as well as in Mali and Senegal in black Africa and in the Maghreb, the Arabo-African countries of Morocco, Algeria, and Tunisia. Within this network, the French educational system was almost totally transferred and adapted to the African reality. In fact, until recently, the Frenchness of the system was ensured and maintained by the employment of *coopérants*, teachers imported from France and given plum assignments, housing, and other perks. This trend is beginning to be reversed as Africans trained abroad are beginning to take the Europeans' places.

Training in Sport Psychology

On the whole the sport sciences have developed only to an elementary level in the Ivory Coast. This is because

the original French professors at the Institut National de la Jeunesse et des Sports (INJS) were *coopérants* trained in nonscientific physical education programs in France. Over the last 10 years, a number of students from the Ivory Coast have been sent to Quebec for undergraduate and master's level training, and two of them specialized in sport psychology. These individuals have thus changed the orientation within INJS from a French to a North American one.

IJNS has a mission of training physical education teachers in the Ivory Coast to work in the country's high schools and colleges. The course of study within this institution is a 4-year program with a practical orientation. To a greater extent, the sport sciences have taken on greater importance, with courses offered in anatomy, physiology, pedagogy, and, since 1985, sport psychology. There are presently discussions about beginning a master's program, but to date this is still in the planning stage.

Students in the INJS are selected through a national contest that results in about 40 candidates each year entering the program. After the first 3 years a student earns a license, and a pedagogical year of practice teaching follows.

In the first year of study, all students take two courses in general and in social psychology, and in the second year, there are broad courses in child psychology and sociology. In the third year, students take a course in motor learning. Fourth-year students take a course in psychosociology in sport as well as a sport psychology unit in a course on sport performance factors. In addition, a large number of courses in pedagogy are required.

Topics of Study. To date, no research in sport psychology has occurred on the soil of the Ivory Coast, although two master's theses by Ivory Coast natives have been completed in sport psychology at the University of Montreal. François Kouablan wrote about the influence of superstition on the performance of Ivory

Coast soccer players whereas Ernest Dagrou looked at the motivation of these same athletes. Dagrou is now studying in a joint Ph.D. program with Lise Gauvin and Wayne Halliwell at Concordia University and the University of Montreal.

Publications

No specialized publications in sport science or sport psychology are produced in the Ivory Coast. Some general articles have appeared in French publications such as *Education Physique et Sport*. In 1991 Dragou published his research on mental training of Ivory Coast athletes in the *International Journal of Sport Psychology*.

The Role of Sport Psychology in the Ivory Coast

Institutions. The INJS is the only teacher training institution in the Ivory Coast. Forty students are taught physical education and rudimentary sport science over a 4-year program.

In addition to training teachers, the INJS also offers coaches specialized courses of study. Graduates are then employed by the high schools and colleges around the country. INJS training parallels but is not equivalent to that of university programs, and courses are not taken in academic departments outside of INJS as occurs in North America. The final program leads to a license in physical education, or Certificate of Professional Aptitude in Secondary Education (CAPES), as is done in France.

Society. There is no specialized sport psychology group, but a sports medicine association Ivory Coast Association of Sport Medicine (AIMS) that meets annually welcomes sport psychology presentations.

Sport Psychology and Top Sport. So far very little has been done to integrate sport psychology into the preparation of top sport programs, mainly because little is known about sport psychology in black Africa. Because traditional cultural and religious values in sport are still prevalent the use of fetishes is still common—for example, hanging small magic-associated objects in the net of the soccer goal.

At the moment, the introduction of a sport psychology course at INJS will help sensitize sport directors and coaches to the importance of sport psychology. Much remains to be done at this early stage in the Ivory Coast, but events are at least going in the right direction.

Perspectives for Sport Psychology in the Ivory Coast

Sport psychology in the Ivory Coast now plays a modest but central role in the national institute for sport. Graduates of the INJS program are now being introduced to this emerging discipline. Though the integration of sport psychology outside the INJS has been slow, the efforts in this country are still leading those of most other black African countries, with the exception of Nigeria.

Morocco

in collaboration with

Baria Abderrahim

Nabli El Hassane
Ecole Normale Supérieure d'Education Physique et Sportive, Casablanca

Moroccan Sport Psychology Résumé

Estimated Number of Sport Psychologists. 7

Prominent Institutions. Ecole Normale Supérieure d'Education Physique et Sportive, Casablanca; Institut National des Sports, Rabat

Privileged Topics. Anxiety, motivation, pedagogy, motor control

Orientation. Educational sport psychology

Publication Vehicle. None

Society. Association of Physical Education and Sport Psychology

A well-known local adage states that Morocco is a country of contrasts, and this applies as well to the field of sport psychology. Actually the term psychology is a buzz word often used daily by coaches, athletes, administrators, and the media, and this is contrasted by the fact that no one has thought of this as a discipline of academic study that might be systematically applied to sport.

A better understanding of the phenomenon of sport psychology in Morocco requires certain information on how sport is organized in both school and community programs in this North African country. One fundamental characteristic of independent Morocco is the extreme youth of its people—nearly two thirds of the population is younger than 20. In this respect, school sport has become a veritable reservoir for community sport. The government needs to invest its resources in the construction of school structures by providing sound infrastructures. However, to adjust to a shortage of trained professionals, the government has decided to establish regional pedagogical centers for physical education and sport (CPREPS) and, more recently, normal schools for physical education and sport (ENSEPS), both with the mission of training physical educators.

The need to promote a clearly defined national sport policy in Morocco incited the government in 1958 to implement a national sport charter, which has become the basis for the organization of community sport. From the cinders of French sport leagues were born various Royal Moroccan Federations under the tutelage of the ministry of youth and sport, through which athletes are prepared at the National Institutes of Sport (INS). Since that time, national sport programs have seen progressive improvement in the infrastructure of sport personnel within the clubs and federations.

Since the 1960s, Morocco has developed some of the best athletes on the African continent within both individual and team disciplines, as evidenced by the numerous world-record performances in track and field by Said Aouita, the charming gold medal hurdler Nawal El Moutawakil at the Los Angeles Olympics, and the representation of its soccer team at various international events. This new dynamism in sport has also resulted in Morocco's leadership in organizing major multisport manifestations such as the Mediterranean Games in 1983, the Pan-Arab Games in 1985, and the Francophone Games in 1989. This form of involvement in the training and organization of elite sport will probably put Morocco into its golden age of sport in the 1990s.

Training in Sport Psychology

At present, there are no specialized programs or any systematic means to introduce sport psychology to high-level coaches and athletes. However, there has been renewed effort in recent years in sport psychology because a number of Moroccans have studied this specialization abroad, in France, Canada, or the United States. Because of this specialized trianing, the theoretical development of individuals in sport psychology, sociology, sports medicine, or sport training will bring about the introduction of these elements into the various schools and institutes in physical education and sport.

The Normal Superior School of Physical Education and Sport (ENSEPS) and the Regional Pedagogical Center for Physical Education and Sport (CPREPS) are both under the aegis of the national educational ministry with the respective mandates of preparing physical education teachers for secondary and primary schools.

At the CPREPS, which are scattered around the country, students take introductory courses over the 2-year program in subject areas such as physiology of exercise,

anatomy, pedagogy, general psychology, and, in some cases, certain notions in sport psychology.

All students at both of the previously mentioned centers receive government grants to study and are guaranteed teaching positions once they graduate. Certain CPREPS conduct a national contest and award certain professors an additional year of study after they have obtained the certificate of professional aptitude in secondary education (CAPES). To qualify, a professor must have had 2 years of teaching experience, taught two special lessons, and passed an oral exam before a jury of teaching inspectors. At the end of the program, the candidate must produce a modest graduation project that is defended before a jury. This additional year of study allows the candidate to receive the normal salary of a teacher and the professor is awarded what is equivalent to a North American bachelor's degree.

At ENSEPS, the training process is a more intensive process that takes 4 years and requires a final exam and a small graduation research project (the latter could be in sport psychology) and leads to the diploma or professor's license at the bachelor's level. A certain number of professors who give the basic sport science courses were originally trained in physical education in France, as was the case in many of the colonized North African nations. There is now a trend in all these countries for native scholars to be trained abroad and to gradually replace the French *coopérants*. These professors, in addition to teaching various sport sciences including sport psychology, also supervise the graduating projects of senior students. Recently, interest in the sport psychology area is increasing because courses in sport psychology and motor learning are an integral part of the curriculum.

At the National Institute for Sport (INS), the 4-year training period is the same as at ENSEPS and follows the same course of study. However, all courses keep in focus the candidate's area of sport specialization. An amalgam of professors, medical doctors, and coaches give courses in the various sport sciences, including sport psychology, as well as in principles of athletic training. Though the situation should change in the next few years, to date very few individuals have been trained to the doctoral level. Still, an increasing number of graduating students have shown interest in doing their projects in sport psychology.

Topics of Study. Because the majority of teaching professors are recycled French *coopérants* who have the equivalent of a general nonscientific bachelor's degree or Moroccans who have not yet completed a doctoral degree, the research areas are either completely theoretical with no experimentation or use only simple forms of experimentation. The theoretical projects are based on the integration of information from the French and North American literature into current practice in physical education and sport.

Topics that receive considerable attention are mental preparation and motivation for competition, anxiety control, and causal attributions for success and failure. Actual experimental research is carried out at either

ENSEPS or INS using either the standardized and translated objective inventories on state and trait anxiety of Spielberger and Martens, or the personality tests of Eysenck and Cattel. Bencheikh has been most notable at ENSEPS in Casablanca, trying to evaluate the psychological characteristics of Moroccan athletes. Baria has also studied elite performers using structured observation grids with which the pre- and postcompetitive behaviors of Olympic, North African, and Middle Eastern Arab gymnasts were compared. His research has been published in both English and French in North America and abroad. He is now studying at the doctoral level the knowledge structure of gymnastic coaches with John Salmela at the University of Ottawa.

Finally, research has been carried out in the field of motor performance, initially by El-Fakir on Schmidt's schema theory and more recently by Nabli on preparation strategies to react quickly. Both of the latter studied with Claude Alain at the University of Montreal, to the master's and doctoral levels, respectively.

Publications

At present there is no specialized Moroccan publication in sport psychology; the only known African one is the 1988 Algerian initiative *Sciences et Technologie au Sport*. It is also possible to publish in the French popularized (*Education Physique et Sport*) or scientific (*Sport et Sciences*) journals, although it is rare to see research in these journals. A few articles, notably by Nabli and Baria, were published as the result of research carried out in Canada in psychology or sport psychology refereed journals. Moroccan professors have written a few general articles on sport psychology, but these have tended to be somewhat philosophical in nature.

The Role of Sport Psychology in Morocco

Institutions. Three types of institutions in Morocco have as a mission the training of individuals in physical education and sport. Two of these are under the aegis of the national education ministry, CPREPS and ENSEPS, and the third is under the supervision of the ministry of youth and sport, at the INS in Rabat.

Both the CPREPS and ENSEPS have a very strong pedagogical rather than sport-centered orientation. The 2-year study program for primary education takes place at the CPREPS, which are found in a number of centers of Morocco, notably in Casablanca, Rabat, Fez, Taza, and Marrakech. Secondary school teachers are prepared over 4 years at the ENSEPS in Casablanca. At the third type of institute, the INS, the preoccupation is with the academic preparation of coaches, administrators, and

supervisors in the area of sport. Within this institute is also the Moulay Rachid National Sport Center, where all of the national teams for sport excellence reside and make final preparations for international competitions.

Association d'Education Physique et de Psychologie du Sport. The appearance of this newly trained first wave of sport scientists has resulted in the recent creation of the Association of Physical Education and Sport Psychology. It is hoped that this association will help sensitize athletes and coaches to the importance of sport psychology in the training and competition process.

Sport Psychology and Top Sport. Presently Morocco's international reputation for its trade of phosphates and sardines and its beautiful sunshine has been surpassed by its acclaim as an international sports nation. Its soccer team is one of the best in Africa and participates regularly in the World Cup. Nawal upset the favorites to win the 400-meter hurdles at the 1984 Olympics and thus altered the role of women in Morocco. But most impressively, Said Aouita has rewritten the world track record books from 800 meters to 10,000 meters. Yet aside from personal coaches' intuition, effective physiological conditioning in a good climate, and inborn talent, there is still no consistent psychological preparation to finish off this process. At the moment, no systematic mental training programs are taught to coaches or athletes, and no third-person intervention has been requested or attempted in anything but a haphazard manner. It is hoped that all of this changes as better trained specialists return to the country from abroad.

Perspectives for Sport Psychology in Morocco

The developmental pattern for sport psychology in Morocco will follow one similar to those of the emerging Arabo-African nations such as Algeria and Tunisia as they wean themselves from mother France. A greater number of young professors are receiving North American postgraduate training in the sport sciences, including sport psychology. This has resulted in more research, more publication, and the creation of a professional association.

In addition, coaches and athletes are increasingly aware that cognitive and emotional factors can make the difference between winning and losing and that methods are available for teaching these skills. The combination of these factors should help guarantee that sport psychology develops into a broader based discipline and becomes an integrated part of physical education and sport practice.

Nigeria

in collaboration with

P. Bola Ikulayo
University of Lagos

Nigerian Sport Psychology Résumé

Sport psychology is in a remarkable state of advancement in Nigeria due to the preferred status it maintains in sport and to the many recent achievements it has made in a short time.

Estimated Number of Sport Psychologists. 12

Prominent Institutions. University of Lagos, National Sport Commission Secretariat

Orientation. Psychometrics

Privileged Topic. Stress management

Publication Vehicle. Conference proceedings

Society. Sports Psychology Association of Nigeria

Nigeria is the most populous country in Africa and as such exerts considerable influence by this as well as through its natural resources. Nigeria's track athletes such as Chidi Imo and Innocent Egbunike are known worldwide, as are its soccer teams.

But very soon Nigeria will also be known in Africa and abroad as Africa's leading sport psychology nation through some ambitious, far-reaching, and energetic initiatives by its leaders in sport psychology. Reading any national chapter in this book reveals that a country's sport psychology activity was usually sparked and maintained by the singular efforts of one or two individuals. What is unique in Nigeria's case is that its sport psychology firebrand is a woman: P. Bola Ikulayo.

The way in which sport psychology began in Nigeria is also unique. As recently as 1984, the government of Nigeria appointed 14 men and one woman, Bola Ikulayo, to the National Sports Commission Caretaker Committee, which was established to study the reasons behind the instability of recent Nigerian sport performances at the international level. The committee set a system of three subcommittees for finance and administration, facilities, and sport development. One recommendation from the sport committee was that each national sport federation have access to media personnel, social/welfare workers, and sport psychologists. To coordinate the activities of the appointed psychologists and psychiatrists, the Sport Psychology Association of Nigeria (SPAN) was formed and given official status, along with the Sports Medicine Association and 22 federations, and an office at the National Sports Commission in Lagos, where it works in close concert with all sport federations.

Training in Sport Psychology

Sport psychology is now offered at all eight Nigerian universities as a compulsory subject for graduation in physical education. At some of the leading postsecondary institutions such as the universities of Lagos, Ibadan, and Ife Obafemi Awolowo, this has been going on at the undergraduate level for 10 years. It is also possible now to pursue master's and doctoral training in sport psychology at these universities as well.

At the undergraduate level, students take a comprehensive sport psychology course that includes sections on learning and feedback, stress and performance, motivation, personality, competition, leadership, aggression, practice conditions, and social and cultural elements. Evaluation of the students' progress is done by a final 2-hour exam as well as a 2,000-word term paper. Students are also encouraged to interact with athletes to assess any personality disorders. This course is complemented by other courses in movement education and motor learning as well as by the other sport sciences. Upon graduation from the university, these students are eligible to qualify as associate members of SPAN.

Top-level students may apply to do a master's degree at certain universities. Again academic excellence is required along with constant interaction with athletes to apply theoretical knowledge.

Students must complete from 8 to 12 taught course units from the following bank of courses: psychological bases of physical activities and sports performance (3 units), psychophysiological dimensions of sports and physical education (3 units), coaching variables in sports (2 units), motivational variables in sport performance (2 units), and stress management and control in sport (3 units). In addition, students specializing in sport psychology are also expected to enroll in a 3-unit course from the psychology department, 2 to 4 units in educational psychology, and 2 to 4 units in sport sociology.

Finally, students take compulsory courses in qualitative research methods and their application and a research seminar and must complete a 4-unit research project. In total, the students must have between 24 and 30 units to graduate. Because of a lack of sport psychology and motor learning equipment, many of the research projects are descriptive in nature. There is also the possibility of a supervised internship with an advisor in a sport setting.

At the doctoral level, students take seminars on advanced sport management, applied psychological analysis, and analysis of sport problems and continue with a supervised internship. The thesis is an in-depth analysis that demonstrates evidence of confident handling of extreme sport situations.

In 1986 and 1987, the first University of Lagos group of master's students graduated and qualified for professional membership in SPAN as sport psychologists. There is a great deal of interest in sport psychology in Nigeria and many applications for these graduate projects in sport psychology.

Topics of Study. At this early stage of sport psychology in Nigeria, it is surprising to see the variety of subject areas that have been presented at SPAN conferences.

A number of studies have been directed to the sport of soccer, Nigeria's national preoccupation. Research has been done on the motivational traits of soccer players (T.A. Adedoja), violence during soccer matches (J.A. Oyewusi), incentives and rewards in playing soccer (A.R. Ogundari), and psychological adjustments during play (P.B. Ikulayo). Other research interests relate to the effects of mental practice on free throws (A. Onifade & A.P. Agbonjimi), fair play (A.S. Sohi & O.O. Omotayo), neuropsychological skill analysis (D.M. Gwany), and conflict management (H.O. Ololade). All projects are very applied and require simple methodologies using little electronic technology. This type of research will evolve as the graduate program gains more maturity over the years.

Nigeria has decided to address concerns that have been neglected in a number of countries relating to what Ikulayo refers to as "dangerous trends of negative psychology." For example, educational efforts are being given to sport teams to discourage belief in and dependence on the supernatural powers of juju, or fetishes, in sport. Another concern deals with elimination of cheating in sport, whether by using overaged athletes in youth sport, using paid athletes, or deliberately intending to injure in sport. These concerns raised by SPAN have important social and moral values for sport and have resulted in a number of recommendations made directly to the National Sports Commission.

Publications

No specialized publication exists for sport psychology in Nigeria. However, the proceedings of the seven national conferences of SPAN have been published in various forms along with various memorabilia such as photos, speeches, official addresses, and research abstracts.

To date, some Nigerian research has been published in journals abroad, and in 1990 Ikulago published *Understanding Sports Psychology*, the first sport psychology book from Nigeria, or from anywhere else in black Africa.

The Role of Sport Psychology in Nigeria

Institutions. The institutional structure for sport psychology is also very special in Nigeria as compared

to elsewhere. Normally, individuals interested in sport psychology lobby and agitate politically for many years to become institutionalized. Links with sport practice are often tenuous and require many years, if not decades, of nurturing.

The reverse situation took place in Nigeria. Sport psychology was just beginning in the 1980s within the universities. Then in 1984, the National Sports Commission Caretaker Committee recommended that sport psychology be an integral part of Nigeria's rejuvenation in sport with the direct representation of Bola Ikulaya, not only as a board member on the National Sports Commission, but also a member of the management committee of the Nigeria Olympic Committee. This has given sport psychology instant credibility as well as a voice in a number of decision-making processes.

From this power base, it becomes a relatively easy task to implement compulsory undergraduate sport psychology courses at the eight different universities in Nigeria that offer physical education programs as well as the three universities that offer graduate programs up to the doctoral level in sport psychology. It also becomes clear why students in these various programs have the rich opportunity to be in close contact with top-level athletes in different supervised settings. One area in which there has been an expressed interest in change is in the provision of a well-equipped clinical facility for the evaluation of and consultation with athletes, upgrading sport administrators, psychosomatic rehabilitation of athletes; and the improvement of lifestyle management and fitness consultations.

SPAN. Never has any sport psychology society started with such a mandate to accomplish so much. SPAN is empowered to have governmentally supported functions for doing research; to monitor, assist, and enhance the sport performance of top athletes; to facilitate ethical behavior of athletes, coaches, and support staff; and to advise on the welfare of the psychological, social, and health-related dimensions of all sport participants. This mandate has enormous scope and foresight, if it can be effectively put into practice.

Membership requirements for SPAN are of four varieties, the most important being professional members who have undergraduate and graduate training in sport psychology and are involved in teaching the discipline or working with top-level athletes. There are also associate members who have only first-degree level or undergraduate training in sport psychology or related areas but are involved with high-level sport performance or coaching. There is also a category for students and a fellow category for meritorious service.

In providing consultation services for the various sport federations, SPAN has again provided some services that appear precocious for such a young group. For example, SPAN is already providing the various sport federations with the names and credentials of all SPAN professionals for potential counseling of their athletes and is setting up regional centers and contacting people in the different states.

SPAN did not at first content itself, as have most other societies, with holding annual conferences. Instead, because of the accelerated schedule of development that SPAN desired, it organized four successful conferences at different Nigerian centers over a 2-year period. Conference proceedings have followed most events, and the response by participants has been very enthusiastic. The 1987 conference was highlighted by the presence of ISSP president Robert N. Singer, who was impressed by the advanced state of affairs of this 2-year-old society.

Finally, the activities of SPAN are supported financially not only by national and state governments, but, interestingly enough, by a number of private-sector sources as well, including banks, holding companies, and transport companies.

Sport Psychology and Top Sport.   Unlike what has occurred in many other countries where sport psychology is distanced from sport practice, in Nigeria sport psychology's reason for being is helping top-level athletes. Thus professors of sport psychology as well as graduate students doing practicums are directly involved with coaches and athletes during training camps and competitions, monitoring the psychological readiness of athletes in various disciplines.

SPAN members have put much emphasis on the ongoing preventive surveillance of athletes during training rather than on corrective short-term intervention. Though the Nigeria Olympic Committee has indeed supported the participation of a sport psychologist at the 1987 All Africa Games as well as at the Seoul Olympics, these decisions were often made at the last minute, which acted against the smooth integration of this service into the competition process. Still, for a group less than 5 years old, these initiatives are unheard of, not only in Africa but in the rest of the world as well.

Perspectives for Sport Psychology in Nigeria

Nigeria appears to be the wunderkind in the international world of sport psychology. The major pieces necessary for success have been put into place, such as national recognition and institutionalization of programs, postgraduate study, and numerous outlets for academic and professional interaction.

If there is one weak link in this whole system, it would be that the quantity and output of the research facilities is not yet up to international standards. Then again, with so much accomplished in such a short time, who could complain about this?

Tunisia

in collaboration with

Taktak Khaled
Ecole Normale Supérieure d'Education Physique et Sportive, Tunis

Tunisian Sport Psychology Résumé

Even though sport psychology has not yet been launched in Tunisia with the same impulse as in other Arabic North African countries, still there has been a recent motivated attempt to prepare specialized individuals abroad in both research and areas of application.

Estimated Number of Sport Psychologists.   10

Prominent Institutions.   Normal Superior School of Physical Education and Sport, Normal Superior School for Coaches, Normal School for Masters of Physical Education and Sport, Normal School for Animators of Physical Activity

Orientation.   Applied research

Privileged Topics.   Stress management, motivation, and psychopedagogy

Publication Vehicle.   *Bulletin Scientifique et Technologique du Sport*

Society.   None

Tunisia perches upon the north central region of Africa, mainly because its geographical situation places it in a favorable position to the western influence of France, the first colonizer of this nation. Even after Tunisia attained its independence in 1956, France was still able to put its educational system into place. Thus today Tunisia continues to run western European–styled education programs with only a few attempts at arabization, along with its Maghreb neighbors Algeria and Morocco.

Gaining a better understanding of sport psychology in Tunisia requires looking at an overview of how sport itself is organized in a number of different milieux. Tunisia is unique in that the average age of its population is less than 20. This young population has now become a fertile base for sport programs, especially in major cities such as Sfax and Tunis. Since 1958, the Tunisian government has invested in the construction of schools and sport installations and has set up the necessary infrastructure of programs for this young population. Along with that investment at youth sport levels in Tunisia has come a modest tradition of international achievement. For example, Mohamed Gammoudi won the 5,000-meter race at the 1968 Mexico Olympics, and Tunisia's soccer team participated in the World Cup in 1978 in Argentina. Presently Tunisia is taking on a greater role in international games held in nearby Mediterranean and francophone countries, especially in swimming, combat sports (boxing, judo, wrestling), and track and field.

Training in Sport Psychology

At the end of the 1960s elementary-level courses in sport psychology were introduced in the professional preparation programs for teachers of physical education and sport. This concern evolved from the programs in psychopedagogy inherited from the French tradition and was based on the philosophical writings of the same authors that still influence French sport psychology.

Only recently have the teachers who give these courses received specialized postgraduate training in the various fields of sport psychology, in either Europe or North America. A number of exchanges of educational specialists with Poland and the USSR have provided professors with socialist ideals. Sport psychology also may soon be taught as an academic discipline within the classic universities of Tunisia when trained specialists from abroad return to fill professorial positions there.

Students who wish to teach elementary school physical education follow a 2-year program of study, taking general psychology and pedagogy courses along with various practical sport courses that make up 50% of the curriculum. Those who wish to work in junior secondary schools take a 3-year program of study, and an extra year is required to teach at the senior secondary level. This 4th year requires a graduating thesis project, which can be in sport psychology. Coaches must also take specific psychopedagogy courses as part of a 2-year course, and people who will supervise play schools for children in all regions of the country take general courses on child development.

There is presently a movement in progress to replace foreign academic teachers, *coopérants*, from France and the USSR with Tunisians who are now studying abroad. These newly trained specialists must possess a doctorate and be able to direct graduating theses for students in the 4-year program.

Topics of Study. As the result of Tunisians going to eastern Europe for doctoral study in Poland and the USSR, three researchers specializing in sport psychology currently work at ENSEPS in Tunis. Fray Hamaida and Agreby Mohamed are best known for their evaluation of the psychological characteristics of Tunisian handball players, whereas Fouzi El Madhi has studied how basketball players differentiate the space, time, and effort parameters of movement.

In addition, a new wave of doctoral students is being prepared at the Université de Montréal using a North American model of research. Mohamed Belgaid and Bahri Mohamed Adel are now studying the effects of anxiety and motivation under the direction of Wayne Halliwell, and Taktak Khaled is working with Claude Alain on the preparation processes necessary to react quickly.

Publications

No specialized publication exists specifically for sport psychology in Tunisia, although sport psychology articles have appeared in the *Bulletin Scientifique et Technologique du Sport*.

Some scholars have taken a number of personal initiatives and have published their doctoral dissertations, the best known of which are Ben Ramdan on sport and Islamic belief, Hawet Mohamed on coeducational practices in sport, and Kamal El Benzarti on sport sociology. No textbooks on sport psychology have been written yet.

The Role of Sport Psychology in Tunisia

Institutions. A number of institutions in Tunisia have the possibility of introducing psychological notions into the study of education, sport, and leisure, and all of them are under the auspices of the ministry for youth and sport. The broadest based programs are situated in Bir El Bay at the National School for Animators of Physical Activity and Sport (ENAPS), which is directed more toward recreation and leisure in nonscholastic programs, including those for preschoolers.

The 2-year program of study for elementary school physical education teachers is offered at the Normal School for Masters of Physical Education and Sport (ENMEPS) at Sfax, the financial center of Tunisia. The 3- and 4-year programs for secondary school teachers take place at the Superior Normal School for Physical Education and Sport (ENSEPS) in the capital city of Tunis, where the Superior Normal School for Coaches (ENSE) is also located.

At present there are no institutionalized programs in sport psychology at the classic universities of Tunisia, although the potential for this will exist when sufficient foreign-trained personnel return home.

Society. No specialized sport science society exists in Tunisia at this time.

Sport Psychology and Top Sport. Sport psychology, along with a variety of other sport sciences, is an integral course for all coaches who study at ENSE. In the 2-year program, coaches are encouraged to expand their sport-specific knowledge in sport psychology so they can provide a comprehensive program package within their given sport. Though research projects have been carried out on top-level teams, so far no instances of specialized psychological intervention for performance enhancement have taken place during training camps or competitions.

Perspectives for Sport Psychology in Tunisia

Sport psychology in Tunisia is beginning to grow as it borrows new technologies from Western Europe and North America. The experimental research now being carried out by graduate students studying abroad should result in more publications and perhaps the creation of a professional association in the near future. In addition, the government now appears to see the benefits of advanced training in the sport sciences. These factors taken together should provide a solid base for the further growth of this discipline in Tunisia.

Chapter 5

LATIN AMERICA
Brazil

in collaboration with

Benno Becker, Jr.
Universidade Federal do Rio Grande do Sul

Brazilian Sport Psychology Résumé

Brazil has taken the leadership for sport psychology in South America through continued work in teaching, research, and counseling at home and through the organization of continental meetings that bring together the disparate elements of the field on this continent.

Estimated Number of Sport Psychologists. 5

Prominent Institutions. Rio Grande do Sol (LAPEX), Rio de Janeiro (LAFEX), and Sao Paulo (LAFISC)

Orientation. Performance enhancement

Privileged Topics. Anxiety, group dynamics, psychotherapy, mental training

Publication Vehicle. *Brazilian Journal of Sport Medicine*

Society. South American Society of Sport Psychology, Physical Activity and Recreation (SOBRAPE)

Brazil is best known in sport for the tremendous world impact of its renowned soccer teams. The name Pele automatically brings to mind the image of improvisational mastery and control that borders on the artistic. As early as 1954, Joao Carvalhaes, a sport psychiatrist, was working with the Brazilian Football Federation in the selection process for referees. In addition, the great Brazilian World Cup soccer champions of 1958 and 1962 had the benefit of working with Carvalhaes as well as Athayde Ribeiro da Silva, another psychiatrist. However, this work with sport teams was limited to the major Brazilian centers from 1958 to 1974 and was specific only to football. Since then, sport psychology has become more institutionalized and has spread its effects to a greater variety of sport disciplines.

Training in Sport Psychology

Brazil's situation in sport psychology is unique in the world, with the possible exception of Italy, because the prime movers in the field were psychiatric specialists in medicine. Since 1975 there have been postgraduate specializations in sport psychology for medical people at institutions in Rio Grande do Sul, Bahia, Pernambuco, Sao Paulo, and Rio de Janeiro. This program takes 6 months and is centered on evaluation, counseling, and mental training techniques. Since 1978, sport psychology has been a compulsory subject in the postgraduate course in sports medicine at the State University of Rio Grande do Sul that consists of 45 hours of courses and 45 hours of research.

In addition, about 45 hours of sport psychology specialization are offered in the 98 Brazilian universities that have undergraduate degrees in physical education. Students can also receive postgraduate training with courses in sport psychology in centers in Parana, Minas Gerais, Brasilia, Santa Catarina, Sao Paulo, and Rio de Janeiro. A number of Brazilians are presently studying abroad, and their return should provide new initiatives for further specialized study.

Topics of Study. The types of topics studied in sport psychology depend on the interests of the individuals at each major center. For example, in Sao Paulo, Sandra Cavasini and Regina Brandao are particularly interested in group dynamics and self-concept of athletes, whereas in Rio de Janeiro, Joao Alberto Barreto is interested in motivation and anxiety. The work of Benno Becker at Rio Grande do Sul centers on mental training techniques using sport for therapy, whereas a group of researchers in the Minas Gerais University, in Belo Horizonte, including Dietmar Samulski, Luis Carlos Moraes, and Rodrigo Nascimento, are studying youth sport and sport as therapy. Samulski was educated in Cologne, Germany, while Nascimento and Moraes did post-graduate work at Florida State University and Michigan State University, respectively.

Publications

No research publication yet exists specifically in the area of sport psychology, but a large number of psychologically related topics have been published in general journals of sports medicine and physical education. The most prominent journals open to sport psychology articles are the *Brazilian Journal of Sport Medicine*, the *Brazilian College of Sport Sciences Journal*, and the *Brazilian Physical Education Journal*. Two sport psychology books, *Sport Psychology* and *Psychology of Sport*, have been published by da Silva and Hadock Lobo, respectively. Benno Becker is presently writing a *Guidebook in Sport Psychology*, and in 1988 Juan Mosquera and Klaus Stobaus published another book entitled *Psychology of Sport*. In addition, textbooks written by a number of American authors, such as Cratty, Singer, Magill, and Lawther, have been translated into Portuguese.

The Role of Sport Psychology in Brazil

Institutions. In 1974, three sport science and medicine research laboratories were created in Rio Grande do Sul (LAPEX), Rio de Janeiro (LAFEX), and Sao Paulo (LAFISC), and within these three centers three laboratories in sport psychology were created.

The design of these three centers was based on certain laboratories in Europe; they provide evaluation services, counseling, and therapy to top athletes and coaches. In addition, sport psychology courses are frequently given here to physicians, psychologists, and coaches.

In addition to providing sport psychology services for Brazilians, Benno Becker has played an active role in all of South America in the promotion of sport psychology, especially in Uruguay, Argentina, Chile, Equador, and Colombia.

The 98 Brazilian universities that offer physical education programs all provide course work to coaches and teachers in the field of sport psychology.

Brazilian Society of Sport Psychology, Physical Activity and Recreation. In 1979, the Brazilian Society of Sport Psychology, Physical Activity and Recreation (SOBRAPE) was founded at the University of Feevale in Novo Hamburgo, and within SOBRAPE four other state societies were formed. Every 2 years SOBRAPE organizes a national congress on specific topics such as the child and movement, the special child, and psychophysical rehabilitation. More than 500 individuals have attended these congresses along with a number of foreign scholars. Most recently, sport federations such as those for the martial arts and tennis have called on SOBRAPE to organize sport-specific congresses on sport psychology and other sport sciences. In 1990 SOBRAPE invited a number of international experts from the ISSP Managing Council to its annual meeting in Belo Horizonte and this initiative added considerably to interest in Brazil.

Sport Psychology and Top Sport. Top-level coaches have the opportunity to take special courses and workshops at the major sport science centers. These meetings deal with psychological evaluation, counseling, and some forms of psychotherapy as well as some alternative methods for enhancing sport performance. Other sessions are arranged for sport psychologists to meet with the athletes to discuss and carry out mental training programs and group dynamics.

In 1988, the Brazilian Olympic Committee asked Benno Becker to carry out psychological profiling of the Olympic delegation to Seoul. This was the first time such an extensive project was carried out. To date, no sport psychologist has ever traveled with the team.

Perspectives for Sport Psychology in Brazil

Sport psychology has had more success being institutionalized in Brazil than anywhere else in South America. Activity has been steady for the last 10 years, though it is localized in the three major centers. There is still a shortage of qualified individuals working in the area, but numbers are increasing with several individuals having studied abroad. Through the efforts of a few leaders in the field, Brazil has succeeded in improving communication with other South American countries, North America, and Europe. It is believed that this cross-fertilization will help reduce the physical isolation that has to date hindered sport psychology in Brazil's growth internationally.

Colombia

in collaboration with

Jorge Palacio
Cali University

Colombian Sport Psychology Résumé

Sport psychology in Colombia is characterized by its attempt to develop psychological services for athletes and coaches and for the development of applied research in a context with very limited resources.

Estimated Number of Sport Psychologists. 15

Prominent Institutions. Instituto Colombiano de la Juventud y el Deporte–Coldeportes, Universidad del Valle, Universidad de Antioquia, Universidad Pedagógica Nacional

Orientation. Applied sport psychology

Privileged Topics. Psychological preparation for competition, sport and human development

Publication Vehicle. None

Society. Sociedad Colombiana de Ciencias Aplicadas al Deporte

Colombia sits on the northwest corner of South America, and within its restricted geographical dimensions a visitor can find extreme contrasts in terrain and temperature.

The coastal beaches are balmy and lush, but 2 hours into the mountainous interior the air is thin and cool and the countryside is ruggedly harsh. This latter setting has provided perfect conditions for training world-class Colombian long-distance runners and cyclists.

Though the South American tradition for excellence in soccer dates back a century, the introduction of psychological intervention in any Colombian sport is a totally new enterprise. In fact, no less than 8 years ago, the first psychologist was called to explore the possibilities of developing a program of research and intervention in the context of a specific agency, the National Institute for Sport and Youth (NISY). At present approximately 10 psychologists are working in different sport psychology programs within the amateur sport system, some as university professors and others as sport consultants for professional teams. These psychologists have explored a number of areas: motor learning, motor development, youth sport, and sport psychology. In the last category, the identification, organization, and provision of psychological support services for athletes and coaches have received special attention.

Training in Sport Psychology

The organization of the Colombian educational system is rooted in the European model. Students spend the first years of study at the university attaining the bachelor's degree in a specific field of academic or professional work. Successful candidates are also eligible to continue with advanced postgraduate degrees, normally open only to people with undergraduate degrees in the same area. Sport psychologists in Colombia are all professionals with specialized training in psychology departments. However, there is no present means of studying in the specific field of sport psychology in the university, although a student's research could be in the field of sport. For the moment, there are still no programs for the systematic training of all coaches in any of the sport sciences.

Coldeportes, a national institute of sports medicine, has been an oasis for most of the people related to sport psychology. Slowly but surely, the number of sport psychologists has increased at the regional offices of this institute. University programs in physical education, child education, and special education have benefited most of the scholars working in the areas of motor learning and development.

Because knowledge is obtained with such difficulty, with most information received from abroad through books, conferences, and the occasional visiting sport psychologist, Colombian sport psychology could best be called psychology applied to sport rather than applied sport psychology.

Topics of Study. Given the constraints for basic research in developing countries, sport psychology in Colombia has been directed toward the design of intervention strategies. However, no systematic information has been recruited from this applied work. Initial attempts were directed toward evaluation of athletes according to the requirements of directors of the sports medicine departments. Later, psychological preparation for competition and special programs to help athletes overcome specific psychological problems became the topics of interest.

Publications

Because development of the field of sport psychology in Colombia has been relatively recent, there are very few publications in the field. This results from the low numbers of individuals active in research compounded by the small number of publishing outlets, so many applied experiences in the field remain unshared.

Jorge Palacio has published in English and Spanish his conceptual research on delivery systems for sport psychology in developing countries.

The Role of Sport Psychology in Colombia

Institutions. Sport psychology activity has been centered at the different offices of the NISY in various regions of the country. However, further development has many financial and political constraints at this institution, and very little new progress is anticipated from this source.

Fortunately, during the last 2 years universities have become more involved and private-sector institutions have shown even greater interest by providing support for recreational and sport activities. It seems that with the growing interest in psychology as a profession and the current involvement of citizens in physical activities, sport psychology, both research and intervention, will be viewed as an interesting new field for the community.

Sociedad Colombiana de Ciencias Aplicadas al Deporte. Until very recently there was no professional association for sport sciences or sport psychology in Colombia. However, in 1988 the Colombian Society of Applied Sport Sciences (COLCIDE) was created and included a sport psychologist on its executive committee. In 1989 a Colombian meeting of sport psychology was held; 40 individuals participated and later formed a Colombian society. It is still too early to evaluate the strength and durability of both organizations, however.

Sport Psychology and Top Sport. To date there have been a number of punctual interventions by a few individuals with top soccer and volleyball teams in Colombia. Sport psychologists have begun introducing research and intervention in sport activities with the approval of coaches and physical educators but with little support from administrators.

One major breakthrough occurred in 1988 when the head of the Colombian Olympic Committee decided that Colombia's delegation at Seoul should include a sport psychologist. Jorge Palacio, a Colombian psychologist who did graduate work in Montreal, was selected on short notice to work with the entire delegation of athletes. This experience proved profitable for the delegation and perhaps will allow sport psychology to trickle down to the more fundamental levels of the training process.

Perspectives for Sport Psychology in Colombia

Sport psychology has but a small toehold on the world of sport and physical activity in Colombia. There is a great need to bring this activity into institutionalized settings for the training of coaches and teachers. Some encouraging individual initiatives and new organizational elements lend promise to the future of sport psychology in Colombia.

Mexico

in collaboration with

Guillermo Dellamary
Private Practice

Roció Balboa
Universidad Autonoma de Nuevo Leon

Mexican Sport Psychology Résumé

As is the case in most of Latin America, sport psychology does not yet have a significant practical foothold in Mexico because of a lack of information and promotion. Inroads have been made recently to initiate sport psychology programs through private initiatives.

Estimated Number of Sport Psychologists. 10

Prominent Institutions. Various sports medicine programs

Orientation. Top sport

Privileged Topics. Autoregulation, group dynamics

Publication Vehicles. Sports medicine journals

Society. Mexican Society of Sport Psychology

Mexico could be the Latin American country with the greatest potential for growth in sport psychology because of its close proximity to the huge numbers involved in the discipline in North America. But perhaps because of the language barrier, economic factors, or both as well as the lack of existing sources of information in the country, this possibility has not yet become reality.

Sport psychology is a relatively new subject in Mexico, and only a few institutionalized independent psychologists have been working in this discipline in the last 20 years. Many of them receive information and influence from foreign coaches who come to Mexico to train athletes for different competitions. For Mexican sport psychologists, sport psychology consists of applying general psychology to the field of sport. Others obtain information through contacts with foreign sport psychologists from North America, Germany, or Sweden or by attending international congresses. A problem for sport psychology in Mexico is that many athletes and coaches still consider sport psychology something they do not need because they are not "crazy." This is due to the relationship some people perceive between psychology, psychiatry, and mental illness, and to the existence of little published information on sport psychology.

Training in Sport Psychology

Traditionally in Mexico, sport has not been viewed as requiring the help of science and technology, so there has been no public or government financial support for activities like sport psychology. Olympic contenders preferred enlisting the advice and training of foreign coaches rather than investing in Mexican coaches and scientific staff.

The present government has begun looking at sport in a new light and has established a National Sport Comission that will implement programs in the various Mexican centers. However, program structures have not yet been created.

At the moment, Mexican universities are not yet aware of sport psychology, so no programs are available. Isolated courses of sport psychology are included in physical education, sports medicine, and coach training programs.

Only a few psychologists who studied abroad have specialized in this discipline. Because of the lack of trained personnel and because institutions for this purpose do not yet exist in the country, there is no special training in sport psychology in Mexico. A number of individuals scattered around the country and the newly formed Mexican Society of Sport Psychology appear capable of guiding development and training in the field of sport psychology, perhaps within the structure of the government's reforms in sport.

Topics of Study. Most psychologists focus their attention on practical techniques used to overcome psychological barriers in sport performance. Others try to use applied group dynamics to solve team conflicts, and others work with different relaxation techniques to reduce anxiety before competitions. Most of these people do not have special training in sport psychology, and because of this research projects are unknown.

Publications

Because of the truly embryonic nature of sport psychology in Mexico, there are only a few potential places for publication in sports medicine journals with only a few articles in the general field of sport psychology and no specialized Mexican publications in this field.

The Role of Sport Psychology in Mexico

Institutions. At present there are few or no institutionalized forms of sport psychology in Mexico. Physical education teacher training includes some general psychological components, but nothing goes beyond this meager level. There has been some discussion about creating an institute for research and teaching sport psychology with the support of private clubs in collaboration with the Mexican Society of Sport Psychology, but this is still in the planning stages.

The formation of a new government policy regarding sport may significantly change the development of the different sport sciences in Mexico.

Mexican Society of Sport Psychology (MSSP). The MSSP was founded in 1988 by Guillermo Dellamary and has only four members, who work in Guadalajara. Presently the society's main activity is the promotion of sport psychology through different courses and seminars in Guadalajara. This nucleus is working very hard to interest more members and permit greater growth.

In March 1988 the society held a sport psychology symposium along with different courses and seminars at which there was modest attendance, perhaps because a network is not yet in place to disseminate information about such activities.

At this moment, the MSSP's most important goal is to organize and unify Mexican psychologists who work in this discipline or are interested in sport psychology.

Sport Psychology and Top Sport. Some private sports clubs are interested in sport psychology, but there is not enough financial support to carry out specialized research in the field. The Atlas soccer club has shown major interest in this regard, especially in Guillermo Dellamary's professional mental training and the development of human potential. In Monterrey, neurolinguistic programming work was carried out by Roció Balboa with the first- and second-division soccer teams of Tigres. There is still resistance to the integration of psychology into Mexico's training and competition programs for top sport. However, Roció Balboa has also accompanied the Mexican Davis Cup team as a sport psychology consultant to competitions in Marbella, Spain. This is believed to be the first instance of a Mexican psychologist accompanying a sport team to an international competition.

Still, most of the Mexican sport community sees sport psychology as something strange and not yet compatible with sport. This support science appears to conflict with conventional wisdom that has come from empirical training and knowledge that dominates the practices in traditional sports.

Perspectives for Sport Psychology in Mexico

A new generation of young students between 20 and 30 years of age is aware that the country's sports will not improve without sport psychology as part of training and competition. It is hoped that eventually these people will have some say in Mexico's different sport institutions and private clubs, and only then will sport psychology be accepted as in other developed countries. Meanwhile, only a few athletes and coaches accept the work of sport psychologists, and the situation appears perhaps the bleakest of any country studied.

Nevertheless, sport psychologists are hopeful that the work within the newly formed Mexican Society of Sport Psychology will assure good results quickly. More diffusion of information and laboratories for experimentation and research are required. Further publication of sport psychology articles in sports medicine journals by the new association may help spread the word to a larger public. Mexico needs the collaboration of international experts to come and train those working in sport psychology.

Chapter 6

NORTH AMERICA
Canada

in collaboration with

Wayne Halliwell
Université de Montréal

Jim McClements
University of Saskatchewan

Canadian Sport Psychology Résumé

Over the last two decades sport psychology in Canada has evolved into an academically oriented and differentiated field of research characterized by sophisticated professional links with both the world of sport practice and mainstream psychology.

Estimated Number of Sport Psychologists. 150

Prominent Institutions. Universities of Alberta, Montreal, Ottawa, Western Ontario, Waterloo

Orientation. Experimental research and psychological skills training of athletes

Privileged Topics. Motor control, motivation, anxiety, cognitive processes

Publication Vehicle. *Canadian Journal of Sport Science*

Society. Canadian Society of Psychomotor Learning and Sport Psychology

The Canadian sport psychology nerve centers are strung out along an 8,000-kilometer tract that borders on the United States. This thin sliver of the country contains 90% of the population and virtually all of Canada's universities, which are the main centers for sport psychology.

The birth of institutionalized sport psychology in Canada can be traced to the arrival of Max Howell at the University of British Columbia in 1954. After graduating from the University of California at Berkeley as Franklin Henry's first doctoral student, Howell accepted a position at the University of British Columbia where he established the first master's degree in physical education in Canada. Wiggins (1984) reports that there he began teaching bits and pieces of motor learning/sport psychology in Canada.

Then in the fall of 1969, Bob Wilberg and his graduate students organized the first Canadian sport psychology meeting under the title of the Psychomotor Learning and Sport Psychology Committee of the Canadian Association of Health, Physical Education and Recreation (CAHPER). Not until 1977, however, was an independent society formed, the Canadian Society of Psychomotor Learning

and Sport Psychology (CSPLSP). This society recognizes Canada's two official languages, English and French, and it now uses the simpler French acronym SCAPPS when referring to itself.

However, it may be possible to trace the first recorded evidence of Canadian sport psychology to more than a decade earlier in 1942 when Emanuel Orlick, perhaps a candidate for the father of Canadian sport psychology, published a master's thesis that gave an overview of the applications of psychology to physical education and recreation.

As previously mentioned, the beginnings of sport psychology took place within an academic setting, almost exclusively within departments or faculties of physical education, kinesiology, kinanthropology, or leisure studies but definitely not within departments of psychology. This development is interesting, especially compared to the situation in Western and to some extent Eastern Europe, where many of the pioneers were trained exclusively in psychology.

These beginnings of sport psychology within sport-related departments occurred almost within a 5-year period at all of Canada's long network of universities in the late 1960s. Although initiatives in sport psychology in many cases had their origins in graduate programs in the United States, these graduates were later distributed across the country in a hiring boom in the late 1960s and early 1970s.

Virtually every university and college now has some type of academic appointment in sport psychology and, in many cases, a number of appointments in the sub-areas of skill acquisition, motor control, social psychology of sport, and psychology of sport competition. This academic dimension has been the most dominant one and according to Len Wankel (personal communication, 1980) has tended to follow "after an identifiable time lag, the foci of study of mainstream psychology."

More recently another dimension of sport psychology has developed that has come from the grass roots of sport practice. Coaches, athletes, and sport federations have expressed a need for some type of psychological input to improve sport performance and to enhance the experience that sport provides. This has resulted in the development of a more applied area of sport psychology that has a definite applied emphasis, as compared to the disciplinary-based "academic" area. The applied area has undergone rapid recent advances to the point where most national teams include an applied sport psychologist as part of their staff. Even at the provincial level, some support is available for coach and athlete education as are some funds for the provision of services.

Both areas, research and intervention, are in a state of flux because the substantive and methodological dimensions are still being critically analyzed by both academics and practitioners. The relative youth of those working in the area and the absence of restrictive academic and sport traditions has given the area some promise.

Training in Sport Psychology

Students can receive specialized academic training in sport psychology or its subareas in nine Canadian universities, in either physical education, educational psychology, or psychology departments but usually simultaneously in all three. Few psychology departments offer specific courses in sport psychology, but a number of their graduates do research in sport and take graduate sport psychology courses in physical education departments. At the University of Montreal there has been an initiative to create a joint sport psychology degree at the master's level, with required course work in both the sport sciences and psychology, but this situation is far from settled.

A high degree of academic mobility in Canada permits students to take course work in faculties other than the ones in which they are enrolled. This is quite different from the situation in continental Europe, where students do not stray from their own faculty's offerings. Thus, students in physical education whose particular interests are in social psychology of sport can benefit from specific courses on the subject within their faculty as well as from appropriate social psychology or sociology courses at both undergraduate and graduate levels in another department. This mobility is such that if a particular course is not offered at a student's own institution in that city, reciprocal agreements with other universities often permit the student free access to these other centers. This principle of academic mobility differentiates the programs of North America and the Commonwealth countries from all others.

Because 85% of all Canadian respondents in the 1981 survey, which was the basis for the first edition of this book, were trained in faculties of sport science or physical education, it is possible to profile the typical student. But because education falls under provincial rather than federal jurisdiction, a number of variations on this model does exist across the country.

A student coming out of high school can enter a physical education or sport science faculty at a university either directly or via a preparatory college program. The student must have appropriate high school grades and in some cases pass physical ability entrance tests. These tests are not as widespread or as stringent as those in Eastern Europe.

The choice of institution depends on whether the student is interested in teaching physical education or doing something else related to sport or human movement that could take place in a setting other than education, such as health, industry, or administration. If administration,

the student might enroll in a department of kinesiology, human kinetics, kinanthropology, or leisure studies. These departmental titles were created in the 1960s and 1970s to reflect alternate directions that movement or sport science could take besides teacher preparation, and perhaps to improve the perceived academic status of what was formerly called physical education.

Within these 3- to 4-year programs, the student usually receives, within the faculty, theoretical courses in motor learning or skill acquisition, psychology of competitive sport, social psychology of sport and leisure, sociology of sport, growth and development, and in many cases associated laboratory and research projects. It is not unusual that students also receive general psychology and child psychology in the psychology department, with the opportunity of taking further required psychology courses at the undergraduate level. Very often students take courses in elementary statistics and, more recently, in computer science. At the end of this program, a student is often required to complete a graduation project, which could be in sport psychology, comparable to a small thesis. The bachelor's degree awarded at the end of this program is oriented essentially toward science, arts, or physical education. This allows a graduate to teach physical education; however, in some provinces an additional year of teacher preparation is required for a teaching certificate. There is also a tendency toward specialized undergraduate programs in teaching, coaching, sport administration, dance, physical fitness, health, and even research at certain institutions.

A student who wishes to continue study in sport psychology at the graduate level applies either to the same university where he or she did undergraduate work or very often to another institution in Canada or the United States. Eighteen of Canada's approximately 30 universities offer graduate study of some form in the behavioral area.

It is a common belief that it is preferable for students to complete at least part of their graduate studies at other institutions to get some breadth of orientation. One exception to this occurs in the province of Quebec where some unilingual French students might tend to stay *chez nous* rather than study in English in another province or in the United States.

No physical education doctoral programs existed in Canada until the first Ph.D. was established at the University of Alberta in 1967, and later at the universities of Montreal and Waterloo in the mid-1970s. Therefore, a large number of the present-day first-generation people in sport psychology went south to study in the United States. Upon their return, they helped to establish graduate programs in Canada that partially checked the flow south, and in certain instances reversed it. This international mobility is a unique feature that has provided Canadian sport psychology with a great deal of cross-fertilization that is lacking in Eastern and Western Europe. In Europe, students tend to study at their initial institute of study, most certainly within their own country.

A master's degree is a 1- to 2-year program of taught courses that can terminate either with or without a thesis. A degree without a thesis is made up of only course work and examinations. This is usually a very broad area of concern, such as teaching, administration, or organization, and is considered more a professional rather than academic program. Normally, this degree would be terminal and the student could not pursue further doctoral studies upon completion of the degree.

A research master's degree is more specific in nature, with less course work and more emphasis on research projects. At certain universities at this level, students can concentrate almost all their courses in behavioral science and research methodology. The course work in the behavioral sciences might include within-faculty courses in skill acquisition or motor learning, motor control, neurological science, perceptual motor or cognitive development, social psychology of physical activity, psychology of sport competition, or hybrids of these subject areas. Master's level courses in perception, learning, personality, social psychology, or other areas are commonly taken concurrently in psychology departments. In addition, students take courses in research methods and a variety of courses in statistics, electronics, and computer science either within or outside the physical education faculty.

Computer technology has advanced to such a point that almost all of the physical education institutions with graduate programs have not only computer terminals linked into the large "number-crunching" central university system but also minicomputers within the laboratories for on-line analysis and programmed experimentation. Many graduate students and professors now possess their own personal computers at home for word processing, electronic mail, computer-assisted instruction, data collection, and analysis.

The thesis at the master's level is usually a single study requiring 6 to 12 months of planning, research, analysis, and writing. The candidate usually defends the thesis before a committee of three to five members; one member often is from the psychology department. In many cases, the candidate and advisor aim to submit this project for publication or to present it at a national conference for peer evaluation and feedback. A master of arts (M.A.), master of science (M.Sc.), master of physical education (M.P.E.), or master of human kinetics (M.H.K.) is awarded depending on the institution.

Doctoral studies again require application and admission to a school that has this type of program. In some provinces, institutions must first apply to a provincial examining board with one outline of what tack the proposed doctoral program will take in sport psychology or the sport sciences. In other provinces, the decision rests with the institution. Of the approximately 30 universities offering physical education programs in Canada, only 7 have formalized doctoral programs: Alberta, Simon Fraser, Toronto, Victoria, and Waterloo in English Canada and Montreal and Laval in French Canada. McGill, York, Ottawa, and Saskatchewan have ad hoc, or special case, doctoral programs but no formalized programs of study.

These studies include advanced course work in the same areas as outlined in the master's program in both the physical education and psychology departments. Further acquisition of academic skills occurs in advanced courses in statistics and computer science. More seminar work or small tutorials as well as open-discussion brainstorming sessions are features of this level of study. Research toward the thesis is often made up of a series of related experimental investigations on a specific theme, rather than a single study, that unite the advisor's competence and the student's interests. Collaboration on research with psychology department personnel is common at this level. Study programs can last from 2 to 4 years depending on the candidate's preparation prior to doctoral studies and the complexity of the data gathering. The doctor of philosophy (Ph.D.) degree is awarded following successful completion of course work, a written and oral comprehensive exam, and a thesis defense.

A very great variety of educational backgrounds is present in the population of Canadians working in sport psychology because they have been trained at a very large number of Canadian and American universities. In 1981, the greatest number of graduates then working in sport psychology in Canada came from the University of Alberta, which has had a doctoral program since 1967. Bob Wilberg and Rikk Alderman taught the majority of graduates who were working in Canada. A sampling of the University of Alberta graduates who have had a significant impact on the development of motor learning and sport psychology includes Claude Alain, Cal Botterill, Eric Buckholz, Bert Carron, Craig Hall, Dennis Hrycaiko, Peter Klavora, Jack Leavitt, Ron Marteniuk, Jim McClements, Rick Frey, Terry Orlick, John Salmela, Geri Van Gyn, Ted Wall, and Len Wankel. However, with the wider distribution of sport psychology programs throughout Canada, this production is now more evenly divided across the major centers. In addition, an increasing number of graduate students from Europe, Asia and, Africa now makes up the cultural mosaic of most graduate programs.

This system has proven successful in producing research that is in many cases of sufficient quality for publication in North American or international sport psychology journals as well as mainstream psychology journals such as the *Journal of Experimental Psychology* and the *Journal of Personality and Social Psychology*. In 1991 Terry Orlick and John Salmela of the University of Ottawa created Canada's first applied sport psychology program with John Partington of Carleton University. At the moment, sport psychology groups in Canada (SCAPPS), in the United States (AAASP), and internationally (ISSP and FEPSAC) are making collaborative efforts regarding certification procedures for clinical sport psychologists.

The Canadian Sportpsych Registry. In Canada, an ad hoc committee of the Canadian Association of Sport Sciences (CASS) under the direction of Murray Smith has facilitated the development of what has been somewhat awkwardly termed the Registry for Sport Behavioral Professionals by lending financial and support services to this project. The registry was created in 1989 to identify "CASS-approved service providers" to prospective clients in the sport community as a measure to improve the availability and quality of services. Athletes, coaches, teams, parents, and sport organizations considering using the professional services of a clinical sport psychologist, educator/counselor, or researcher will be given the names of approved professionals, but the registry will not make direct referrals. This registry was created to be a means for sport psychology to determine its own future by bringing all the prime movers in sport psychology together in a nonadversarial environment. The whole process was created and administered by representatives from CASS, SCAPPS, Sport Canada, and the Canadian Psychological Association, which served on the review board.

The initial registry, while well-intentioned, did not receive much professional support, with many of the most active consultants not attempting to register. Because of this inertia in the registration process, in 1991 CASS asked a committee chaired by Terry Orlick to revamp the registry.

The new registry, the Canadian Sportpsych Registry, has but one category—the Registered Sportpsych Consultant—and was created only for the registration of effective applied sport psychology consultants. Registration requires being a permanent resident of Canada, having a postgraduate degree in a related area, having demonstrated sport experience and sport science knowledge, participating in applied internships or having done effective consulting, and completing the documented application, inluding client feedback.

The purpose of the registry is twofold: to identify people in Canada who can help athletes and coaches with mental training and performance enhancement and to promote the continued development of high-quality consultation services for athletes/performers and coaches working in Canada.

A Registry Board evaluates applicants and unsuccessful candidates are given suggestions to take before reapplying, which may include course work or supervised field experience.

The Registry Board has no legal power to control or to restrict general practice in sport psychology. However, individuals who wish to work with Canadian teams through the Sport Science Support Program are required to show evidence of maintained registry status. Registered individuals will also be eligible for funds to attend annual continuing education workshops.

Topics of Study. In 1979, a content analysis of the research done by Canadians and published in North American sport psychology publications was published in the book *Coach, Athlete, and the Sport Psychologist.* This analysis was based on 10 years of research presented at the annual Canadian and American symposia and conferences. The summary does not exhaustively cover all published sport psychology research, because some individuals choose not to publish within conference proceedings, preferring instead to try established sport psychology or psychology journals. The rejection rate of these publications at times is from 50% to 70%, so some research was not reported. Still, the breakdown does reflect the overall picture of research in Canada.

Of the 332 reported studies, 56.6% were in the area of motor learning and motor performance. The great majority of these studies were theoretical in nature; that is, they were testing theories in motor memory, motor control, or movement organization. Recent symposia at the SCAPPS annual conferences have covered topics such as response suppression, aging, imagery, and attention as well as reviews on information processing. A review of the free communication papers from 1985

to 1987 revealed that 55.2% of them were in the areas of motor learning/control and motor memory. Very little of this research was involved with gross motor or sport activities. Most research used tasks that have simple movements of a few centimeters in the attempt to experimentally isolate the theoretical variables.

Of the remaining 144 studies in 1979, 77% were in the area of the psychology of sport competition, and 23% were in the social psychology of physical activity. A very wide range of topics was noted in what could be considered mainstream sport psychology. The areas of personality, attitudes, competitive anxiety, and achievement motivation were the most frequent topics in sport psychology, whereas social facilitation in sport led the social psychological field. Symposia offered at the 1985 to 1987 conferences addressed the questions of exercise adherence, youth sport, mental imagery, intrinsic motivation, and functional electrical stimulation. A similar pattern of research would be evident in the United States given that no clear differences can be found between these neighboring countries in their research activities.

Publications

The first sport psychology publication in Canada is believed to have been by Emanuel Orlick, who produced a master's thesis at McGill University in 1942 entitled ''Psychology for Education in the Field of Physical Education and Recreation.'' This thesis highlighted contemporary psychological issues such as ''precompetitive jitters'' in a broad overview.

No specific sport psychology journal is published in Canada, although a number of articles in the area regularly appear in the *Canadian Journal of Sport Sciences.* Since 1981, the Coaching Association of Canada has published a monograph called *SPORTS: Science Periodical on Research and Technology in Sport.* Issues in sport psychology have accounted for 40% of the publications, addressing the areas of elite-level preparation, strategy, feedback, goal setting, motivation, leadership style, youth sport, and autoregulation.

In 1988, John Salmela of the University of Ottawa became coeditor with Alberto Cei of Italy of the *International Journal of Sport Psychology.* This journal has streamlined its editorial policies and has tried to establish a niche to report studies from a broad spectrum of international scholars and cross-cultural research as well as publish special monothematic issues. An important addition for French-Canadians is that the journal now solicits articles in the French language, and English manuscripts include multilingual résumés.

Probably the greatest volume of sport psychology information in Canada has been published in proceedings of the annual SCAPPS symposia over a 10-year period that were edited by Williams and Wankel (1973), Rushall (1975), Bard, Fleury, and Salmela (1975), Kerr (1977), Landry and Orban (1978), Klavora and Daniel (1979), Klavora and Wipper (1980) and Klavora and Flowers (1980), Nadeau, Halliwell, Newell, and Roberts (1980), Partington, Orlick, and Salmela (3 volumes in 1983), and Wankel and Wilberg (1983). Though the editorial and publication standards of these volumes are somewhat uneven, they still contain a wealth of information on the development of Canadian sport psychology. No further publications from the SCAPPS meetings have been attempted, probably because of the increased numbers of specialized journals in sport psychology and motor learning.

Canadians have published a number of impressive volumes in both the academic and applied areas of sport psychology and its subdisciplines. In the academic areas, Marteniuk's *Information Processing and Motor Skill* (1976), Alderman's *Psychological Behavior in Sport* (1974), Carron's *Social Psychology of Sport* (1979), and Kerr's *Psychomotor Learning* (1982) have received considerable scientific and academic acclaim. From the applied viewpoint, Orlick's trilogy *In Pursuit of Excellence* (1980, 1990), *Psyching for Sport* (1986), and *Psyched* (1986) with John Partington, as well as Klavora and Daniel's *Coach, Athlete, and the Sport Psychologist* (1979) and Rushall's *Psyching in Sports* (1970), have proven useful for both coaches and athletes. One other excellent source of practical sport psychology information is the coaching certification manuals used by the Coaching Association of Canada, a group that to date consists of more than 360,000 amateur coaches. The United States and Australia have adapted the Canadian model for the certification of coaches to their own specific needs.

The Role of Sport Psychology in Canada

Institutions. The university system is presently the heart of sport psychology in Canada, though recently some activity has been going on outside these circles. The university structures across Canada are remarkably similar to those in the United States although decidedly different from those of the European system. A newly graduated Ph.D. student in Canada is cut loose from the parent institution and faces the uncertainty of the open job market. This was not much of a problem in the late 1960s and early 1970s when university programs were expanding and creating sport psychology positions. In the late 1970s things tightened up, and graduates began seeking alternative employment in industry or government. In the early 1980s, Canadian universities suffered from severe budgetary restraints that restricted hiring. The young physical education professors hired during the 1960s are now beginning to reach retirement age with the option of early retirement. More sessional and tenure-track positions have been created in the last half of the 1980s and the trend is expected to accelerate in the 1990s.

Once graduates have obtained their doctoral degrees, they are basically qualified to work at a university at the assistant professor level. This position is without job security, or tenure for 3 to 6 years until a committee of peers judges the candidate's contributions in teaching, research, and university and community service. If the evaluations are positive, the candidate can be given tenure and often is promoted to associate professor. After another minimum 6-year period at this level, the candidate may then be promoted to full professor.

These practices differ from Western Europe, where a graduate with a doctorate is often hired as an assistant at the institution where he or she completed studies, although it is rare to be hired as a professor at the same place. In Eastern Europe, a student secures employment before choosing to embark upon doctoral studies.

In a 1981 survey, Canadian sport psychologists were asked to name in order of importance the institutions that prepared students in the psychology of sport and physical activity. It was not surprising that the three top-ranked institutions were those that had doctoral programs: the universities of Alberta, Waterloo, and Montreal.

Though universities have provided the main impetus for the development of sport psychology in Canada, another Canadian institution, the Coaching Association of Canada (CAC), has greatly reinforced the importance of sport psychology for sport practice. This governmental body was formed to upgrade the standard of coaching in Canada. One of its components is the National Coaching Certification Program (NCCP), through which coaches in all sports get a standard course in sport organization, teaching, and sport science, including sport psychology. There are five levels of certification, each including theoretical, technical, and practical aspects. This is followed by specific technical programs within the coach's sport with specific sport psychology input.

Canadian Society for Psychomotor Learning and Sport Psychology (SCAPPS). This group was founded in 1969 by Bob Wilberg as an afterthought to the first Canadian sport psychology symposium. The SCAPPS acronym is the more reader-friendly French version. This group initially fell within the auspices of a special-interest group of CAHPER. Within this structure, functioning was somewhat difficult because, among other things, not all sport psychologists with roots in psychology were interested in paying dues to a physical education group. In 1977, SCAPPS became a separate society from CAHPER and this allowed more independent functioning, collection of dues, and unhindered organization of its functions.

SCAPPS's main activity has been the organization of an annual 3-day symposium each fall. These symposia have centered around invited speakers from the parent disciplines of psychology or from the various areas of motor learning, motor control, social psychology of physical activity, and psychology of sport competition. Attendance has varied from less than 100 to about 300, depending on the location in Canada. A significant number of Americans attend this conference.

The society's annual meetings have also been held in conjunction with larger meetings of the sport sciences such as the CASS, NASPSPA, and ISSP. All of these exchanges in North America result in a vibrant environment for the exchange of ideas.

The stream of conference proceedings the SCAPPS meetings have generated are the responsibility of the conference chair. In the earlier years, the conference chair became the next society president; however, these functions have now been separated and a new president is elected yearly, and publication can be centrally controlled. This is similar to the North American procedures in NASPSPA where new people take their turn in the harness, but very different from the European sport psychology societies in which the more pronouncedly fixed social structure establishes a venerable leader for life. This perhaps keeps the field on a steady course, but the vital force that comes with the involvement of new blood is lacking. A SCAPPS newsletter is sent to members quarterly, including local news, professional issues, upcoming events, and invited articles and editorials.

During its early years, SCAPPS had a somewhat supercilious attitude toward other sport science and even sport psychology groups at home and abroad. Recently, however, it has developed a more mature attitude of cooperation with a number of other sport science bodies. Though the membership rejected an early attempt to merge with NASPSPA, the two groups now coordinate planning regarding conference sites, choice of speakers, and combined events. Whereas the society told the ISSP in 1974 that it wanted nothing to do with them, in 1981 they both were involved in organizing their Fifth World Sport Psychology Congress, and now the ISSP journal is partially housed in Atlanta. In the earlier years, SCAPPS resisted collaboration with CASS. During the 1980s, CASS made a concerted effort to draw all the sport sciences under their umbrella organization. However, at the 1984 Kingston annual conference, SCAPPS decided to remain an autonomous society. The society has also been coordinating work with CASS and Sport Canada on testing standards and the registration of ''Sportpsych'' consultants. Annual membership dues for SCAPPS are $40 for professionals and $5 for students. The society is an open one with a membership of approximately 120.

Sport Psychology and Top Sport.   There is considerable sport psychology input in top sport, but very little of it has the same organized intensity that was once believed to occur in Eastern Europe. Still, there is probably more direct intervention with top athletes in Canada on a per-capita basis than in any other Western country. At the 1984 Olympics, more than 20 different individuals worked with teams that participated at either Sarajevo or Los Angeles. Terry Orlick and John Partington's survey of the effectiveness of these interventions provided revealing material in the first year's issues of *The Sport Psychologist* as well as in their book *Psyched*.

The most pervasive type of sport psychology for top sport is the educational variety. All coaches, whether trained at university or through the club system, must be certified by NCCP certification programs. As outlined previously, there is a heavy emphasis on skill analysis, group dynamics, stress management, and leadership in these programs so that coaches' knowledge bases expand as they move from Level 1 through Level 5. To date more than 360,000 Canadian coaches have passed through at least Level 1 of this program.

The CAC has two other programs that allow developing coaches to upgrade their academic qualifications in sport science in general and sport psychology in particular. The first is through coaching scholarships. A promising young coach is paid to study at a university with an academic resource person who has a sport science specialization and a specific interest in the coach's particular sport discipline. A number of these resource people have been sport psychology specialists. The second program is the apprentice coach program. A young coach is paid to work with a master coach in his or her sport and at the same time is associated with a sport science institution to pick up the appropriate knowledge in key problem areas of sport psychology and the other sport sciences.

The number of full-time coaches in Canada has increased, many at the provincial and local levels. These coaches tend to be well educated and are much more aware of applied sport psychology. Many of the younger coaches have second-generation experience because they worked with sport psychologists when they used to compete themselves. This combined with the widespread use of sport psychologists at the national team level has led to increased acceptance of clinical and educational applications.

Individual sport federations have attempted to incorporate sport psychologists or performance consultants from the sport sciences into their long-range planning for Olympic Games and world championships. Sports such as canoeing, gymnastics, swimming, wrestling, skiing, and sailing have acquired, on a contractual basis, a sport psychologist who works with coaches and athletes during both the training and competition processes. Others have started high-performance centers with sport psychologists consulting and working with athletes and coaches. It appears that this type of activity will be on the increase as more students are trained in the applied areas of sport psychology.

CAC surveys have shown that coaches and administrators consider sport psychology the most important area of concern in the sport sciences that can contribute to the immediate needs of coaches and athletes. The status of sport psychology was greatly enhanced in 1980 when the Sports Medicine Council of Canada, the body that intervenes with top Canadian international delegations, voted in principle that someone with applied psychological skills training in sport psychology should accompany the Olympic delegation. Previously, only medical personnel were involved in this capacity. This was a modest step by Eastern European standards, but it was a starting point.

The important relationship between sport and applied sport science has been clearly stated in publicity brochures of the Fitness and Amateur Sport Division of Sport Canada. For example: ''Competitors and coaches need applied research from the sport scientists to advance training methods.''

Perspectives for Sport Psychology in Canada

The areas of psychomotor learning and sport psychology, to borrow this dual Canadian title, have evolved from their beginnings in the late 1960s. This has been most dramatic in the academic area, where it has achieved broad-based sophistication and certain international acclaim.

It appears that this research progress within the various disciplines that make up the field of sport psychology will continue to evolve with the addition of new applied and clinical programs of graduate and cross-disciplinary studies. The orientation of this research may continue to change, with themes arising from within the realms of sport rather than shadowing the trends of mainstream psychology. In this regard, researchers may use a more qualitative approach that taps the experiences of athletes, coaches, and sport participants to further our understanding of human behavior in sport and physical activity settings. Terry Orlick and John Partington have already used such an experiential approach to assess the effectiveness of sport psychologists' work with Canada's teams at the 1984 Olympic Games at Sarajevo and Los Angeles.

One aspect worth future observation is the direction that the psychomotor learning component of this group is taking. Increased specialization and sophistication is taking this research further and further away from the underlying applied issues within the physical education faculties that house many of these programs. The necessity of advancing basic theoretical areas may be balanced by more immediate practical applications arising from the reality of performance in sport and physical activity, which is the raison d'être of these institutions.

Probably the area of greatest growth will be within the applied areas of sport psychology. With the increased involvement of government in applied sport science research, it appears that this will be the growth area for funding and possibly for jobs. With federal and provincial funding agencies seeking answers to pragmatic questions such as the high dropout rate in youth sport and exercise settings and the mental readiness of Canadian Olympic athletes, contemporary applied sport psychology researchers will undoubtedly spend more time in the field than in the lab. This emphasis on professional rather than academic dimensions will probably depend on the development of the delicate issue of certification of sport psychologists, or sport behavior professionals. There will probably be an increase in the amount of field testing of the various sport psychology procedures to evaluate their effectiveness in applied settings. A greater educational emphasis on long-term prevention will replace much of the present crisis intervention at top sport levels. Finally, it appears that the populations that will benefit from sport psychology attention will spread from junior and top-level athletes to the extremes of the very young and the very old in settings outside the competitive one.

United States

in collaboration with

Robert N. Singer
University of Florida

American Sport Psychology Résumé

Sport psychology in the United States has rapidly emerged as an important academic and professional subject, taught mainly within physical education or movement science departments. Recent years have seen the proliferation of academic and professional societies, journals, and printed and audiovisual materials. Strong leadership in the field is now attempting to resolve problems of fragmentation, definition, and application.

Estimated Number of Sport Psychologists. 750

Prominent Institutions. Universities of Illinois, Wisconsin, and North Carolina as well as Arizona State and Michigan State universities

Orientation. Empirical research and applied sport psychology

Privileged Topics. Wide variety of topics in motor control, learning and development, social psychology, performance enhancement, educational sport psychology

Publication Vehicles. *Journal of Motor Behavior, Journal of Sport and Exercise Psychology, Journal of Sport*

Behavior, The Sport Psychologist, Journal of Applied Sport Psychology, The Research Quarterly for Exercise and Sport

Societies. North American Society for the Psychology of Sport and Physical Activity, Association for the Advancement of Applied Sport Psychology, Division 47 of the APA: Exercise and Sport Psychology

Some countries are difficult to understand because they present to observers two-dimensional façades that look good from afar, but when you dig a little deeper you find they are far from good. The United States is different. It is difficult to completely understand the United States for a different reason. Americans examine themselves, and let others examine them, with sometimes embarrassing honesty. In 1981 a group of leading American sport psychologists described their discipline in a manner that is still appropriate today: ''It is fragmented and poorly organized,'' says Bob Nideffer. ''Has come a long way, but still has a way to go,'' suggests Bob Singer. Bruce Ogilvie laments: ''There is little in the way of an organized attempt to provide the services that are most in demand at this time.'' Or from Tom Tutko: ''Research is scattered and has a shotgun look.''

Along with this critical self-analysis, sport psychology is also characterized in a more positive, forward-looking perspective by Dan Landers "as thriving in terms of both theoretical and applied research"; by Walter Kroll "as emerging and maturing into recognized respectability"; and by Bill Straub as "developing into an important area of the behavioral sciences." What it all boils down to is that sport psychology in North America is struggling through both great spurts of adolescent growth and the accompanying identity crisis.

The birth of organized present-day American sport psychology can be pinned to the day before the April 1966 meeting of the national American Association of Health, Physical Education, and Recreation convention in Chicago. At that time a steering committee of Canadians (Richard B. Alderman, Donald A. Bailey, and Gerald S. Kenyon) and Americans (Roscoe C. Brown, Bryant J. Cratty, Warren R. Johnson, Jack R. Leighton, Arthur T. Slater-Hammel, and Leon E. Smith) was struck to explore the feasibility of a North American sport psychology society. In September 1966, at the meeting of the managing council of the International Society of Sport Psychology (ISSP) in Barcelona, Warren R. Johnson and Arthur T. Slater-Hammel applied for the next ISSP congress in Washington for the yet-to-be-created American sport psychology society that was to become the North American Society for the Psychology of Sport and Physical Activity, or NASPSPA. The appearance of the first *NASPSPA Sport Psychology Bulletin*, edited by Rikk Alderman in January 1967, was one of the organization's first official signs of life.

However, the history of U.S. sport psychology actually goes back more than 50 years earlier to the 1920s when Coleman R. Griffith was appointed director of the Athletic Research Laboratory at the University of Illinois. Griffith may well have established the first sport psychology laboratory in the world. There would be some argument, however, from Germans who claim the Berlin sport psychology laboratory organized by Carl Diem and led by Schulte and Sippel in 1920 was the first. Or from the Soviets, who would say that A.T. Puni established the first Institute of Physical Culture in Leningrad in 1925. The Japanese might even discuss the pioneering work of Mitsuo Matsui in Tokyo in 1924. However, it does seem clear that Griffith's 1926 book *Psychology of Coaching* was the first published psychology text dealing with sport, and that Sippel's 1926 book *Body-Spirit-Mind: Fundamentals of the Psychology of Physical Activity* was the first to relate psychology and physical education.

Prior to Griffith's appointment a number of articles were written about sport psychology and motor learning, the earliest being Frances A. Kellor's 1898 publication in education *A Psychological Basis for Physical Culture*, which included a number of experimental studies on motor learning, particularly on reaction time and transfer. The years between the pioneering work of Griffith and the beginning of the boom in the 1960s were spotted and bare. Notable exceptions occurred, however, in the general consideration of sport problems from a psychological standpoint in the 1950s by John Lawther as well as the very strong fundamental force of Franklin M. Henry of the University of California at Berkeley in the area of motor learning. Henry, whom Schmidt called the father of motor learning in America, initiated a course

entitled "Psychological Basis of Physical Activity" in 1935 that still exists today. In 1981 Henry and G. Lawrence Rarick were elected as the first NASPSPA Distinguished Scholars.

During the 1950s and 1960s, Henry supervised a number of graduate students who have been and still are influential in the field in Canada (Alderman, Carron, and Marteniuk) and in the United States (Schmidt and Stelmach). Maxwell L. Howell, now a prominent sport historian in Australia, was Henry's first motor learning student—a remarkable demonstration of academic flexibility and mobility. Thus, the roots of the modern field of sport psychology sprang from the work in motor learning initiated in the mid-1960s and later differentiated into the many active subunits that characterize the present state of the field.

Training in Sport Psychology

Physical education departments and their offspring accounted for the academic training of 61.8% of all respondents to the 1981 survey in the first edition of this book, whereas psychology departments prepared only 16.8%. In 1989 Ron Smith reported that the AAASP membership was made up of approximately 50% from physical education and 50% from psychology. This can be compared to the overall percentage of psychology-trained individuals in continental Europe, which is closer to 30%.

The academic preparation procedure for individuals going through the physical education program from the undergraduate to the doctoral level in the United States is almost identical to that described in the Canadian section. However, some subtle differences occur in the United States because of the intimate relationship in this country between physical education and intercollegiate athletics. In Canada, intercollegiate athletics is an amateur, non-revenue-producing affair. In the main, athletics and academic physical education programs merely share the same buildings with little other interaction. In the United States, intercollegiate athletics is a multimillion-dollar business. American college football teams fill to capacity stadiums of up to 100,000 spectators and generate considerable local, state, and even national interest. A large number of revenue-producing football and basketball athletes used to enroll in physical education departments in the 1950s and 1960s before the academic disciplines were well developed, and academic standards were compromised to keep them eligible to play. As a result of this phenomenon, a stigma was often attached to physical education departments at the undergraduate level.

Perhaps for this reason in the early years of modern sport psychology in the United States an overcompensation occurred in academic sport psychology that was not present in Canada. In 1981, this phenomenon translated into a higher proportion of theoretical work in the United States (74.5%) versus Canada (65.8%); decreased involvement in sport-related, practical, para-academic experiences for American (20.8%) versus Canadian (33.3%) graduate students; and more taught course work

(66.6%) for the former than the latter (59.9%). Updated figures on current curricula are not readily available.

This emphasis has had the very positive effect of producing a high-quality researcher who is even competitive within university, academic, and scientific circles. These individuals with advanced academic and research skills have been termed "educational sport psychologists." This brand of sport psychologist may have its greatest exponent in the world in the United States.

All those questioned in 1981 on the future directions of the academic preparation of students in sport psychology suggested an increased emphasis on some type of applied experience in the field. These suggestions were in two categories: (1) that both psychology- and physical education–trained graduates undertake more research within applied settings rather than focus exclusively within the laboratory, and (2) that both groups receive increased specialized training in the counseling or clinical aspects of sport psychology. These prognoses proved very accurate, because the field of sport psychology took on a more applied bent with the creation of a new applied association and two new applied journals.

On the first point, it was found in 1981 that only 20.8% of students prepared in physical education departments had any para-academic experiences such as fieldwork, clinics, or workshops as compared to 52.8% of the psychology students. In 1986, Michael Sachs and Kevin Burke edited a directory of graduate programs in sport psychology in North America that indicated that of the 95 programs listed, 55 had directed or supervised fieldwork in sport psychology. This desire to become intimate with sport reality was a phenomenon that surfaced not only in North America, but also in Eastern Europe, where sport psychology programs are already leaning heavily in this direction.

Nideffer, DuFresne, Nesvig, and Selder (1980) indicated that most sport psychology training programs failed to provide services in sport performance enhancement, psychological assessment, communication processes, crisis intervention, sport program development, and clinical therapy. Viewpoints differ on how to rectify this situation. Some suggest that students take double degrees in physical education and psychology to gain a more comprehensive view of both fields, as has occurred in Eastern Europe. Over the last 5 years, integrated cross-disciplinary programs were created at the University of Washington in Seattle and Michigan State University in East Lansing that allowed physical education graduate students to acquire clinical experience in internship training programs in American Psychological Association (APA)–accredited psychology departments.

One final point worth mentioning regarding sport psychology training is the role that North American universities play in the education of sport psychology graduates from Southeast Asia, Oceania, Africa, the Middle East, Europe, and South America. Though countries such as the Soviet Union do not accept certain foreign students from non-allied countries, the North American institutions appear to have had a greater impact given the numbers alone. In addition, books by Singer, Cratty, and Lawther have been translated into a number of foreign languages and have a profound effect

on training of individuals in this field in developing countries.

Topics of Study. The label "sport psychology" is an appropriate umbrella term for most countries in the world, because sport is considered an area of application of psychological principles, whether in the social, differential, perceptual, or learning areas of psychology. However, in the United States "sport psychology" is not as comfortably used in the sport-centered generic sense, because until recently a discipline-centered approach has predominated. This concentration on sport psychology as an academic discipline has fractionated the field into smaller subdisciplines. The strong North American tendency in mainstream psychology toward specialized theoretical research is also reflected in the many narrow spheres of interest of present-day sport psychology research.

From a very broad perspective, in the mid-1960s the field of motor learning split into a discipline-centered narrower area of motor learning and motor control as well as a sport-centered field called sport psychology. The earlier field of motor learning initially centered on areas such as the practice conditions (massed-distributed, whole-part, etc.) necessary for learning gross motor skills. When the available theoretical models such as Hull's proved inadequate for the explanation of learning phenomena, the field of study narrowed to motor performance assessment using information processing models. Again a narrower focus beyond the behavioral level followed, which brought the scientist's attention to the neural mechanisms of motor control.

The use of engineering constructs to elaborate movement theory has produced a field of research that is extremely complex and mathematical. For a time a void was left in the territory previously occupied by researchers interested in the area of learning of gross motor skills, until the late 1970s and early 1980s when researchers such as Michael Turvey and Scott Kelso began talking about coordinative structures in ecologically valid movement areas.

The 1987 NASPSPA membership report showed that of the 629 members, 326 were interested in sport psychology (51.8%), while motor learning and control was the central focus of 195 (31%). The smallest membership sector of 108 (17.2%) worked in motor development. The area of sport psychology was empirically based and also developed into a specialization. With the creation of the new applied sport psychology group AAASP, the field was further fractionated into three specialized areas—the social psychology of sport, health psychology, and intervention/performance enhancement. The last group has now also begun to fill the void that motor learning scholars once occupied. The subject areas of concentration, imagery, attention control, and signal detection in sport are now being enveloped within sport-centered "sport psychology."

In summary, sport psychology is an appropriate umbrella term for most work going on in the rest of the world, because it is basically sport-centered. However, in North America "sport psychology" is but a subunit of the area called "the psychology of sport and physical activity," the name from which the latter part of the acronym NASPSPA is derived. The division also shows up in the Canadian Society of Psychomotor Learning and Sport Psychology. The direction the two groups have taken has appropriately incited leaders like Rainer Martens to say, "I believe North America has by far the strongest research and empirical base in sport psychology, but Eastern Europe and the USSR probably do more application."

Several individuals have raised this issue of application as an inherent weakness in laboratory-based research. Martens, himself an empirical sport scientist turned applied sport psychologist, pleaded in 1979 for a movement into the real world of sport practice in "From Smocks to Jocks" (Martens, 1979). Again in 1986, Martens maintained his forward thinking by criticizing the orthodox methods used to study sport psychology. He suggested that sport psychology should include the use of idiographic approaches, introspection, and field studies.

Recently individuals trained in physical education as well as those trained in psychology have shown a great deal of interest in the intervention/performance-enhancement aspects of sport psychology. There is still quite a bit of discussion regarding the line of demarcation between the teaching of cognitive skill and clinical intervention. This is also the most prickly area in terms of professional competence and territorial rights, in both psychology and sport. The recent work in the area of health psychology has led to a new branch of applied sport psychology. The main thrusts to date are the study of the psychological outcomes of participating in sport and exercise programs within the wellness concept, as well as the motivation for exercise adherence. Researchers are also giving attention to the psychology of injuries by considering their diagnosis and prediction based on the participating athletes' psychological makeup.

Finally, the overall distribution of research topics in the United States is very similar to that described in the Canadian section. A glance at the key words in the Who's Who section also shows that North America in general and the United States in particular has the greatest variety of innovative, specialized, and intriguing areas of sport psychology.

Publications

The United States is the home of the competitive publication game of publish or perish. This phenomenon has resulted in a wide range and depth of publications in the form of articles in psychology and sport psychology journals, conference proceedings, book chapters, and books. Wayne Halliwell and Lise Gauvin have kept an updated list of sport psychology resources and report that there were over 100 specialized sport psychology books by Americans in print in 1989.

In 1981 Bryant J. Cratty admitted to having written "40-plus" books, including his landmark books—in motor learning, *Movement Behavior and Motor Learning* (1964); in sport psychology with Miroslav Vanek, *Psychology of the Superior Athlete* (1970); and more recently

in movement education for special populations and in social psychology. (The number of books by Cratty was updated in 1988 to "50-plus"!) As an indication of the impact of these early publications, Robert Singer's classic *Motor Learning and Human Performance* was voted one of the top 20 books in all of education in 1968.

The 1970s witnessed specialization in publication with popular books, mainly by physical educators, in motor learning and performance by Richard A. Schmidt, Robert N. Singer, and George Stelmach; in social psychology of physical activity by Martens; and in sport psychology by Fisher, Harris, Landers, Martens, Nideffer, Ogilvie, Singer, Straub, and Tutko. A unique contribution to clinical sport psychology is R.M. Nideffer's *The Ethics and Practice of Applied Sport Psychology* (1981).

The expansion of the production of sport psychology publications makes citing individual authors difficult, but Cratty, Straub, Singer, Martens, Weinberg, and Harris have had multiple publications. A number of sport psychology publications by American physical education–trained individuals have appeared in leading academic and popular psychology journals such as the *Journal of Experimental Psychology*, *Journal of Personality and Social Psychology*, and *Psychological Reviews*. Specific sport psychology journals were also developed in the area of motor skill, such as the *Journal of Motor Behavior*, as well as in the area of sport psychology, such as the *Journal of Sport and Exercise Psychology*, the *Journal of Sport Behavior*, and the more recently created *The Sport Psychologist* (1987). The last journal was formulated as a refereed publication vehicle open to a variety of traditional and nontraditional research methods and is concerned with the professional practice of sport psychology. The most recent sport psychology publication is the *Journal of Applied Sport Psychology*, the biannual publication of AAASP, which produced the first issue in March 1989. From 1973 to 1979, the annual conference of NASPSPA led to published proceedings and an impressive series entitled *Psychology of Motor Behavior and Sport*. This publication, however, proved uneconomical in this form and was not continued after 1980.

The Role of Sport Psychology in the United States

Institutions. Sport psychology in the United States has its primary and almost unique home within the university structure. This situation is an advantageous one for the generation of new knowledge within the ideal academic setting of the American university system. However, the United States seriously lacks an organized system to deliver this knowledge to coaches, athletes, and other beneficiaries as has occurred for 25 years in Eastern Europe and more recently in Canada.

Observers must appreciate the enormity of the American university and college network that covers the country to explain the diversity of research that comes from the United States. There are presently more than 400 programs of physical education at the university level in the United States with approximately 150 having contributed to the education of the Americans sampled in the first edition. The 1987 NASPSPA membership report indicated that 136 different schools produced the individuals currently working in the field. A 1984 NASPSPA survey of graduate programs indicated that 17 American universities offer postgraduate study up to the doctoral level in all three NASPSPA interest areas, and 36 specifically in sport psychology. Though there were talented mentors all around the country, most of the sport psychology action is concentrated in three distinct geographical areas, and within these areas certain traditionally strong centers have attracted exceptional people.

The eastern seaboard from Maine to Florida is one area of strength, with the largest number of graduates, according to the NASPSPA membership report, coming from Florida State University (20) where Bob Singer worked with his colleagues, followed by Penn State (15), Virginia (13), Columbia (10), and Tennessee (10). Other East Coast institutions of note are Louisiana State University and the universities of Georgia, Maryland, Massachusetts, and North Carolina at Greensboro.

The midwestern United States contains the second cluster of prestigious sport psychology universities, according to the NASPSPA sample. The University of Illinois at Champaign can probably be considered the premier sport psychology program in the country, and 26 of its graduates are NASPSPA members. Tradition supports this ranking given that Coleman R. Griffith set up the sport psychology program at the Athletic Research Laboratory at the University of Illinois in the 1920s. This center has since attracted scholars such as Rainer Martens, Karl Newell, Glyn Roberts, and Dan Gould in sport psychology. The University of Wisconsin (21) has also been classed in the top five institutions due to the work of Bill Morgan and George Stelmach. However, other Big Ten universities such as Iowa (15) and Michigan (10) have also been productive.

Finally, the West Coast is the site of the third concentration of sport psychology activity, with the University of Oregon producing the most graduates (23). The University of California campuses in Davis (10) and Southern California (10) are recognized as having strong programs, as are centers located at Arizona State University and the University of Washington. Washington offers an accredited sport psychology option in the psychology department with Ron Smith and Frank Smoll providing the research and intervention skills.

In spite of the breadth and depth of sport psychology in the United States, the country does not yet have an effective system to deliver this knowledge to the sport participants—the coaches, parents, and participants. An analogous body to the Coaching Association of Canada, with its coaching periodicals, bibliographic searches, and coaching certification programs, does not exist in the United States. Although corporate-sponsored publications on topics such as youth sport have been attempted along with private-sector coaching effectiveness programs, there is no stability for long-term commitment within this system. The lack of contact between sport psychology and real-world problems in sport and physical activity is due in part to the lack of government intervention in the system. Though sport psychology has begun to be accepted at the academic level, much needs to be done to bring this information to the sport participants.

The Sport Psychology Academy of the AAHPERD was created in 1979 to act as a bridge between sport psychology theory and practice. Its tasks are to translate sport psychology information from research to the applied level and to communicate the needs of the sport community from the grass-roots level upward. Although this academy is made up of 2,700 people who are actively interested in sport psychology, its exact frame of reference and means of functioning are still unclear at this early date. It may, however, help provide one type of delivery system for sport psychology to teachers and coaches.

Societies. The North American Society for the Psychology of Sport and Physical Activity (NASPSPA) is probably still the single most influential academic professional society in the world focusing on the psychology of sport and physical activity, with a 1988 membership of about 650. This honor is due to advances in both the academic and the professional areas of sport psychology, with an accent on the former rather than the latter. NASPSPA's impact in the realm of sport has, however, been somewhat diluted since 1985 with the creation of the Association for the Advancement of Applied Sport Psychology, or AAASP, with its membership of over 500, many of whom also belong to NASPSPA. In addition, there have been some attempts within NASPSPA to distance itself from the term "sport" in its name and substitute a broader generic term such as "motor behavior" or "motor science."

The origins of NASPSPA were in effect the result of a bit of crisis management by the pioneers of sport psychology in the United States, especially Arthur Slater-Hammel, the founding president. These individuals were rushed into organizing the second ISSP congress. In 1967 a national society had to be formed to properly organize this congress for a mostly European audience. In effect, the staging of this international meeting accelerated progress within the society. Since its 1973 meeting in Allerton Park, Illinois—the first meeting the society held independently of AAHPERD—NASPSPA has consistently organized solid conference programs with top speakers from various fields of psychology. One feature of the Allerton conference was Bob Singer's challenge for the future directions of the field, many of which are still valid. Each conference from 1973 to 1980 resulted in a reviewed and edited publication of full papers entitled *Psychology of Motor Behavior and Sport*.

NASPSPA membership tends to break down into three interest groups: sport psychology, motor learning and control, and motor development. In 1987 the largest percentage of the 629 members of NASPSPA was in the interest area of sport psychology (51.8%), followed by motor learning and control (31%) and motor development (17.2%). All members receive annually the three newsletters plus reduced subscription rates for the *Journal of Motor Behavior* and the *Journal of Sport and Exercise Psychology*. There are no membership requirements other than payment of annual dues of $20 (U.S.) for faculty and $5 for students. The society has prepared a code of ethics and guidelines for testing human subjects to be used as frames of reference for monitoring members' professional activities.

NASPSPA has also established two special research awards of merit for members at opposite ends of the career spectrum: the NASPSPA Distinguished Scholar Award for individuals who have demonstrated long-term contributions to research, and the NASPSPA Early Career Distinguished Scholar Award for those who have shown advanced development at an early stage of their scientific careers. The first award is restricted to those who have worked for 25 years beyond a doctorate, and the second is for those who have worked no more than 5 years after receiving a doctorate.

Nowhere else in the world has a professional sport psychology society undertaken such a broad mandate and carried out such a string of accomplishments. Only the German ASP, the Canadian SCAPPS, and, potentially, AAASP are within the same category of organization. The balance of professional and academic responsibility may be changing because sport psychology in North America is now also being directed by another association because of decisions NASPSPA made.

The AAASP was created because the membership of NASPSPA decided to concentrate solely on scholarship and not deal with the expanding scope of professional issues in sport psychology, a concern that Singer had in 1973. This decision was made after public deliberations on the issue by leading NASPSPA scholars appeared in the newsletter in 1983 to 1984, resulting in a mail vote by the membership against expanding NASPSPA's mandate into applied concerns.

As a result of this decision, an organizational meeting of AAASP was held at the 1985 NASPSPA conference in Gulfport, Mississippi, and an executive board was formed with John M. Silva elected as inaugural president. AAASP was created to promote research and examine professional issues in three areas of applied sport psychology: intervention/performance enhancement, health psychology, and social psychology. The following October an organizational meeting was held in Nags Head, North Carolina, where the functions of the three subcommittees were outlined.

In October 1986 the inaugural meeting of AAASP was held at Jekyll Island, Georgia, where 250 of the associations initial 350 members met for 3 days of lectures and workshops. This successful meeting was followed by annual meetings in Newport Beach, California, in 1987; Nashua, New Hampshire, in 1988; Seattle, Washington, in 1989; and San Antonio, Texas, in 1990.

The composition AAASP's membership was very balanced in terms of the academic preparation of its members, with 45% having been trained in physical education and 43% in psychology. AAASP members receive a glossy biannual newsletter and a reduced subscription rate for the *Journal of Applied Sport Psychology*, which first appeared in March 1989.

In 1986 the American Psychological Association created a new subgroup—Division 47, Sport and Exercise Psychology, as the result of lobbying by William P. Morgan of the University of Wisconsin, who became the first president of this division. The president-elect, also a physical education–trained scholar, is Daniel M. Landers of Arizona State University. Robert Singer was asked to make a keynote address at the APA conference in Atlanta in 1988, probably the first time sport psychology has had such a platform in this mammoth organization. Interest appears to be growing within mainstream psychology in the field of sport; in 1989 the number of apportionment ballots expressing interest in the area was just marginally above the percentage necessary for their first seat on the APA council. Developments within this sphere will be of great interest in the future.

Finally, though the International Society of Sport Psychology (ISSP) is not a North American organization, since 1985 the president (Robert Singer), general secretary (Glyn Roberts), vice president (John Salmela), and NASPSPA representative (Richard Magill) have been North Americans. The world situation in sport psychology has also changed rapidly since 1985 due in part to the efforts of the ISSP in the following domains: the creation of *The Sport Psychologist* in 1977; the revamping of the *International Journal of Sport Psychology* in 1988; the creation of an ISSP newsletter in 1990; the stimulation of national and continental societies around the world; and the organization of the first ISSP conference held in Asia—in Singapore in 1989.

Sport Psychology and Top Sport.   The last several years in the United States have seen an increased interaction between top-level sports and sport psychology. The slow progress in this area may have been partly because so much emphasis has been given to making the area academically respectable. Thus, little energy remained for this area of concern. But in all probability this weakness can be reduced to three factors: the lack of defined career structures in sport, poor communication, and inappropriate professional training.

Amateur sport in the United States is based on elaborate, diverse organizational systems that are not under governmental control as in Canada and Eastern Europe. Thus, for a time no career structure was built into sports from a central sport organization. Now the United States Olympic Committee (USOC) has begun to form a master plan at an executive level that covers all sport and sport science support. American amateur sport has traditionally been left in the hands of individuals with varied interests and orientations, rendering the systematic implementation of sport psychology on a large scale next to impossible. The Coaching Effectiveness Program, a private-sector program that has many parallels with the Canadian coaching certification program, is being set up through U.S. YMCAs to reply to this need at the grassroots level.

The second point, previously dealt with, is the difficulty in adequately preparing sport psychologists for the types of intervention required at this level. Specialists trained in physical education faculties may have situational empathy with sport reality, but they often lack adequate preparation in intervention skills developed within supervised settings. Psychologists trained outside sport are methodologically strong but situationally weak. In addition, the latter may have limited or no knowledge about sport science, including the specific work developed by sport scientists in the field. Cross-disciplinary collaborations in physical education and psychology may provide the necessary internship both populations require.

The number of sport psychologists working with amateur teams at the Olympic level has grown slowly over the last few years. The first assignments were made for the 1976 Olympics by the USOC after consultation with respective federations; however, the Elite Athlete Program of the USOC for the 1984 Games was the first systematic attempt at assigning sport psychologists to teams. Eleven individuals were matched with teams according to interests, needs, and geographical location: Bruce Ogilvie (volleyball), Jerry May (alpine skiing), Dan Landers (archery and shooting), John Adderson (boxing), Andrew Jacobs (cycling), Herbert Fensterheim (fencing), Rainer Martens (nordic skiing), Richard Suinn (women's track and field), Betty Wenz (synchronized swimming), Robert Nideffer (men's track and field), and Mike Mahoney (weight lifting). In addition to their work with specific teams, two of the consultants, Nideffer and Wenz, were contacted by 45 other athletes, indicating the need of such intervention at moments of high psychological tension.

Besides these Olympic participants, individuals such as Dan Smith, Bob Singer, and Ken Ravizza have worked with, respectively, the Chicago White Sox, the Cincinnati Reds, and the California Angels in professional baseball. In 1981 Tom Tutko, who has worked with more than 20 professional and 25 college teams in various capacities, said that the idea of making a living from clinical sport psychology without another form of institutionalized support was farfetched. This is probably still true. Interestingly, Bruce Ogilvie, one of the founders of sport psychology's modern age, has worked 30 years in this area and has never charged a fee for his services.

There have been various forms of sport psychology input at the USOC training center in Colorado Springs, Colorado, but this is not the type of ongoing sport-specific support that has proven effective in Eastern Europe. Recently, however the Sports Medicine and Science Program of the USOC hired Shane Murphy as the first full-time sport psychologist at the Olympic training center. Changes in the programs and the implementation of sport psychology in top sport will still be centered in the universities where most of the sport psychology activity is already in place. This activity will also become more entrenched as an integral part of year-round training and competition as the training of applied sport psychologists improves.

Perspectives for Sport Psychology in the United States

Sport psychology in the United States has enjoyed rapid growth over the last decade within the academic system because increasing numbers of young, energetic individuals have defined the area and created their respective niches. Great advances have been made methodologically and professionally, so the future seems bright.

However, it appears that a saturated job market for postgraduate students will cause a leveling off in the areas of motor learning and control and motor development. In sport psychology, however, student enrollments from the United States and especially from abroad, have increased considerably in recent times. The task facing new graduates will be seeking out or creating alternate areas of professional involvement—perhaps engaging in entrepreneurial efforts in amateur or professional sport, expanding roles within sport businesses and health clubs, or working as counselors and educators in the community.

Because of retrenchment, academic efforts will be held to greater accountability for the needs of society, and this may result in an increased emphasis on action research, field projects, and alternate areas of intervention. Sport psychologists must convince potential consumers that well-trained specialists can help them enhance performance, increase their enjoyment of participation in exercise and sport programs, and realize personal potential.

The various areas of sport psychology will also continue to demarcate their territorial limits with greater precision as the different interest groups become more active. It is hoped that the interactions between the various bodies will be nonconfrontational to allow for productive growth.

Finally, sport psychologists worldwide will have a growing interest in the issue of requiring workers in the field of sport psychology to have professional qualifications. This will be especially critical in terms of the required competencies that must be developed by professionals and academics within the sport sciences and psychology.

References

Martens, R. (1979). From smocks to jocks: A new adventure for sport psychologists. In P. Klavora & J.V. Daniels (Eds.), *Coach, athlete and the sport psychologist* (pp. 156-162). Toronto: University of Toronto.

Nideffer, R.M., DuFresne, P., Nesvig, D., & Selder, D. (1980). The future of applied sport psychology. *Journal of Sport Psychology*, **2**, 170-174.

Wiggins, D.K. (1984). The history of sport psychology in North America. In J.M. Silva and R.S. Weinberg (Eds.), *Psychological foundations of sport* (pp. 9-22). Champaign, IL: Human Kinetics.

Chapter 7

SCANDINAVIA
Denmark

in collaboration with

Jørn Ravnholt Peterson
Danish Sport Federation

Danish Sport Psychology Résumé

Since Denmark hosted the 6th ISSP World Congress in 1985, sport psychology in this country has risen from a nonexistent sphere to one that holds the attention of athletes, coaches, and organizers at all levels. Hence, educational courses in sport psychology for these groups have grown popular and the Danish Sport Federation now offers them. In addition, applied programs have been developed for many of the national sport bodies, and research is just beginning to see daylight.

Estimated Number of Sport Psychologists. 7

Prominent Institution. Danish Sport Federation

Orientation. Sport for all and elite sport

Privileged Topics. Competition and sport for all

Publication Vehicles. *Focus, Idrætsliv*

Society. DIF study group

An observer cannot help but like the Danish people; they are so enthusiastic in their undertakings in sport and life. They reveal a very ultramodern side of their nature that contrasts with the traditional setting steeped in history in which they live. Modern freeways whisk people over the places that still hint of Hamlet or Viking warriors.

This same tug-of-war between the contemporary and the traditional occurs in the general area of sport science, particularly with regard to sport psychology. Denmark has had a long tradition in the area of physiology of exercise at the Royal Danish School of Gymnastics under the guidance of notables such as Asmussen and now Saltin. But there has been little interest at a comparable level in the behavioral sciences. The traditional body-centered sport science approach has not yet shifted toward the social sciences, and it appears that at the institutional level it is in no hurry to do so.

However, in recent years, to paraphrase Shakespeare, there has been a breath of fresh air in Denmark in sport psychology, emanating from the official Danish Sport Federation (DIF), which decided to host the 6th ISSP Congress in 1985, as well as from Team Danmark, the government-funded institution established in 1985. In 1988 DIF and Team Danmark set up a sport psychology study group with the seven most active Danish sport psychologists. This may be the only way of spurring development outside the sport science structures that do not seem to want sport psychology. The Danish Society of Sport Psychology, founded in 1980 by Arno Norske, now has little or no input in the development of sport psychology in Denmark.

Training in Sport Psychology

No specialized training exists in sport psychology in Denmark due in part to the strong emphasis schools of physical education place on the physiological sciences. Thus Danish universities have no chair in sport psychology, no professors in sport psychology, and next to no research in sport psychology. If, however, Denmark does experience a shift toward the behavioral sciences, the pattern, judging from the evolutionary processes that have taken place throughout the rest of Scandinavia, might follow this route.

Denmark is one of the few countries in Western Europe and Scandinavia that maintains the traditional old European university structure. At the head of each department is the professor who holds the chair position. Venerable scholars attain such positions only after long years of research and writing. The study profile for an individual wishing to make it to the top is long and hard. The basic degree is the candidate, which takes 5 to 6 years to complete and is comparable to a master's degree. Next is the licentiate degree, which may take another 3 to 4 years of nonformalized study and is equivalent to a North American Ph.D. The final step is the doctorate, which is another 7 to 10 years of lengthy research and writing. This compares to the doctor of science degree in Eastern Europe or the habilitation in Germany and Austria.

In that there is no sport psychology chair in Denmark, this stream of development is purely theoretical. Because this long, arduous academic system tends to burn people out through both work and old age, it has since been revamped in both Sweden and Norway so that higher education is accessible to more people in a shorter time. Changes have been proposed, but it may be a long time before they are carried out.

Besides Jørn Ravnholt Petersen, who obtained his master's degree in sport psychology from Pennsylvania State University, to date in Denmark only a few individuals working in sport psychology with sport as their focus have studied to the candidate level in psychology departments. However, the few active sport psychologists all have solid backgrounds in sport, an important asset in counseling. No special sport psychology training exists for professional preparation within the field, but the Royal Danish School of Gymnastics offers limited pedagogical psychology to physical education students.

In preparation for the 6th World Sport Psychology Congress of the ISSP held in Copenhagen in 1985, the DIF held a number of lectures and clinics to the top coaches of the Danish Sport Federation. DIF and Team Danmark have hosted similar seminars in other sport sciences on a yearly basis since then, and each time sport psychology has been the most discussed sport science.

Topics of Study.

Because no real program of study in sport psychology exists in Denmark, nor very much evidence of systematic research within university psychology departments, only a few examples of punctual research can be cited.

In the early 1980s Lars Skovland completed his candidate of psychology degree in the psychology department of the University of Copenhagen, specializing in the area of conflict among players within the top Danish soccer teams. In recent years others have followed this same route. Kim Jensen (1989) completed his candidate of psychology looking at the relationship between attention-concentration, performance, and arousal-stress. Aside from scattered research projects that touch on sport done within the psychology departments, little scientific literature in the behavioral sciences has been published in the Danish language. However, members of the DIF/Team Danmark study group have conducted more investigations and plan more in the near future.

Publications

Arno Norske (1980) published the first Danish book on sport psychology that was fundamentally patterned after Vanek and Cratty's book *The Psychology of the Superior Athlete*. DIF (1984) had Willi Railo's book *Best When It Counts* translated from Norwegian into Danish, and more recently Jens Hansen (1986) with *The Art of Coaching*, Freddy Gleisner (1986) with *Mental Training in Sport*, and Jørn Richter (1989) with *Applied Sport Psychology—Status and Future* have updated the Danish literature since the days of Arno Norske. One type of publication that has not been used for sport psychology to such an extent anywhere else is the popular sport press. The news media have shown great interest in the mental aspects of sport, and numerous publications have focused on this "new" dimension in Danish sport. The amount of printed material may seem amazing given sport psychology's lack of institutionalization and the relative paucity of research. Even the proceedings of the Copenhagen ISSP Congress in 1985 were published in Sweden in English, so even this major event left little concrete legacy.

The Role of Sport Psychology in Denmark

Institutions.

In May 1988 the Danish Sport Federation and the government, recognizing a growing need, funded an institution for elite sport called Team Danmark. This brought the country's leading sport psychologists together to form a sport psychology study group. The group was asked to (a) contribute to the development of relevant activities within sport psychology, (b) teach sport psychology through DIF and Team Danmark courses and seminars, (c) consult with athletes and coaches on the psychology of training and competition, (d) take the pulse of the international developmental tendencies in sport psychology, and (e) report on new information learned from various seminars and congresses. Consequently, the study group has begun to develop educational programs in sport psychology for coaches and athletes. Educational programs and counseling to national sport bodies increasingly involve members of the study group, and the results are starting to show promise.

Sport Psychology and Top Sport.

Counseling of both individual athletes and teams at all levels is becoming more common. The study group is available for and is very much involved in counseling the top Danish athletes as a service for Team Danmark.

Finally, members of the study group have now joined the ISSP, FEPSAC, ASP, and AAASP, and six persons participated in the 7th ISSP Congress in Singapore in 1989. All of this ensures that sport psychology will continue to provide a flow of fresh air to Danish sport.

Perspectives for Sport Psychology in Denmark

Probably the single most important factor that can accelerate the advancement of sport psychology in Denmark is the discipline's formal institutionalization within some existing structure. This goal, however, is still not in sight. The buoyant enthusiasm of sport psychology's devotees can carry things a long way, but there are limits to the level that can be achieved without some formal structure. However, the DIF and Team Danmark study group now has an opportunity to work with the other sport sciences. This collaboration may open now-locked doors to institutionalization. For the moment, it appears that the future of sport psychology depends on the energy and interest of a few Danes who appear to be swimming upstream. Structural changes may be essential before fatigue and frustration set in.

Finland

in collaboration with

Juhani Kirjonen
University of Jyväskylä

Finnish Sport Psychology Résumé

Sport psychology may be at a more advanced level in Finland than anywhere else in Scandinavia, at least as far as institutionalized research is concerned. However, structural integration between those doing sport psychology research and those applying sport psychology to top athletes is still lacking.

Estimated Number of Sport Psychologists.   25

Prominent Institution.   University of Jyväskylä

Orientation.   Empirical research and applied work

Privileged Topics.   Top-level sport and sport participation patterns

Publication Vehicles.   *Scandinavian Journal of Sport Science, Stadion*

Society.   Finnish Society of Sport Psychology

Individuals interviewed from the four Nordic countries in the first edition of this book were unanimous in citing Finland as Scandinavia's leader in sport psychology. Once again the ingredients for success are government support and institutionalized positions in sport psychology.

The Finnish government gives a relatively high level of direct support to research in sport psychology on the condition that it have broad social aims and relate to mass participation and "sport for all." At least four full-time positions in the behavioral sport sciences are concentrated at Finland's main physical education center in Jyväskylä, which is amply equipped with laboratories, a library, and a fine resource center. Centered in Helsinki is another group of more applied individuals concentrating their efforts on high-performance sport. The two groups are quite separate not only in direction but in professional background as well. The Helsinki group was originally stimulated to action in the 1960s by Friedrich Blanz, who was primarily interested in top-level sport psychology. Though both groups are active, two factors tend to reduce the impact Finland has had on the international sport psychology scene. The first is Finland's physical isolation; it is linked with only Norway and Sweden to the west at latitudes well beyond the arctic circle and with the Soviet Union to the east. The second is its cultural isolation resulting from the incomprehensibility of the Finnish language to anyone but a Finn.

Training in Sport Psychology

The basic educational pattern followed by university students who will eventually specialize in sport psychology is similar to that in other Scandinavian countries. After studying at the gymnasium, or high school, and after passing the necessary exams, the student can apply for entry into the faculty of sport and health sciences at the University of Jyväskylä, the only institution in Finland where an individual can study in the area of the psychology of physical activity and sport. Admission requirements are very stringent, with an acceptance rate of about 1 in 30.

The program of study takes about 5 years and is comparable to a master's degree. In the Jyväskylä program, a student has the option of specializing in physical education, coaching, public health, or sport administration and does 2 to 3 years of undergraduate course work. Within this curriculum are a number of courses in sport pedagogy and sport psychology. The student then takes about 2 more years of specialized study during which he or she does research and prepares a thesis topic.

Since 1979 a specifically institutionalized professorship in sport psychology has existed at Jyväskylä and was first held by Jorma Tiainen. After Tiainen's tragic death in 1983, Juhani Kirjonen took over this position in Jyväskylä in 1986. Risto Telema holds a second professorship in the educational aspects of sport psychology. Nowhere else in Scandinavia is there such a concentration of institutionalized expertise.

In 1970 it became possible to complete a doctorate at Jyväskylä with a special concentration in sport psychology. Normally the doctorate takes another 4 to 6 years of specialized study. Interestingly, the licentiate degree, or half doctorate, also serves as a decision point at which a student chooses to stop or to continue on for the full term of study. Foreign students can also qualify for study in this program if they have the necessary prerequisite course work.

One factor that appears to limit efficiency in educational pursuits and the quality of experiences in both sport and psychology is the lack of crossover or academic mobility between faculties. Physical education undergraduate and graduate students have little direct study in psychology faculties, and vice versa.

A number of sport institutes also exist in Finland in smaller centers, such as Vierumaki and Pajulahti, where more basic training is given to "sport instructors" who then become part-time coaches in amateur sport. These institutes also provide sport psychology content within these more abbreviated courses of study.

Occasional research projects have been carried out in sport in the psychology departments at the universities of Jyväskylä, Helsinki, and Tempere but not within formalized programs of study.

Though the preceding profile covers those persons interested in sport psychology within a physical education and psychology research context, a significant number of people also work in applied sport psychology, mainly in Helsinki. These individuals have been trained in either psychology or psychiatry departments and have an interest in top sport. The Finnish Society of Sport Psychology, with its members centered mainly in Helsinki, has given a number of clinics and courses in sport psychology to interested coaches over the years, but members do not engage in research.

Topics of Study.   Analysis of the areas of concern in sport psychology in Finland must consider the two distinct reference groups: the Jyväskylä researchers and the Helsinki applied sport psychologists.

The Jyväskylä University group basically depends on funds from the governmental agency, the Finnish Research Council for Sport. The Finnish government has provided substantial support for research projects that have broad social implications in physical education rather than solely in top sport. This results in investigations that benefit the entire Finnish population. The research has dealt extensively with the reasons for participation in sport and physical activity. These studies use large representative samples of the Finnish population. This psychopedagogical approach is a direct result of this tendency in the researchers' training in sport psychology within physical education departments. The Finnish Research Council has handsomely supported this research during both the data collection and the follow-up periods by giving the researchers support to travel abroad to communicate the results.

The Helsinki group appears to have another orientation, with their funding coming from top sport federations. This group is primarily composed of general psychologists and psychiatrists, in a 2 to 1 ratio, who operate with private rather than public funds. Their work can be characterized as clinical with a certain amount of psychometric research on top-level athletes.

Publications

In the 1960s and early 1970s only one journal, *Stadion*, was available for the dissemination of information on sport and physical education. However, it was published only in Finnish, and thus its impact was limited to within Finland itself.

In 1980, the Jyväskylä group initiated a new publication, the *Scandinavian Journal of Sport Science*. The collaboration of a Scandinavian editorial board gives it broad support, so research from this area of the world can now be shared with the rest of the international sport science community. The journal is published in English and appears to be of high quality from both academic and production view-

points. The Finnish Research Council has financially supported the publication of individualized sport psychology research reports to ensure that this information reaches a broader Finnish market.

Book publication is a very expensive affair in Finland because the target population is so small. All sales are limited to within the country's borders. Sport federations have used Railo's *Mental Training* from Norway to some extent, but Blanz's *Psychology of Sport Training* (1973) is the most widely used book written by a native Finn.

The Role of Sport Psychology in Finland

Institutions.   Though there is scattered sport psychology activity in the universities of Turku, Tempere, Kuopio, and Helsinki, the most promising location for the development of sport psychology is at Jyväskylä. The creation of a professorship specifically in the area of sport psychology was an important start. However, the untimely death of Jorma Tiainen in 1983 was a serious setback for all activity in the area. Juhani Kirjonen was hired as his replacement only in 1986 and much consolidation and rebuilding had to be done.

Finnish Society of Sport Psychology.   This group was founded in 1976 under the direction of Friedrich Blanz. It is the focal point for the previously mentioned Helsinki group that centers its attention on psychological support systems for elite sport. Most of these psychologists and psychiatrists carry out their work in association with a specific sport discipline, but usually as a pastime without remuneration. The group is made up of about 100 active members who meet a couple of times a year to discuss their work with top-level athletes. Interested coaches and athletes also take part in the seminars that are usually held in Helsinki. This society became affiliated with FEPSAC, the European sport psychology federation, in the late 1970s.

Sport Psychology and Top Sport.   Though elite sport is the central focus of sport psychology in most Eastern European countries, it is of less interest in Finland, at least as an area of academic research. A few dedicated individuals have occasional sport psychology input into elite sport. Track and field has benefited from ongoing sport psychology consultation since the mid-1970s through the work of Pekka Salmimies, a psychiatrist. Coaches' and athletes' personal problems are dealt with in a clinical setting, and various relaxation and mental training techniques are employed. These interventions take place during both training and competition phases.

The sports of cross-country skiing, shooting, and bowling have also had varying degrees of sport psychology input. The Finnish Society of Sport Psychology has an overall aim to have a sport psychologist associated with each of the sport federations. But at the moment, no specialized course exists for academic preparation in the field of clinical intervention in sport psychology.

Perspectives for Sport Psychology in Finland

The future for sport psychology in Finland is potentially very bright because it has in place many of the necessary components essential for professional and academic growth: the existence of a professorship in sport psychology at the University of Jyväskylä; the initiation of a sport science journal in English that can reach out to an international market; the availability of modern library, laboratory, and research support systems in sport psychology and the other sport sciences; and the presence of financial support for these undertakings from the Finnish Research Council.

It still appears that the situation could improve through the creation of better professional and academic bonds between the two sport psychology groups centered in Jyväskylä and Helsinki. In a country of only 5 million people, there must be a consolidation of efforts to create new lines of communication that would allow the growth of mutual benefits, both theoretical and practical.

Norway

in collaboration with

A. Morgan Olsen
Norges Idrettshogskole

Norwegian Sport Psychology Résumé

Almost all the sport psychology activity in Norway takes place in one center in Oslo. Though it has many institution-aligned benefits not present elsewhere in Scandinavia, Norway still does not have a total program in sport psychology that has reached its full potential.

Estimated Number of Sport Psychologists. 10

Prominent Institution. Norges Idrettshogskole

Orientation. Top-level sport and general topics in sport

Privileged Topic. Psychoregulation

Publication Vehicles. Several books

Society. Norwegian Society for Sports Research

Compared to most other Western countries, Norway has had a head start in sport psychology. Because Norway got into the sport psychology movement at the ground floor via A. Morgan Olsen, an observer might expect to find within the country a broad array of interactive components forming a complete sport psychology package. Though most of the components for such a package are in place, they do not quite function in unity. Norway seems to have a moderate desire for success in top-level sport. Many Norwegians would like their athletes to do well, but not at any cost, as is evidenced in parts of Eastern Europe. So consideration is given to the psychological dimensions of sport, but not on as wide a scale as elsewhere. The load falls mainly on the shoulders of two people.

A. Morgan Olsen holds the first chair and is Scandinavia's first and only full professor in sport psychology. His involvement with the ISSP dates back to the founding meeting in Rome in 1965, at which he was named the group's vice president. The second most well-known person is Willi Railo, who has acquired a reputation throughout Norway and even neighboring Sweden and Denmark as an excellent speaker and a kind of sport psychology evangelist for top-level sport.

These two individuals represent the two most essential steps for the initial growth of sport psychology: institutionalization and broad-based acceptance by sport. Two other psychologists, Olav Nøkling and Odd Kjørmo, have also been actively working at the Norwegian College of Physical Education and Sport since the early 1970s.

Training in Sport Psychology

It is possible in Norway to receive an education comparable to a master's degree program with a form of specialization in sport psychology at the Norwegian College of Physical Education and Sport. Study in sport is independent of the university system but is considered equivalent to it. Because of certain opportunities for academic mobility, it is also conceivable that an individual could concentrate in sport and have a minor in psychology. The Norges Idrettshogskole (Norwegian College of Physical Education) is Norway's main center for sport psychology. Situated in a lovely setting near the Hollmenkollen ski jump, the school has an impressive complex of gymnasiums, library, and laboratories. Typically physical education students study 2 years in all subject areas that form the basis for teaching. If a student desires, he or she can then study 1 more year to acquire advanced training for increased competence and the possibility of a higher salary. This year could be directed to practical work with the handicapped or to a specialized area of sports medicine, physiology, or sport psychology. Following this year, the student devotes 2 to 2-1/2 years to research in an area of the sport sciences. This special training is comparable to a master's degree and enables a person to work as a sport lecturer, sport administrator, or coach or in the military.

To date, 15 to 20 of the approximately 160 graduates of this program have specialized in sport psychology. The existence of four people on staff with interests in the broad area of sport psychology provides potential for growth in the area. A doctoral program is now in operation, and candidates in this program can specialize in sport psychology.

Though about 10 people in Norway possess doctorates in an area of the sport sciences, no one has studied directly in a formal program of sport psychology. Most often their course of study was in educational psychology or pedagogy, and this was later broadened into sport psychology. The course of study for the old European style doctorate in Norway is the arduous 6 to 7 years of nonformalized education that is still prevalent in Denmark but that Sweden abandoned in 1975.

Topics of Study. Initially Norway was best known internationally for the in-depth bibliographical work in sport psychology Olsen carried out in collaboration with Paul Kunath of East Germany. More recently, Railo's clinical observations and work in psychoregulation have received much acclaim across Scandinavia. In association with the master's course, a number of surveys, experimental studies, and bibliographic investigations have covered a lot of sport psychology territory, though little of it has been in-depth.

Publications

No specialized journal exists for sport psychology or for the sport sciences in Norway. It has been suggested, however, that the new *Scandinavian Journal of Sport Science* may fill an essential need for communication in these countries.

Presently workers can publish vulgarized research in the physical education journal of the Norwegian college. Some sport psychology papers from Norway, especially by Olsen, have been published in various international journals.

A. Morgan Olsen is another sport psychology pioneer as evidenced by his 1958 text *Psychology and Sport*, probably the first book published in Scandinavia in the discipline. Railo's 1972 sport psychology textbook *The Psychology of Training and Competition* has been widely used by coaches and teachers as the basic text in sport psychology in Norway. It gives a broad overview of the field with simple language and illustrations but is based mainly on earlier American texts. This book also apparently filled a need in Sweden, where its translation has been widely used. Railo's second book (1982), *Best When It Counts*, summarizes much of his clinical experience and

has been translated into several languages, including English.

In addition, Olav Nøkling published two editions of *Psychology With Respect to Sport* (1980, 1987), and Odd Kjørmo wrote *Children and Youth in Sporting Environments* (1977) from a social psychology perspective.

The Role of Sport Psychology in Norway

Institutions. Norway's hierarchical university system has three levels, each with different degrees of potential involvement in sport psychology. At the top of the hierarchy are the traditional universities, in which research in sport has been only sporadically carried out in the psychology departments. However, no formal courses exist in the area of sport psychology.

The Norwegian College of Physical Education and Sport is at the same functional level as the universities; it is one of the technical colleges along with those for engineering, veterinary science, and other vocational pursuits. Here most of the sport psychology teaching and research is carried out. Some individuals in social psychology who are interested in sport are also at the faculty of psychology in the University of Bergen. Also associated with the Norwegian college are a number of centers for the disabled where researchers do work with special populations.

Finally sport is taught at some regional colleges within the applied disciplines, but where little research is carried out.

Norwegian Society for Sports Research. Although an estimated 20 individuals in Norway are interested and academically prepared to a certain level in sport psychology, no formal sport psychology society exists, and thus there is no separate forum to discuss research in the area. Psychologists can join the Norwegian Society for Sports Research, however. This situation may seem somewhat paradoxical given that Norway has two things many countries with emerging sport psychology structures do not have: acceptance of sport psychology by sport and governmental agencies, and the existence of an institutionalized sport psychology chair and academic program. It has been suggested that certain differences of opinion among the various top-level personalities involved in sport psychology prevent Norway from reaching its optimal level of sophistication. The fact that some Norwegian teachers travel annually to Sweden for the Swedish sport psychology meetings of the Swedish Association for Behavioral Sport Science (SVEBI) indicates a need for some formal sport psychology structure. Norway remains the only country in Scandinavia and Eastern and Western Europe (with the exception of Albania) without a professional sport psychology society.

Perhaps the 1989 election of Marit Sorensen, a physical education professor at the Norwegian College of Physical Education, to the Managing Council of the ISSP will be the catalytic agent to bring together the pieces of this organizational puzzle. A meeting for January 1991 has been tentatively set to create, at last, a national Norwegian society.

Since 1981 multidisciplinary conferences in the sport sciences sponsored by the Norwegian Society for Sports Research have been held at different locations in the country featuring invited speakers from Europe and North America. The 1986 meeting was entitled a "Nordic" conference, thus expanding its scope, and was held in Lillehammer, the site of the 1994 Winter Olympics, on the topic "Sport, Sex, and Gender." Further initiatives of this nature would likely provide a useful mechanism for sharing ideas on sport psychology and related topics.

Sport Psychology and Top Sport. The sport federations of Norway have a good relation with the sport sciences, including sport psychology. At present various applied sport science areas are being used in each federation to give some additional support and guidance. The services of sport psychologists have often been secured for general sport psychology courses for a broad number of sports. On occasion, a few sport psychologists have carried out more specific clinical work in selected sports, but these occurrences have been infrequent. There is ample financial support for both clinical work and research as a result of Norway's central committee for research funding, which organizes and funds research from pool money bet on soccer matches. It is hoped that about

1% of the total budget, of $750,000 to $1.5 million or about 5 to 10 million Norwegian crowns, will be annually directed in this area. Most of this funding goes toward purchasing equipment and hiring technical support personnel.

No official sport psychology support staff regularly accompanies Norwegian teams to international games. Perhaps broadening the base of people working in the applied areas would have a bigger impact on the total Norwegian sport perspective. The universal goal of having one sport psychology individual with each team is far from a reality in Norway.

Perspectives for Sport Psychology in Norway

It is somewhat a mystery why sport psychology is still not operating to its full potential in Norway in that finance, sport psychology programs, and full-time sport psychology appointments are not problems as they are in other countries. Some catalytic agent seems to be missing that can tie this all together into an effective unit. All the components for success appear to be in place.

Sweden

in collaboration with

Erwin Apitzsch
Lund University

Swedish Sport Psychology Résumé

Sport psychology in Sweden has diverged onto two separate paths during its early period of growth. The broader one cuts a swath through the social aspects of sport whereas the narrower one concentrates on high-performance sport. The future for sport psychology in Sweden is promising in that more and more sport psychology programs are springing up in universities across the country.

Estimated Number of Sport Psychologists. 10

Prominent Institutions. Stockholm Institute of Education; Universities of Lund, Örebro, Göteborg, and Umeå

Orientation. Sport participation and top-level sport

Privileged Topics. Social needs in sport and psycho-regulation

Publication Vehicles. *SVEBI Journal, SVEBI Yearbook*

Society. Swedish Association for Behavioral Sport Science (SVEBI)

In Canada advertisements employed to stimulate the general population to participate in physical activity read: "The 30-year-old Canadian is as fit as the 60-year-old Swede." Whether true or not, this statement does underline the important role that sport and physical activity play in Sweden. Not only does this interest in sport manifest itself at the competitive level, but perhaps more importantly it is also present in Swedes' day-to-day life patterns. Projects involving thousands of participants regularly take place on fitness trails, during orienteering meetings, or on cross-country ski networks.

Sweden also enjoys a first-class sport science reputation, especially in the area of the physiology of exercise. The research and publication of P.-O. Åstrand and his co-workers in this field have brought this country of only 9 million people into a privileged position in the world of sport science. Sport psychology has thus had tough competition in earning its place in the sun, because financial support for all the sport sciences comes from one place, the Sport Research Council. At the beginning of the 1970s there was little else but exercise physiology, but over the last decade research has spread into the behavioral sciences. This development has been unique in that the individuals in charge of the development of the field were often trained in sport pedagogy; the research had broad social aims and the work was spread throughout.

The roots of sport psychology in Sweden go back to the pioneering work of Sten Henrysson and Torbjörn Stockfelt, who first brought a psychological perspective to sport science. A number of localities are very active in sport psychology: Lund in the south, Göteborg and Halmstad on the west coast, Örebro and Stockholm in central Sweden, and Umeö up near the polar circle. Specific contributions to top-level competitive sport have also increasingly surfaced in a number of localities.

Training in Sport Psychology

Over the last 10 years a number of formalized courses of study were created in both the existing physical education and the psychological courses. Because the greatest number of sport psychology individuals in Sweden have come from either sport pedagogy or physical education, first this study profile will be traced and then other variations will be mentioned.

After completing gymnasium, the equivalent of North American high school, the student enters the university physical education program. Physical education is now part of the university program, but it previously was not. The university program is based on a point system in which each semester is worth 20 points, or 20 weeks of study, over 4 semesters, or 2 years. Because the physical education degree requires only 80 points, a makeup year at a university, often in pedagogy, is necessary if the student wishes to attempt postgraduate study.

Presently discussion is taking place regarding the addition of a 3rd year to the physical education degree during which the student could specialize in sport psychology or other disciplines.

Over the last 10 years, pedagogical departments have offered university sport psychology courses at the universities of Göteborg and Umeä and the University College of Halmstad. Göteborg offers 6 points in the area of sport and the individual, and 5 points in the psychological analysis of the sporting individual. Graduate-level courses are also given in motor learning and motivation in sport. In the 100-point program at Halmstad, 8 points are given in sport psychology, 6 in the psychology of well-being, and 20 points are awarded for a small thesis. In addition, students can take courses in research methodology, statistics, and computer science. Up until 1985, the University of Umeä offered 40 points in sport psychology, which has since been increased to 100 points in a single course called "Educational Psychology of Sports." It is a popular program that had over 300 applicants in 1988, of which the annual allotment of only 30 students were admitted.

Certain changes have occurred in higher educational training since the educational reform of 1975. Previously, as is still the case in Denmark and to some extent in Norway, three levels of academic promotion existed: the candidate, which is between the North American bachelor's and master's; the licentiate, which was comparable to a Ph.D. and thus open to only a few; and the docent, which was awarded if the candidate's habili-

tation, or extended research series, was of sufficient quality. The programs have now been updated and shortened to provide a greater number of people access to these higher degrees. With the educational reform, the new doctorate is a Ph.D. and falls somewhere between the levels of licentiate and docent.

There are two types of professors in Sweden: extra professors, who have nonpermanent status, and full professors, who are associated with a permanent chair. In the area of the social sciences of sport, the first extra professorship was established in 1983 at the College of Gymnastics and Sport (GIH) in Stockholm by means of a 3-year grant from the Swedish Research Council in behavioral sport research. Since 1986 this extra professorship has been financed by GIH and the Teacher's College in Stockholm, and the title of the award changed to sport pedagogy. The professorship is currently held by Lars-Magnus Engström.

For years sport scientists involved in behavioral research argued that this area had been neglected and required greater support for research. This argument reached the point that in 1987 several members of the Swedish Parliament indicated that this form of sport science research was lacking in the country. Parliament thus enacted the establishment of four new full professorships, the first one in sport pedagogy at the University of Umeä in 1989. This full professorship is Sweden's first in the behavioral sciences, and the third in Scandinavia, after Norway (A. Morgan Olsen) and Finland (Juhani Kirjonen).

Two streams of preparation in sport psychology now occur in Sweden. The first takes place after the physical education degree and the additional makeup year. A student who shows promise will be supported by a professor in a faculty of pedagogy. After perhaps some specialized courses in sport psychology and methodology and 4 to 5 years of research, the student earns a Ph.D. Very often this degree is in the general area of pedagogy.

In the second stream, the psychology student takes specialized courses in sport psychology at the postgraduate level and then does a dissertation in the area of sport. This has occurred in, for instance, Örebro, where the psychology and physical education departments have a close relationship. Where previously there was little academic mobility between sport and psychology departments, it is now possible for students from both faculties to participate in the others' courses. This streamlining again has reduced the time necessary for the cross-disciplinary study that is the heart of preparation in sport psychology. Similarly, the department of applied psychology at the Lund University has now started a 20-point course in sport psychology that will be increased to 40 points in 1990.

It is also possible for sport coaches, in Örebro at least, to study sport psychology in the evenings on a part-time basis or by correspondence; that is, the 20-point course is spread out over a 2-year period and thus progresses at about a quarter of the speed of a normal one.

Future preparation in sport psychology will probably change with regard to both broad-based social research as well as that specific to top performance. Engström, who works in a full-time research capacity at the Stockholm Institute of Education, points out that the field of sport psychology will become even broader, reaching into the areas of sport for the handicapped and across the life span. Greater efforts in cross-disciplinary research will result when the academic mobility between faculties is further increased, thus allowing students to "read," or take courses, in other faculties.

Topics of Study. There is no predominant topic of study in Sweden, but rather a broad range. In the Lund region, a broader sociological perspective on sport is being carried out. Also in Lund, Erwin Apitzsch coordinated an international project on anxiety in sport that was published as a FEPSAC report in 1983.

At the Stockholm Institute of Education, Lars-Magnus Engström has been directing a longitudinal study of the sport behavior and participation patterns of a Swedish sample from the teenage years to the early 20s. In Örebro, Lars-Eric Unestähl is actively involved in research and consultation in the area of self-hypnosis, relaxation, and ideomotor training. The impact of these methods has been great because cassette tapes in various languages are available to guide top athletes in developing these techniques.

Sweden's strong experimental tradition of exercise physiology has probably influenced directions in sport psychology research in this country. In fact, Gunnar Borg's work in perceived exertion at the University of Stockholm has provided a multidisciplinary view of the psychology of exercise that is used around the world. Göran Patriksson in Göteborg has done extensive research into the psychological effects of physical education on children, and Sven Setterlind of Karlstad has done extensive work on the benefits of relaxation programs to elementary schoolchildren. Workers at the Department of Education in the northern city of Umeä have carried out a wide variety of research projects on violence, morality, and doping control (Martin Johansson); evaluation (Ingemar Wedman); mental processes of physically active women (Anita Wester-Wedman); conditions for women in top sport administration (Eva Oloffson); and anxiety in sport (Bo Molander).

Publications

A growing number of varied publications in sport psychology have been generated over the last decade in Sweden through the physical education and sport science journals. Up until 1967 only a dozen articles had been published; since then there have been hundreds. The Swedish Association for Behavioral Sport Science (SVEBI) began publishing its own triannual journal, *Idrottsforskaren* or *The Sport Researcher*, in Lund in 1976. This society also publishes an annual 180- to 200-page yearbook on its activities.

Swedes have published several books on sport psychology, namely, *Idrottspsykologi* (1969) by Stockfelt and an applied sport psychology book by Unestähl on mental training. The translation of Norwegian Willi Railo's *Training and Competition Psychology* (1972) is also popular in Sweden. In 1983 Apitzsch edited an international compilation on anxiety in sport for FEPSAC, and in 1984 Göran Patriksson and Sven Setterlind published a monograph

entitled *To Cope With Stress in School*. Finally, in 1987 Patriksson published *The Children in Sport: Sport Habits, Stress and Drop-outs*.

The *Scandinavian Journal of Sport Science*, edited in Finland since 1981, has provided a useful means of making Swedish research accessible to a broader population of scientists in the Nordic countries and abroad.

The Role of Sport Psychology in Sweden

Institutions. A number of university cities house pockets of sport psychology activity across Sweden. At the University of Lund, sociological research in sport relates to stratification and sport preference. Anders Ostnäs also edits the *SVEBI Journal* from its birthplace in Lund. Erwin Apitzsch, the founding president of SVEBI, works as a psychological counselor and researcher. Sport psychology activity can also be found in Göteborg in the area of attitudes and socialization in sport; and, as mentioned previously, there is activity in Örebro, Halmstad, and Umeä.

Stockholm, of course, has the greatest potential for development in sport psychology because it is the nation's capital and is home to a variety of governmental and educational institutions. At the Stockholm Institute of Education, Engström and two assistants carry out full-time research from a psychopedagogical point of view. And at the University of Stockholm, Gunnar Borg works within the psychology department on topics of motivation and perceived exertion. The pedagogic institution for physical education also has the potential for research, but to date this has not been realized. The University of Örebro hosted a week-long gathering of international sport psychologists in June 1985 prior to the ISSP Congress in Copenhagen. This initiative by Lars-Eric Unestähl provided an interesting forum for free exchange between close to 400 individuals.

Finally, the Swedish Confederation of Sport has decided to fund several sport development centers throughout the country, with bridging the gap between research findings and their application and influencing the type of research undertaken among their goals. This project will be carried out in the 1990s to provide a forum for coaches and researchers to develop elite sport in Sweden.

SVEBI. The Swedish Association for Behavioral Sport Science, the accepted voice for sport psychology in this country, was formed in Lund in 1974 and founded in Örebro in 1975. After an initial period of difficulty, SVEBI is now receiving some funding for annual meetings from the Sport Research Council.

This organization has grown to the point that it now has close to 200 members and attracts up to 130 people to its annual conferences. The group is made up mainly of physical education people trained in sport pedagogy, with a few sociologists and about 10 trained psychologists. About 10 individuals holding Ph.D.s are active in the group.

Members of SVEBI have also been very active in both continental and international sport psychology associations. Erwin Apitzsch has been a member of the Managing

Council of FEPSAC, the European continental federation, since 1979 and its secretary general since 1983. Lars-Eric Uneståhl has been a managing council member of the ISSP for Sweden since 1981 and was the program chair for the 6th ISSP Congress held in Copenhagen in 1985.

Though the future looks bright for this young group, its directive forces must generate even greater energy to increase the authority and credibility of SVEBI's voice within the various government and educational associations in relation to sport practice.

Sport Psychology and Top Sport. The number of individuals working with elite sports people in Sweden remains relatively small. The most prominent is Lars-Eric Uneståhl from Örebro, who has had extensive contact with a number of Swedish athletes, mainly in swimming and track. His main focus is psychoregulation based on the principles of relaxation, activation, self-hypnosis, and ideomotor training. He worked with the Swedish Olympic gold medalist in swimming at the Moscow Games as well as with a number of other national delegations in his world travels. Because his services are widely requested, he has produced and sold an effective set of tapes on the preceding procedures, available in English, German, and Swedish.

More recently Apitzsch has been consulting and doing research with a number of elite soccer teams in the country and with British athletes of international caliber, and Leif Isberg has been working closely with ice hockey.

Perspectives for Sport Psychology in Sweden

Sweden has a vibrant if still not completely integrated mosaic of activity in sport psychology that appears to be on the verge of progressing rapidly into a more coherent program. Perhaps the creation of sport development centers around the country will be the catalytic agent necessary for bringing coaches and scientists together. The existence of SVEBI may be the vehicle that will sensitize the general public to the psychological dimensions of sport and physical activity.

Chapter 8

WESTERN EUROPE
Austria

in collaboration with

Susan S. Etlinger
University of Vienna

Karen Heitzlhofer-Lackner
University of Klagenfurt

Austrian Sport Psychology Résumé

By international measures, a small handful of enthusiasts pioneered Austrian sport psychology in the mid-1970s. But in contrast to many countries just developing in sport psychology, Austria can already boast institutionalization of sport psychology in mainstream psychology as well as research and intervention in applied settings at both the organizational and individual levels.

Estimated Number of Sport Psychologists. 15

Prominent Institutions. University of Vienna, University of Klagenfurt

Orientation. Empirical research for everyday applications

Privileged Topics. Psychophysiological diagnostics, counseling

Publication Vehicle. *Sportsmedizin*

Society. Öesterreiche Arbeitsgemeinschaft für Sport Psychologie (ÖASP)

Early in 1970, H. Rohrcher of the University of Vienna began to voice his conviction that the processes of training and competition in sport are decidedly part of psychology's domain and that Austrian sport suffered from a lack of psychological input. He was the chief proponent of an institutionalized form of cooperation between sport and psychology in Austria. Unfortunately, however, Rohrcher died in 1972, leaving the legacy of his foresight to his successors.

Up until this point, for all practical purposes the realm of counseling and advising of Austrian athletes in high-performance sport was left by default to the field of sports medicine. This group was already strong and active, supported by a long tradition of work and research in the fields of physiology, drug detection, morphology, and growth. In fact, L. Prokop of Vienna, head of the School of Physical Education at the University of Vienna, was one of the vociferous pioneers opposed to athletes' use of performance-enhancing drugs. He had also long been the head of the medical commission of the International Olympic Committee, serving as an expert on doping issues. But these sports medicine perspectives merely grazed the psychological dimensions by including only the psychiatric ones. Though the Austrian psychiatric tradition has produced the likes of Sigmund Freud and his disciple Alfred Adler, the Austrian psychological tradition has always been distant from the field of psychiatry.

The incumbent to the vacated chair for experimental and applied psychology in Vienna was Giselher Guttmann, an adept athlete who had grasped the implications of Rohrcher's initiative. At the same time, Guttmann's young graduate student, Karen Heitzlhofer, who completed a research project on rock climbers, showed the direct link between psychological variables and motor performance. Coincidentally, in 1979 Heitzlhofer received a survey questionnaire from the first edition of this *Sourcebook*, and she realized that many countries had sport psychology societies. She thus became the catalyst for Austria's formal entry, led by Guttmann, to the world sport psychology stage. On September 28, 1979, Rohrcher's dream of creating an Austrian sport psychology society was realized with the establishment of the Öesterreiche Arbeitsgemeinschaft für Sport Psychologie (ÖASP). By formalizing the movement, the founding members also consolidated the disjointed efforts of like-minded but isolated colleagues who were unaware of the existence and work of others. To use Heitzlhofer's words, "Sport psychology began in Austria as a rather diffuse idea." Since the inception of the idea by Rohrcher and its realization by Guttmann and Heitzlhofer, the group of activists, although growing in influence, has remained relatively small.

Training in Sport Psychology

The training profile for someone interested in doing sport psychology research or teaching at the university level is comparable to that of the Federal Republic of Germany. To date no specific training within a specialized sport psychology course exists. Sport psychology in Austria exists more as a private initiative and postgraduate topic, or as the reserve of interested master's and doctoral candidates in physical education or psychology. Students in the Institute for Sport Pedagogy, future certifiable teachers of physical education at the secondary level, also receive tutelage in sport psychology under Professor Guttmann, but this does not yet qualify them for postgraduate study in the field.

After completion of college or preparatory high school (gymnasium), a prospective student of sport psychology would begin to study for a 4- to 6-year period of basic training at the institute of either physical education or psychology at the university, after which he or she could research a topic in sport psychology for the master's degree. Under recently effected jurisprudence, a doctoral candidate can now work as a university assistant under the direct supervision of the departmental professor. After approximately 6 more years of research and publication, the candidate must present a total package of sufficient quality and quantity to successfully qualify for candidacy for a habilitation (*venia docendi*). In Austria, completion of the habilitation gives status equivalent to that of the North American tenured associate professor. This status allows the graduate to be a member of the examiners' commission, supervising graduate degrees for aspiring candidates. Normally, an individual does not receive this habilitation at the same university in which his or her own studies were completed; rather, it is often awarded by another university seeking the individual's services. This convention increases academic mobility in the German-speaking community: in the five Austrian universities, within the university systems of the Federal Republic of Germany, and in the German cantons of Switzerland.

Despite the many developments, sport psychology does not yet hold an assured place in the university system because there is not yet a university chair in the field, and stable courses of study are not yet a reality. Progress is still being carried out at the word-of-mouth level. Interested students know that they will find open doors for these topics at Vienna or Klagenfurt, no matter what.

Topics of Study. At the time the ÖASP was formed in 1979, when sport psychology first became part of a formalized organization, it was found to some surprise that a number of dissertations already 25 years old focused on the personality of athletes (Schimanek in 1954 and Seist in 1953). The earliest applied Austrian dissertation in sport psychology was by Ivath in 1968 on the subject of mental training in sport. These early projects shared empirical rather than theoretical approaches in the areas of sport talent identification, modeling of behavior, overcoming fear, and taking risks, and attribution of success and failure in sport.

The 1970s saw a greater diversification of topics with Baumhackl in 1974 looking at the effects of mental training and age of performers on different practice schedules; the relationship between activation and physiological tension and motivation by Ortner in 1972 and Guettel in 1974, respectively; and the changes in types of motivation by nonathletes, top athletes, and "fitness athletes" by Voigtleiter in 1975. In addition, Paul Weingarten has been doing a variety of projects in applied sport psychology using psychodiagnostics, and Karen Heitzlhofer has been studying in the area of group dynamics.

The formation of ÖASP in 1979 spawned a still greater variety of projects on the physiological indices of exercise performance as well as on hooliganism in soccer. The ergopsychometric method first studied by Heitzlhofer and Lackner in the late 1970s has been used more recently to separate so-called "training champions," whose performances decrease in competition, from top-level performers (Beiglböck, 1983). In 1983 Bischof showed that top performers were most consistent when their successes were due to internal attributions that were unstable, such as willingness to go all out. In 1988 Philipp completed a field study in ice hockey in which he showed that top performers had consistent control over their feelings whereas training champions tended to "boil over" in competition.

The year 1989 was a special one in Austria, when the late American Dorothy Harris, the first recipient of a research Fulbright scholarship in sport psychology, spent her sabbatical in Vienna studying with Susan Etlinger the effects of rhythmic movement on brain waves and well-being.

Publications

As might be expected given the discipline's present stage of infancy, no specialized journal for sport psychology exists in Austria. It is possible, however, to publish sport psychology articles in the Austrian journal *Sportmedizin* that traditionally has been biologically rather than behaviorally oriented, as well as in *Zeitschrift für angewandte Socialpsychologie* and *Psychologie in Öesterreich*. A number of sport psychology dissertations have been published in the German sport science journals *Leistungssport* and *Sportwissenschaft* as well as in the mainstream publications *Zeitschrift für experimentelle und angewandte Psychologie* and the *German Journal of Psychology*. No Austrian-authored books yet exist in sport psychology, but a number of chapters have been published in a variety of books and proceedings, the most notable being Guttmann's "Ergopsychometry: Testing Under Physical or Psychological Load" in the *Encyclopedia of Psychology* (1984). Sport psychology reports can also be found in sport and hobby journals in the popular literature.

The Role of Sport Psychology in Austria

Institutions. Sport psychology is presently housed within the psychology departments of two Austrian universities, in Vienna and Klagenfurt. The fact that it is within psychology rather than sport departments makes this situation unique in Western Europe. However, sport psychology lives by the efforts of individuals and is not yet in the form of an accredited program under the direction of a sport psychology chair.

Guttmann, Etlinger, and Heitzlhofer also have professional ties with the Institute for Sport Pedagogics, which trains physical education students. Within this institute, a form of educational psychology is introduced into students' pedagogical experiences. However, no research activities in sport psychology are yet evident. The first formalized sport psychology input was given by Paul Weingarten and has been presented within this empirical educational context rather than within the university psychology departments.

Finally, Austria has a recently constructed well-equipped *Bundesleistungssportzentrum* (high-performance sport center), developed as a live-in center for elite Austrian athletes (in tennis, cycling, swimming, fencing, handball, track and field, judo, and wrestling). A similar winter sport facility exists in the city of Stamms in the Tyrolean Alps. In this setting coaches and athletes have access to sport psychologist Paul Weingarten, who has a part-time paid appointment at this training establishment.

Öesterreiche Arbeitsgemeinschaft für Sport Psychologie.

In 1979 the paperwork for the Austrian Work Group in Sport Psychology (ÖASP) was completed, thus giving this body registered and recognized status in the area of sport psychology by the Austrian Ministry for Health and Culture. Though sport psychology societies exist in many countries of the world and are often made up of self-proclaimed experts, few have received this level of official status from their governments.

At the first meeting, the society's aims were quite clear: to carry out research in the various fields of sport psychology and to provide sport psychology input for sport teams. The priority, however, is unequivocally with the academic dimensions of sport psychology. The society's membership is open to university-trained people who have accomplished academic work in sport psychology and to sport people who have an interest in psychology.

The first president, elected at the inaugural meeting, was Giselher Guttmann, who has carried out this role up to the present. The 15 full members and four supporting members meet annually and have been active at various scientific events in Europe, such as FEPSAC, and in North America.

Sport Psychology and Top Sport.

In a country as compact as Austria, a centralized sport school for top-level performance makes sense. Such an institute for high-performance sport exists in Vienna specifically for the summer sports. Another institute in Stamms concentrates on winter sports. An agreeable home environment has been created at these centers to attract potential sport talents. Athletes can live in the center, study, recreate, and train in the most modern sport facilities. It is often somewhat difficult, however, to attract top talents to this setting, because many parents with traditional family-oriented values wish to keep their children in the home environment.

During the past decade, the work at these centers has changed from that of carrying out empirical research to the use of counseling, group dynamics, organizational psychology, and performance enhancement. Karen Heitzlhofer has been very active in this function. As a measure of the Austrians' faith in the developing field of sport psychology, Weingarten accompanied and consulted with the Los Angeles Olympic delegation in judo, fencing, canoeing, archery, and shooting and helped the group from this traditionally Winter Games country achieve an unprecedented Summer Games realization: a gold and a silver medal.

Perspectives for Sport Psychology in Austria

The groundwork for a multilevel approach to make inroads into a number of dimensions has been set in Austria. The quantity of work accomplished is modest, but the quality is high. The broadening of the sport psychology bases within the established structures of sport and education remains to be achieved. The main restriction, as is often the case, is a financial one. But it has become obvious to more and more people that sport performance is mentally determined, and there has been an increasing call for services in this direction. As more and more aspiring sport psychologists complete their work at the universities, these intervention roles are becoming more common.

Belgium

Belgian Sport Psychology Résumé

Sport psychology in Belgium has had a moderate degree of success, especially in the aspect of interdisciplinary concerns of broad-based problems arising from the real sport environment, as well as in certain initiatives in private enterprise.

Estimated Number of Sport Psychologists. 15

Prominent Institutions. Institute voor Lichamelijke Opleiding of the Catholic University of Leuven; Free University of Brussels

Orientation. Interdisciplinary research

Privileged Topic. Sport games learning

Publication Vehicle. *Hermes*

Society. Belgian Society of Sport Psychology

In any country, an observer has to understand the underlying values of its people before attempting to unravel the complexities of its sports system. Belgium is particularly interesting because it has two founding peoples, the Dutch-speaking Flemish and the French-speaking Walloons. If you listen to a Walloon characterizing the Flemish, you will hear words such as predictable, unemotional, but organized. If you hear a conversation from the opposite perspective, the Walloons are said to be less organized, emotional, but creative. Each group has qualities that the other both admires and dislikes.

These different values even translate into the programs within Belgium's separate sport institutes for the Flemish and the Waloons. Belgium, as a country intimately involved in the world mosaic of the sport sciences, is more complex than most, not only because of its bicultural and bilingual makeup but also because it is the center of an intriguing interplay of international sport science and sports medicine forces.

A disciplinary-centered sport science dimension washes across the bicultural-bilingual aspects of the country with the resulting effect of an interaction of languages and cultures, hard science and soft science, disciplinary implosion and cross-disciplinary explosion, and a wide variety of strong personalities in both sport science and sport psychology.

It has been observed in Belgium, and often elsewhere as well, that in sport science, the biological sciences, led by medical science, take an upper hand over the behavioral sciences. The result is that hard-data people who measure fiber types, heartbeats, or nostril widths assume roles of dominance over soft-data people who measure tactics, feelings, or motivational levels. For this reason, even though sport psychology in Belgium is vibrant by Western European standards, its international existence is only now beginning to be felt outside its own borders.

Training in Sport Psychology

No specialized postgraduate program exists in the discipline of sport psychology under that specific name. However, a content analysis of the graduating theses from the Catholic University of Leuven, the most active Belgian institution in the behavioral sport sciences, reveals that much of the work falls into what can be considered mainstream sport psychology. Even if the programs do not bear discipline-specific names such as sport psychology, we can still consider that sport psychology training occurs in Belgium.

Within the physical education institutes, students follow an integrated program of study that covers the wide range of sport sciences as well as sport-specific concentration. This approach is somewhat unique in that a student selects an area of sport activity, and it becomes the focus of study—for example, swimming, gymnastics, team sports, or track and field. This content area is then studied with a variety of sport science techniques. Certain sport activities, such as swimming, lend themselves more readily to analysis by physiological or biomechanical techniques, whereas the area of team sports has been approached with tools from sport psychology.

A student in these institutes selects a work group based on his or her special interests and then seeks the disciplinary expertise from the most appropriate sport sciences. Sport psychology content is introduced by means of appointed individuals from the university psychology department who are assigned to the physical education institute. Rigid limits on academic mobility keep sport students within their own department rather than allowing them to take courses directly from the psychology department. The appointed psychologist may not have an extensive background in sport and usually has no specific sport psychology training. The result is an overall lower level of sport psychology sophistication from a disciplinary point of view. However, this is compensated to some extent by the students' intimate involvement with the content area and its potential problem areas.

The resulting sport psychology structure appears to be a question of either strong methodology in psychology but low levels of sport sensitivity, or vice versa. Perhaps disciplinary protectionism within the institutes is the villain in this situation.

Each student's program of study terminates with a specific study that is comparable to a master's thesis. Students can also study up until the doctoral level, resulting in a Ph.D., at these same institutes. At this level, all study is directed toward the research for the thesis, and the candidate takes no specific course work. Compared to North American standards, the students do not receive as much specialized course work from the parent discipline of psychology or from the technical-specific support areas such as computer science, electronics, and statistics. This tends to weaken the overall end product.

Topics of Study. Analysis of each Belgian entry of the "Who's Who in Sport Psychology" usually reveals one or two psychological descriptors that are connected with a particular sport activity. This in itself is the main distinguishing feature of sport psychology in Belgium—the intimate relationship it holds with sport practice. The majority of the work done at Leuven is directed toward learning and the optimization of learning in sport situations. Behavioral analyses of sport are coupled with laboratory evaluation of such phenomena as cognitive strategies, decision making, and anticipation. There is also a sprinkling of projects in the areas of personality, body image, superstition, causal attributions, stress, and motivation that are within the mainstream of sport psychology research.

At the Free University of Brussels a concerted effort in the area of psychomotricity and in adapted physical education has also gained some international recognition.

Publications

There are no specialized sport psychology periodicals published in Belgium at the moment, although the review *Sciences et Motricité* had a promising but brief life in the motor skills area. Some sport psychology topics are published in the periodical *Hermes* out of Leuven and others in the Brussels publication *Sport*.

Perhaps the most prolific authors are Jan-Maria Pauwels and Stephen Swinnen from Leuven, who have published a number of books in the area of the psychology of sport learning and performance. Pauwels's books have been directed to learning in handball and other sport games, and Swinnen's articles on cognitive style have been published in North America. Czeslaw Wielki from the French University of Louvain, as compared to the Flemish Leuven, has received much acclaim for his publications in more than a dozen different countries relating sport psychology and volleyball. Luc Lefebvre has also published widely on some unique topics in both psychology and sport psychology, most recently related to enhancing business performance through sport and exercise.

The Role of Sport Psychology in Belgium

Institutions. The institutions that deal with sport psychology, or in some cases with "psychological kinanthropology" and the like, are situated mainly in the cities of Brussels, Leuven (Louvain), Leiges, and Ghent. Judging by the number of publications in international sport science journals, it seems that the Flemish universities in Brussels and Leuven lead the field. The Brussels center is known worldwide, especially in the area of physical anthropology and biochemistry of exercise. The Leuven institute is especially strong in its broadly concerned brand of sport psychology and also in sports medicine.

The French institutions in Belgium have taken on a less structured approach to sport from a sport science point of view, instead putting sport into a more philosophical or phenomenological-pedagogical perspective that is interesting to read but difficult to quantify or replicate.

Belgian Society of Sport Psychology. There appears to be some confusion regarding the status and perhaps even the existence of the Belgian Sport Psychology Society. Of the six questionnaires analyzed in 1981, three respondents stated that they were members, even executive members, of this society, whereas three stated that no society existed. It seems that the Belgian society, until 1987 led by Luc Lefebvre, was indeed made up of 12 to 15 individuals who did not include any of the members from the Leuven or Brussels institutions. It was, however, recognized as the Belgian representative to FEPSAC. Judging by the annual reports, it appears that this renegade society's main focus is private enterprise in sport psychology; it has given 20-odd 3-day seminars to large corporate sponsors. Little of its research has surfaced in mainstream sport psychology publications.

More academic is the francophone Association for Research in the Psychology of Sport (ARPS), which in a large part has been guided by Belgians. This group meets annually in Europe to present and discuss research, and its 1987 meeting in Brussels attracted more than 200 participants. It is still unclear what the future holds for these two forces.

Sport Psychology and Top Sport. To date there has been little known applied sport psychology work with top-level individuals in Belgian sport and little official contact on a broad-based level between the sport federations and those with sport psychology expertise. This may be because sport psychology is buried deep within the dominant area of kinanthropometry. One striking exception, however, is a close collaboration between sport and sport science in the area of swimming at Leuven, where a multidisciplinary research team is doing in-depth diagnostic research on top swimmers from Belgium, France, and Germany.

Perspectives for Sport Psychology in Belgium

It is difficult to predict in which direction things will develop in Belgian sport psychology for certain historical reasons. From the earliest times, the two founding cultures had very different ways of looking at the world. It appears now that research in the French- and Flemish-speaking institutions is beginning to find a common ground and that a unique Belgian hybrid may result.

The second factor that makes clear predictions difficult is sport psychology's dominance by the field of kinanthropology. Other countries have shown that disciplinary progress can be made within a broad sport science framework only when subdisciplines such as biomechanics or sport psychology have functional autonomy from parent sport science organizations.

The final unknown factor relates to the hermetic sealing off of psychology departments from the physical education institutes. Opportunities for more academic mobility must be increased so that students in sport and sport psychology can have direct access to psychological course work and the expertise of the psychology department. Likewise, psychology students could profit from the situational peculiarities of sport by having access to courses in sport science.

France

in collaboration with

Hubert Ripoll
Institut National du Sport et de l'Education Physique, Paris

Edgar Thill
Université de Clermont-Ferrand

French Sport Psychology Résumé

Sport psychology in France is in a phase of building its institutionalized base within the university system. Recent changes in the structure of the field of physical education have permitted sport psychology to develop as an academic discipline.

Estimated Number of Sport Psychologists. 63

Prominent Institutions. Institut National du Sport et de l'Education Physique (INSEP), Université de Clermont-Ferrand, Teaching and Research Unit in Physical Activity and Sport (UFRAPS) in Marseilles and Montpelier

Orientation. Differential and cognitive psychology

Privileged Topics. Evaluation, imagery, neuropsychology, clinical psychology

Publications. *Science et Motricité, Sciences et Technologie des Activités Physiques et Sportives* (STAPS), *Education Physique et Sport, Education Physique et Plein Air*

Society. La Société Française de Psychologie du Sport

One of sport psychology's earliest organized events was initiated by Frenchman Baron Pierre de Coubertin, the father of the modern Olympic Games. In 1913, de Coubertin organized in Lausanne an international congress of psychology and physiology directed toward sport. His intention was to introduce psychological analysis into sport to counterbalance the *"animalism"* of physiological and technical approaches. Between this earliest of initiatives and modern-day practice, a great number of radical changes have occurred in the educational system that have influenced the development of physical education and sport psychology to make it unique.

But then most things that are French are like nothing else in the world: the quality of French food and drink, the creative mastery of French design and engineering. France's most pronounced characteristic, however, is its richness of both written and spoken communication. French expression tends to be more circular compared to either German or North American forms, which tend to be more linear. Conversation and writing in French tend to explore all the subtleties of both the subject matter and the communication medium to produce convoluted but extremely rich relational portraits. In contrast, Anglo-Saxon communication tends to get right to the point and is often stripped of all but the essential elements.

In the formative years of sport psychology during the 1960s and 1970s, French sport psychology was also characterized by this relational nature because of its close ties with philosophy and humanism. This philosophical orientation was important in that workers in the discipline could consider the interaction of sport, society, and the universe from a broad perspective.

During the 1980s France underwent a rapid evolution in the field of physical education that had an enormous impact on the development of sport psychology. Though the field is still adjusting to these structural changes, it is now beginning to prosper in its own unique way.

Training in Sport Psychology

Before 1981 a mechanism that specifically prepared individuals in the area of sport psychology did not exist in France. This was simply because there was no specific postgraduate preparation beyond what was equivalent to undergraduate training in the Science and Techniques of Physical and Sport Activities (STAPS).

In 1981 the ministerial structures that regulated sport and physical activity became reorganized. The state secretary for youth and sport had authority over all that was related to the preparation of coaches and instructors of sport and leisure activities, whereas the ministry for national education was in charge of the academic preparation of physical education teachers at the undergraduate and postgraduate levels.

Coaches and instructors enter the 20-odd regional centers for physical education and sports (CREPS) once they have finished their secondary education at a *lycée* and have received the baccalaureate. These centers provide trained coaches for the various sport federations during the 2-year period of study. This program includes a modest amount of input from the area of sport psychology. Two regional centers, in Aix-en-Provence and Bordeaux, have sport psychology laboratories.

At the national level, the National Institute of Sport and Physical Education (INSEP) in Paris has a sport psychology unit where four sport psychology specialists work on the questions of sport talent development and identification. In addition, students there also receive an introduction to sport psychology from these specialists. Coaches in France do not receive university postgraduate training. Physical education teachers, however, are prepared in the teaching and research units for physical activity and sport (UFRAPS) at 19 major centers in France after completing their secondary education. The students at these institutes take the first 2-year preparatory cycle and receive their diplomas for general university study

(DEUG) in a program that includes basic sciences, including general, developmental, and social psychology. The students can then either take the second cycle for the license to become a certified professor of physical education and sport (CAPEPS) or enter a 2-year master's program.

Those who select to study for the license receive course work in various nationally determined areas such as psychophysiology or sociopedagogy. At the end of the program of study, the 2,000 graduating students take a national examination, and the top scorers are selected to fill 250 to 300 professorial posts.

Those who decide to take the second cycle master's program study for 2 years and complete a project that can be in sport psychology, depending on the competencies of the professor at the UFRAPS. Only 50 professors are spread across the 20 units, and each center does not always have a specialist in sport psychology.

Since 1985 students have been able to continue for the third cycle, or the doctorate, in the area of science and techniques of physical activity and sport (STAPS). This study includes 1 year of qualification for the diploma for advanced studies, equivalent to a master's degree (DEA) and 3 more years of research on a specialized subject area. The completion of these studies is equivalent to a Ph.D. and allows the individual to work at a university as a conference master, which is a lecturing position. To achieve the status of professor, an individual must demonstrate specific research capacities. This then allows the person to direct doctoral dissertations. An individual can also do research in the area of sport while working within a postgraduate university program in psychology, though this is rarer.

One final force in the universities has contributed to sport psychology, and that has been within the psychophysiological research area. At a number of institutions in France, experimental research is being done in many of the areas that make up the field of human performance, motor skill acquisition, and perception. The most notable research is at the National Center for Scientific Research (CNRS) in Marseilles, where Jacques Paillard and his associates have been doing neuropsychological and motor control research for years, sometimes in the field of sport.

Topics of Study. Workers in France have given special concern to a wide number of areas with a certain amount of international acclaim. The most prestigious work group is situated in Marseilles under the direction of Jacques Paillard at the CNRS Institute of Neurophysiology and Psychophysiology. For more than 30 years this institute has done research in motor processes as well as a number of projects in perception and decision making in sport.

Hubert Ripoll at the INSEP in Paris has followed a similar orientation, consistently researching a number of areas of expert perception in skills, such as table tennis, using complex eye movement recorders. The same institute has been keeping a strong focus on sport talent identification and evaluation for a number of years using various psychometric procedures. Also of note at INSEP, in 1987 Guy Missoum developed a projective test specifically for sport situations that may have been inspired by early work in the same area by Michel Bouet in the 1960s.

In Clermont-Ferrand, Edgar Thill, perhaps France's foremost sport psychologist, has been constructing, validating, and applying a sport-specific personality inventory, *Questionnaire de Personnalité pour Sportifs*, which was designed to evaluate specific traits and motivation of athletes. This test has been translated into English, Bulgarian, Russian, Portuguese, Spanish, and Japanese. In addition, Thill's approach includes giving athletes a variety of personality, imagery, projective, and perceptual motor tests.

Publications

No specialized journal yet exists solely for sport psychology in France, though the volume of material in the French language is beginning to warrant one. Two relatively new sport science journals publish sport psychology research. *Sciences et Technologie des Activités Physiques et Sportives* (STAPS) is edited in Grenoble by Pierre Chifflet, and *Science et Motricité* is edited at INSEP in Paris for the Association of Researchers in Physical Activity and Sport (ACAPS). Also, a more established INSEP journal, *Education Physique et Sport*, often includes some interesting articles of an applied nature dealing with psychopedagogy and sport.

During the early years in sport psychology, the best known books were by Michel Bouet of Rennes, who wrote sociological treatises such as *Les Motivations des Sportifs* (1969) and *Signification du Sport* (1968). Also during that period, the late Georges Rioux, who was perhaps the most renowned authority on de Coubertin, compiled an impressive list of accomplishments from his original work in psychology at the University of Tours. Besides directing a number of young leaders who are now researching and publishing in sport psychology, such as Raymond Thomas and Edgar Thill, he also published, with colleague Raymond Chappuis, two French philosophical classics: *Les Bases Psycho-pédagogiques de l'Education Corporelle* (1968) and *Eléments de Psychopédagogie Sportive* (1972). The book gives a cross-sectional view of this new area in France and reflects both extremes from philosophy to the hard sciences. A similar overview of research projects carried out in France was published in Alain Von Hoff and Robert Simonnet's *Recherches en Psychologie du Sport* (1987).

With the increase of academic rigor and postgraduate study at the UFRAPS in France has also come a large improvement in the quality of recent scientific publications. For example, Hubert Ripoll and Guy Azemar from INSEP edited in 1988 an impressive volume entitled *Neurosciences du Sport*, which brings together the expert knowledge from INSEP in Paris and Paillard's CNRS group in Marseilles to center on the themes of information processing and decision making in sport. In 1991 Ripoll was also the editor of a special double monothematic edition of the *International Journal of Sport Psychology* on information processing and decision making in sport. Also of note, and related to Ripoll's and Azemar's book, are Jean-Pierre Famose's *Apprentissage Moteur et Difficulté de la Tache* (1990) and Bernard Jeu's *Analyse du Sport* (1987), both of which do a task analysis of sport. Finally, Luis Fernandez has written an applied book for sport performance enhancement, *Savoir Gagner: La Réussite en Compétition* (1988), and Guy Missoum and Jean-Marcel Habouz used the neuro-linguistic programming techniques for the same goal in *Piloter Sa Vie en Champion* (1990).

The Role of Sport Psychology in France

Institutions. Three institutions have made real contributions to sport psychology in France: INSEP, the university-associated UFRAPS, and the CNRS center in Marseilles. INSEP is an impressive sport complex in the Bois de Vincennes near Paris that was created for the training of top athletes and the education of coaches and teachers. This center is under the jurisdiction of the state secretary for education, youth, and sports. It now has a team of four sport psychologists and medical doctors who have established a protocol for the detection, evaluation, and training of athletes. INSEP has provided leadership in conducting research and publishing, and it is now governed by the ministry of education, but it provides no possibility for postgraduate study. However, some sport psychology course work is given to coaches and teachers within this framework, and educators and instructors can come to the institute for a year of upgrading.

The UFRAPS, or institutions for the preparation of physical education teachers, are situated in 19 major centers in France and currently offer courses in sport psychology and related areas. Because of the recent creation of second- and third-cycle graduate programs, sport psychology should begin to grow over the next few years as more and more professors are hired to do research and teach in the area.

The CNRS is a world-famous institution whose center in Marseilles has been studying motor and visual coordination for four decades under the direction of Jacques Paillard. Many of Paillard's students have also been interested in sport, so a substantial body of literature on vision and decision-making processes has come out of this independent laboratory.

La Société Française de Psychologie du Sport (SFPS). The SFPS was founded in 1973 and reorganized in 1988, replacing an earlier sport psychology society that was established and then floundered. This group numbers 63, with 13 of the members working in the Paris area. It has organized on a regular basis either study days or colloquiums at various centers in France on themes ranging from the philosophical (sport and the progress of man, Olympism and sport consciousness) to

the more concrete (team cohesion, sport journalism). The largest and most successful congress was held in 1990 in Montpelier with close to 300 participants. Delegations from France have been active at every international sport psychology event both abroad and at home. In 1969 the European sport psychology umbrella group, the Fédération Européene de la Psychologie des Sports et de l'Activité Corporelle (FEPSAC), was founded on French soil in Vittel. The French delegate to this group is presently Edgar Thill.

Sport Psychology and Top Sport. As is the case in many Western European countries, France has offered only limited sport psychology support to top athletes, mainly at INSEP where coaches and athletes have access to the human resources at this institution. More recently, the team of psychologists at INSEP has begun to take a more behavioral approach to benefit coaches and athletes at various training camps and clinics. Luis Fernandez has recently been involved in providing performance-enhancement support to top-level athletes using sophrology techniques that combine visualization with relaxation, while Guy Missoum has done practical work with neuro-linguistic programming.

Sport for so long has been monopolized by technicians and medical personnel that athletes and coaches have had some resistance to the adoption of applied programs by practitioners or by governmental agencies.

One clear exception to this has been the work of Bouvet and Digo, who since 1950 have worked in association with the French Skiing Federation. They have continuously monitored the development of top-level skiers, keeping medical, personality, and behavioral records and providing various forms of clinical support during both training and competition.

Perspectives for Sport Psychology in France

The diversity and individuality that makes the French culture so distinctive is also reflected in the sport psychology of this nation. From the point of view of philosophical expression, nowhere else has sport and its relation to the mind been discussed from such diverse viewpoints in so rich a terminology.

However, for a number of years this very diversity has limited the development of a coherent voice in sport psychology from either the research or the applied point of view. Great changes have been made in the French educational structures in the 1980s, allowing sport science, and in many instances sport psychology, to be taught within university structures. Though still only a limited number of trained specialists in sport psychology can teach and direct research in the area, the structural potential is now in place, and observers can anticipate much growth in this field.

Germany

in collaboration with

Jürgen Nitsch
Psychologisches Institut Köln

Hans Schellenberger (for the former GDR)
Deutsche Hochschule für Körperkultur (DHfK)

Editor's note: The dramatic changes sweeping Europe are best symbolized in the reunification of Germany. This reunification has shaped and reshaped every aspect of German life, and the study of sport psychology is no exception. Indeed, in the transformation of German sport psychology, the only surety is change. So rather than reporting information that is half-known and quickly obsoleted, we will instead report the prevalent conditions of sport psychology in Germany's western and eastern regions just prior to the momentous events of October 3, 1990.

Sport Psychology Résumé of Western Germany

Sport psychology in the FRG is still without a doubt more advanced than anywhere else in Western Europe from the point of view of active individuals, levels of institutionalization, and publications. Academic initiatives have integrated sport psychology not only into the practice of sport but also into mainstream programs in psychology.

Estimated Number of Sport Psychologists.   163

Prominent Institutions.   Deutsche Sporthochschule, Cologne; Universities of Berlin, Bochum, Frankfurt, Heidelberg, Kiel, Saarbrücken, Tübingen, and München

Orientation.   Empirical and applied research

Privileged Topics.   Broad range of topics related to sport and school, health, rehabilitation, and high performance; in particular, action regulation and psycho-regulation

Publication Vehicles.   *Sportpsychologie, Leistungssport, Sportunterricht, Sportwissenschaft;* the book series *Betrifft*

Society.   Arbeitsgemeinschaft für Sportpsychologie (ASP) in der Bundesrepublik Deutschland

Germany was the birthplace of modern experimental psychology and perhaps even sport psychology. Experimental psychology can trace its roots back to Wilhelm Wundt's first laboratory for psychology in 1879 in Leipzig. In 1977 Karl Feige of Kiel cited dissertations by Schultze and Benary dated 1897 and 1913 that respectively dealt with human movement and the ''psychological theory of sports.'' The first sport psychology laboratories were created in Berlin during the 1920s within the Deutsche Hochschule für Leibesübungen. The first institute for sport psychology chaired by a professor was founded in 1965 at the Deutsche Sporthochschule Köln.

In the late 1950s a few articles began to appear in sport psychology, and thus began a period during the 1960s of slow but steady growth that could not be attributed to any one central figure, as in most other countries, because it was more widespread and spontaneous. A single event, however, caused the accelerated growth of sport psychology in the FRG—the Munich Olympic Games in 1972. Sport psychology was caught up within the heady creative spirit of the German people who were eager to show the world how they had successfully rebuilt their nation. A number of recent graduates from sport science and psychological institutes grouped together in 1969 and formed the Arbeitsgemeinschaft für Sportpsychologie (ASP).

In 1970 a governmental sport science agency, the Bundesinstitut für Sportwissenschaft (BISp), was created to interface sport federations with sport science. Sport psychology was a special section of the agency's department of ''applied science.'' The early 1970s saw the creation of more than 30 sport science institutes across Germany. The 1980s have been the period of the most rapid growth in sport psychology, as measured by the number of meetings and publications, within the context of *Sportwissenschaft*, or sport science.

The nature of *Sportwissenschaft* in the western half of Germany is unique, and an observer must understand it to appreciate the special brand of sport psychology that exists in this country. Sport science is an interdisciplinary field that investigates the phenomena of sport with the methods of the natural sciences and the humanities. ''Since sport science is also a behavioral science, it originates in and reflects sport practice,'' stated Grupe in 1980 when interviewed for the first edition of this book. The sport science leaders in the FRG believed that methods arising from the sport sciences would be different from those that come from the parent disciplines. The solutions coming from sport practice will ultimately be derived from newly created methods that have roots with the parent disciplines but are sensitive to the specific and special nature of the sport environment. This accent on multidisciplinary investigations initiated by the needs of sport is a specific characteristic of the FRG's traditional sport science approach. Of particular interest is how the German sport and sport science systems will be modified with the reunification of East and West Germany.

Training in Sport Psychology in Western Germany

Sport plays an important part in the total school program in the western half of Germany, beginning in elementary school and continuing right up through the university level. The older term *Leibesübungen*, or physical education, has been changed to *Sportunterricht*, or sport instruction, with the broadest interpretation given to the word sport. One unique feature that has been observed within some states is the opportunity to choose sport as a field of concentration while in gymnasium, or high school. Within this option are lectures on the theory of sport, including a special sport psychology section. The final gymnasium exams leading to the *Abitur*, or diploma, also include written exams in sport theory.

During the educational reform of the late 1960s and early 1970s, the Deutsche Sporthochschule Köln was accorded the rank of a university. This was and still is the premier institute in both sport science and sport psychology in the western half of Germany, and most probably in Europe. At the same time, institutes for physical education were upgraded to institutes for sport science or an equivalent name, and full professorships were created in sport science and in sport psychology.

Within this newly created structure, students could study in the broad area of the sport sciences and receive a number of courses in motor learning, sport pedagogy, and sport psychology. Though these courses provide a good overview for students who will go on to teach physical education, they provide insufficient depth of knowledge for those wishing to do postgraduate study.

Those students who wish to continue their education with a specialization in sport psychology are normally hired in some capacity as assistants at an institute. At this time they teach some undergraduate courses and prepare their dissertation research. These candidates receive no other formally taught information in sport psychology as occurs in North America at both the master's and the doctoral levels. This system does have some inherent weaknesses, although the candidate maintains close contact with the professor in tutorials and research projects.

In the 1970s, when many professorships in sport psychology were first created, the professors directing the research often had been trained only in physical education or sport science and not specifically in psychology. They were sensitive to the problem areas in sport, but their expertise was less developed from a psychological point of view.

Curricula began to change in the mid-1980s, however, when ASP, the professional society for sport psychology in the FRG, set a common program of study in association with the Association of General Psychologists (BDP) in the area of sport psychology. This allowed psychologists to receive advanced training in sport psychology, including the areas of psychological aspects of school sport, performance sport, health sport, and rehabilitation sport as well as in sports medicine and sport practice.

The university faculties or institutes are more rigidly compartmentalized so there is little mobility between academic disciplines. Students in sport psychology in a sport science institute cannot take courses to fit their specific needs from a psychological institute in the "cafeteria" style prevalent in North America. But as a result 20% of active sport psychologists in the ASP have double qualifications in psychology and sport science. Thus, a student must enroll for another 3 to 5 years in the psychological institute once he or she terminates the sport studies. However, a section on sport psychology does not yet exist in the final examination in psychology, though students studying in applied psychology have made a number of personal initiatives to do their final exams in this area.

The tutorial professor-student consultation may be good for individualized direction, but it can suffer from a lack of consistency across the country. There is no specific curriculum in sport psychology common to all sport science institutes. Various curricula have been established since 1966 in sport psychology for the training and the advanced training of the more than 6,000 coaches who are studying at the Coaches School.

Once the candidate completes and defends the dissertation, the doctoral degree is awarded as the "promotion." After this step, the individual often remains as an assistant at the same institute until he or she completes an additional qualifying step of habilitation, which usually results in a published book or collection of works that is judged by peers. This step may be roughly equivalent to that of receiving tenure in North America. An individual arriving at this level annexes the title "professor" to that of "doctor" on all forms of communication. Once habilitation is completed, the candidate waits until a professorship at another institute becomes available.

A large number of available positions were quickly filled by a group of relatively young sport scientists in the 1970s, so the career outlook for new candidates with doctoral degrees is relatively bleak. New professorships, however, are created from time to time in specialties such as sport pedagogy and sport psychology as well as in the sport sciences, and are available to graduates often within the institution they attended as students.

Topics of Study.   A glance at the key words from the Who's Who section respondents from the western half of Germany indicates that many of the subject areas are essentially based on mainstream preoccupations within the reality of sport practice. Many of the descriptors relate to topics that fall within the scope of physical education, as well as to a number of psychology fields of discipline-based research that is intent on theory testing.

The underlying philosophy that has evolved within the German concept of sport sciences is that the ultimate solutions to sport-related problems will emerge essentially from sport with the support of the disciplined-based parent sciences such as psychology. In recent years, the variety of research themes has expanded to the point that they are more or less comparable to those seen in North America.

Differences do exist, however. One peculiarity of German research as viewed from a North American perspective is its holistic nature. Germany adopts a phenomenological overview that is relational in nature whereas a more analytical-reductionist optic holds a privileged position in Canada and the United States. This translates methodologically in the former case to circular, statistical approaches based on correlational type analyses and the systems approach that lend themselves to a wider philosophical interpretation. In the latter case, the narrower analytical approach is best adapted to hypothesis testing that is conceptually more linear than circular and that can result in more specific, albeit narrower, analyses of data.

The large number of book publications that come from the western half of Germany represent the region's dominant areas of study in sport psychology. Certain general trends override the individual specialties within each institution. First, a large concentration of work is directed toward youth sport in the schools and clubs. Following this thrust is the study of top-level sport, with special emphasis on sport-specific training. Related to this topic is a large body of work that deals with psychoregulation in competitive sport. There is also a strong emphasis on movement education, retraining, and sport for the disabled. Finally, a heavy concentration of research takes place in the area of motor abilities and sensorimotor processes. Academic efforts appear to reflect equitably both the broad values of the society and the specific competencies and interests of a number of individual researchers.

Research tends to favor topics that the BISp considers important and therefore underwrites, as determined by the various needs the BISp foresees. Research topics that have been funded include: aggression, violence, and talent detection in sport; psychoregulation and self-motivation training; and underlying cognitive and emotional processes in movement behavior. The ultimate direction of sport psychology in a city or state is determined by the local institutes' decision to carry out either a discipline-based approach (motor learning, social psychology) or a problem-based approach (top athletes, disabled people, children).

Publications

The growth of the area of sport psychology has been mirrored by the publication rate over the last 20 years. Hahn estimated that during the period 1960 to 1969 there were perhaps 50 publications and 10 investigations in sport psychology. In the 1970s these figures increased to approximately 700 publications and 120 research projects. Judging by the annual ASP report to FEPSAC, the European sport psychology group, during the mid-1980s close to 20 books were published annually in various areas of sport psychology and associated areas.

A growing number of overviews in the area of sport psychology can now be considered classics in the western half of Germany. Perhaps Feige's (1973, 1978) or Gabler's (1971, 1976) books initially served as milestones in the development of this area. More recently more general textbooks that fill this need have been pub-

lished: Eberspächer's (1982) *Sportpsychologie*; Bierhoff-Alfermann's (1986) *Sportpsychologie*; Baumann's (1986) *Praxis der Sportpsychologie*; and Gabler, Nitsch, and Singer's (1986) *Einfürung in die Sportpsychologie*.

As a result of BISp's very intimate support of sport psychology research, a large number of published proceedings and sets of readings have been realized in the former FRG. It is evident that no other Western European region has such a demonstrated record of sport psychology publication as the FRG. An impressive amount and quality of research and philosophical points of view is published on a regular basis in the internationally known journals *Sportwissenschaft*, *Leistungssport*, and *Sportunterricht*. Since 1987 ASP has published *Sportpsychologie*, a glossy sport psychology journal that tries to bring together theory and practice. Compared to other Western European regions, in the sport psychology of western Germany has the highest profile within the context of the total sport science backdrop.

The Role of Sport Psychology in Western Germany

Institutions. Perhaps the institutions that make the FRG unique in the Western world are Deutsche Sporthochschule Köln and the Bundesinstitut für Sportwissenschaft (BISp), or the Federal Institute for Sport Science. The Deutsche Sporthochschule was created in 1947 for education and research in sport science and is made up of 18 scientific institutes. Presently more than 6,500 students are enrolled as coaches and teachers. The BISp was created in 1970 as a federal institution within the ministry of the interior. The BISp's official functions are described in their brochure as follows: "The Federal Institute initiates, plans and coordinates research projects, promotes the evaluation of research which may be of immediate practical value, cooperates in the providing of sports facilities by building and maintaining them at the federal level, develops conceptual models for sport and recreation facilities and for sport equipment, and finally, is responsible for the organization of central sport documentation and information on the federal level." One particular section on applied science includes the following work groups: sports medicine, sport biology, sport psychology, sport pedagogy, sport sociology, the science of coaching, and the science of movement.

This institute has been very dynamic, and the work group in sport psychology, ably directed by Erwin Hahn, has been particularly active. Individual research projects are funded through the BISp if they fall into the priorities established by the institute. Of the 2.2 million deutsche marks available for research, about 200,000 ($160,000) go to sport psychology. An average project may run for 2 to 3 years and be supported to the extent of 50,000 to 80,000 deutsche marks a year. This money goes toward salaries to assistants, travel, and material and equipment purchases. Financial support is also available for the publication of research findings in the distinctive red-and-white BISp series.

A large number of sport institutes exist in which sport psychology is being carried out in varying forms and intensities. The consensus is, however, that the Deutsche Sporthochschule with its Sport Psychology Institute is the largest and most active in the western half of Germany. This institute is, of course, at an advantage in that it is one of the best physical facilities for sport in the world, with more than 6,500 students in a variety of teaching and coaching programs.

The Sport Psychology Institute in Cologne is directed by Jürgen Nitsch, a psychologist, and has a total staff of 19, including academics, assistants, an engineer, secretaries, and some part-time people. It has a definite experimental approach that is in many ways similar to the direction of North American laboratories. A pedagogical institute is also associated with the sport psychology institute; it tries to do more applied work in school sports. The main experimental thrusts in the sport psychology laboratory are in the areas of biofeedback during performance, psychoregulation and other forms of autogenic training, and tests for motor behavior processes for fine and gross skills.

Along with the Deutsche Sporthochschule, Cologne also has the Trainer Academy, to which top-level coaches return for updating in the sport sciences. A step or two behind Cologne are the sport science, rather than sport psychology, institutes in Heidelberg and Tübingen. Both these institutes are guided by strong individuals trained in the sport sciences but with definite interests in sport psychology. Hermann Rieder in Heidelberg was the first director of the BISp and is president of the sport psychology society of western Germany, ASP. On staff at Heidelberg is a trained psychologist, an individual in sport pedagogy, and assistants in both sport psychology and motor behavior. The main sport psychology focus in Heidelberg is special populations, psychoregulation, counseling, and studies in kinesthesis.

At Tübingen Ommo Grupe, president of BISp and the main force behind the highly successful Munich Olympic Sport Science Congress, directs the sport science institute. Tübingen has attempted to avoid fractionating research into narrow disciplines by adopting a problem-oriented approach that requires integrated sport science solutions. Researchers here consider areas such as talent identification, movement analysis, and play, using sport psychology and the other sport sciences as appropriate. Tübingen's sport science institute also has a trained psychologist as well as technical support staff. What makes Tübingen unique in the country is the close relationship between the sport science and the psychological institute. In many cases throughout the country, such relationships are either negative or nonexistent. Some academic interdisciplinary exchanges occurred in this respect in Tübingen.

Other strong centers of sport psychology activity in the former FRG are in Bochum, Darmstadt, Frankfurt, Kiel, and Munich as well as in a number of smaller centers.

Arbeitsgemeinschaft für Sportpsychologie (ASP).
The Work Group for Sport Psychology, or ASP, is without a doubt the best organized and most active sport psychology society in all of Europe or Asia. The ASP would perhaps compare favorably with the American (NASPSPA) or the Canadian (SCAPPS) sport psychology groups in terms of hosting regular meetings, undertaking professional projects, and having an active membership.

Formed in 1969 as the brainchild of two psychologists, Willi Essing and Erwin Hahn, who were participating in the 2nd ISSP Congress in Washington, DC, in 1968, the ASP as a work group was designed to guide researchers in the FRG. Hermann Rieder was able to get the group moving quickly in the right direction as its first president in that he was also director of the BISp. In 1972 when an Eastern European country defaulted on organizing the FEPSAC sport psychology meeting, the ASP agreed on short notice to do so. To date the ASP has organized 22 national or international scientific meetings.

The ASP's managing council selects the site and theme of the annual congress. This provides a stimulus for regional research, because a special part of the congress is devoted to the host institution's own work. Every few years, the scope of the ASP Congress widens into an international meeting. At least four ASP publications have come from these international meetings, and another six from national ones. In 1991 ASP will again collaborate in hosting the FEPSAC Congress in Cologne. The topics of psychological training and sport for health have dominated discussion in recent years, and much attention has also been given to school sport.

To qualify for membership in the ASP, an individual must have accomplished work in sport psychology and must be recommended by two members. Annual dues are 70 deutsche marks ($56). The total membership is about 165. Approximately 38% of the members were trained in sport science, and 62% come from psychology.

Sport Psychology and Top Sport.
The history of sport psychology in the FRG has not included very many intimate relationships between top-level athletes and sport psychologists. At the 1972 Winter Olympics in Sapporo, Reiner Kemmler accompanied the German alpine ski team as a psychological consultant. Hans Eberspächer played a similar role for the entire German delegation at the 1976 Montreal Olympics, an experience that he termed "too little, too late" because of its last-minute nature. Since that time several sport psychologists have become involved in either an ongoing or a short-term nature, in, for example, track and field, gymnastics, fencing, bowling, tennis, the pentathlon, and swimming.

Within the Deutsche Sportbund (DSB), or the German Sport Federation, is a scientific commission that has regular sport psychology input into workshops and courses and that tries to provide services for top-level athletes.

At the moment, the gap appears to be narrowing between sport psychology theory and the practice of sport psychology with top athletes. Members of the ASP initiated a revision of the sport psychology content in the curriculum for top coaches. Recent developments by the DSB have resulted in the creation of Olympic training centers. A growing number of highly specialized, discipline-centered sport psychology books have been published on subjects such as self-regulation and stress, personality, and aggression. But some of these sport psychology books are reportedly still written in an overly formal style with academic jargon that is difficult for the average coach to understand.

An integration of sport psychology into the academic preparation of psychologists used to be lacking. Since 1986, an advanced training course of 270 hours established by the ASP and the BDP allows psychologists to come into close contact with the field of sport psychology.

Perspectives for Sport Psychology in Western Germany

The period of rapid growth in sport psychology is over; now a period of consolidation will follow. This must occur because most of the sport psychology positions in university institutions in the western half of Germany have been filled by relatively young people. The market is now saturated. This in itself presents a special problem because new graduates now have difficulty finding work. There is little mobility from job to job as occurs in North America.

Because sport psychology is a relatively new area, the researchers are attempting to establish their academic credentials by upgrading their work in the eyes of both psychologists and the other sport scientists. The variety and quality of the work in sport psychology will improve with the new opportunities for academic mobility between the sport sciences and the parent disciplines. The possibility that sport scientists can do course work and research within the psychology departments is anticipated, and the benefits of this cross-fertilization to both psychology and sport have been clearly demonstrated in North America. This controlled growth within the sport institutes will inceasingly be integrated with the existing sport structures so that all components of this complex structure will reach their full potential.

Perhaps of greatest interest will be sport psychology's evolution in a united Germany. The combination of East Germany's pragmatic psychology and West Germany's sophisticated laboratories and funding networks could produce formidable results.

Sport Psychology Résumé of Eastern Germany

Sport psychology has played a key role as part of the interdisciplinary science team and as a branch of applied psychology. However, since the democratization of the country and its fusion with West Germany, the future of the sport scene is at best unpredictable.

Estimated Number of Sport Psychologists.   40

Prominent Institution.   German College for Physical Culture and Sports (DHfK) (before January, 1991)

Orientation.   Coach education, research in high-performance sports, sport talent, school sport, mass sport

Privileged Topics.   Action-oriented concept of sport psychology, development of personality, processes in motor learning, psychoregulation

Publication Vehicles.   *Theory and Practice of Physical Culture, Scientific Journal of the DHfK, Medicine and Sports*

Society.   Fachverbund für Sportpsychologie

After World War II, a socialist state developed on German ground in the center of Europe—the German Democratic Republic (GDR) with its 17 million inhabitants. A comprehensive and planned promotion of high performance sports allowed the GDR to take a leading position as a sporting nation, as demonstrated by its success in Olympic Games and world championships. The German Sports and Gymnastics Union (DTSB) made the greatest contribution to the development of sport. In its statutes it has set itself the goal of uniting all athletes in the country on a voluntary basis and affording all sports-minded individuals an opportunity to participate in sport in accordance with the right proclaimed in the Constitution. Currently, about 3.5 million people, or 20% of the population, are members of the DTSB. The desire for sport participation has been widespread in this country but clearly the fall of the Berlin Wall on November 9, 1989 shook every aspect of German life. October 3, 1990 saw the official reunification of Germany and in its wake some tough decisions must be made in sport science. An independent commission will distinguish between the genuine scientists and the Communist hacks. Who can say what the next decades will bring for sport in Germany?

The eastern half of Germany still has a well-organized system of sport for children and young people. Kindergartens make ample provision for exercises and games to arouse children's enthusiasm at an early stage. In general, school physical education is taught for 10 years just like any other subject, by specialist teachers with a four-year academic qualification.

Almost all schoolchildren participate every year in qualification competitions for the mass sport participation event, the Spartakiad. The best performers in the different sports and age groups compete at 2-year intervals in selected events to determine the most promising candidates. The most talented can, with the consent of their parents, join training centers and sport clubs to improve their special abilities. With the help of specially qualified coaches and constant medical care, they prepare for international competitions and championships. Before January of 1991, most coaches were trained at the DHfK in Leipzig. Apart from providing training in selected sports, the program covered educational theory, psychology, sports medicine, biomechanics, administration, general theory and methodology of coaching, and foreign languages.

On January 1, 1991 the reunified German government ordered the closing of the Leipzig institution since it was so costly to run. It was also regarded as a negative symbol of the overindulgence of the GDR in high-performance sport.

Klaus Heinemann, a noted sociologist from Hamburg, reported in a survey at the 1990 Sport for All conference in Italy that the GDR also grossly inflated the importance of the sport program for the masses. Actually, on a per capita basis, the FRG had over 13 times more sport halls and 7 times more indoor pools than the GDR. In addition, the participation rates of East Germans in physical activity were low, especially for women and the uneducated.

Sport psychology has developed in the GDR as an applied discipline of psychology and as an integrated part of sport science. Sport psychology as an applied discipline is closely connected with general psychology and other psychological disciplines as far as its development of theory and methodology are concerned. The comprehensive understanding of sport task demands requires extensive interdisciplinary cooperation between training methodologists, pedagogues, sociologists, physiologists, sport physicians, and others. Sport psychology is also necessary for the training and further education of physical education teachers, coaches, sport physicians, and sport administrators as well as for the operational work in all fields of sports and research.

Training in Sport Psychology in Eastern Germany

Until January of 1991, sport psychology was taught at the DHfK in Leipzig, where Wilhelm Wundt founded the first experimental psychology laboratory in 1879. There are eight other sections for sport science at the universities in Halle, Greifswald, Rostock, and Potsdam. Whereas the DHfK trained coaches for the DTSB, the other sections focus on training physical education teachers for schools. All sport students are instructed for some 140 hours in sport psychology and have to pass a final examination in the subject. Students especially interested in sport psychology can write their diploma work in this field. Sport psychology knowledge is also offered in courses for coaches at eastern German administrators of the DTSB, and courses for upgrading physicians in their training to improve their specialized qualifications.

Up to 1986, about 2,000 foreign coaches, sport scientists, and administrators from 88 countries received training or continued their education in the GDR sport system. More than 40 foreigners have acquired diplomas or doctor of science degrees in sport psychology.

A specially talented and interested physical education teacher with a diploma can also acquire after the 4 years of studies both the academic degrees Dr. of Pedagogy

and Dr.Sc. in Pedagogy over 3 or 4 years by studying in the field of sport psychology. In addition, every psychologist with a university diploma is able to work as a sport psychologist if he or she is interested in sport and acquires additional qualification in sport science. Many sport psychologists have double qualifications in psychology and physical education.

Topics of Study. Basic trends in eastern German sport psychology arise directly from the multidimensional demands of physical culture and sport. The scientific branch of sport psychology at the DHfK, directed by Paul Kunath, was responsible for the theory and further development of sport psychology. Over recent years, a number of topics had been considered. The main focal point, the nature of cognition in athletes, was carried out under the direction of Hans Schellenberger. Athletes thus enhanced their training methodology by understanding the importance of information processing in sport. Cooperation and communication processes were also investigated in sport games and used to determine sport aptitudes and to select young athletes for a given sport.

At the sport science section of the Friedrich-Schiller University in Jena, R. Pöhlmann is also examining psychomotor processes. Apart from certain "applied basic experiments," researchers are investigating tasks using sensorimotor training and considering their effectiveness in practice in school physical education lessons as well as in high-level training and competition. At the Martin-Luther University in Halle, Gerd Konzag has analyzed cognitive components in sport games. H. Ilg from Greifswald University is also especially concerned with tasks having different psychic loads and their effects on the motivation of schoolchildren in physical education lessons from grades 1 to 4 in a general polytechnical school. At the Research Institute for Physical Culture and Sport, Renate Mathesius has been studying problems of movement regulation and motivation for participation in sport by means of questionnaires, observation, and other methods. This investigation has revealed the nature of motivational forces and the level of consciousness of the athletic needs of different age groups.

Workers at the Research Institute for Physical Culture and Sport at the DHfK also studied in detail the effects of psychic loads and the capacity to resist stress as well as the development of these physical and mental capacities. This aspect of sport psychology had resulted in the application of psychoregulatory procedures that were of very special importance to sport performance.

At the various sports medicine institutions in eastern Germany, sport psychologists also work on practical problems concerning why people participate in sport. By means of psychodiagnostic and psychoregulative procedures, the importance of health-producing effects is being examined in school sport, mass sport, training, exercise, and competition. This outline of the main topics of study does not mean that the institutions are considering only these questions. Each sport psychologist also has his or her own special subject area. On one hand this specialization is necessary for the effective support of an athlete, and on the other it aids in the formation and further education of physical education teachers and coaches. Independent of research, most sport psychologists are also concerned with other tasks, like the psychological aspects of other aspects of personality development as well as the development of other aspects of theory, methodology, and psychodiagnostics.

Publications

Some 20 sport psychology studies appear annually in the scientific sport journals of eastern Germany, especially *Theory and Practice of Physical Culture*, the *Scientific Journal of the DHfK*, and *Medicine and Sports*. Since the beginning of the 1970s eastern Germans have also written a number of books, such as *Contributions to Sport Psychology*, Volumes I and II, by Paul Kunath (1972; 1974); *Psychology in Sport Games*, by Hans Schellenberger (1981); *Research Methods in Sport Psychology*, by Brigitte Schellenberger (1969); *From Start to Finish*, by Frank Schubert (1982); and *Sport Psychology for Coaches, Instructors, Administrators, Physical Education Teachers and Sport Physicians* by Kunath and Doil (1985).

The Role of Sport Psychology in Eastern Germany

Institutions. At the DHfK, all of the elements present in the basic Soviet model described in detail in the Czechoslovakian section were in place; that is, the Institute for Physical Culture, the Research Institute, and the Trainer Academy. What appeared to be different was the streamlining of the system and the efficient tying together of the elements into a functional whole. Sport psychology was implemented at all levels of education, research, and application.

The lines of authority between the DSTB and DHfK were clear, as were the aims of the programs, and this results in what was clearly the premier sport organization package in the world.

Fachverband für Sportpsychologie. At the end of the 1960s sport psychologists in the GDR formed a special commission of the Scientific Council of the State Secretary for Physical Culture and Sports. Apart from sport psychologists at the research institute for physical culture and sports, representatives of the sport science section at the universities and pedagogic colleges are also concerned with sport psychology. In addition, psychologists from the sports medicine service and other social institutions and organizations of eastern Germany belong to this special commission. Since 1974 the special commission has held annual sessions that serve to provide its members further education, scientific discussion, and exchange of opinions. The special commission was responsible for the coordination and promotion of sport psychology work at the DHfK until the fundamental political changes that occurred on November 9, 1989 when the Berlin Wall began to be dismantled.

The process of democratization in sport psychology

swiftly followed the Berlin Wall incident: On January 25, 1990 the Fachvenband für Sportpsychologie (Specialized Union of Sport Psychology) was formed as a sovereign society. Hans Schellenberger was elected spokesperson until the first autonomous congress. Membership included elite athletes' sport psychologists, who were previously quarantined to keep a tight lid on "secrets." This group provides a welcome new locus of control: Before the revolution, the Central government was so strict that the state secretary for physical culture and sport had to approve every word in this section!

In 1965 the the GDR's sport psychologists were among the founding members of the ISSP in Rome and of FEPSAC in Vittel. Since then, the GDR's sport psychologists have been represented on the managing councils of both associations. They regularly take part in international congresses, conferences, and symposia on sport psychology and work as editors, members of organizational committees, and chairpersons at these events. At the 7th FEPSAC Congress in Bad-Blankenburg, GDR, Paul Kunath was once again elected president of this association.

Since 1972 Paul Kunath has led the sport psychology section of the Association for Psychology of eastern Germany, thus allowing sport psychologists to take an active part in scientific discussions on the development of mainstream psychology.

Getting a definite handle on applied sport psychology in eastern Germany is difficult: In the past, much information was suppressed or falsified. For example, on my 1980 visit, I was told the GDR had no sport psychology laboratories; on my 1987 visit, I was whisked through 16 laboratories but given no time for questions or much observation; and a visit today would doubtless reveal far more. But great strides have been made from when the only information released on elite athletics in the GDR was the innocuous paragraph that follows.

Sport Psychology and Top Sport. All coaches who attend the DHfK study sport psychology as part of their professional preparation. However, it was estimated that only 50% of the coaches request special services from sport psychology specialists. Still, an increasing number of individuals are taking advantage of trained members of the DHfK. Individuals can be assigned to work with individual teams throughout the training and competition process. In most cases intervention occurs through the coach, who teaches various methods of psychoregulation. In rare cases the sport psychologist works directly with an athlete.

Perspectives for Sport Psychology in Eastern Germany

With the reunification of Germany on October 3, 1990, one might safely guess that a hybrid of West Germany's funds and technology and East Germany's hands-on experience should produce a sport psychology superpower.

Great Britain

in collaboration with

Stuart Biddle
University of Exeter

British Sport Psychology Résumé

After the initial peak in the early 1970s and a decline until the 1980s, the current atmosphere in sport psychology is positive and productive, particularly in the applied field. A number of young sport psychologists have entered the field and provided much-needed enthusiasm. The low productivity rate in publications in the applied area remains a cause for concern; however, there is still a strong tradition in motor skill research. Recent positive advances include a formal code of conduct and a register for sport psychologists.

Estimated Number of Sport Psychologists. 40

Prominent Institutions. Bedford College of Higher Education, Birmingham University, Liverpool Polytechnic, MRC of Cambridge University, University College of North Wales, University of Exeter

Orientation. Applied, cognitive, and social psychology

Privileged Topics. Motor learning, performance enhancement, social cognition

Publication Vehicle. *Journal of Sports Sciences*

Society. The British Association of Sports Science (BASS)

As in almost every other aspect of science and culture, Great Britain has made some form of significant contribution somewhere in its long tradition. This is also true for sport psychology and especially within the area of skill acquisition. This tradition has continued in Britain in that most institutions have maintained this focus in postsecondary education.

The postwar discoveries of the concepts of information processing and cybernetics translated in the 1950s and 1960s to advances in the area of skill acquisition, mainly at the laboratories of the Applied Psychology Unit of the Medical Research Council at Cambridge University. The research and human performance models of Bartlett, Craik, Broadbent, Welford, and Poulton provided conceptual frameworks for skilled performance that are still continued today.

Near the end of the 1960s, Leeds University became the academic heart and mind of what was to become the golden era of sport psychology in Great Britain. A strong program of research, publication, and professional activities was started within the modest laboratories at Leeds under the direction of H.T.A. Whiting. In 1976 Whiting left for a new position in the Netherlands and returned to the University of York in 1989.

In this wake, sport psychology began to flounder for a period. In recent years it has taken on a new life. In addition, the nature of the teaching of sport psychology has broadened considerably, especially in the areas of performance enhancement and social cognition. National conferences are dominated by the current interest in mental training, arousal/anxiety regulation, and social cognition, mainly in attribution theory. A recent thrust has also been made in topics related to children and in exercise psychology.

Training in Sport Psychology

It is possible for individuals to receive specialized training in certain areas of sport psychology right up to the doctoral level in Great Britain. But there is no formally recognized route for the training of applied sport psychologists. Indeed, the national psychology society, the British Psychological Society (BPS), has little contact with sport psychology, although in 1988 there was one sport-centered symposium at the annual BPS conference. One of the problems is that many of the prominent members of the British sport psychology community do not qualify for graduate, associate, or chartered status of BPS.

A young student's career normally begins at an academy, or secondary school, where he or she must obtain the necessary number of certified courses (GCSEs) to graduate. To go on to university, another year in the "6th form" is taken to obtain the necessary "A levels" or "highers" that a given institution requires. This may vary from 2 to 4 highers, depending on the number of applicants and the prestige of the institution. There are two options for someone interested in studying in physical education: the university, or the polytechnics and colleges of higher education (HE).

Some prefer university study because a certain amount of status is still attached to academic training at a traditional institution. It is somewhat ironic that until the early 1970s physical education departments in universities in Britain were often no more than sport or recreation services, with not a great deal of academic research. However, over the last few years a number of academic reforms have thrown colleges of education and polytechnics together. This resulted in curriculum reforms that appear to have upgraded the quality of the programs. Because the new polytechnics and colleges of HE must have their programs validated or authorized by the external Council of National Academic Awards (CNAA), this evaluation tends to be quite severe. Universities, on the other hand, validate their own programs and can be more lenient.

Within the undergraduate programs of either institution, a student in physical education receives taught course work in skill acquisition, general psychology, motor development, and sport psychology. These courses are not specializations but only a part of these degrees. Real specialization does not occur until postgraduate study. A student with high first-class honors in the undergraduate program, however, can go directly into doctoral work, bypassing the master's level.

A master's degree can be either a taught course of six subjects, which does not require a thesis, or a research option, which must be negotiated with a specific adviser at an institution. In the early 1970s, Leeds University was the only institution with a specific planned sport psychology option that included courses in theory of physical education, motor impairment, measurement, psychology of skill acquisition, and sport psychology. The situation has improved regarding the broadening of the scope of the motor skill/development work of the 1980s into the applied areas with sport as a focus.

The University College of North Wales with John Fazey and Lew Hardy, as well as Liverpool Polytechnic, has been productive in turning out graduate students at the master's and doctoral levels in sport psychology. What makes doctoral studies unique in Great Britain is that a doctoral research grant is awarded to an individual professor based on the quality of a submitted project. This individual then advertises for a student who will be supported by the grant for a number of years of research. This is different from the North American system in which certain departments, rather than individuals, are awarded doctoral programs.

There are still excellent programs of study within psychology departments in motor learning and control, especially at Oxford with Peter McLeod, at Cambridge with Alan Wing, at Lancaster with Mary Smyth, and at Edinburgh with David Lee. An increasing number of young, and not so young, sport psychologists are obtaining graduate degrees through part-time study while at the same time teaching in other undergraduate programs. To an increasing degree, British candidates are obtaining doctorates with a specialization in sport psychology, although a large percentage of good undergraduates are also studying in North America.

Topics of Study. In light of the effect that the Leeds program has had on all of Great Britain, the area of motor skill acquisition was for many years the dominant theme in research. Up until the 1980s Leeds graduates generated the only real concentration of research in the British Isles. In that Whiting's students are now spread around the country, the skill acquisition area still reverberates, but not with as much intensity, because many of these graduates went into vacant administrative positions in developing departments of physical education. The position at Leeds was later filled by David Sugden, who collaborated with Jack Keogh of UCLA in the areas of motor development and deficiencies.

The motor skill tradition has continued within psychology departments, however, with far-reaching work being carried out by David Lee and Mary Smyth in vision and sport at the universities of Edinburgh and Lancaster, respectively; Donald Broadbent and Peter McLeod at Oxford University; and Alan Wing at the MRC unit at Cambridge. John Kane has contributed a significant amount of research in the area of personality and sport, especially during the mid-70s.

Leo Hendry of Aberdeen was one of the most consistent of all the British sport psychology researchers over an extended period in the 1970s. In the 1980s he changed his slant more to broader educational issues in the areas of adolescent sports participants, leisure, social behavior, and the mass media.

The area of applied sport psychology has become important recently, with researchers giving special interest to mental training programs, anxiety/arousal control, and social cognition. Though at present the research base is rather small, there is a broader interest in the wide range of issues that are central to sport psychology.

Most recently, there has been an increased awareness of the role of the psychological benefits of exercise, and Nanette Mutrie in Glasgow and Stuart Biddle at the University of Exeter have begun such research. A potential area of growth is in psychophysiology, in which David Collins of St. Mary's College and Nick Smith of Crewe & Alsager College have been recently working. Another promising area is the research going on in youth sports, mainly by Jean Whitehead and Martin Lee at the Bedford College of Higher Education.

Publications

Aside from the significant publications in the area of motor skill provided by British psychologists D.A. Broadbent, A.T. Welford, and E.C. Poulton, Great Britain has contributed at least two classics to the psychology of skill acquisition literature: the late Barbara Knapp's *Skill in Sport* (1963) and John Whiting's *Acquiring Ball Skill* (1967). Beginning in the early 1970s Lepus Books published a series (*Readings in Sport Psychology, Movement Studies, Aesthetics in Sports*) edited by Whiting, Brooke, and Hendry that has received some acclaim.

Individuals interested in sport psychology, such as Tony Byrne, Richard Cox, John Fazey, and Lew Hardy, have contributed sport psychology content to a number of coach education monographs published by the National Coaching Foundation and the Scottish Sports Council.

In 1990 Cox published a second edition of his well-received book, *Sport Psychology: Concepts and Applications*, while H.T.A. Whiting collaborated with F.C. Bakker and H. van der Brug on a book with the same title. Also in 1990, J. Graham Jones and Lew Hardy published *Stress and Performance in Sport*.

Researchers interested in motor skill development have continued to maintain the strong British track record in this domain. Mary Smith and Alan Wing published an in-depth book on motor control in 1984 titled *Psychology of Human Movement*, and David Sugden published the comprehensive motor development book *Movement Skill Development* with Jack Keogh of UCLA.

One book that received great public acclaim and national press coverage was *Sporting Body, Sporting Mind* by John Syer and Christopher Connolly, based on their work with famous sports teams and individuals. Most recently, Peter Terry published a mental training book entitled

The Winning Mind (since translated into Italian), and Lesley Cooke and John Alderson published *Anxiety in Sport*.

No specialized sport psychology journal exists in Great Britain simply because there is not a sufficient volume of researchers to warrant this. The *Journal of Human Movement Studies* was originally based in England but its seat was transferred to Holland when Whiting changed institutions. This journal was appropriate for sport psychology studies with movement as their central theme. Now it is possible to publish in the *Journal of Sports Sciences*, a journal edited by Thomas Reilly of Liverpool Polytechnic.

A number of physical education journals published in England, Scotland, Wales, and Ireland also have occasionally published applied sport psychology articles. Some British authors have published abroad in foreign journals, but this has been an exception rather than a rule. The inclusion of the likes of Martin Lee and Stuart Biddle as editorial and review board members of *The Sport Psychologist* and the *International Journal of Sport Psychology* might have positive long-term effects on sport psychology publication production in England.

The Role of Sport Psychology in Great Britain

Institutions. Perhaps the greatest sport psychology legacy that John Whiting left to Great Britain was the number of quality students that he produced in his graduate program at Leeds. Because Whiting's students were among the first homegrown individuals possessing doctoral certification, they were immediately snapped up into the vacuum of the educational system that then had few qualified people with advanced training. In many cases, Whiting's top students were hired at polytechnics or colleges: Alderson at Sheffield, Sanderson at Liverpool, Sharp at Jordon Hill, and Morris at Leeds Polytechnic. The tradition had continued at Leeds University with the work of David Sugden in motor development. These individuals are good for the institutions, helping polytechnics evolve from sometimes being ''academic burial grounds.'' In the 1970s, the academic restructuring caused new life to be brought into sport psychology by some individuals within polytechnics. And only a few clearly defined centers of expertise, such as exercise physiology, have difficulty attracting research funds. In fact Bedford College of Higher Education has established an Institute for the Study of Children in Sport, a multidisciplinary research and consultancy unit, where Lee and Whitehead have focused their initial work on motivation, attributions, and moral behavior.

At the university level, the most consistent output in the social sciences over the last 20 years has been from the University of Aberdeen, where Leo Hendry has steadily turned out good work in the social psychology of sport within a broad educational context. The motor skill research laboratories from the traditional centers at Cambridge and Oxford universities have still maintained

their position with mainstream psychology, although various sport skills are often the focus of study.

British Association of Sports Sciences (BASS). In 1966 and 1967 Bill Steele of the University of Manchester was the prime mover behind the founding of the British Society of Sports Psychology (BSSP). He became its first president and was succeeded by John Whiting. The golden years of the BSSP were in the early to mid-1970s, when Whiting teamed up with John Brooke of Salford and organized annual meetings that drew large numbers from home and abroad. These were organized around a concept of establishing a forum for academic sport psychology presentations. Activity in the BSSP declined in the late 1970s when Brooke moved to Canada and Whiting to Holland.

After a difficult period in the early 1980s, the BSSP took on a more active role on the international sport psychology scene, especially with the European FEPSAC group. BSSP was assigned to do a bibliographic compilation on the subject of anxiety and sport in 1983 with the financial support of the Sports Council, and it was finally published in 1987.

In 1985 the BSSP merged with other groups into the British Association of Sports Sciences (BASS) and held its first joint meetings with physiology, biomechanics, and an open section dealing with multidisciplinary issues at the West Sussex Institute of Higher Education. The sport psychology section was initially chaired by Frank Sanderson and subsequently by Stuart Biddle.

The reorganization brought with it new vigor, and this eventually streamlined the administration of the sport sciences. The conferences were more viable and allowed for cross-disciplinary interaction, and BASS was also able to produce a 35-page newsletter triannually. In addition, links were facilitated with the National Coaching Foundation (NCF) and the Sports Council. In 1988 BASS acquired the services of a paid administrator based at the NCF, and guidelines are being drawn up to coordinate each section's consulting activities with the national sports governing bodies. The future may see BASS broaden out from the narrow sport performance field into the allied areas of health science. BASS has also permitted the organization of consecutive annual student conferences in sport psychology with about 15 papers and one invited keynote speaker.

Perhaps the most significant advance in the professional dimensions of sport psychology has been the drawing up of a code of conduct for sport psychologists and a register of sport psychologists. The code of conduct has guidelines regarding competence, consent and confidentiality, psychological testing, research ethics, and personal conduct. The code of conduct was the initiative of the Sports Council's Sport Science Advisory Group under the chairmanship of John Annett.

The register has been proposed as a means to define the best set of practical and academic qualifications to practice sport psychology. At the moment, the British Olympic Association's Psychological Advisory Group, made up primarily of clinical psychologists, is the only group to work with national teams. Yet members of this group do not interact significantly in the BASS meetings. The creation of these more formal links should facilitate future interactions between all players in sport psychology.

Sport Psychology and Top Sport. In 1978 at the Commonwealth Games in Edmonton, the host nation, Canada, for the first time in Games history beat both England and Australia in the final standings. Outcries were published in the British press charging professionalism, bionic athletes, and Svengali-type forces directing the Canadians. It appears that Great Britain, the birthplace of many modern sports and games as well as the concept of fair play, has been slow to enter the modern age of marriage between sport and sport science.

The Sports Council has recently called on competencies of clinical psychologists in the psychological preparation of the international squads. This, combined with the introduction of sport psychology components into the National Coaching Foundation programs, is moving sport psychology slowly but significantly onto the playing fields of Great Britain.

Perspectives for Sport Psychology in Great Britain

The Whiting-Kane era of British sport psychology, focusing on motor learning and personality research in the 1960s and 1970s, is long gone, at least within the physical education context. It has been replaced by a new guard of people interested primarily in applied interventions in sport psychology along with research considerations in youth sport and health. Regrettably, the research output is still low, although the profile of sport psychology has never been higher in the public eye. This lack of research input is potentially hazardous if all energy is directed toward application. Nevertheless, the future looks promising. Young blood has been recruited, and if these individuals can be channeled in the right direction and not asked to spread themselves too thin, the situation may change for the better. The money to sustain such optimism, however, remains an eternal problem. At the time of this writing, however, it is probably fair to say that British sport psychology is entering its second era with extreme optimism, promise, and new professionalization.

Greece

in collaboration with

Yannis Zervas
University of Athens

Greek Sport Psychology Résumé

Sport psychology is beginning to become a recognized academic discipline that is growing at a modest rate. The potential for new development would be even greater if there was more collaboration between the different working groups at the universities and the institutes.

Estimated Number of Sport Psychologists. 15

Prominent Institutions. University of Athens, Hellenic Sport Research Center

Orientation. Descriptive and empirical research

Privileged Topics. Motivation, personality, mental practice, violence in sport

Publication Vehicles. *Sport Psychology, Sport Science (Theory and Practice), Physical Education and Sport*

Society. Hellenic Society of Sport Psychology and Applied Neurophysiology (HESPAN)

Greece is not only the cradle of the Olympic Games but also the cradle of psychology. Aristotle's (384–322 B.C.) book *About Psyche* is the first systematic work in the history of psychology. He examined in the scientific manner of the time various psychological phenomena and noted the relationship between soma (the body) and the psyche (the mind). Since that time Greece has undergone many political, social, and economic changes that have greatly influenced education and sport science.

The first interest in sport psychology was expressed in Greece in 1964 when Pantelis Kranidiotis, a neurologist and psychiatrist, began to participate in various international meetings, symposia, and conferences dealing with sport psychology. But sport psychology truly emerged in Greece in 1981, when it was identified and recognized as a distinct academic subdiscipline in the university setting.

Training in Sport Psychology

At the beginning of this century, Yannis Chryssafis, a pioneer of physical education in modern Greece, made a systematic effort to revive the ancient concept of educating youth through physical training and sport. For many years since, physical education in Greece has been directed mainly toward the practical preparation of teachers. During the last decade certain physical education teachers have begun to contribute to the scientific development of sport psychology and sport in Greece.

All the professionals who work in sport psychology in Greece were trained abroad, mostly in the United States, Canada, West Germany, and Great Britain. The majority took undergradute studies in physical education and then continued with graduate studies leading to master's and doctoral degrees in sport psychology. Since 1981 courses in motor control and learning as well as in sport psychology have been included in the curriculum of the school of physical education at the University of Athens. At that time the first sport psychology laboratory was also established there. Yannis Zervas spent much time and effort first to convince the administrators of the field's importance and then to establish both the courses and the laboratory. Two years later similar efforts were made in the University of Thessaloniki in northern Greece.

All undergraduate students in physical education are required to take courses related to general psychology, motor control and learning, and sport psychology. However, because there are 4,000 undergraduate students in the program, professional contact time with each student is necessarily limited.

Graduate programs began in Greece in 1987 with six graduate students enrolled in the section of sport psychology. All graduate work must be focused in the area of sport coaching; at this time none have graduated and moved into the field.

At present another 15 graduate students are studying sport psychology abroad. Most of them have scholarships from the government, so they have to come back to work in state schools and institutions. An intensive governmental effort has been made to improve the training of sport psychology graduates, and Greece is just beginning to see the benefits.

Topics of Study. The primary concern of sport psychology is to help athletes learn, perform, and enjoy sport activities. To achieve these goals, much effort in the new graduate programs is directed to the study of motor learning, personality, motivation, stress, and anxiety as well as social psychological topics such as sport ethics, leadership, cohesiveness, and sport violence. Youth sport is also a primary concern of the universities of Athens and Thessaloniki. During 1988, Greece introduced its own system for sport talent identification, and sport psychology has played a significant role in the development of this system.

However, Greeks do not forget their past. Historical research is always an attractive field of study. We can explain present situations and predict the future by studying and understanding past events. Some of the questions to be answered include the following: How were athletes in ancient times mentally and psychologically prepared and motivated for highly competitive

events? How were sport participants affected by religious beliefs and other social factors? How were some mythical and incredible achievements accomplished?

One other original area of interest was created to encourage teachers and students to understand violence in sport. Thus the University of Athens and the Hellenic Society of Sport Psychology and Applied Neurophysiology have announced awards for the best research projects that attack this problem area.

Publications

Articles and papers in sport psychology have appeared sporadically in various Greek publications, with most of these publications being psychopedagogical in nature. A relatively productive period of development in publications began in 1984. During these last years five books have been published, most of which are used as textbooks in schools of physical education. Moreover, four journals deal in various degrees with sport psychology.

The *Journal of Sport Psychology*, published by the Hellenic Society of Sport Psychology and Applied Neurophysiology (HESPAN), was first published in 1984 and presents articles on sport psychology, sport sociology, sport pedagogy, and philosophy. The *Journal of Sport Science: Theory and Practice* is published by the Hellenic Sport Research Institute and also covers the sport sciences. Two other journals, *Athlitismos* and *Physical Education*, deal with teaching and sport in general. Research papers and bibliographical surveys in sport psychology are published mainly in the *Journal of Sport Psychology*.

The Role of Sport Psychology in Greece

Institutions. Because of continuing development in the field of sport, a reform is going on in this country. The training of physical education teachers has been upgraded to the university level. According to the new law relating to schools, this training aims at (a) the acquisition and transmission of knowledge through research and teaching; (b) the formation of responsible human beings with scientific, social, cultural, and political sensitivity who are capable of pursuing a scientific and professional career; (c) the resolution of the country's social, cultural, and developmental needs; and (d) the contribution to the process of continuous education of the people. It is hoped that sport psychology will play a significant role in the realization of these goals.

In Greece there are four departments or schools of physical education and sport science in the universities of Athens, Thessaloniki, Thrace (Komotini), and Serres. A serious problem, common to all schools, is the enormous number of students and the lack of means and facilities. This year the universities of Athens, Thessaloniki, Komotini, and Serres have 4,300, 4,200, 2,000, and 1,500 students respectively enrolled in their physical education programs. Only two of these schools, Athens and Thessaloniki, have established sport psychology sections combined with organized laboratories. These laboratories serve as research and training centers for undergraduates and centers for the psychological preparation of top-level athletes. However, the logistical problems of having a laboratory with more than 4,000 students must certainly be formidable.

In 1977 the Hellenic Olympic Committee established the Hellenic Sport Research Center to promote sport from a scientific viewpoint. Vassilis Klissouras, an exercise physiologist formerly at McGill University, was the founder and first director of this center. One component of this institute is the sport psychology section that in 1980 was equipped with contemporary, even state-of-the art, laboratory facilities. Anastasios Stalikas, a clinical psychologist, has been in charge of this laboratory since that time. Stalikas carries out psychodiagnostic assessment of personality and psychomotor abilities. The athletes can also practice psychoregulation with biofeedback devices in extremely well-equipped facilities.

However, one problem area that haunts Greek sport psychology in Athens is the lack of contact between the university and the Sports Research Center. There could be a dynamic research climate with selected students from the university doing internships on projects with national teams at the Sports Research Center in the quiet setting at Kifisias. These two elements, however, remain separate because of social conflicts between the two organizations.

Hellenic Society of Sport Psychology and Applied Neurophysiology (HESPAN).

In 1978 Pantelis Kranidiotis suggested the formation of the HESPAN to act as Greece's professional association. HESPAN was initially involved in the organization of various lectures concerned with themes in sport psychology. In 1980 HESPAN organized its first seminar on autogenic training, run by Yannis Xenakis, a psychiatrist. The first HESPAN symposium was held in 1983 during the inaugural National Conference of the Hellenic Society of Physical Education Teachers.

HESPAN has paid a lot of attention to athletes' physical and emotional well-being. In addition, violence in sport is a matter of great concern to this society, and as such it published a special issue on sport violence in 1989.

So far HESPAN has 30 members, but unfortunately very few of them are directly involved in sport psychology on a day-to-day basis. Those who apply for membership have to show interest in sport psychology and accomplish some scientific work. The establishment of HESPAN has contributed to the development of both national sport psychology and international cooperation in this domain. Greece was accepted as a member of FEPSAC on September 10, 1983, and hosted a managing council meeting in Athens in 1988.

Sport Psychology and Top Sport. Until now only a small number of top-level athletes have received psychological services directly from sport psychologists. The use of psychologists in counseling and the psychological preparation of top-level athletes seems to be still in its infancy due to a gap between the universities and sport federations. However, in recent years coaches, athletes, and administrators have shown a great deal of interest in sport psychology and have of their own initiative practiced mental training in the laboratories of the Hellenic Sport Research Institute.

Anastasios Stalikas has also accompanied the Greek delegation as the team sport psychologist to major competitions such as the 1987 Mediterranean and 1984 Olympic Games.

Perspectives for Sport Psychology in Greece

Sport plays an increasingly significant role in the total picture of Greek life. The measure of this significance is reflected in the government's involvement in sport and in supporting services that are necessary for accelerated growth. Up to now Greece has achieved some of the necessary prerequisites for full development. However, because sport psychology is a relatively new area, more organization and better education, research, and international connections are needed. The establishment of graduate programs in sport psychology would provide an impetus for advanced professional specialization. Professionals in sport psychology today are in a much better situation than they were some years ago. The market has just opened. Sport psychologists have numerous opportunities for employment at federations and clubs. Attractive positions for doctoral graduates studying abroad are available in the universities and research centers.

Finally, since Greece was not selected for the centenary 1996 Olympic Games, its sports scientists and sport psychologists will now have to seek new directions in which to develop their energy and skills.

Italy

in collaboration with

Ferruccio Antonelli
Dipartimento di Medicina dello Sport

Alberto Cei
Scuola dello Sport

Italian Sport Psychology Résumé

Sport psychology in Italy has broadened its attempts at understanding top athletes by adding coach and psychologist education to the existing psychodiagnostic and medical framework. The most important concentration of activity is still in Rome, but other centers have been flourishing.

Estimated Number of Sport Psychologists. 350

Prominent Institutions. Dipartimento di Medicina dello Sport, Rome; Scuola dello Sport; Dipartimento di Psicologie dello Sport; Istituto Superiore di Educazione Fisica; universities of Rome, Bologna, Milano, Padova

Orientation. Psychodiagnostics, counseling, mental preparation, applied and coaching research, youth sport

Privileged Topics. Psychopathology, group dynamics, cognitive neuroscience, psychometrics, gender research

Publication Vehicles. *International Journal of Sport Psychology, Medicina dello Sport, Movimento, SDS-Rivista di Cultura Sportiva*

Societies. Associazione Italiana di Psicologia dello Sport (AIPS), Societa Italianà di Psicologia (SIPs)

''Rome or death,'' said the great leader Garibaldi during the unification of Italy, and with regard to Italian sport psychology, again Rome becomes the central focus of attention for many reasons. First, the central driving force has been Ferruccio Antonelli, a Roman psychiatrist. Second, the predominant sport psychology interest in Italy has traditionally been top sport, and the Italian Department of Sport Medicine and the Central School of Sports are situated in Rome. The sport psychology situation in Italy is a very particular one and has no comparable model in the world. The phenomenon of sport as a health-building activity or as a popular national pastime for men and women of all ages has not been a traditional part of the Italian culture, as is the case in Scandinavia, for example. Not until recently has the population become sensitized to the positive aspects of participation in sport. For centuries people believed that sport was dangerous, causing bone fractures, or that sport participation could injure the female organs.

This historical lack of a popular participatory sport in this culture resulted in the development of a narrow focus in the area of sport psychology, namely, understanding the elite male athlete. The adoption of the mental health perspective that was first used to consider top competitors was natural in that Antonelli and many

of his associates were psychiatrists or medical doctors. The consequences of having a homogeneous medical orientation has created a collective perception of the sportsperson that is unique in the world.

Both Antonelli the man and Rome the city hold special places in the history of the young discipline of sport psychology. In 1963 Antonelli and three other Europeans, Michel Bouet of France and José-Maria Cagigal and José Ferrer-Hombravella of Spain, met during a sport psychology session at a sports medicine congress in Barcelona. There they proposed the staging of a similar event with an international scope specifically in sport psychology. Antonelli attributed the idea to Ferrer-Hombravella, although Antonelli organized the first congress in Rome in 1965.

At that time the International Society of Sport Psychology (ISSP) was founded, and Antonelli was elected its president. Later, in 1969, during Antonelli's second term at the helm of ISSP, he and his close friend and publisher Luigi Pozzi initiated, again from Rome, the *International Journal of Sport Psychology* (IJSP), which was to become the official journal of the ISSP. Finally, in March 1974 after Antonelli stepped down as ISSP president, having served two terms, once again in Rome he and his associates formed the Associazione Italiana di Psicologia dello Sport (AIPS), and Antonelli was elected president.

Training in Sport Psychology

Though Italy was the birthplace of international sport psychology in 1965, no specific and extensive training existed in the area until 1974, and it still has not yet flourished on an extensive scale.

In Italy, as in many Latin countries (Portugal, Spain), the medical profession provided the first established scientific support system for sport. What is unique here, however, is the predominant number of medical people involved in the area of sport psychology. Many doctors still consider this involvement only a hobby, because no one is able to work at this in a full-time capacity. The second group of sport psychologists is made up of a variety of individuals with backgrounds in philosophy, psychology, sociology, and physical education.

Before the AIPS initiative in 1974 in Italy, most sport psychology personnel acquired their training through on-the-job experience by working with athletes or by meeting together professionally rather than through specialized academic preparation.

For the medical population specializing in sports medicine in Rome, Antonelli has given a single course in sport psychology at the University of Rome since 1962. From the 1960s to the late 1970s, the health model, that is, psychodiagnostics by means of projective techniques, was the privileged orientation for this training, whereas little or no emphasis was given to the experimental or educational models used elsewhere. Only since the late 1970s have university departments of psychology across the country witnessed specialization. However, the exact role of the psychologist in Italy has not been clearly delineated in relation to the dominant providers of mental health services, the psychiatrists.

Little preparation in sport psychology existed for trained psychologists in 1981. But in 1982 and every year since, AIPS has offered intensive courses that include 240 hours of theory and practice and a final practical exam of techniques learned taken before a panel of experts. To date many individuals, averaging between 40 to 45 successful candidates a year, have passed this exam, thus allowing themselves to be called sport psychologists, which is not legally appropriate in Italy. AIPS maintains a yearly update of this sport psychology register much as does the USOC in the United States and the CASS in Canada.

In the past in Italy, as was the case in many other Western European countries, at first the energy of a few individuals fueled the interest in sport psychology, and then a structure soon had to be created to institutionalize these activities. Voluntary efforts had to be replaced by full-time, paid positions at the major centers.

Presently there are full-time sport psychologists working at the School for Sport and at the Department of Sport Psychology, both at CONI. Perhaps more importantly there is talk about creating two sport psychology chairs at the faculties of psychology in Padova and Rome. This has been in response to the ever-increasing numbers of theses doctoral candidates have written in the area. In addition, the National University Council of the Ministry of Education is discussing the possiblity of creating a school of the psychology of sport and motor activity in the universities of Florence and Padova. It is clear that sport psychology is still very much on the move in Italian academic circles.

Coaches, or "technicians" as they are called in Italy, follow various courses organized by the School of Sport in Rome or in their own region. Physical educators are trained in 12 nonuniversity Superior Institutes of Physical Education (ISEF). A psychology course is one of the basic subjects within this school system. At the moment in Italy, the sport technicians play only a consumer role in sport psychology; they receive information through technical updates in clinics and courses. But already, the image of sport has changed dramatically in the public eye, and the role of these individuals may be the next to evolve once they have earned a higher level of professional respectability.

Topics of Study. A glance at the key words submitted by the Italian respondents reflects the heavy preoccupation with the psychiatric model—for example, deviance, personality, and psychodiagnostics. This is of course understandable given the medical backgrounds of the founders of sport psychology in Italy. Though observers might consider the spectrum of study some-

what restrictive, the intensity of these efforts cannot be questioned.

Antonelli has in his office the test batteries for all Italian Olympic athletes since the 1956 Games in Melbourne. This data base is made up of a series of projective tests, such as the Middlesex Hospital questionnaire, the Machover Draw-a-Person test, the Koch-Stora test, and the Banati-Fischer test. Emphasis will continue to remain on the elite athletic population, and study in other areas will likely not proliferate unless structural changes in sport science are implemented within Italian institutions of higher learning.

More recently, topics of study such as attention control, self-efficacy, and group cohesion, which are popular in North America, are beginning to appear in the Italian sport psychology literature. This is probably directly because more and more graduates from psychology rather than medical departments are becoming active in sport psychology. The former departments are better aware of current research areas that are being studied abroad.

Publications

Because sports medicine has held such a prestigious place in Italian society and sport psychology in Italy was dominated by medical doctors, it is understandable that there are ample means of publication in the country. For example, the proceedings of the biannual AIPS meeting have always been published either through local publishing houses (Società Stampa Sportiva) or as a supplement to the *IJSP*. Publication of individual work when appropriate is also possible through the sports medicine journals.

Since 1985 AIPS has published a glossy journal specializing in sport psychology called *Movimento*. It includes popular as well as research articles and is distributed to 5,000 subscribers. This journal is similar in many ways to the German publication *Sportpsychologie*, which began in 1987. In addition, nearly every edition of the School of Sport's publication *SDS-Rivista di Cultura Sportiva* has an article on sport psychology.

Single publications in sport psychology with international repute have also originated from Rome. The best known is the classic 1,300-page proceedings of the 1st ISSP Congress, *Psicologia dello Sport* (edited by Antonelli). One of the most impressive sport psychology books written in Italy or elsewhere is Antonelli and Salvini's *Psicologia dello Sport* (1978; 2nd edition, 1987), which has an authoritative section on psychodiagnostics that is unique in the world. However, it has limited accessibility because it was published in Italian. This has decreased its effect on the international market.

Two recent publications have appeared in the *Psyche and Sports* series from Luigi Pozzi Publisher. The first by Antonelli is entitled *Readings in Sport Psychology*, and the second by Alberto Cei is called *Mental Training*. The latter is an original initiative that resembles many of the North American applied sport psychology "how-to" books.

In 1990 Francisco Salibere, Bruna Rossi, and Gabriele Cortili wrote *Fisiologia e Psicologia degli Sport* with Mondadoci Publishers. This book provides the best source of neurosciences for athletic purposes. Finally, the School of Sport publishes special monographs, or *Dispense*, on areas such as group dynamics, motor learning, cognitive processes, and performance enhancement.

The Role of Sport Psychology in Italy

Institutions. The personalities of the major figures in Italian sport psychology as well as the social halo that surrounds the medical profession have allowed the work of these doctors in sport to be seen in a very positive light. The sports medicine center in Rome has had an impressive record of giving attention to athletes for more than 25 years. This service has been held in high positive regard by athletes because it has been at once useful, nonthreatening, and free of charge. The media as well as the athletes have reported on this work enthusiastically.

Now the appearance of specialized courses in sport psychology within the universities and intensive training and refresher courses at the sport institutes and schools augurs well for the further development of more institutionalized dimensions in sport psychology.

Associazione Italiana di Psicologia dello Sport (AIPS). This group, made up of psychologists and physicians, has been active; it met biannually first in Rome in 1974 and since then it has met on a regular basis at various centers in every corner of the country. Each meeting has centered on a specific theme—for example, youth sport, group dynamics, and psychoregulation—and has always resulted in some form of publication. Antonelli was succeeded by Mascellani as president of AIPS from 1978 to 1984 and remained honorary president until he was reelected president in 1984, a position he has held to the present. In addition to the biannual meetings across Italy, the AIPS also organizes a yearly "Roman Days" meeting in the spring, when 100 to 150 interested persons listen to selected lectures from noted experts in Italian sport psychology.

In addition to holding meetings, AIPS also provides specialized courses and certification and publishes *Movimento*, as described previously. It has about 350 members, approximately 100 of whom are certified sport psychologists. One potential source of conflict with the AIPS certification process is specific legislation that prevents non-psychologists (i.e., medical doctors) from calling themselves psychologists.

In 1988 the Società Italiana di Psicologia (SIPs) began a special section in sport psychology under the direction of Alessandro Salvini of Padova University, and in April 1989 the section held its first symposium. The inclusion of the field of sport psychology within mainstream psychology represents a major step in the recognition of the discipline. Since now the possibility of teaching the subject at the universities exists, another umbrella group may have to be created to include AIPS and SIPs members so that competent researchers and clinicians can work together.

Sport Psychology and Top Sport. In some Western European countries sport psychologists cannot get close to elite athletes. In Italy, the two groups have been working hand in hand for 25 years. The confidence that has built up has progressed to the point that athletes more frequently request the services of the center in Rome. In the early years, Antonelli and colleagues provided all services free of charge, but there are more and more paid positions working with top athletes as well as club teams. The increased institutionalization of this process resulting in more full-time employees will standardize such important areas as record keeping and statistics and will allow the introduction of other psychological interventions to complement the diagnostic methods.

Perspectives for Sport Psychology in Italy

When first questioned in 1981 in the first edition of this book on what initiatives in Italy could cause changes in the development of sport psychology, Antonelli replied, "The image of sport in the mind of the Italian population." In fact, sport is no longer perceived as an idle pastime for men but rather as a health-giving alternative life activity for men and women of all ages, and this has already changed the image of sport psychology to the general public.

The restructuring of the universities and the creation of specialized chairs in sport psychology will surely be the most effective way of accelerating positive growth in the area, along with the recent modifications in institutionalized sport science. The new doctors in psychology have now found their own niche in a society previously dominated by medical science. Sport psychology has progressed a long way internationally since modern-day activity began in that 1965 congress. Italy is not being left behind.

Netherlands

in collaboration with

Frank C. Bakker
Free University, Amsterdam

Adri Vermeer
Free University, Amsterdam

Dutch Sport Psychology Résumé

Sport psychology in the Netherlands has traditionally been limited to research in a university setting. More recently, however, the discipline has spread to a broader applied sport setting.

Estimated Number of Sport Psychologists.   25

Prominent Institution.   Vrije Universiteit

Orientation.   Interdisciplinary experimental research

Privileged Topic.   Complex motor actions

Publication Vehicles. *Journal of Human Movement Sciences, Geneeskunde en Sport (Medicine and Sport)*

Societies. Dutch Society for the Scientific Study of Sport (VWSL), Dutch Society for Sport Psychology (VSPN)

Holland has a long, rich tradition in sport with roots in the everyday activity of its people. The foreigner is impressed by the orderly procession and constant flow of bicycles along the special pathways that cover the nation's billiard table–like surface. This well illustrates that movement activities are still very central to life in Holland in spite of their decreasing importance in modern society.

As in other countries, many people in the Netherlands participate in sports in some way or another. There is an extended network of professional and semiprofessional organizations for virtually all kinds of sport. From the 1970s until the present, an increasing number of people have participated in sport outside of formal club systems. This is especially true for cycling, running, and speed skating.

Holland has a well-organized physical education system that is virtually autonomous. Five academies turn out broad-based physical education teachers who have only a smattering of psychological knowledge, the depth of which varies depending on the philosophy of the particular academy. The major difference between the Dutch orientation and that of most other countries is that in Holland physical education at the academies and the university sport science programs are virtually independent of each other. However, some changes have taken place in isolated situations, and closer cooperation between academies and universities will likely be realized within the next 5 years.

It might also be expected that the education of coaches, which is presently the primary responsibility of the sport federations themselves, will be less isolated from both universities and academies, which are being urged to expand their range of service training because the present job market for physical education teachers is rather unfavorable. Some academies have already extended their curricula, for example, and have developed a coaching program. On the other hand, federations that organize coaching courses commonly ask for the expertise of graduates in sport science.

Interest in sport psychology is growing in Holland. Athletes and coaches seem to have become less skeptical about sport psychology, reversing a viewpoint that dominated in the Netherlands until about 1980. Books on sport psychology and mental training are gaining in popularity, and some kind of mental coaching or mental training is more or less accepted now. An increased interest in sport psychology is also apparent among students in the sport sciences.

Training in Sport Psychology

The particular structure of academy-based physical education, which is separate from university-based sport science or psychology, is gradually changing. Until 1985 those who decided to go into physical education studied psychological dimensions that were mainly within the confines of pedagogy. Within this training stream no academic postgraduate training was possible in sport psychology or in any other sport science discipline.

As a result of government regulations, there is now more academic mobility, and students at an academy can attend graduate courses at the university and participate in academic postgraduate training. Because this opportunity is very new and universities and academies are not yet prepared to fully exploit this new situation, only a very few students have been able to take advantage of it, although their numbers are steadily growing.

For physical education students interested in the academic area of the sport sciences such as sport psychology, the most common path is still to enroll in a university-based program of study. This can take place in one of two general settings. The first option is to follow a normal course of study in the psychology department of a university and direct attention to a sport topic. No specific program of study exists within these traditional structures, so the final product of this process is at best uneven in quality. Roughly estimated, annually two or three students in the whole country choose to study sport psychology in this way.

The second and more structured alternative is the department of psychology in the faculty of human movement sciences of the Free University (Vrije Universiteit) of Amsterdam. The structure of this faculty appears to be unique in the world. It is not directly associated with the training of physical education teachers, although movement is still a central focus. There are both pure and applied dimensions to the research, which by definition of the faculty is interdisciplinary.

This interdisciplinary program was set up in 1971 as a discipline-based program directed toward the study of human movement. Psychological research is conducted in association with other disciplines such as functional anatomy, physiology, educational science, health science, and theory and history of human movement. These collaborations are also carried out to varying degrees within applied and pure areas of study.

The goal toward which students of the faculty of human movement strive during their 4 to 6 years of study is the attainment of the doctorandus (Drs.), which is equivalent to a good master's degree in North America. Graduates of this program acquire an interdisciplinary background in movement-related topics that qualifies them for a career as a research assistant in the human movement sciences; as a professor in the physical education academies or academies of physiotherapy; or in psychomotor therapy, ergonomy, or sport or school administration.

From 1972 to 1989 H.T.A. Whiting, now at the University of York, has been chair of the department. He has 10 coworkers who collaborate on research projects and teach various topics on psychology related to human movement. This teaching program within the department contains three streams: human movement psychology, behavioral medicine, and sport psychology. Frank C. Bakker has most recently taken over responsibility from Whiting for this last area. A growing number of students are interested in the sport psychology area, which contains a basic program in psychology and the psychology of motor control and learning, and courses in the classical topics of sport psychology such as motivation, personality, and aggression. Students who choose the sport psychology stream participate in one of the department's research projects or set up and carry out their own research proposals as far as they fit into the research program of the department.

Within the faculty, a considerable number of students are also interested in psychomotor therapy and sport for the disabled. They follow a doctoral program in one of the other departments of the faculty, namely, the department of educational sciences; they are supervised by Adri Vermeer.

Students can also carry out Ph.D. work within the faculty of human movement sciences in sport psychology. Opportunities for doing Ph.D. work have greatly increased since the faculty opened a graduate school of human movement sciences in 1988.

Topics of Study. The Netherlands has a tradition of research in the area of movement that predates the existence of the faculty of the Free University. In the 1940s the work of Buytendijk influenced many early researchers, including the prominent Russian Bernstein.

The department of psychology organizes its research following the research tradition that Whiting initiated in a program entitled "Complex Motor Actions." This program embraces five subprograms: the acquisition of motor skills, the teaching of motor skills, evaluation of movement patterns, individual differences, and the conceptualization of human actions. Much of this work uses sport tasks even when the research work is considered more fundamental. A recent innovation in the program is the development of a project area based on a natural-physical approach to movement control (self-organizing systems). The inauguration of a graduate school will lead to a considerable extension of this work, with sport psychology research playing a greater role in the department.

The department has extensive research facilities. The laboratory space of the departments of functional anatomy and educational sciences totals about 800 square meters. Other departments in the faculty will engage in multidisciplinary research, and as such research support is also available for physiological, biomechanical, and anatomical methods.

Publications

A relatively large number of sport psychology articles are published in the Dutch language in *Geneeskunde en Sport* (*Medicine and Sport*). The main areas of research related to fundamental problems occurring in complex movements are also published in international psychology journals.

Between 1984 and 1988, more than 100 research articles, chapters, and books were published by members of the department of psychology. Among the books are *Human Motor Actions: Bernstein Reassessed by Whiting* (1984) and *Sportpsychologie* by Bakker, Whiting, and van der Brug (1984). The latter book was published in English by Wiley in 1990. Whiting is also editor in chief of the *Journal of Human Movement Studies*, a publication that carries considerable weight internationally.

The Role of Sport Psychology in the Netherlands

Institutions. Sport psychology is formally studied at the faculty of human movement sciences of the Free University in Amsterdam, which offers a broad-based, multidisciplinary program in human movement studies that is structured to present among other things sport psychology in its broadest form. Formalized programs, specialized research apparatus and methodologies, and university structures assure the discipline's stability and growth.

Individuals can also study topics in sport psychology within the program of the psychology department of the universities of Groningen, Utrecht, Leiden, and Nijmegen or at any of the other Dutch universities, although no formalized course of study exists at those institutions.

Dutch Society for Sport Psychology. Initiated by the Dutch Psychological Association, a working group on sport psychology was founded in 1987. In this group psychologists, sport scientists, researchers, and psychologists practicing mental training for top sport worked together.

The working group aimed to structure the development in sport psychology in the Netherlands and to develop a formal institution wherein researchers in sport psychology and practitioners of mental training could meet and cooperate. This resulted in the formation of the Dutch Society for Sport Psychology (VSPN) in 1989. Important goals of the VSPN are to organize sport psychology congresses and symposia and to initiate the development of postgraduate sport psychology courses aimed at practical aspects of sport psychology.

The Dutch Society for the Scientific Study of Sport (VWSL) is an informal interdisciplinary sport science group that also meets occasionally for symposia and within this structure provides sport psychology an interesting forum for discussion.

Sport Psychology and Top Sport. The strongest sport science influence in Dutch elite sport has been within the area of sports medicine. Since the 1928 Olympic Games in Amsterdam, sports doctors have been associated with Dutch Olympic teams. This long tradition has resulted in a formal specialization in sports medicine within a university program of study.

Until 1980 the role of sport psychology in elite sport was somewhat minimal. Coaches and athletes no longer seem to view sport psychology with skepticism, and presently several psychologists, including Peter Blitz, the father of applied sport psychology in the Netherlands, are still involved in mental training and mental coaching.

However, there are not yet formalized postgraduate courses on the practical aspects of sport psychology, and any type of career in sport psychology and elite sport is still somewhat unstructured. One of the primary tasks of the VSPN is to adapt to improve this situation.

Perspectives for Sport Psychology in the Netherlands

The development of sport psychology in the Netherlands shows some promise. The university structures for sport psychology are sound. In the faculty of human movement sciences, sport psychology is one integrated part of an intricate, multidisciplinary program that centers its attention on both applied and theoretical study of human movement. This academically oriented structure is gaining the respect of sport psychology colleagues on an international scale and appears to be leading into an era of rapid growth.

Interest in sport psychology is growing. Athletes and coaches seem to have lost the skepticism that predominated in the Netherlands until 1980. Now they more commonly ask for some kind of psychological support—for example, in mental skill training. The gap between theory and practice, although far from closed, has narrowed. The foundation of the Dutch Society for Sport Psychology reflects these developments.

Portugal

in collaboration with

Antonio de Paula Brito
Institut Superior de Educacao Fisica

Sidonio Serpa
Institut Superior de Educacao Fisica

Portuguese Sport Psychology Résumé

Portugal has taken its first major steps toward a full professional and academic program in sport psychology. The creation of a new society, a new journal, and a new program of study has generated encouraging results in the field.

Estimated Number of Sport Psychologists. 25

Prominent Institutions. Institut Superior de Educacao Fisica (ISEF), Sports Medicine Center of General Directors of Sports, Faculdade de Mortricidade Humana

Orientation. Broad overview of sport psychology

Privileged Topics. Sport psychology and high-level sport

Publication Vehicles. *Boletim da Sociedade Portuguesa de Psicologia Desportiva, Ludens, Motricidade Humana*

Society. Sociedade Portuguesa de Psicologia Desportiva

Portugal is a small, developing country pinched between Spain and the Atlantic Ocean. In former times, Portuguese sailors had access to the New World by the sea, and their considerable skill as sailors allowed them to bring back many riches from abroad. At present those interested in sport psychology are searching the reaches of neighboring countries for information, but now travel is more expensive, and the treasures they return with are not guaranteed to hold their value as they once did in Portugal.

As is usually the case in Western Europe, the progress of Portuguese sport psychology rests on the shoulders of a few active individuals. Fortunately, in Portugal these individuals are also influential in the appropriate higher institutions of sport and education, so the energies they expend result in creation and action, not just frustration. The area of sport psychology has rapidly matured in

Portugal, due mainly to the efforts of Antonio de Paula Brito and his associates. In a relatively short time, much has happened in sport psychology since its origins in 1965.

Training in Sport Psychology

Portugal may have one of the most complex administrative and academic structures in the world. This is because the "venerable" university structures created in the 16th century have maintained their venerable values. These structures and values are juxtaposed with others arising from a more radical modern era beginning in the 1970s.

For example, the capital city of Lisbon is home to the "classic" university for medicine, law, letters, science, and pharmacy; the "technical" university for engineering, agriculture, economics, administration, physical education, and architecture; the "new" universities mainly for the social sciences; the "Catholic" universities with small specialized courses; and the "free" universities that offer private, tailor-made courses.

Even with all these differences in structure, there is still relative equality in the programs' degrees and the difficulty and length of study. For example, students can obtain a medical degree at either a classic or a new university and a psychology degree at either the Superior University of Applied Psychology or within the faculty of letters of the classic university.

All programs are monitored by one central body, the Secretary of State's General Direction for Higher Learning. When a student completes studies in psychology, a licensing board accredits him or her to work in the profession. Strangely enough, there are two accrediting licensing boards, or syndicates, for medicine.

All students follow the same basic course of study to receive their first academic degree or License, which takes from 5 to 6 years: two or three years of study in common nuclear, or core, subjects; two more specialized years of study; and finally a selection of options available within the student's area of specialization. To teach in the school systems, an individual must have a university license or must have taken the course of higher education schools, after which follows one year of probationary work in the school system. At this level of study at the ISEF, a student receives sport psychology input in the areas of general, developmental, and learning psychology as well as in the more specialized areas of motor learning, sport psychology, and motor development. In the final year of the license, two special one-semester courses are offered in sport psychology.

Advanced training in a specialization of sport psychology has been available since 1979 at the ISEF leading to the mestrado, or master's degree. This study program takes place over an additional 2 years. At present, the ISEF at Lisbon has a sport psychology laboratory in which sport psychology courses and research are carried out. Often this research is done in collaboration with sport institutions, federations, and clubs.

A program reform in 1980 created opportunities for postgraduate doctoral studies within the ISEF. Previously doctoral candidates had to study abroad in one of the neighboring Latin-speaking countries—France, Spain, or Belgium. In the future sport psychology may also become a specialization at the psychological institutes.

Topics of Study. At the moment sport psychology is in a stage of program consolidation, and no real major emphasis can be noticed. A more general educationally based approach is being used to sensitize the coaches and physical education students at ISEF to the importance of sport psychology in the total sport picture.

However, Sidonio Serpa has recently began a program in the attributions of male and female athletes, and at the same institution there are also a number of projects on the reaction states of athletes.

Publications

Since 1980 an annual *Boletim da Sociedade Portuguesa de Psicologia Desportiva* of about 50 pages has been circulated by the Portuguese Sport Psychology Society and directed more to academics and coaches. This has been an interesting collection of short articles, translated works, and sport psychology news from around the world. It's not pretty, but it is effective. Considering the total amount of information that is transmitted from such a wide variety of sources, it appears this publication is the single best international bargain in sport psychology.

Over the years there have been a number of psychologically related publications within the *Ludens* journal of ISEF, which caters mainly to the physical educator. There is also a journal dedicated to basic motor processes called *Motricidade Humana*.

The Role of Sport Psychology in Portugal

Institutions. Recent years have brought an impressive development of sport psychology in Portugal at the institutional levels. These rapid advances have come both from below, through the athletes, coaches, and teachers requesting these services; and from above, through the far-reaching steps taken by the leaders in government and sport psychology.

At the moment sport psychology input is offered to physical education students enrolled at ISEF, and there are now possibilities for postgraduate specialization in sport psychology at the same institution. The area of sport psychology has recently benefited from the upgrading of programs, and this has put sport psychology a step and a half ahead of the other disciplines in Portugal. These reformulations resulted in the creation of a Faculdade de Motricidade Humana, which is freer to research fundamental aspects of movement rather than being limited to the physical education context.

The university hierarchy appears quite similar to that found in North America. An individual can advance up the university ladder by becoming, with the appropriate qualifications, a monitor with a bacherel; an assistant with a license; an auxiliary professor with a doctorate; a professor agregado (associate) with a doctorate after earning promotion through a specific competition; and finally, a professor catedratico (full) after competition among former directors and department heads.

Sport psychology is also one of the dimensions of the Sports Medicine Center, an organism that provides support to top-level Portuguese athletes. A multidisciplinary team concept is available, including counseling in the applied areas of sport psychology.

Sociedade Portuguesa de Psicologia Desportiva.
In the late 1970s the Portuguese sport psychology society was formed in Lisbon with the intent of creating its own place within the already existing field of sports medicine. The present membership totals 80, with approximately 25 active individuals, and is made up mainly of coaches and teachers. A few sport journalists are also members, a dimension that is unique to Portugal. This allows the ''word'' to be spread to a much larger population. In addition the society has a most important inner core of people who are trained in psychology or medicine and work at the specialized sport institutions.

There are three classifications of members in the society: ordinary members, emeritus members, and honorary members. The society has organized seminars and workshops, sometimes in collaboration with colleagues from abroad. Over the last few years, Robert Singer from the United States, Gloria Balagué from Spain, and Pierre Lacoste and John Salmela from Canada have visited and lectured for varying periods. The Portuguese have been much more active in the last few years in attending conferences abroad to present their research.

Sport Psychology and Top Sport.
Though at the moment there are not a large number of trained individuals in sport psychology, some federations have sport psychologists working with elite-level athletes.

The main way that sport psychology is presently used at the various sport-oriented institutions is through the educational mode; that is, by sensitizing and teaching the individuals involved in the areas of sport psychology. Some clinical approaches have also been used, along with interventions involving mental training and coach assessment.

Because the programs and structures for sport are already in place, it appears that the impact of sport psychology on top sport will increase as more Portuguese students trained in applied sport psychology begin to emerge from the new postgraduate programs.

Perspectives for Sport Psychology in Portugal

Now that the groundwork has been carefully prepared, the total picture for sport psychology in Portugal appears promising. The first step of creating an awareness of sport psychology's importance has been established. This has been realized through the implementation of programs at two levels—the physical education institute and the sports medicine center.

At the moment, sport psychology in Portugal is intent on developing coaches, sport administrators, and the media who have an interest in the area. Increased interest is also coming from graduates from psychology who are interested in sport. These developments indicate that in the near future the most important sport teams will begin to integrate psychological personnel into their staff.

Spain

in collaboration with

Joan Riera
Instituto Nacional de Educacion Fisica de Catalunya

Spanish Sport Psychology Résumé

Sport psychology has been in an upswing in Spain for the last 10 years with the establishment of a number of institutionalized positions in sport institutes and universities, publications, and professional activities. The impetus of the 1992 Olympic Games in Barcelona will also accelerate the development of more applied areas of concern.

Estimated Number of Sport Psychologists. 40

Prominent Institutions.
Instituto Nacional de Educacion Fisica de Catalunya (INEFC); Instituto Nacional de Educacion Fisica (INEF), Madrid; Autonomous University of Barcelona; University of Granada

Orientation.
Pedagogical, coach education, cognitive research

Privileged Topics.
Motivation, talent identification

Publication Vehicles.
Apunts de Medecina de l'Esport; Apunts de Educacio Fisica

Society.
Federacion Española de Asociaciones de Psicologia de la Actividad Fisica y el Deporte

Spain got in at the ground floor in the development of international sport psychology, remained somewhat disorganized for most of the 1970s, and then demonstrated a remarkable turnaround from the early 1980s to present.

The force behind these many changes in sport psychology was the remarkable team that developed in Barcelona in Catalunya. This team brought about a number of important changes, especially through the institutionalization of the field in both the sport and the psychology departments.

Historically, sport psychology at the international level was conceived in Barcelona in 1963, although the birth did not take place until 2 years later in Italy. During a sports medicine meeting, José-Maria Cagigal and José Ferrer-Hombravella of Spain, Ferruccio Antonelli of Italy, and Michel Bouet of France discussed their common interests in the psychological aspects of sport and speculated as to the feasibility of organizing a world sport psychology congress. At that time no known national associations in the field existed anywhere in the world. Two years later, Antonelli organized this congress in Rome, which drew more than 300 participants. This meeting resulted in the founding of the International Society of Sport Psychology (ISSP) and the election of Antonelli as its first president and Ferrer-Hombravella as secretary general.

The Spanish involvement in this initiative resulted in a flurry of activity by Ferrer-Hombravella and other associates, including Cagigal and Roig-Ibañez. This core of individuals was then instrumental in obtaining and organizing the 3rd World Sport Psychology Congress of the ISSP in 1973 in Madrid. But despite the success of the congress and the resulting publications, this event failed to leave a significant legacy of sport psychology in Spain. The lack of any formal, collective sport psychology activity resulted in some lean years, with only sporadic activity occurring during the 1970s.

At the beginning of the 1980s, a small group of enthusiasts led by Gloria Balagué in Barcelona began to face the problem of bringing sport psychology to the forefront, first at the INEF in Barcelona and then throughout the rest of Spain. Today many of the structures that were lacking in the 1970s are now in place, and sport psychology is a rapidly evolving concern that will undoubtedly be further stimulated by the Olympic Games in Barcelona in 1992.

Training in Sport Psychology

Until 1982 Spain's situation was similar to that occurring in much of western continental Europe, whereby the field of physical education had to battle against old university traditions and had not yet achieved parity in terms of academic status. Whereas specialists in education received their training at the university, physical education students were prepared at non-university-status INEFs in Madrid and Barcelona. All of this changed in 1982 when the INEFs gained university status, which then allowed them to prepare academic programs for second-cycle (master's) and third-cycle (doctorate) study in sport psychology and other disciplines. In addition, the number of centers in Spain housing INEFs has increased from the initial ones in Madrid and Barcelona to new centers in Granada and Lleida in 1983; Pais Vasci in 1986; and Galicia, León, Canarias, and Valencia in 1987.

Each program in physical education at the INEFs consists of specialized courses in child and general psychology, sport psychology, motor learning, motor development, and pedagogy. There is considerable interest in the field of sport psychology due partly to its new university status and partly to the small nucleus of Catalonians—Joan Riera, Josep Roca, and Gloria Balagué—who have actively stimulated academic activity in the area after completing their own doctoral studies in the early 1980s.

One other aspect in the recent development of sport psychology in Spain is the opportunity since 1982 for graduate study within the psychology departments for the second cycle at the Autonomous University of Barcelona, where Jaume Cruz is active. The third cycle at the University of Barcelona began in 1989 and is unique in that the program is organized in collaboration with the INEF, the Autonomous University, and Direction General of Sport. A 2-year period of study occurs, with half the course work theoretical and the other half applied. Candidates are admissible from programs of both physical education and psychology.

These initiatives demonstrate remarkable progress when compared to the relative stage of development of the field of general psychology in 1980. At that time Gloria Balagué, the dynamic young sport psychologist at the Barcelona INEF, was only the third graduate from the psychology department of the University of Barcelona. Her initiatives at that time allowed 4-year psychology students to become involved in in-service training in sport psychology at the INEF. This spark developed into the present collaborations between the INEF and the universities in Barcelona.

Balagué has since completed her doctorate in the psychology department at the University of Illinois, where she now lives, but she maintains close contact with her native Spain.

One other area in which sport psychology can be taught is in the area of sports medicine. Sports medicine in Spain began in 1959 and has been most active in the Barcelona center. At one time this field had been more of a hobby for most medical doctors, because no specialized university study program existed. However, since 1987 there has been a specialization in sports medicine in Madrid, Barcelona, and Oviedo. This program of study lasts 3 years and incorporates sport psychology units along with a number of practical field experiences. About 50 candidates are enrolled in this program that also has personal fitness and a sports background as admission requirements.

Topics of Study. Presently a number of groups of people are doing research in sport psychology activity in a number of centers in Spain. At the end of the 1970s most research was limited to the individual efforts of those working at the INEFs in Barcelona or Madrid. The Barcelona INEF has been the most active center because Balagué, Riera, and Roca were the first to finish their doctorates in the area and were working at the center. Balagué initially had an interest in psychometrics of sport ability but then continued her studies in attribution patterns of elite athletes. Josep Roca's interests are in the area of motor learning and development, and Joan Riera has concentrated on psychological processes of competitive sport and motor learning. At the Autonomous University of Barcelona, Jaume Cruz is interested in the behavioral aspects of youth sport coaching. The influence of Ferrer-Hombravella and later Roig-Ibañez in the 1960s gave Barcelona this head start in Spain that it has maintained until the present.

This early sport psychology program was then integrated into the activities of the INEF Barcelona Medical Control Center. A sport psychology laboratory established by Roig-Ibañez at the INEF was used for the psychodiagnosis of sport aptitude by means of paper-and-pencil tests as well as a variety of laboratory measures of reaction times, depth perception, concentration, and vigilance.

At this early stage of development, no clear research foci have emerged from the traditional INEF at Madrid or from the newer INEFs created throughout the rest of Spain.

Publications

Sport psychology articles have been periodically published in the quarterly journals *Apunts de Medecina de l'Esport* and *Apunts de Educacio Fisica* of Barcelona and the *Revista de Investigacion del INEF* of Madrid. The creation of a functional sport psychology society with annual meetings has stimulated an increase in the number of sport psychology articles appearing in these journals.

The first Spanish sport psychology publication that had great impact internationally was the three-volume set *Psicologia del Deporte* (1976–1977), which was the product of the 1973 ISSP Congress in Madrid. The editor of these proceedings was P. Piernavieja.

José-Maria Cagigal, the Spanish sport psychology pioneer and former head of the Madrid INEF, has been the single most productive individual in the country. Cagigal, who died tragically in a plane crash in 1983, published seven books on diverse topics, including *Sport, Pulse of the New Age* (1972), *Man and Sport* (1957), and *Sport, Pedagogy and Humanism* (1967) as well as others on sport and aggression and sport and society. These books are both academic and popular, reaching many thousands of Spaniards. The works of a number of foreign authors such as Cratty, Rioux, and Antonelli have also been translated into Spanish.

More recently, a number of textbooks that could be considered more scientifically rigorous have been published in the areas of motor development (Ona, 1987; Roca, 1982; Ruiz, 1988), reaction times (Roca, 1983), and sport psychology (Marrero, 1988; Palmi, 1984; Riera, 1985).

The Role of Sport Psychology in Spain

Institutions. Sport psychology remains principally in the hands of the many INEFs that have been developed in all parts of Spain, beginning with Madrid in 1968 and Barcelona in 1976. In the capital city of Madrid, the INEF is bigger in terms of its physical plant and the number of students it can accommodate. Thus the potential to

effect greater change should lie with Madrid, especially with its ready access to government resources. However, changes in direction within the INEF has retarded the possibilities for smooth and progressive advances in sport psychology. Barcelona has had more continuity, especially in terms of research, with the succession of Ferrer-Hombravella, Roig-Ibañez, Balagué, and now Riera and Roca.

The medical control center at Madrid carries out as a matter of course evaluations of top athletes from medical, physiological, perceptual, and psychological points of view. Because of this broad range of services, many sport federations use this center for diagnostic investigation as well as for clinical purposes.

The recent initiation of sport psychology specializations into university structures also promises to provide a new source of potentially refreshing input to the work being carried out at the various INEFs. These changes indicate that Spain has probably been one of the most progressive countries in Europe in changing the institutionalized nature of sport psychology.

Federacion Española de Asociaciones de Psicologia de la Actividad Fisica y el Deporte. In 1977, just prior to the 4th World Sport Psychology Congress of the ISSP in Prague, a Spanish sport psychology society was founded on paper. However, not until 1980 did this group become functional by holding its first general meeting with an accepted constitution and a new program of activity.

At that time, Balagué hoped to accomplish three things through this society: (a) to bring people interested in sport psychology together to stimulate some concerted activity on projects of common interest; (b) to provide a common voice to other sport science groups, and (c) to create a potential go-between for new programs in sport psychology, within either the universities, the INEFs, or sport federations.

In the next 5 years dramatic organizational changes occurred and all these goals were indeed accomplished. In 1983 the Catalonian Society was formed, and its first congress was held in Barcelona. The next year congresses in both Barcelona and Madrid followed. Each year thereafter, annual meetings were held at various centers in Spain, during which Spanish research was presented and to which foreign guests were often invited. In 1987 the Spanish Federation of the Psychology of Sport and Physical Activity was formed in Granada; the group included associations from 11 different centers or regions, and Joan Riera was elected president. Each section is autonomous, and the development of the federation now depends on the progress of each component.

Sport Psychology and Top Sport. Spain has been able to establish a program of medical support mainly at the Barcelona and Madrid INEFs, which has provided a variety of diagnostic profiles for coaches and athletic administrators that enable them to gauge an individual's relative state of training and performance compared to established norms.

Part of this procedure includes evaluation of the sensory, perceptual, and intellectual variables that contribute to successful performance in a given sport. The appropriateness of each set of tests, however, has yet to be validated in terms of how these measures relate to sport performance. In addition a clinical service in problem solving, psychoregulation, and group dynamics has been implemented when requested. Most of this activity is possible because of the close relationship between sport psychology and the sports medicine unit in the Barcelona INEF.

A small number of individual sport federations have hired consulting psychologists or psychiatrists with varying degrees of success. The most common treatments have been the teaching of concentration and relaxation techniques along with some attempts at group dynamics. Public, top-level, and general sport centers have hired a number of sport psychologists to enhance performance. Though applied sport psychology is perhaps the weakest component to be developed to date,

there is great promise that its role will intensify with the approach of the Olympic Games in Barcelona in 1992.

Perspectives for Sport Psychology in Spain

Since 1981 Spain has taken very impressive steps beyond what was then a crossroads in its development. Whereas the situation was tentative during the early years, everything now appears to be stable and promising. Sport psychology is taught within INEFs and universities where an individual can now receive postgraduate training. The upcoming 1992 Olympic Games promise to increase the sport federations' interest in sport psychology in their attempts to do well in front of their home crowds. Finally, the structuring of a federated sport psychology society permits national communication while allowing local initiative to flourish within the best possible overall situation.

Switzerland

in collaboration with

Guido Schilling
Swiss Federal Institute of Technology, Zürich

Swiss Sport Psychology Résumé

Sport psychology in Switzerland can be characterized by its reorganization and establishment of structures to allow a dynamic group of individuals to study applied problems in sport. More recognized sport science programs and new positions at the university level have resulted in new growth in sport psychology in this country.

Estimated Number of Sport Psychologists. 35

Prominent Institutions. Swiss Sport School Magglingen; Swiss Federal Institute of Technology, Zürich

Orientation. Educational

Privileged Topics. Aggression, anxiety, fair play, coaching, counseling

Publication Vehicles. *MPT* (Human Potential Training), *Bulletin Suisse des Psychologues, Magglingen-Macolin*

Society. Association Suisse de Psychologie du Sport (SASP)

To best understand sport psychology in Switzerland, an observer needs some very general background information on this Western European country. This small nation is unique in that it is made up of 26 cantons, or provinces, each with its own particular traditions, ethnic

makeup, and predominance of one or two of Switzerland's four official languages (French, German, Italian, and Romansh). Each canton is responsible for its own educational system with the singular exception of sport education, which is organized at the national or federal level. The separation of physical education or sport education into a central jurisdiction is linked to the fact that at one time physical education was closely tied to military training, and there are obvious advantages in having this type of central control in terms of the consistent application of policies. Some inconveniences also arise from this special status for sport, or more specifically for sport psychology, because the sport sciences, perhaps indirectly due to their special status, do not yet hold a very healthy place in the university system. This causes certain difficulties in sport psychology in Switzerland, especially regarding long-range planning.

However, in 1986 Guido Schilling, one of the prime movers in Swiss sport psychology, moved from the Swiss Sport School Magglingen (ESSM) to the Swiss Federal Institute of Technology (ETH) in Zürich, and sport psychology in Switzerland has already begun to feel the effects of this transition.

Training in Sport Psychology

No specialized programs in the area of sport psychology exist in Switzerland, and only because of the singular efforts of interested individuals within university settings has a small nucleus of serious activity been created. The majority of the approximately 35 individuals who are active in sport psychology are graduates from psychology departments who were permitted to do their master's or doctoral dissertations in the area of sport. In some cases, psychologists later on became interested in the area of sport, perhaps because it was an area of greater social recognition. In a more limited number of cases people trained in physical education schools at a later date became interested in psychology. Thus for most people sport psychology is still just a hobby.

For the moment, training in sport psychology has been given a boost now that Guido Schilling has taken over as the physical education director at the ETH in Zürich. This institute now has elements of sport psychology at a number of different levels.

ETH Zürich founded a center for research and counseling in sport, and it now offers a number of services in the field of sport psychology. The most important unit is a course in human potential training that includes activation, concentration, recreation, and relaxation training for athletes. In addition, the institute offers short courses and clinics to coaches and publishes a number of documents for administrators. Presently it is still extremely difficult for a person trained in physical education to switch to a psychology faculty, because the physical education courses are not sport science–based but are of a more practical, nonacademic nature.

The ESSM in Magglingen as well as other centers around the country have given certain courses for coaches in sport psychology under the auspices of the newly reformed Association Suisse de Psychologie du Sport (SASP). For example, members of SASP gave successful courses about improving methods for coaches of elite athletes as well as fair play for directors of federations.

Topics of Study.   Because there are few institutionalized programs in sport psychology, the research tends to be short-term rather than ongoing, with limited spheres of concentration. Nevertheless, past efforts have included the areas of personality of athletes, cognitive processes in sport, and athletic aggression.

The 1983 European sport psychology meeting of FEPSAC was held in Magglingen, Switzerland, and centered on the theme of emotions in sport. This event proved to be a catalytic agent in generating more coherent research directions in Switzerland. A major initiative introduced and promoted the concept of fair play in sport in Switzerland.

Publications

The most accessible means of communication for general sport psychology information appears to be the publication *Magglingen-Macolin*, edited by the ESSM. Individuals can also publish in the *Bulletin Suisse des Psychologues*, *MPT* (Human Potential Training) the *Swiss Journal of Sport Medicine*, or some of the German or French revues such as *Leistungssport* and *Education Physique et Plein Air*. In addition monographs are published in the series *Information Entraîneur* that is made available to coaches at clinics and courses usually held at Magglingen.

Two of the most influential "Swiss-made" publications resulted from the edited proceedings of international meetings held in Switzerland. In 1974 Schilling and Pilz edited a book called *Psychologie Sportive—Pourquoi? (Sport Psychology—What For?)*, the product of an international symposium in Magglingen containing a compilation of Swiss research. And in 1985 Schilling and Herren edited two volumes, *Excellence and Emotional States in Sport* and *Contemporary Concepts in Sport Psychology*, based on the 1983 FEPSAC congress. Just prior to this Congress, the FEPSAC publication *Anxiety in Sport*, edited by Erwin Apitzsch, was published and launched at the congress.

The Role of Sport Psychology in Switzerland

Institutions.   The ESSM in Magglingen began the first programs in sport psychology in Switzerland, due primarily to the efforts of Guido Schilling, who has served on various occasions as the president of the Swiss sport psychology group and of FEPSAC as well as treasurer of the ISSP. This unique school merits discussion in that it has played such a dominant role in the early development of Swiss sport psychology.

The ESSM is a multifunctional school that serves as a national training center, technical coaching school, administration and documentation center, research institute, and technical organ for the Swiss army. Through this institute, a vast network of instructors, athletes, coaches, and administrators in sport can be updated and upgraded in a first-rate physical facility laid out in an astoundingly beautiful natural setting. In his former role as ESSM's director of information, Schilling kept his fingers on the pulse of the Swiss sport situation while maintaining a high profile in sport psychology.

One unique feature of the ESSM is its youth sport program *Jeunesse et Sport*, which provides an equal-opportunity environment for young people 14 to 20 years old to receive quality sport training in more than 30 sport disciplines ranging from mountain climbing to judo.

The close physical proximity of all corners of Switzerland coupled with the Swiss people's industriousness and natural love of sport could make this country a leader in sport psychology if the institutionalization of sport science would begin in greater earnest. Schilling's appointment in 1986 as director of ETH Zürich might provide the stimulus for the implementation of these stable forms of academic preparation and research.

Association Suisse de Psychologie du Sport (SASP). The Swiss sport psychology group has existed since 1968 and was initially guided mainly by Schilling's initiatives. In 1984, however, this group became more formal, holding annual courses and conferences as well as different small meetings around the country. Originally SASP was a subgroup of the Swiss Society of Sports Medicine. A few years earlier Schilling had been quoted as saying, "There is no doubt that the connection to 'big brother' medicine is of great value." It appears that the perceived value of this relationship soon changed because few actual benefits accrued from this association, a situation that has also occurred in other countries around the world.

In 1987 the group was one of the founding members of the Federation of Swiss Psychologists (FSP), a professional association. Now membership requirements for SASP are academic qualifications in psychology and an interest in sport. Perhaps this new liaison with a group that has more compatible goals than does medical science will stimulate the professional growth of sport psychology. There is also talk of the formation of a Swiss sport science association, but this has not yet materialized.

Sport Psychology and Top Sport. In the 1988 report of activities of the SASP, an item appeared concerning the seeming disinterest of those responsible for elite sport regarding the inclusion of psychologists in preparations for the Olympic Games. Whereas medical doctors and physiotherapists were an accepted part of the preparation process, the Swiss authorities did not yet appear to be aware of the role that the systematic preparation of emotional and cognitive dimensions could play within preparation and performance procedures.

However, some inherent drawbacks in the preparation of Swiss sport psychologists may again be due to the lack of university programs in this area. It becomes exceedingly difficult to pick up practical experience, especially of a clinical nature, if the formal sport science structures are nonexistent. The only roles left are educational ones, whereby coaches or athletes obtain the most recent sport psychology information at clinics and symposia.

The lack of clinical experiences arising from sport is due in part to Switzerland's small number of athletes. This makes earning a livelihood through sport psychology on a consultation basis very difficult. Still, some individuals are already working with rowers, parachutists, table tennis players, and skiers on a volunteer basis. In addition, the Swiss national soccer team has a former player who is now a psychologist, Lucio Bizzini, working with the team.

Perspectives for Sport Psychology in Switzerland

Sport psychology in Switzerland has made progress over the last few years, but it has been quite slow to evolve. Could it be that the cantonization in this geographically isolated country is also present in sport science? The small step of introducing an additional area, sport psychology, into the sport sciences that is outside the jurisdiction of sports medicine still appears to be impeding the long-term evolution in this field in Switzerland. The establishment of the center for research and counseling in sport at the ETH Zürich is perhaps an important step. It seems evident that once this situation is normalized through the insightful and efficient conduct of the present policies, Switzerland will assume a role of leadership in sport psychology that will surpass in importance by many times the country's small physical size. The new attempts at the scientific upgrading of sport psychology in the preparation of psychologists and physical education teachers might also bring their commitment to sport into the scientific laboratory, an approach that has been very successful in North America.

Chapter 9

EASTERN EUROPE
Bulgaria

in collaboration with

Filip Genov
Georghi Dimitrov Institute of Physical Culture

Bulgarian Sport Psychology Résumé

Sport psychology in Bulgaria is perhaps the classic remaining example of the Soviet model that is directed almost totally toward high achievement in top sport and that has born the fruits of its labor.

Estimated Number of Sport Psychologists. 127

Prominent Institutions. Georghi Dimitrov Institute of Physical Culture, Sofia; Institute of Physical Culture, Varna

Orientation. Research and preparation for top-level sport

Privileged Topic. Prestart states

Publication Vehicles. *Vaprosi na Fiziceskata Kultura, Psihologia*

Society. Bulgarian Society of Sport Psychology of the Bulgarian Union of Physical Culture and Sport

The Socialist countries in Eastern Europe are anything but monolithic clones of the Soviet Union. A great deal of difference can be seen and felt in the degree to which the prototypic "system" is implemented. But Bulgaria is perhaps the country that fits most clearly into the mold of how a socialist country is expected to act. In some respects, Bulgaria is more Catholic than the Pope.

The great deal of information control encountered in Bulgaria for this project makes it somewhat difficult to write accurately about the country. It can only be assumed that the basic patterns in structure and function are similar to the Soviet model described in detail in the next section on Czechoslovakia.

In spite of the radical changes in the communist world during 1989 and 1990, Bulgaria has proven resolute in its traditional political orientation. Though the November revolt ousted Todor Zhivkov, free elections in June 1990 instated a reformed communist party.

For many centuries Bulgaria was ruled by the Turks. The agriculture-based society did not foster a broad university tradition, except among the bourgeoisie in the classical areas of study. After the revolution, Institutes for Physical Culture were established in the major centers of Sofia and Varna and in the smaller centers of Burgas, Pleven, and Rusi.

Training in Sport Psychology

Sport psychology in Bulgaria began immediately after "the victory of the Socialist revolution" in 1948. At that time a directive from the Party stated that there would be special development in the area of physical culture for the masses with the aid of the sport sciences, including sport psychology. Thus, the Institute for Physical Culture was established in Sofia, and a special division was created to teach this subject matter to coaches.

In that no university tradition in sport existed prior to the revolution, Filip Genov was the first Bulgarian to obtain advanced training in Moscow, where he achieved the doctor of science degree. Genov is now the professor in Sofia and the dominant sport psychologist in the Bulgarian system, representing the country on the managing councils of both FEPSAC and the ISSP.

The educational levels of diploma, doctor of physical culture (comparable to a master's), candidate of science (comparable to a Ph.D.), and doctor of science (comparable to habilitation or tenure) are described fully in the section on Czechoslovakia. Presently in Bulgaria 45 people hold the doctor of physical culture certification. A few individuals have also received all their training within psychology, pedagogy, and medical departments.

In 1966 laboratories were established in the institutes across the country to monitor top-level athletes and do a certain amount of research. Controlled experimental studies are considered less important than field research that has an immediate impact on sport performance. In contrast to this approach among the Socialist countries is Hungary, which is also interested in theory testing.

Topics of Study. Three main topics dominated research in Bulgarian sport psychology from 1980 to 1985. All three relate to the achievement of top sport performance. The first is the psychological preparation of athletes for competition. This involves analysis of both the demands of the sport and the psychological characteristics of the athlete. Subsequent to this, tailor-made training procedures are drawn up in consultation with the coach. Athletes can be redirected to other sports if a mismatch occurs between their particular makeup and the nature of the activity.

The second area of concern is the effect of sport training on the athlete's psychological development. This refers to the shaping of the athlete's behaviors for the social good of Bulgaria. In other words, the athlete is supposed to be transformed into the model Socialist citizen, with the task being victory to reflect the advantages of the Socialist system. Bulgarians present many papers on this theme of achieving the ideal Socialist personality.

The third area of concentration has been on-site psychological readiness for competition. This is probably the area of Bulgarian sport psychology that is the best-known abroad, due to the extensive writing on the pre-start state by Genov and his associates. Researchers have considered the phenomena of both relaxation and anxiety reduction as well as activation or energy mobilization during these key moments of competition.

In addition to the preceding themes, the 1985 to 1990 plan includes psychological requirements of the national team coach, psychological requirements in physical education classes for children, and psychological barriers for high-class achievements.

There has also been mention of research into the "psycho-recreation" of the masses that would result from their participation in physical activity. However, it was reported that efforts in this direction are simply not as pronounced because of the great emphasis that is put on top-level sport.

Publications

As often occurred in the Socialist countries, a Russian expert, in this case Dimitrov Oshanov, was sent to help set up the programs until 1955. Smieskol reports that until 1959 only 20% of Bulgarian publications dealt with top sport. This rose to 40% between 1959 and 1970 and to 70% in 1971. It is quite possible that the rate is even higher now.

As is the case in the other Socialist countries, no specialized publication in sport psychology exists. All types of sport science information is published in *Vaprosi na Fiziceskata Kultura* and sometimes in the mainstream journal *Psihologia*.

Genov has reportedly written 16 books on various aspects of sport psychology and sport. He has also given a special emphasis to weight lifting, the national sport of Bulgaria. Bulgarians have published well over 1,000 sport psychology articles in various forms since the revolution, mainly in sport science journals from Socialist countries.

The Role of Sport Psychology in Bulgaria

Institutions. The prototype Soviet sport system that is described in the Czechoslovakian section is in place in Bulgaria. The Bulgarian Union of Sport and Physical Culture is the ruling body under which the Institute of Physical Culture functions in its educational role. This institute gives specialized courses in coaching, physical education, and rehabilitation. In association with this body is the Research Institute, which was created in 1954 with the aim of preparing athletes for competition. Specialized sport psychology units appear in both the teaching and the research institutes with some individuals working at both. No contacts with the psychology faculty exist as in Czechoslovakia and in eastern Germany.

Committee for Sport Psychology of the Bulgarian Union for Sport and Physical Culture. This committee was founded in 1962 with the goals of making concerted efforts on selected psychological problems in sport as well as introducing coaches and athletes to new psychological perspectives. The membership is now reported to be 127 and is made up mostly of coaches, teachers, medical doctors, and 40 sport psychologists.

The active individuals in this committee have been well supported by the Bulgarian sport leadership in terms of sponsorship to scientific congresses in Eastern Europe and even abroad. At the 1979 FEPSAC meeting in Varna, 22 Bulgarians presented 60 papers. More recently papers have been published from meetings in a number of Socialist countries as well as in Copenhagen, Magglingen (Switzerland), Eugene (Oregon, USA), Acapulco, and Sydney.

Sport Psychology and Top Sport. The predominant feature of Bulgarian sport psychology is its close relation with top sport in all phases of the training and competitive processes. Athletes can even be forbidden to compete if it can be shown that they will crack under stress. The procedures used for monitoring the training process at the Research Institute are drawn up by the sport scientists and coaches on the Council for Top Level Sportsmen. Along with evaluations in physiology, biochemistry, and doping control are a number of sport psychology measures. The capacity of cognitive functions under various work loads are evaluated as indicators of overtraining. A large number of psychomotor tasks requiring tracking, reaction to complex stimuli, tension control, steadiness, and movement accuracy are employed along with some paper-and-pencil tests of personality. The methodological approaches used at each of the centers tend to be the same. This unified approach is more feasible within such a centrally controlled system.

The great degree of success that Bulgarians have enjoyed in boxing, shooting, gymnastics, wrestling, and weight lifting has been attributed in part to their psychological training. All top-level athletes receive a 30-hour course in psychoregulation for competition that is made up of 16 hours of theory and 14 hours of practice. The athlete's ability to use these techniques is evaluated both subjectively and objectively using various monitoring devices.

Various stress tests used for diagnostic purposes within the Research Institute are able to pick up early indications of overtraining that go undetected by physiological measures. Top athletes are also tested just before and following competition. Bulgarians are now also using biofeedback-based, self-monitoring devices during actual competition.

In addition, during the year prior to the Olympics a sport psychologist is released from all other responsibilities to work full-time at the Research Institute with the athletes. For each of the major sports, a sport psychologist is directly involved throughout the whole training and competition process. It is anticipated that this individualized attention will increase so that all sports receive similar treatment.

Perspectives for Sport Psychology in Bulgaria

The tendency in Bulgaria to concentrate energy on top sport appears to be ever on the increase. The importance of sport psychology in the total sport achievement picture has been established, although admittedly the hard-science physiologists still have more clout in the decision-making processes for athlete selection.

Though the area of psychoregulation, especially during the prestart condition, has received special attention, it appears that new thrusts into the areas of psychotherapy and psychoprophylaxis will be developed. The overall sport psychology emphasis in Bulgaria is somewhat limited in scope but is admittedly effective within these limits. Given the stability of communism in Bulgaria, too, one would expect sport psychology in Bulgaria to continue in its present course.

Czechoslovakia

in collaboration with

Miroslav Vanek
Charles University

Bohumil Svoboda
Charles University

Czechoslovakian Sport Psychology Résumé

The field of sport psychology in Czechoslovakia is internationally one of the best rounded in terms of productivity and breadth of study. The programs also maintain credibility in sport and in psychology as well as with colleagues from both the Socialist and the Western worlds.

Estimated Number of Sport Psychologists. 50

Prominent Institutions. Faculty of Physical Education and Sport (FTVS), Charles University, Prague; FTVS, Comenius University, Bratislava

Orientation. Personality and group processes of top athletes

Privileged Topics. Psychoregulation, personality, sport games, coaching, motivation, sport for all

Publication Vehicles. *Teorie a Praxe Telesne Vychovy, Acta Universitatis Carolinae Gymnica*

Society. Working Group of Sport Psychology of the Czechoslovak Psychological Society

It was on the newly constructed auto route from Prague to Bratislava in 1980 that I was first introduced to Grigory Potemkin and his style of work. Potemkin was a court favorite and lover of the Russian tsarina Catherine the Great while at the same time he held the finance minister's portfolio. Rather than directing allocated money to the building of factories, as Catherine believed, he put these funds into his own pocket. One day, Catherine decided to visit these new installations to see how her money was being spent. Potemkin was in a bind, but he acted quickly. He ordered workers to hurry out to these vacant lots and construct facades to represent the facto-

ries he had supposedly built. Shortly afterward he transported Catherine in a carriage and showed her these two-dimensional villages from afar, confining her to the roadway perspectives. Catherine was content, and the phrase ''Potemkin villages'' was coined to represent showy presentations of prefabricated prettiness that have no real substance.

On the road to Bratislava, Miroslav Vanek, then president of the ISSP, told me that I would not see any Potemkin villages on my visit to Czechoslovakia, and I believe that this was so. The openness and thoroughness of visits and discussions in Czechoslovakia make this perspective on a Socialist nation probably the most accurate. In light of the dramatic yet peaceful change of November 1990 and Vaclav Havel's subsequent election, communist hegemony is now over. However, many structures of the past remain to be evaluated and perhaps changed.

In that most activity in the other Socialist nations is based on this Soviet model, I will refer to Czech structures and programs rather than repeat them, and only differences or variations from the pattern will be noted. Of course, one should remember that though many structures remain to be changed, the Marxism that underlay them has been seriously challenged.

Sport psychology in Czechoslovakia is in a special position because it draws from many sources in both the East and the West. As an organized field of study within a sport psychology society or committee, sport psychology here has a history of close to 30 years. Basic techniques of an applied nature and program structures have been adopted from the Soviet Union, yet good contacts with Western Europe and North America have allowed this source of sport psychology offerings to temper the basic model. Distinct research departments and ties to the Academy of Sciences give Czechoslovakia one of the most well-rounded sport psychology packages in the world.

Though there are many similarities between the Czech

and Slovak structures and those of other Socialist countries, the people in place make the difference in the smooth coordination of all the elements. In Czechoslovakia, effective people who are judiciously placed provide leadership both within the country and abroad.

Training in Sport Psychology

Training in sport psychology in Czechoslovakia has been carried out through the university faculties of physical education as well as in the department of psychology in the philosophy faculty, with the greatest number taking the former route. In 1952 a resolution of the government and the Party suggested the introduction into the physical education movement of "the well-established system of socialist physical education, resting on the scientific bases of Marxist and Leninist ideas, which have brought the Soviet physical culture to the most progressive and advanced level in the world." The collaborators on this chapter now make it clear that Marxist-Leninist ideas no longer serve as the basis for training in physical education. Whereas the greatest single concentration of courses in Czechoslovakia, the GDR, and Poland, as in the other Socialist countries, used to be in the area of political education, since the November 1989 democratization this socialist content has been totally removed from the program. At the undergraduate level, courses in sport psychology and pedagogy in Czechoslovakia make up 5% of the total course hours.

A student can complete undergraduate work in physical education after 5 years of full-time study in either teacher training for secondary schools in physical education and another subject, in sport training and coaching, or in military training. The diploma in physical education is the basic degree and is equivalent to a bachelor's degree in North America.

After acquiring the diploma, a student can do specialized postgraduate work in sport psychology or in another sport science as well as in the previously mentioned teaching and military streams.

An individual wishing to obtain advanced scientific postgraduate training must take a rigorous set of entrance exams. Courses are taken in a specialized area along with research that leads to the thesis. Students take no cross-disciplinary courses in the psychology departments, however, as this program is limited to the confines of the physical education faculty. This lack of academic mobility is a feature of all sport psychology programs in the Eastern European countries.

After 1 to 3 years of study, the thesis is evaluated by two professors, and then the student takes a final set of exams. Vanek believes this training is equivalent to that for the North American master's degree, although the academic title presently received is the doctor of pedagogy.

The next step up the ladder is equivalent to the Western Ph.D., but it is called the candidate of science, or the C.Sc. Normally a candidate for this position is already employed by a sport institute of some kind and studies while working. The system prevalent in North America

of studying while being either self-supported or supported by student loans is foreign to this part of the world. An individual is always employed in an institute while taking on parallel studies, a system that has the advantage of supervised internships and built-in on-the-job training.

A candidate must apply to the appropriate academic authorities and if accepted must sit for an oral exam to become an "aspirant." It goes without saying that prior to November 1989 a person did not get this far without being a good Socialist citizen. There is then a minimum 3-year internship with a professor while research is carried out. There are also comprehensive examinations in socialist philosophy, languages (Russian and one other), and basic information in the other sport sciences as well as the individual's own research or dissertation. After achieving this degree an individual can then tack on the C.Sc. designation after his or her name. Normally, this degree is conferred when the candidate is about 40 years old.

The next level of academia, attained by only a few, is the doctor of science, which is granted when the individual has published a great deal. The qualification for this level appears as a monograph, a new collection of works, or a book, and a committee composed of individuals who already have this award evaluate the work and the candidate's external references.

According to Vanek, by the time a person has achieved this level and the extra 1,000 crowns each month that goes along with it, "the hair, the teeth, the sex are well on their way to disappearing." Finally, all remaining vestiges of youth have gone by the boards when someone is elected to the prestigious Academy of Sciences. However, democratization may streamline this process. Indeed, 11 of the 13 party-member deans at Charles University were removed from their posts after the democratization, due to their Communist ties. The Physical Education Department was one of the two faculties involved.

Topics of Study. "The solution of the projects of the State Plan and the Ministerial Plans is mostly the concern of the habilitation theses, dissertation theses, of the postgraduate, doctorate papers as well as the degree theses of the students." This statement from the Charles University prospectus for the Faculty of Physical Education and Sport indicates two important features of the Socialist sport system prior to the revaluation of November 1989: the existence of state 5-year plans for research, and the means by which these plans get carried out.

The State Plan is a broad set of guidelines drawn up for research in every area of scientific concern, including physical education and sport. Within the overall theme, a number of interrelated subthemes are elaborated that are further broken down into smaller units that may be tackled by individual projects. For example, the development of the Socialist personality has been the theme of a broad line of research in Czechoslovakia from 1980 to 1985. This theme is then divided into methodology sections, developmental considerations, theoretical formulation, and so on. These directives are formulated from the appropriate scientific committee of the Academy of Sciences. These directives from above, however, are only guidelines, and researchers have input from below to create smaller projects, to modify the subsections to match their skills, and to generate new but related projects. In the 1985 to 1990 5-year plan, an innovative project was brought forward so that more than 1,000 elite athlete-students were given a series of 16 lectures regarding increasing motivation and creativity in sport performance. This demonstrates that the topics vary from the theoretical to the very practical.

This plan is distributed and certain centers are given responsibility for specific areas. Thus, a professor working in one subsection directs his or her students into the orientation of the State Plan for their theses, papers, or dissertations. The choice of the specific subarea is left with the student; however, the main sector of the student's work is already delimited.

This system has obvious advantages and disadvantages. The advantages include having a collective attack on a broad area of concern; interrelating a number of methods, dispositions, and disciplines in a common direction; and knowing more or less what everyone is doing and how that relates to one's own research. Disadvantages include the potential stifling of individual initiative through overplanning and regimentation, reducing the intellectual excitement of choosing the orientation of research, and minimizing the possibilities of discovering something really new and revolutionary. Such disadvantages can lead to mundane research.

Likely, however, the procedures for planning research will be radically changed to emphasize personal initiative over collective planning.

Research within the main center of Charles University in Prague in the late 1970s and early 1980s was in the area of the personality of top-level athletes. Vanek and associates in this area wrote a major volume based on evaluations of more than 6,000 Czech athletes. This work is tied into other clinical work of a psychodiagnostic nature on the anxiety control of top athletes during competition by Machac and his workers.

More recent research by second-generation staff members has been directed toward achievement motivation (Hosek and collaborators), the social aspects of team unity (Slepicka), game strategy (Svoboda), emotions in sport (Machac), and psychological and physiological bases of youth sports (Kodym).

The other major center is at Comenius University in Bratislava, where a greater emphasis is put on talent selection and youth sport by Machac and his collaborators. A research tool to measure cognitive processes and perceptual abilities under various loads and types of stressors is unique to this institution. The research efforts of Valkova and Man, respectively in the smaller centers in Olomouc and Budejovice, are beginning to produce interesting results that compare favorably with those of the main institutions in Prague and Bratislava, though they have considerably less support from a technical viewpoint.

It is clear in Czechoslovakia, as Vanek reports, that the physical education institutes have attached "the greatest theoretical and practical importance to the problem of the psychological preparation of the athlete for contests and the investigation of the psychological basis of athletic activity." Much of this research is carried out in field settings using clinical techniques. Carrying out theoretical research is not a priority, but finding areas of application for this information is important. The other factor that predisposes sport psychology toward this applied approach is that there is little or no laboratory space for sport psychology in the physical education institute.

This research in laboratory settings has, however, been carried out in association with the stress laboratory in the psychology department in Prague, which is now situated in the philosophy department. At this laboratory under the direction of Dr. Miksic, athletes, patients, and even the Czech astronauts are put under a series of stressors for 6 hours that tax the perceptual cognitive and motor capacities along with various pressures of time, social comparisons, and threats of punishment.

Publications

No specific periodical in sport psychology is published in Czechoslovakia, but as in most Eastern European countries there is a special publication in the "theory and practice of physical culture" series, in this case, *Teorie a Praxe Telesne Vychovy* and *Acta Universitatis Carolinae Gymnica*. Sport psychology publications make up a significant part of this prestigious journal.

In addition an impressive series of book publications reaches back over 50 years during the bourgeoisie years and through those of Socialism and back to democracy. In 1932 Chudoba published *The Psychology of Training* based on his experiences in the United States. It is ironic that the 1970 classic *Psychology of the Superior Athlete*, which helped popularize sport psychology to the North American public, was written by Miroslav Vanek and Bryant J. Cratty, based on Vanek's experiences with Czech athletes.

Vanek has published a number of books on the psychology of physical education (1956, 1963), personality (1974), and sport psychology (1980, 1984, 1988). Ivan Machac in Bratislava also has a long history of publication specifically in sport psychology, having written seven books and edited seven, the first released in 1962. Vaclav Hosek has written topical books on the psychological resistance to failure in sport (1979) and achievement motivation (1982, 1986), as well as a number of edited volumes. More recently, there have appeared *Psychology of Coaching* by Pavel Slepicka (1985), *Achievement Motivation* by Frantisek Man (1986), *Volitional Effort in Sport* by Anton Rychtecky (1987), and *Psychology of Sport Games* by Bohumil Svoboda (1986).

Book publication can occur through the university press and is important not only for the dissemination of scientific information but also as the essential means of receiving academic promotion. So things are no different in this respect here than anywhere else in the world. Ironically current Czechoslovakian sport psychology bases itself upon Western rather than Soviet schools of thought.

The Role of Sport Psychology in Czechoslovakia

Institutions. A number of sport psychology structures are similar throughout most of the Eastern European countries. In that I had the greatest accessibility to these structures in Czechoslovakia and spent the most time there, I will elaborate them in more detail in this section and refer to this section for the other formerly Socialist countries. The basic structure, of course, is from the Soviet Union, but the means of functioning varies from country to country.

At the top of the heap is the Academy of Sciences, the body that creates the State Plan and its research directions for the various scientific fields, including the physical education subdisciplines such as sport psychology. Within the Academy of Sciences are full-time individuals who carry out only theoretical research. If these individuals also teach, they have 500 hours of research work, whereas full-time researchers have a load of 2,000 hours a year. Some types of theoretical research in sport psychology might be carried out here, but this is rare. The former director of the psychology institute of the Academy of Sciences, Miloslav Kodym, has also previously carried out extensive work in talent identification in sport psychology.

The directives from this body and the Council of Science of the Czechoslovakian Union of Physical Education and Sports channel the applied research to be carried out in the faculties of physical education and sport. This research in sport psychology is mainly through the dissertation work of graduate students or academics looking for promotion within the faculty. However, each faculty has an associated research institute; these were created in all Eastern European countries to provide for the needs of top athletes. Full-time researchers or part-time individuals borrowed from the physical education faculty carry out psychological diagnosis, clinical treatments in psychoregulation, and talent identification. Theoretical research is sometimes combined with this work, but that is most often the task of the Academy of Sciences.

Some sport psychology research can also be found in the psychology departments of the universities, which are very much separate from physical education. More cross-fertilization does now occur, however, especially since the opening of university functioning after the 1989 political revaluation.

Similar structures at the university level are found at Prague and Bratislava, where specific sport psychology chairs exist within the faculties of physical education. At the other smaller centers, eight Czech and five Slovak in all, there are chairs only in physical education and lecturers in sport psychology.

Committee of Sport Psychology. In 1953 Miroslav Vanek created a special section or committee of the Czechoslovakian Union of Physical Education and Sport (CSTV) in the area of sport psychology. This could be the oldest working group in sport psychology in the world, with the possible exception of one in the Soviet Union. However, since the political changes of 1989 the CSTV has been dissolved and the future of each component has to be redefined.

In the Western sense of the word, no sport psychology societies existed in the Socialist countries; rather they were committees. They were small groups whose members were selected by the committee. It was not open to just anyone who wished to become a member. An individual had to possess a certain amount of academic credibility as well as be able to march in turn to the prevailing political piper. The group met several times a year to discuss sport psychology research, but it did not hold open congresses as occur in the West. For example, in its 1985 FEPSAC report the committee reported holding six different seminars with between 11 and 62 invitees attending on themes such as the scope of motivational problems in top achievement sports and characteristics of the notion of mental stress. Changes will be radical in this means of functioning within the new structures that have yet to be created.

One unique feature in Czechoslovakia is the creation in 1960 of a sport psychology section of the Czechoslovakian Psychological Association that Vanek first chaired and that was subsequently chaired by Hosek. This has assured that sport psychology remains on sound theoretical underpinnings as well as receives credibility from the psychological community. This dual citizenship in sport and psychology has also been observed in the GDR and in North America. Finally, the Academy of Sciences also recognizes a small section with psychology as an applied area of concern, which gives it the ultimate stamp of approval.

One very dynamic chain of events occurred between 1973 and 1985 when Miroslav Vanek served as the successor to Ferruccio Antonelli as president of the ISSP. Vanek was able to democratize this international society by bringing new, younger players to the managing council to replace earlier pioneers who were often only political figureheads. This new dynamic allowed greater interaction between the East and the West and the spreading of sport psychology out of Europe and North America to other areas of the world. When Vanek's term finished in 1985, the Czechoslovakian sport psychology scene admittedly stagnated a bit without "Mirek" at the head. Recently, however, the next generation has caused a resurgence in sport psychology. In fact, Machak has spread the influence of sport psychology at Comenius University in Bratislava because he is prorector of this institution. In addition, another sport psychologist, Vacslav Hosek, has been named dean of the faculty of physical education and sport at Charles University in Prague. Hosek's position remained firm even after the 1989 democratization process.

Sport Psychology and Top Sport. By Western standards, the theoretical sophistication of Czechoslovakian sport psychology research may be questionable, but there is little doubt that the gap between theory and practice is relatively small. It is often stated here, as in other Eastern European countries, that the volume of research information coming from the West is simply applied to sport situations in the East. There is little need to do more, given these countries' stated priority of winning medals.

Vanek has accompanied Czechoslovakia's Olympic delegations from the Tokyo Games in 1964 through the 1980 Moscow Games as the team sport psychologist while working specifically with the ice hockey team on an ongoing basis. In addition, Svoboda has been attached to the national basketball program since 1977, and Slepicka and Hosek were respectively attached to volleyball and shooting. In most cases, however, specialists in sport psychology interact with athletes only occasionally and for limited periods for special research projects or if particular problems arise. Such voluntary relationships will probably change little in the new political environment.

Twenty sport centers for top athletes exist across Czechoslovakia, each with a resident sport psychologist. To be admitted to these live-in centers, the athletes have discussions with the sport psychologists and take various personality tests designed to weed out those who appear psychologically unstable. Once accepted into the system athletes are equipped, fed, and given full living and training accommodations.

Top athletes receive special attention at the research institutes where they can receive clinical diagnoses and learn techniques for psychoregulation as well as receive full medical, mechanical, physiological, educational, technical, and financial support. Central control over sport in this manner streamlines the procedures for achieving excellence. These centers regularly offer seminars for coaches containing psychological material, mainly on team processes and psychoregulation.

Perspectives for Sport Psychology in Czechoslovakia

The elements for the advancement of sport psychology are all in place in Czechoslovakia, and it appears that the quality of the activities rather than their initiation and implementation continues to be the main challenge. The close ties with psychology that have been established ensure that progress will advance at a controlled rate so the quality of psychological interventions do not suffer as the result of meeting short-term needs in sport. There has been an increased emphasis on perfecting clinical tools during the academic preparation in sport psychology. Some also hope that long-term study of athletes throughout and following their careers occurs in a systematic, multidisciplinary fashion to facilitate the compilation of a data bank on these individuals.

Still, the greatest need on the part of those working in sport psychology is upgrading the theoretical, experimental, and psychological aspects of their training within the physical education faculties. This should occur as the total university program is being reorganized within a democratic, westernized orientation. The existence of Potemkin villages in the area of sport psychology was not apparent to me during my visit to Czechoslovakia. These villages do exist both in the East and the West, however, but the political evolution in this and other Eastern European countries has spurred a new honesty that makes these false structures things of the past.

Hungary

in collaboration with

Pál Rókusfalvy
Hungarian University of Physical Education

Hungarian Sport Psychology Résumé

Sport psychology in Hungary is unique compared to the work in the other Eastern European countries in that it is firmly rooted in experimentally controlled laboratory research as well as in psychological support systems for top athletes.

Estimated Number of Sport Psychologists. 15

Prominent Institution. Testnevelési Föiskola, Budapest

Orientation. Experimental

Privileged Topics. Perception and talent identification

Publication Vehicle. *Testnevelési Föiskola Közlemények*

Society. Sport Psychological Section of the Hungarian Psychological Society

Hungarians are a wonderful, fiercely independent people who appear to march to the beat of a different drummer compared to their neighbors. This independence from other Eastern European traditions is evident in a broad variety of everyday life activities and filters down to their choice of sport activities and even to their orientation in sport psychology.

An observer senses something tantalizingly different about Budapest, the capital city divided by the Danube into the mountainous older section of Buda and the flat, more contemporary district of Pest. In the small, dimly lit wine cellars and restaurants foreigners can only randomly point to items on the menu written in incomprehensible Hungarian, a language distantly related to Finnish and little else. Still, these adventures always result in an intriguing blend of new tastes and textures that enchant the visitor.

The Hungarian sport tradition is also unique, with demonstrated excellence in sport activities that by North American standards are not exactly mainstream: fencing, water polo, and paddling. The domination of boxing for decades by László Papp now finds an analogy in the stranglehold that for close to 20 years first Zoltán Magyár and now Zoltán Borkai have had on the pommel horse, the most peculiar and difficult men's gymnastic event. So it is not surprising that sport psychology in Hungary does not fall into the mainstream of the sport psychology orientations that predominate in Eastern Europe. Rather than being tied to clinical consultations and the preparation of top athletes, Hungarian sport psychology is attempting to advance psychological science through controlled laboratory research. Indeed, László Nádori, former FEPSAC executive and dean of the Hungarian College of Physical Education, was elected a member of Parliament for Budapest in 1989—the first free elections since the war. Current economic liberalization will hopefully improve academic and applied sport psychology, which have deteriorated over the last 10 years of communism.

Training in Sport Psychology

The academic and sport structure in Hungary is based on the Soviet model, although the means of implementing the programs are very different. And surely the democratic elections will impact the present academic regime, introducing even greater differences or possibly complete change. But for the moment, as is the case in most of Eastern Europe, the Hungarian College of Physical Education, or Testnevelési Föiskola, is the central institute for the preparation of teachers and coaches. The college staff members and researchers have received more training in psychology departments than occurs in most other Eastern European countries.

Often graduates from the college go on to study in the Institute of Pedagogy and Psychology (ELTE) of the University of Budapest so they have both practical sport experience as well as theoretical preparation in psychology. This bridge between the two areas probably accounts for the high level of sophistication evidenced in Hungarian research. There also appears to be a greater emphasis on receiving taught courses at the postgraduate level rather than only carrying out dissertation work.

Topics of Study. In that sport psychology in Hungary was late in developing compared to the other Eastern European countries and was directed by individuals trained in psychology, it is understandable that the discipline has advanced with a strong theoretical orientation. This orientation is based to a greater extent on psychological theory rather than political ideology.

A strong thrust is in the psychophysiological domain, in which a number of perceptual and decision-making variables have been studied using athletes from different sports. Researchers measure static and dynamic peripheral vision, visual acuity, cue discrimination, and reactions to various stimuli under sophisticated and controlled laboratory conditions. The main reason for this work was to obtain the scientific data, although certain diagnostic services were offered to top-level athletes.

Another pronounced interest is the area of multidisciplinary analyses of talent identification in sport. A theoretical conceptualization of the demands of sport activity has been elaborated along with the psychological profiles that best match up with successful performance in each discipline.

Certain psychophysiological correlates of personality, such as anxiety, have also been monitored during competition in sport using telemetry techniques. Some pathological aspects of the personality structure have been diagnosed with the help of personnel from the Sport Hospital.

Publications

Although no specific publication in sport psychology exists in Hungary, many psychological articles have been published in the Hungarian School of Physical Education quarterly, *Testnevelési Föiskola Közlemények*. Other work has been published on sport in journals of psychology in impressive numbers.

Many books have been written on sport psychology in Hungarian, such as those by Hepp, Nádori, Nagy, and Rókusfalvy. However, the unique linguistic structure of the Hungarian language limits communication with other nations. Fortunately, most top Hungarian sport psychologists have multilingual skills, and their respective contributions extend across their national borders in foreign language journals. In addition, Rókusfalvy's comprehensive 1980 book, *Sportpsychologie*, which brought together research from the Soviet Union, Eastern and Western Europe, and North America, was published in German in the GDR. A number of individual research papers have consistently been presented at various international conferences in Europe and abroad based on the research at the Hungarian College of Physical Education.

The Role of Sport Psychology in Hungary

Institutions. Most sport psychology activity is centered in the capital city of Budapest around the Hungarian School of Physical Education, which plays the role of educating teachers and coaches. A number of full-time researchers and support personnel carry out their theoretical research and provide diagnostic services for the top sport teams that train in the complex. Neighboring the physical education complex is the Sport Hospital, in which physiotherapy, medical, and psychiatric services are available.

The institutional structures in Hungary are like those described in detail in the section on Czechoslovakia. A great deal of crossover occurs between the psychology departments of the university and the College of Physical Education in terms of professional exchange and interdepartmental study.

Sport Psychology Section of the Hungarian Psychological Society.

Hungary is similar to the GDR and Czechoslovakia in that its sport psychology section is part of the psychological society, not the physical culture society. But, as in the other former Socialist countries, membership in the sport psychology committee has been restricted rather than open. Annual meetings since 1981 have provided a forum for the discussion of a variety of subject areas.

For example, at the 1986 meeting papers were presented in the diverse areas of school and health psychology, attitudes toward sport, visual efficiency, gender research, psychoregulation and psychotherapy, and computer technology in sport psychology. László Nádori, Pál Rókusfalvy, and some associates have represented their country at FEPSAC and ISSP meetings as well as at congresses in different parts of Eastern Europe.

However, change is on the way. In 1989, an independent sport psychology society with open membership was created. But change may be slow. Until the country's 20% inflation rate is controlled, sport psychology may have to wait for more funds.

Sport Psychology and Top Sport.

Compared to the other Eastern European countries, Hungary does not provide as much systematic support in sport psychology for its top athletes. Though there have been sporadic attempts at clinical work with teams and individuals, this appears to be less widespread and organized than has been observed in Bulgaria and the GDR. Close contact between coaches, athletes, and sport psychologists does, however, occur through the courses in these subjects at the Hungarian College of Physical Education.

Perspectives for Sport Psychology in Hungary

The sport psychology scene in Hungary has been late in developing compared to the neighboring Eastern European countries. Deep roots in the psychology departments have resulted in an orientation that in many respects makes sport psychology in Hungary resemble the North American rather than the Socialist model for research. It appears that continued sophistication in research and theory building in sport psychology will continue to color the next few years. There has been some concern regarding reorganization of the programs so that top sport performers can receive more clinical psychological services rather than just serving as subjects for laboratory investigations.

Poland

in collaboration with

Jadwiga Klodecka-Rozalska
Institute of Sport, Warsaw

Polish Sport Psychology Résumé

Poland has had a long history of sport psychology. In recent years a greater amount of research has occurred using approaches from both the East and the West. Activity levels in both research and applied sport psychology have increased as the work climate in the country has stabilized.

Estimated Number of Sport Psychologists.   50

Prominent Institutions.
Institutes for Sport and Academies of Physical Education (Warsaw, Poznan, Krakow, Wroclaw, Gdansk, Katowice, Gorzow Wielkopolski, and Biala Podlaska).

Orientation.
Top and youth sport, rehabilitation, recreation and tourism

Privileged Topics.   Many various topics

Publication Vehicles.
Kultura Fizyczna, Wychowanie Fizyczne i Sport, Sport Wyczynowy, Biology of Sport

Society.
Sport Psychology Section of the Polish Scientific Society of Physical Culture (ISPS-PTNKFI)

The tourist brochure for Warsaw told the whole story: ''You must come at night to see the spectacular Sound and Light Show at the Royal Palace. But it was not necessary in Warsaw to be introduced to this new French technology. Over our history, we have witnessed on our doorsteps our own brand of sound and light shows.''

There is a wry fatalism about the people of this nation that has served as the battlefield for the rest of Europe throughout the ages. The tanks roll in, the bombs fall, and Warsaw is flattened. Then the old town photographs and plans come out, and the city is reconstructed, stone by stone, until an exact replica stands in the same place. Sport psychology has had a long history in Poland. But this history, as everything else, has been interrupted by the activities of the wars.

Solidarity's first appearance was crushed in the early 80s by military communist rule. But in 1989, Solidarity won the first free elections, and now the new market economy is struggling to regain lost ground. Understandably, sport at the elite level has been downplayed but mass participation in sport for health is better funded.

Evidence of sport psychology publication dates back to 1899 when Piasecki, a medical doctor, applied known psychological principles to physical education. From 1907 to 1926 Jarosynski wrote about the role of sport psychology in physical education with special reference to emotional control and character development. Before World War II, three academies of physical education were created in Warsaw (1929), Poznan (1919), and Krakow (1927). The Warsaw Akademia Wychowania Fizycznego (AWF) was not the first created but remains the biggest and perhaps the most influential in Poland.

Today the AWF in Warsaw is one of the largest academies of this type in the world. This is all the more remarkable because it also was completely demolished after World War II. The AWF brochure mildly understates its case when it says that the war "interrupted the activities of the Academy" when in fact its research institute, laboratories, gymnasiums, sport facilities, and book collections were destroyed. Sport psychology in Poland always has to be put within this context of destruction and rebuilding. The work tensions experienced at the end of the 1980s have now eased, especially in academia, and robust activity levels are now combined with serious reflection on new directions in the field.

Training in Sport Psychology

In 1979 the AWF in Warsaw celebrated its 50th anniversary, dating back to its earliest institutional form as a 2-year vocational school in physical education. This was increased to a 3-year course in the 1930s that was equivalent to a university degree. During World War II clandestine physical education classes were also organized in Poland, and teachers' courses were even carried out in officers' prisoner-of-war camps. In 1946 the courses were again reopened despite the mass reconstruction of the didactic and sport facilities.

The postwar period brought into place the Soviet model of physical culture, with the creation of various departments and chairs in 1952. In 1954 the present 4-year master's degree was introduced and its curriculum is similar to that outlined in the Czechoslovakian section. Within the options of physical education, coaching recreation, tourism, and rehabilitation, students get course work in the areas of developmental psychology, sport psychology, and clinical psychology, respectively. Students cannot yet pursue specialized study in a sport psychology concentration with taught courses. Rather, an individual either does postgraduate studies within a psychology faculty and chooses sport as the subject of study, or, since 1959, studies in the AWF for a doctorate in physical education. The lack of interdepartmental

mobility in Poland and in any other Socialist country prevents students from doing simultaneous study in sport and psychology faculties.

Some individuals, such as Jacek Gracz, Jadwiga Klodecka-Rozalska, Marek Wielochowski, Tadeus Rychta, and Teresa Raczkowska-Bekiesinska have studied in both faculties, but this requires at least 8 years of training at this level and then from 5 to 10 years to complete a doctorate. The academic steps have been described in the Czechoslovakian section.

Poland was an important source of sport psychology information in the 1981 edition of this book, because this country contributed by far the greatest number of questionnaires (33) of any of the Socialist countries. In this respect, they had the strongest collective socialist voice for suggesting how their training procedures might be improved. Of the 29 respondents who wished to change something in their training, 48% said they wanted more practical experience integrated into their academic preparation. It is significant that 45% hoped to have increased experimental, laboratory, and specialized theoretical training in sport psychology. A smaller percentage (17%) wanted more clinical work in psychotherapy, and others wanted increased knowledge and contact with foreign research and scholars (10%). Finally, some expressed the desire to increase academic mobility to shorten study programs to a more reasonable period.

Since the initial survey many of these recommendations have been acted upon. For example, in 1984 at the 25th Jubilee of the Polish Psychological Society, a special session was devoted to how to upgrade the image of sport psychology from the viewpoints of both general psychologists as well as from sport participants.

Topics of Study. Polish research is well developed not only in sport psychology but also in the other areas of sport science. Within the academies of physical education (AWFs) and the Institute of Sport, multidisciplinary research has occurred in a major longitudinal twin study designed to evaluate the inherited and environmental components that contribute to sport performance as well as in a number of other major projects. Polish sport scientists are also world-renowned in biomechanics, physiology, and sociology.

In a publication summarizing the research in Poland, Geblewicz, Nawrocka, and Rychta outlined four areas of concentration in Polish sport psychology research. The first area is applied psychomotor learning. Researchers have carried out a great deal of work on the role of attention during the learning and performance of athletic movements.

The second concentration is the study and control of mental states during the prestart phase of competition. The Polish scientist Rotkiewicz was one of the first researchers to introduce autogenic training into the field of sport. Related work on concentration processes and resistance to stress was also initiated in Poland.

The third emphasis borrowed from Soviet research on the personality of athletes and making the best match between this dimension and specific sport activities, along with work in individual differences, temperament, and psychophysiology of sport. Finally, the Poles have adopted certain North American trends in their study of sport in the areas of preference, sport motivation, self-efficacy, psychoregulation, and psychosocial aspects of physical activity. Poland admittedly borrows approaches from the East and the West to profit from the best of both directions of knowledge and practical experiences.

The scientific components at the different academies are now entering into increasingly complex interactions between sports and between sport science disciplines. Common research projects are being conducted between sport activities on a single psychological dimension such as emotional states, or need for achievement. There is also a tendency toward interdisciplinary research on a single problem such as talent identification or peaking to evaluate the relative importance of the various sport sciences for each sport.

Publications

Although no specific sport psychology periodical exists in Poland, at least three well-known journals publish sport psychology articles: *Kultura Fizyczna, Sport Wyczynowy, Wychowanie Fizyczne i Sport*, and, most recently, *Biology of Sport*, in English. Researchers can also publish in institutional journals at each of the eight physical education academies.

In addition to the long line of individual research published since the 1920s, a few thematic overviews in sport psychology have also been published in Poland: Korolczak-Biernacka's *Activity and Behavior of Sportsmen in Difficult Situations*; Dracz's *Psycho-social Conditions of Tennis*; Czajkowski's *The Tactics and Psychology in Fencing*; Staworska's *Psychological Diagnostics in Top Sports*; Zdebski's *Psychology of Mountaineering*; Olszewska's *Outline of Work Psychology and Rest*; Zmudski's *Reactivity Levels and Success During Start Periods of Weightlifters*; Rychta's *Personality of Sportsmen*; and finally, Pieter's classic *Urgent Problems in Sport Psychology*. In addition, the well-known journal *International Review of Sport Sociology* is also published at the AWF in Warsaw.

The Role of Sport Psychology in Poland

Institutions. The institutional setup in Poland is similar to that found in the other Socialist nations. Major academies of physical education appear in Warsaw, Krakow, Wrotaw, Gdansk, Katowice, Poznan, and Biala Podlasky along with a number of affiliates in smaller centers. Elsewhere, Poland created a scientific sport institute for multidisciplinary study of top-level sport, similar to the research institutes found elsewhere. The first Research Institute of Physical Culture (1953–1971) was created in Warsaw and professors of the academy carried out the initial work on a volunteer basis. At present the department of psychology of the Institute of Sport in Warsaw, which was created as an independent scientific institute in 1977, is working within the Five-Year Research Project for Sport (1986–1990) related to psychoregulation, youth sport, cognitive and motivational processes, personality and talent identification,

selection in sport, psychomotor learning, temperament, evaluation in sport, and adaptation to physical effort.

Sport Psychology Section of the PTNKF. There is no special subdiscipline for sport psychology in the Polish Psychological Association as exists in the German Democratic Republic and Czechoslovakia, although sport psychology sessions are included in the annual meetings of the Polish Psychological Society, which has 2,000 members.

In addition, the Polish Scientific Society of Physical Culture (PTNKF) created in the early 1970s a special sport psychology section (SPS) that became active after the 1977 ISSP Congress in Prague. This section included as members about 50 psychologists and a larger group of about 100 teachers and coaches. The SPS has set the official objectives of spreading the word of achievements of sport psychology theory and practice, initiating cooperative research in Poland and internationally, and organizing forums for the exchange of information.

The SPS has also begun to organize monothematic meetings in the major centers of Poznan, Krakow, and Warsaw on subjects such as emotions, personality, social psychology, recreational problems of rest, and psychoregulation. The Polish delegate, Wilstoria Nawrocka, was also present at the inaugural meeting of FEPSAC in 1969 in Vittel, France, and has continued to participate in annual international meetings of FEPSAC and the ISSP. At the 7th Congress of FEPSAC in Bad-Blankenburg, Jadwiga Klodecka-Rozalska was elected to the managing council of FEPSAC.

Sport Psychology and Top Sport. Since the 1964 Tokyo Olympics, Polish specialists in sport psychology have been working in conjunction with top athletes, either directly within the clubs or at the sport academies. The main emphasis for these interventions has been developing forms of psychoregulation such as autogenic training. The scientific departments work in both diagnostic and clinical aspects of top sport performance. Those athletes who qualify to be financially supported with food, accommodations, training, and education at one of the academies also have psychological support services available.

Poland under Solidarity approaches sport in more measured fashion. While communist Poland all but ignored sport for the masses, the new Poland funds sport-for-all projects. However, it also seeks to maintain the pinnacle of elite athletics: Solidarity cut jobs for sub-elite athletes while continuing to support those at the top.

Such aid is given at the discretion of the coach and in turn is a function of the coach's confidence in the sport psychologist. Athletes are administered a wide variety of paper-and-pencil as well as perceptual motor laboratory tests to provide diagnostic profiles for analysis. Trained clinical psychologists are also available for psychoregulation sessions and general counseling.

Polish academics have tried to improve the image of sport psychologists who work with top-level athletes. For example, in 1984 Dominiak wrote an article in *Sport Wyczynowy* questioning some practices entitled ''Sport psychology—science, technique or quackery.'' Further discussion, especially in the mass media, has been directed toward realistic expectations for sport psychology and top-level sport. This sort of self-analysis indicates the presence of a healthy evolution of the field in Poland. As it has been observed elsewhere and is again outlined in this country, psychologists who have no background in sport have difficulty integrating into the sport environment because they do not understand the prerequisites for performance and do not speak the same language as the athletes.

There are now attempts to integrate one sport psychology specialist into each of the top teams, especially for the Olympic sports. At the moment, sports such as basketball, modern pentathlon, volleyball, tennis, fencing, boxing, judo, wrestling, table tennis, cycling, gymnastics, rowing, and shooting have sport psychology support.

Perspectives for Sport Psychology in Poland

In that Poland is a very liberal country by Eastern European standards, the central directives for control are not as apparent as in more orthodox societies such as Bulgaria or Romania. This has resulted in increased academic freedom and a diversity of research and intervention that is unique. The quality is definitely there, and more attention to the broad-based implementation of a sound mixture of theory and practice is underway.

As in so many other dimensions of Polish life, the sport programs are in a continuous process of rebuilding and attaining solidarity, and sport psychology in this light is no different.

Romania

Romanian Sport Psychology Résumé

Sport psychology is an essential concern of an interdisciplinary team of sport scientists who are directing their efforts to the achievement of top sport performance. However, recent political and economic problems have severely hampered their effective action.

Estimated Number of Sport Psychologists.   14

Prominent Institution.   Institute for Sport and Physical Culture, Bucharest

Orientation.   Multidisciplinary support for top athletes

Privileged Orientation.   Psychoregulation

Publication Vehicle.   None

Society.   Sport Psychology Committee

My expectations were high before entering the country that produced Count Dracula in the 16th century and Nadia Comaneci in the 20th. Aside from the fictitious accounts of Dracula's blood-sucking activities in the Transylvanian Alps, it was also discovered that he really did rid the country of thieves and gypsies. Nadia, in turn, rid the world of stereotypes as to the degree to which young female athletes could achieve sport perfection.

It became evident upon visiting Bucharest why sport perfection could be achieved in this nation of 25 million people. Romania has an eccentric approach to most things in life, including sport and sport psychology. Romania takes the best features of the Soviet sport model and adapts them to its own system without blindly accepting all dimensions. Romania formerly maintained open communication channels in sport not only with countries that are ideologically acceptable by Soviet standards, but also with taboo nations such as Israel and China. Thus, all doors used to be open to this country.

However, the brutal overthrow and execution of the Ceausescus threw the country further into an economic and political tailspin. The neo-communist government elected in 1990 has further isolated Romania in Eastern Europe.

The history of sport psychology in Romania dates back to 1932 when Zapan studied the learning capacities of athletes and nonathletes. A chair in sport psychology existed with the implementation of the Soviet system in 1948. During this first period from 1948 to 1955 methods and fundamental concepts were elaborated. The next phase, from 1955 to 1962, was an experimental one that revolved around the evaluation of the theoretical strength of the earlier work. The final era from 1962 into the 1980s was one of production in sport psychology through the publication of books and articles. Underlying the academic development of sport psychology was the application of this information within an applied framework.

Priorities for sport excellence are quite clear in Romania, as are the directives of how sport psychology should be integrated into this process. Sport psychology is a tool used in conjunction with the other sport sciences to win medals. This is similar to the policy statements in this area for Bulgaria, and the Soviet Union.

Training in Sport Psychology

The study profile for a future sport psychologist in Romania is similar to that described in the section on Czechoslovakia. However, additional data on entering the university program from secondary school is presented to complement the standard socialist profile.

The people who teach and practice sport psychology in Romania all came through the psychology department. This has resulted in individuals working in the field who have good theoretical backgrounds in psychology but often little situational experience in the sport environment. However, a number of leading figures in Romanian sport psychology have earned double qualifications, first in sport and later in psychology. This is somewhat more difficult to accomplish now because of tighter restrictions on academic mobility.

Any graduate from secondary school must take an aptitude test before admission to the university. In psychology this evaluation is in the areas of political philosophy, history, biology, and psychology. Students gain entrance to the Institute of Physical Culture by taking a pass-fail physical aptitude exam, a pass-fail medical exam, a pass-fail test of specific sport mastery, and an exam in biology. Both streams take 4 years of university study; however, students cannot pursue a doctorate in the Institute of Physical Culture, though it is possible in psychology.

A graduate in psychology could find employment possibly in an Institute of Physical Culture or at a research institute. An individual who has some degree of success at this institute can apply for doctoral studies. This system provides the following advantages: (a) An individual is assured of a position after graduation, (b) a candidate has already demonstrated promise for future work, thus allowing the dead wood to be filtered out, and (c) it is more likely that the candidate will do graduate work in an area that is immediately relevant to sport practice.

Although no sport psychology courses exist within psychology departments, students can take some postgraduate courses through the Institute for Physical Culture. Since 1965 all coaches and physical education students have received specialized courses in sport psychology, sport pedagogy, and skill acquisition.

Topics of Study.   Although early sport psychology research and writing was based on the theoretical reactions of teaching and top-level performance, this has changed in recent years to a more pragmatic approach. Romania has adopted a focus on top-level performance and its maximization, similar to the focus of Bulgaria and the Soviet Union.

Mihai Epuran can be credited with changing in 1951 the theoretical conceptualization of sport psychology in the Socialist countries from ''moral volative preparation,'' as advanced by the Russian A.T. Puni, to ''psychological preparation.'' Moral-volative training is a heavily loaded ideological term that unites the orthodox communist idea of striving to do well for the system through sport

achievement. Psychological preparation, however, is a more integrated term that includes the cognitive, affective, and volitional dimensions of performance.

The interdisciplinary nature of applied research is an important feature of Romanian sport psychology. The procedure begins with forms of psychodiagnosis and continues through personality and intelligence testing and evaluations by other specialists in physiology and medicine. Some psychological or, if necessary, psychiatric counseling is available at the research institutes. But most practical interventions are in the area of psychotonic training; that is, relaxation and activation.

Using cybernetic models, Epuran and Horghidan have conceptually developed research on systems for learning and teaching basic skills. Holdevici has proven useful a battery of psychodiagnostic tests for the selection of young talent for high-level sport. Moscou's work with anxiety of sports participants in competitive situations has been published both within and outside Romania and the Eastern European countries. Other research on the psychological makeup of the coach and referees by Stanculescu has been particularly interesting.

Publications

No specialized sport psychology publication is available, although articles of a psychological nature are often published in a general physical education journal. Although Epuran has published a total of nine books and edited another two over a 30-year period, his 1968 book *Psiholigia Sportolui* is considered the classic.

The Role of Sport Psychology in Romania

Institutions.   The standard Soviet model in sport organization has been implemented in Romania and used to advantage. The educational division is in the Institutes for Physical Culture, and here coaches and teachers receive information on sport psychology. A scientific unit is also situated in either the Academy of Science or the Pedagogical and Psychological Research Institute, and a practical component that comes from within the Research Institute is designed as a support system for top athletes. All of these components are interrelated. There is also some sharing of personnel, equipment, and information resources in this system. Other support personnel are available in electronics, equipment, or construction, depending on the task at hand.

Sport Psychology Committee.   The supreme voice in Romanian sport, the National Committee for Physical Culture and Sport, has a coordinating commission for scientific work. One of the committees it coordinates is the Sport Psychology Committee, which has existed since 1968. The committee is made up of eight sport psychologists and coaches who meet periodically for methodological meetings. No conferences or symposia are held, presumably because in a centrally governed country where most of the activity is in one city, everyone knows what everyone else is doing.

Sport Psychology and Top Sport.   Sport excellence pays great dividends in Romania as it has in the rest of the Socialist countries. Although the collectivity of the nation certainly benefits from success in Olympic Games through the reflected glory the political system receives, it is common knowledge that successful coaches and athletes get their share of material wealth. Nadia Comaneci reportedly received five cars and a house for her success at the Olympic and world-championship levels. Release from military duty can accompany outstanding sport performances. All of this is no secret and may be the ultimate motivational stimulus for athletic achievement. But more importantly, it is the support system potential and the material wealth over the long preparation period that succeeds in Romania, rather than the on-the-spot desire to win at the moment of competition. And in Romania, this long-range preparation is at its best.

Sport federations have access to whatever sport science support they want, but not all sports select sport psychology support. However, it is strongly implanted in gymnastics, swimming, shooting, athletics, rowing, weight lifting, handball, water polo, and soccer. If a sport federation wishes to have increased scientific or sport psychology support, the following steps occur in Romania, and presumably elsewhere in Eastern Europe.

First, a team makes contact with a sport psychologist and a financial contract for services is drawn up. The athletes are observed in training and competition and the psychologist holds discussions with the coaches. An interdisciplinary team then carries out diagnostic evaluations in all areas of the sport sciences, including certain measures of personality and intelligence. Clinical sessions on appropriate training and competition behaviors along with sessions in group dynamics occur. Then the most important sessions in psychotonic training are carried out for 3 months. This begins with Schultz's autogenic training using self-perceptions of heaviness and warmness to induce and monitor achievement of relaxation. This is followed by different forms of self-hypnosis for emotional control in competitions.

In certain cases, the sport psychologist uses hypnosis to maximize rehearsal strategies on difficult individuals. Holdevici reported that in a group of shooters who were tested using the Harvard scale of hypnotic suggestibility, the best and the most intelligent shooters were most easily hypnotized. The word hypnosis, however, is replaced by the term "deep relaxation" so the athletes do not feel threatened. In more informal settings, athletes often freely contact the sport psychologist to discuss personal problems.

Some restrictions, however, are put on the psychological interventions that occur with the athletes. First, most of the testing has occurred with lower level athletes. There is a tendency not to "fool around" with top-level athletes too extensively, because they often use their own effective "naive" self-control strategies. Second, sport psychologists try not to attribute success directly to these techniques, because a failure may result in athletes' rejection of them. Rather, the techniques are introduced as one of many forms of help that is available if requested.

Another of Romania's innovative support dimensions is the inclusion of a methodics specialist on the sport science team. This individual is a general sport technician trained in the Institute of Physical Culture who understands both sport science and the sport activity. This person's task is to observe, calculate, and present to the coach in summary form various dimensions such as amount of work time, emotional behaviors, rates of success/failure, or other measures appropriate to the objectives of the program.

The coach, of course, is the central figure and can take or leave the advice of the methodics specialist or any other sport science personnel. If, however, the coach refuses to take the advice and the team or athlete continues to fail, the coach can be strongly criticized.

Perspectives for Sport Psychology in Romania

Romania has cut a clear path of where it wants to go in terms of athletic excellence. The role that sport psychology is to play in this adventure is quite explicit. Earlier work in more fundamental areas of psychology has tried to build a foundation for the present situation. The people now in place are running hard, but are moving faster than the bureaucratic forces that tend to bottleneck their progress.

The future of the area of sport psychology lies, as do most things, within the context of the social demands of the country during this dark period in Romanian history. The people currently in charge hope that despite present economic hardships and political turmoil, greater advances will more than counteract small steps backward and that more emphasis will be given to youth education, youth guidance in sport, and even more applied research.

Soviet Union

in collaboration with

Valdimir M. Melnikov
Institute for Physical Culture, Moscow

Soviet Sport Psychology Résumé

Sport psychology in the Soviet Union is a highly institutionalized movement directed toward athletic performance enhancement through applied research and clinical intervention as well as a broad base of empirical research. Programs instituted in this country have served as the model for the other Socialist countries.

Estimated Number of Sport Psychologists.   200

Prominent Institutions. Leningrad Scientific Research Institute for Physical Culture, Moscow Central Institute for Physical Culture

Orientation.   Assistance of top athletes

Privileged Topics.   Personality psychograms, psychoregulation

Publication Vehicle. *Teoriia i praktika fizicheskoi kultury*

Society.   USSR Sports Psychology Federation

Before the revolution in Russia, there was practically no scientific research in physical education and sport. In 1909, however, Leningrad scholar P.F. Lesgaft outlined the necessity for developing children to harmonize perceptions of time, space, and motor patterns. Immediately after the revolution, the State Central Institute for Physical Culture opened, and a mechanism for the training of specialists in physical education was implemented in the Soviet Union. This system would later serve as the model for many other countries in Eastern Europe. The intensity of efforts in applied sport psychology increased during the 1950s and 1960s when the Soviet Union again appeared on the international sporting scene. During this period greater investments in research institutes were made and analogous structures were also implemented within the other Socialist nations. Now with *glasnost* and *perestroika* the future of the discipline is less clear.

Training in Sport Psychology

The academic preparation system described in detail in the section on Czechoslovakia derives directly from the system that was first established in the USSR. During the 1930s and 1940s, the basics were established at the main Institutes for Physical Culture in Moscow and Leningrad. These centers later spread across the Soviet Union so that there are now 25 institutes of physical culture and 56 pedagogical institutes. During the 1950s, the Research

Institutes were also established to generate new knowledge in the area of top sport performance.

A student is permitted entry into an institute of higher learning after taking entrance examinations in physics, chemistry, Russian language and literature, and demonstration of physical education aptitude. The degree of physical aptitude required of the candidate varies with the prestige of the school. Admission to the pedagogical institute requires good health and general physical development and level 1 of the GTO badge. The GTO badge is a sport classification certification that was started in 1930 and stands for "Ready for Labor and Defense." Entrance to an Institute of Physical Culture requires the preceding qualifications in addition to a second-class GTO rating; that is, a time of 11.5 seconds for the 100-meter run, or a 2-hour, 56-minute marathon.

Candidates wishing to study at the prestigious Moscow State Institute for Physical Culture require a first-class GTO rating; that is, a 11.0-second 100-meter run or a 2-hour, 40-minute marathon. The program of study takes 4 to 5 years and includes psychology in each year. During teaching practicums in the first year, the students are given certain tasks that include familiarization with certain psychological states that affect performance, such as high levels of anxiety. Second-year students take a 140-hour theoretical course that deals with general psychological principles, developmental psychology, pedagogy, and certain elements of sport psychology. In the third year, a course of social psychology of sport is given that requires a research project using different subject samples. Finally, in the last year students give attention to demonstrating how psychological practice must change as a function of different sport demands. Final oral examinations at the end of the program are taken in the areas of Marxism-Leninism, theory of physical culture, physiology, and a specialized subject, which could be in sport psychology. No academic degree is awarded, such as a B.A.; rather, graduates earn the title of *prepodavatel*, meaning teacher or instructor.

Exceptional students can enroll in a postgraduate department, or *aspirantura*, at either a university or an institute of physical culture of research. Entrance exams again include political philosophy, a foreign language, and an exam in the student's specialty, such as sport psychology. During this 3 years of study the student must pass more advanced exams, termed the candidate minimum, in dialectical and historical materialism and in his or her specialty. The candidate must complete and publicly defend the dissertation, demonstrating both new findings of a scientific and practical nature and the candidate's ability to carry on independent research. The academic degree, candidate of science (C.Sc.), is then awarded with the proviso that the student master completely the Marxist-Leninist philosophy while participating actively in political and educational work. Candidates can also carry on these studies by means of correspondence courses. However, the percentage of dissertations successfully completed is somewhat lower for those taking correspondence courses (52%) as compared to those in regular programs (77%). The C.Sc. is equivalent to a North American Ph.D.

Individuals can also take a special postgraduate or postdoctoral 4-month course in psychotherapy at the Kharkov Institute of Physician's Perfection. The doctor of science (D.Sc.) can be awarded to individuals holding the C.Sc. or the title of professor who have publicly defended a dissertation based on collected works, or a completed original textbook. An individual can also earn the title of professor or dotsent, the equivalent of associate professor or senior lecturer, through this advanced scholarship.

Finally, all degrees and academic titles are approved by the Higher Certification Commission for the Ministry of Higher and Secondary Specialized Education. The commission may not approve an awarded degree and can even revoke degrees and titles in cases where the candidate's works have not been of concrete use in the field of research, or if the works do not have value for science and production. A number of students from Eastern European countries as well as from China, India, Cuba, and Algeria have also completed programs of study for advanced degrees. A number of Soviet scholars have also taught for extended periods in various developing countries.

Topics of Study. All research topics fall within the 5-year plan of the Committee of Physical Culture and Sport and the Committee for the Science and Technology of the USSR Council of Ministers. For example, from 1971 to 1975, one plan involved all 25 institutes for physical culture and a total of approximately 4,500 pedagogical-research staff, among whom were 84 doctors of science and 1,093 candidates of science. It can be assumed that these numbers are higher now, so it is clear that the scientific preoccupations of the state profit from this immense work force.

One of the major preoccupations of Soviet research has been the establishment of athletic psychograms, or representations of an ideal psychological personality profile for a given sport. Fieldwork on athletes' behavioral stability using various reliability measures is carried out in both training and competition. Indexes of cooperation and obstruction of teammates have been compared during competition and training using behavioral techniques. Development of appropriate personalities is important not just for sport performance, but also for being a complete member of society.

The other major emphasis in Soviet research is in the area of the psychological preparation of athletes for competition. This includes work in psychoregulation, decision making, and tactical preparation. Examples of this last type of research can be seen in Puni's (1980) book, *Sport Psychology*, that was recently translated into English. Much of this work can be used as reference studies for research in skill acquisition and perception in sport.

Melnikov has outlined the trend that will occur in Soviet sport psychology research from now until the year 2000. Though the dominant themes of the athletic personality and psychoregulation will be maintained, greater emphasis will be put on the educational and social benefits of participating in sport and physical education through lifestyle changes of the ordinary person.

Publications

No single journal exists for sport psychology in the Soviet Union, but a significant number of psychological publications appear in the classic periodical that sets the model for those in the other Socialist countries, *Teoriia i praktika fizicheskoi kultury*, and the *Psychological Journal of the Academy of Sciences of the USSR*.

In a review article on sport psychology that appeared in the *Journal of Soviet Research*, Rodionov reported in 1979 that nearly 2,000 works were published between 1971 and 1975 in the area of sport psychology. Most of these publications are data based, though some of them are of the ideological-political rather than empirical scientific variety.

Hanin reveals that the translated works of North American publications are also very popular in the Soviet Union. He tells of how 45,000 copies of Vanek and Cratty's *Psychology of the Superior Athlete* sold out in 10 days, and the same is expected for books by Martens, Nideffer, and Singer that will also soon be translated and published.

Many books that are published annually are printed in large quantities and still sell out quickly. Of the current group of active researchers the most prominent works are by Melnikov and Yampulsky (*Introduction of Experimental Psychology of Personality*), Filatov (*Emotional and Mental Preparation of Athletes*), and Plakhtienko and Bludov (*Systemic and Structural Analysis of Sport*).

The Role of Sport Psychology in the Soviet Union

Institutions. The basic institutional structure explained in the section on Czechoslovakia finds its master pattern in the Soviet Union, but to a much greater degree of implementation. Whereas two to five Institutes of Physical Culture are the rule in most Socialist countries, the Soviet Union has 21, and 56 pedagogical institutes. These institutes educate and prepare teachers and coaches. Sport psychology specialists have heavy teaching loads at these centers and do some research as well.

Most other research occurs at the Research Institutes, where the staff members are relieved of teaching duties. The institutes in Moscow and Leningrad are well known and thus tend to attract the best people. However, centers with proven research capacity also exist in Kiev, Vologograd, Cheliabinsk, Alma-Ata, and Erevan.

USSR Sports Psychology Federation. As in the rest of the Socialist countries, there is a sport psychology committee to which members are appointed depending on their academic or scientific competence. Up until 1987, this committee organized a variety of scientific events at different locations in the Soviet Union. Normally, two or three hundred specialists in the field would attend to listen to lectures or present papers. The structure of the group has now changed into a federation format, whereby a number of local associations are under the umbrella of the USSR Sports Psychology Federation. The late Victor Plakhtienko became chairman of this new federation in 1988 and then suddenly passed away the next year. It is hoped that the new structure will facilitate communication.

Sport Psychology and Top Sport.

Khudadov reported in 1977 that ideal performance models are constructed for individuals and team sports that include important psychological dimensions. These models are translated into diagnostic evaluations that include a number of complexes, or factors of psychological variables that are evaluated in laboratory or "nonspecific" environments. During training, telemetry is used to monitor psychological states, whereas direct behavior observation is used in competition. Using these blocks of information, the athlete's psychogram can be diagnosed for potential areas in which remedial clinical work can be carried out if required.

Individuals in sport psychology are trained in clinical aspects within specific sports using known psychological techniques developed in the laboratories or taken from the literature. Rodionov reported in 1977 the use of psychoregulatory techniques, relaxation, activation, hypnosis, self-hypnosis, and imagery. These techniques are well known in the West but are thoroughly applied and used in the Soviet Union. Presently, small bio-feedback apparatus are commonly used during training, and their use by Soviet and other Socialist athletes was reported during the Moscow Olympics.

One final noteworthy point in the clinical use of sport psychology concerns the education of the coach in these techniques. The sport psychologist only rarely makes any direct intervention with the athletes. Direct intervention occurs only when the coach or athlete specifically requests it in a difficult problem area. The sport psychologist is an accepted part of the training and competition process due to the longstanding tradition that has united science and sport.

Perspectives for Sport Psychology in the Soviet Union

Sport psychology in the Soviet Union has always held a position as one of the leading and most promoted of the applied branches of the psychological sciences. The complex structure of the research institutes and the institutes of physical culture at a large number of centers in the Soviet Union, all with sport psychology units, makes it the biggest integrated national network in the world. However, the size of the country and regional particularities make communication a major problem.

It is anticipated that the next years will produce more of what has taken place in the past. Large national programs will focus on selected sport psychology topics. But some people also feel that *perestroika*, or the new openness, will also affect sport psychology. Future concerns will be directed not only to top-level athletes, but also to the common good of the recreational sport participant.

Yugoslavia

in collaboration with

Ljubisa Lazarevic
Faculty for Physical Culture, Belgrade

Yugoslavian Sport Psychology Résumé

Sport psychology in Yugoslavia is still in a state of relative infancy in comparison to its Eastern European neighbors. Although analogous structures are in place, implementation of procedures has been very slow in coming.

Estimated Number of Sport Psychologists. 15

Prominent Institutions.
Institute for Physical Culture (Belgrade), Faculties for Physical Culture (Belgrade, Zagreb, Novi, Sad, Ljubljana)

Orientation. Support for top sport

Privileged Topics. Psychoregulation, psychodiagnostics, counseling

Publication Vehicles. *Sportska Praksa, Fizicka Kultura, Kineziology*

Society. None

Yugoslavia was guided by its leader Marshall Tito until 1980 on a careful course that straddled the fence between socialism and capitalism. Though the structures on the surface once wore the trappings of the system from the East, scratching a little deeper reveals that most of the functions are similar to those of the West.

This is also true in the area of sport and sport psychology. The Soviet-inspired system of Institutes of Physical Culture, Research Institutes, and "physical culture" publications are all in place here.

Training in Sport Psychology

The educational system is not based exactly on the Soviet model outlined in the Czechoslovakian section. There are some similarities, however, because in a number of institutes and faculties of physical culture psychology plays an important role. At these institutes both independent and interdisciplinary research is carried out, along with the preparation of top athletes and the education of teachers and coaches. Some recent limitations have been placed on the preceding activities because of limited financial resources dedicated to sport science.

People working in sport psychology have first been trained within a university program of study in a psychology department. Their study is then completed specifically in sport psychology within the institutes for physical culture, the main centers being in Belgrade and Zagreb.

Doctoral dissertations have been carried out in a number of applied areas of sport psychology within departments of both psychology and physical culture. A unique feature of Yugoslavian education is that a number of locally trained Yugoslavian experts have left the country and taken teaching jobs abroad in more favorable conditions. Travel restrictions both in and out of Yugoslavia are by far the most liberal of the Socialist countries. This is also true for most other dimensions of Yugoslavian life. This more relaxed brand of socialism may result in an increased amount of individual freedom, but it is not conducive to the optimal development of sport psychology in the future. The number of individuals working in sport psychology is relatively low, which may reflect a lesser interest in athletic excellence in the country as a whole. Perhaps Yugoslavians do not feel the need to prove themselves on the sport fields, believing instead that there is just not enough to be gained by these investments in sport science.

Topics of Study. Research does occur in sport psychology within the Faculties for Physical Culture, the Institute for Physical Culture, the Research Institutes, the institutes for mental health, and the universities. Because there is a freer exchange of information with the West, many of the subject areas sound like Western terminology: "competitive anxiety" is used rather than "prestart state," and "stress management" rather than "energy mobilization."

The research is limited in quantity and fairly mainstream by Eastern European standards. The topics of personality of sports participants and coaches, psychoregulation, and motivation in sport predictably lead the field.

Publications

Seven journals in sport science and sport practice have been the main means of communicating sport psychology information in Yugoslavia, *Sportska Praksa* and *Kineziology* being the two national publications. In addition, a version of *Fizicka Kultura* is published in each of the federal republics (Belgrade, Skoplje, Titograd, Novi, and Sad).

A number of books treating diverse areas of sport psychology have been written in Yugoslavia, with those by Lazarevic, Paranosic, Bacanac, Momirovic, and Stefanovic the most prominent.

The Role of Sport Psychology in Yugoslavia

Institutions. The Faculties for Physical Culture prepare coaches, teachers of physical education, and specialists in rehabilitation. Study up to the doctoral level can occur within this system. Promotion and academic degrees are identical to those described in the section on Czechoslovakia. Specialized research is carried out at the research institutes, and preparation of top-level athletes occurs at the Institute for Physical Culture with all the appropriate support services and monitoring devices for top-level athletes, including counseling in sport psychology.

Society. Yugoslavia is the only Eastern European country that does not have a special committee for sport psychology. The relatively small number of people involved in sport psychology, a floundering educational system, and lack of funds explain this situation.

Sport Psychology and Top Sport. Although the Research Institute in Belgrade and various Faculties for Physical Culture provide evaluation services for the top teams that request their aid, the volume of business is considerably lower than that in the more conventional Socialist countries. Lazarevic and Bacanac have, however, accompanied Olympic delegations and have worked with a number of top Yugoslavian athletes.

Perspectives for Sport Psychology in Yugoslavia

It appears that Yugoslavia's course steered away from mainstream socialism has given everyday life a different, relaxed flavor not seen elsewhere in Eastern Europe. This free and easy attitude seems to have been transmitted to the perspective on sport, sport science, and sport psychology. Due to the restrained number of employed sport psychologists in the country, the field is somewhat stagnant. Work continues in the areas of research, coach education, and direct intervention with various teams. Still, the precarious position of sport psychology will be determined by economic restraints placed by the government on science and education.

Part II

INTERNATIONAL FIGURES IN SPORT PSYCHOLOGY

Chapter 10

THE WORLD WHO'S WHO IN SPORT PSYCHOLOGY

One of the fundamental necessities in the professional development of an emerging discipline such as sport psychology is communication. Within one's own country it is relatively easy to keep up to date on what colleagues are doing in other parts of the country in terms of writing, researching, and counseling.

Usually the lines of communication are quite accurate, though not always direct; in professional circles the rumor grapevine is exceedingly fast-moving and surprisingly accurate. The speed of communication often results from the competitiveness in academic circles fed by traces of professional envy. Communication is exceptionally rapid following the rejection of an article for publication, a negative decision regarding promotion or tenure, the presentation of a lackluster paper at a conference, or worse, inexcusable fumbling on a question following a presentation.

This Who's Who is for those people who need information on people in the field but do not have the advantages of close circles of sport psychology grapevines, physical proximity to colleagues, computerized information-retrieval systems, access to travel funds, or multiple language skills.

The World Who's Who in Sport Psychology was conceived as a tool to facilitate human communication around the world in sport psychology. To accomplish this, I created individual profiles with a sufficient number of elements that permit someone interested in a specific item in the area of sport psychology to localize this item or individual and to make contact by either physical, electronic, or postal communication.

Format of the Who's Who

The structure of the individual profiles was formulated in the following manner:
La Fong, Carl H.,[1](Ph.D.)[2], Faculty of Sport Psychology; Verdun University, 513 Richard Avenue, Verdun, Quebec[3], Canada[4], (514-768-5076)[5], (514-768-5077)[6], LAFONG@UMTLVR.BITNET[7], E,F(s), G(R,W)[8]; Group dynamics, cooperative games, humor[9]

Guide

1. Family name, given name, and initials
2. Highest academic degree
3. Address label
4. Country
5. Telephone number
6. Fax number
7. Electronic mail address
8. Language skills
9. Key words

Certain clarifications of each of the nine points in the guide will permit their most efficient use.

1. Family and Given Names. Entries in this section begin with the individual's surname or family name followed by the first or given name along with the initials. The addition of the given names where possible is a change from the last edition, which used only initials. This was an attempt to further personalize the Who's Who.

In the case of entries from certain Arabic and Asiatic countries that put the surname before the given name, the surname is still reported in the preceding manner. Thus, Professor Ma from China would be addressed as Professor Ma Qi-Wei.

2. Academic Degree. Entries in this field were restricted to what was judged to be the highest academic degree earned by the respondent. In cases where the highest degree was unknown, two were included. Inconsistencies occurred when the highest degree was unknowingly omitted and a lower one chosen. Respondents sometimes inaccurately judged the equivalence of earned degrees, such as Cand. psych., and what they believed to be a North American equivalent, such as M.Sc. or Ph.D.

3. Address Label. This entry is made up of the second, third, and fourth lines of the address label, excluding the country. The variations in the length of entries for this dimension are the result of my inability to determine the essential or redundant aspects of the address. Japanese entries in particular have long address labels that are difficult to shorten.

4. Country. In cases where a country is known by different names, the name used was chosen in accordance with what the majority of respondents from that country used. Prefixes such as ''the dominion of'' or ''the people's republic of'' were dropped, except for the two Germanies.

5. Telephone Number. The telephone number was entered, sometimes with the inclusion of locals and extensions. In certain cases, area codes for countries are either present in separated or fused form, or absent. Users are advised to determine area codes for specific cities through overseas or long-distance telephone information services before calling.

6. Fax Number. The same caveats apply to use of fax number as to use of phone number. Many entries have no fax number.

7. Electronic Mail. A number of individuals now use electronic mail, or E-mail, to communicate instantly via the various international institutionalized computer networks such as BITNET in North American and EARN in Europe. This cheap, efficient system requires that the user have a user address (e.g., LAFONG) as well as a physical address (e.g., UMTLVR for the University of Montreal VAX Research System) joined together by the "at" sign (@).

Those individuals who do not yet have access to an E-mail network should first of all contact an institution with a computer link for electronic mail. Most universities and many government agencies with mainframe computers have access to an E-mail network. Once this contact is made, the person wishing to be part of the network must have a specific address created to receive mail from anywhere in the world. At present the most efficient way of being part of an international network is to send a message to the E-mail network of the Association for the Advancement of Applied Sport Psychology at the following address, and you can then send and receive messages to anyone in the network within hours. E-mail address: SPORTPSY@TEMPLEVM.BITNET

8. Language Skills. Entries in this category reflect both the individual's nominal language skills as well as the degree of proficiency in each language. Full competency in a language is represented by the code letter (s) for that language followed by a comma. Partial competency in the language is represented by the code letter followed by specifications in parentheses in the following manner: Reading skills (R), speaking skills (S), and writing skills (W). Seldom-cited languages are reported fully, such as Kisswahili, Turkish, and Thai. Codes were assigned to the most frequently found languages as shown in Table 10.1.

Table 10.1 Who's Who Language Codes

A	= Arabic		
AFR	= Afrikaans	K	= Korean
ARM	= Armenian	L	= Latin
B	= Bulgarian	M	= Mandarin
BS	= Bengali	MA	= Malay
C	= Czechoslovakian	N	= Norwegian
CA	= Catalan	PU	= Punjabi
CAN	= Cantonese	POL	= Polish
CHI	= Chinese	POR	= Portuguese
D	= Dutch	R	= Russian
DAN	= Danish	ROM	= Romanian
E	= English	S	= Spanish
F	= French	SC	= Serbo-Croatian
FIN	= Finnish	SE	= Serbian
FL	= Flemish	SO	= Sotho
G	= German	SAN	= Sanskrit
GAELIC	= Gaelic	SLOVAK	= Slovak
GRE	= Greek	SLOVENE	= Slovene
H	= Hungarian	SW	= Swedish
HEB	= Hebrew	T	= Tamil
HI	= Hindi	U	= Ugboshi
I	= Italian	UK	= Ukranian
IN	= Indonesian	UR	= Urdu
IND	= Indian	W	= Welsh
J	= Japanese	Y	= Yoruba

9. Key Words. This entry provided respondents with the opportunity to recall five key words that best characterize their work in the psychology of sport and physical activity. Modifications were made to certain entries due to translation difficulties, such as "bringing up" changed to "development"; consistent usage, "elite sport" changed to "top sport"; and consistent length of entries, such as "motor learning with children" changed to "motor learning" and "children" as separate entries. I attempted to standardize key words using as a guide the German BISp's *European Inventory of Sport Research Projects* (1970–1977) edited by Hans Fleischer in Cologne.

The Compilation of the Who's Who

The present Who's Who was compiled based on the original 858 entries that were included in the first edition. These entries were maintained in a data base and updated as people moved from one institution to another. In addition, an individualized mailing was sent to all the 1981 entries so they could make any changes to their Who's Who data. A blank entry form appeared regularly in *The Sport Psychologist* as well as in a number of national sport psychology newsletters. Finally, Who's Who forms were often present in the registration packages at various national and international congresses.

In addition to this process of continual updating, Human Kinetics performed one final update of the entries. Any entry preceded by a star (★) was flash-updated as of January, 1991.

How Can You Best Use the Who's Who?

The Who's Who in Sport Psychology was first conceived as a coercive means of encouraging people around the world to reply to the initial survey. It has turned out to have the potential to be much more. The two major functions that come immediately to mind are communication and retrieval.

Communication. One of the most difficult tasks I had in organizing the survey and the interview was determining how to contact these people. There now exists a list of people from many countries who have taken the time to cooperate with me, and now with you, by completing their forms. This already seems to be a good selective factor for contacting people who take time to complete professional tasks, such as replying to this survey. Here are some ways you may not have thought of to use this list for communication:

For Mass Communication. If you have a conference, a meeting, a book, or a paper that you want people to know about, send your information to the people in the Who's Who. A number of sport psychology publishing houses will have self-stick labels already made up with these entries. Or make up your own labels.

For Special Interest Communications. By scanning through the interest areas of those in a specific geopolitical area, you can access a subpopulation of people interested in one of the same areas as you. You can then cross-reference these selected entry numbers with another of your key words, and you will get a smaller subgroup with two interests in common with you. Obviously you'll have a much larger group if your key words are "personality" and "competition" then if you cross-reference "heroes" and "orienteering."

If these people selected by your sorting process can read your language, you can send them a reprint, letter, or holiday greeting. If they speak your language, you can telephone or E-mail them. This is also a useful tool for those who wish to set up sabbatical trips abroad.

Retrieval. It is often important to be able to rapidly dig up specific information in a given area without having to seek computer access. Here are a few ways to retrieve information that could prove useful:

For New Areas. Those people who always like to be on the fringe or in the avant-garde of sport psychology can always look for key words that are cited only one or two times. If the entry number leads you to a little-known sport psychology person, you're on the fringe; if it's a sport psychology heavyweight, you're avant-garde.

For Well-Trodden Areas. This might be a useful tool for a graduate student wishing to find an area, and an associated name to reference, in the mainstream of sport psychology that offers a small niche to fill with a thesis. First pick a broad area that your advisors might feel comfortable with, like mass media, and then cross-reference it with an obscure key word such as gambling, and the search leads you to Garry Smith.

For Conference Speakers. It is often difficult to select an appropriate conference speaker who knows a specific topic and speaks the right language. If the topic is narrow enough and you've done your cross-referencing, you're in business!

For Social Comparison. People are often interested, for purely personal reasons, in just what their colleagues want others to think they are doing. Now you know!

For Visual Identification. A number of entries have been complemented with photos. This will allow you to attach a name to a face and help to personalize these people's sport psychology contributions.

Publisher's Preface to the World Who's Who in Sport Psychology

As noted in the author's preface, this international who's who of sport psychologists emerged from a lengthy process of gathering and verifying data from professionals worldwide.

To the names listed in the 1981 edition we added the myriad entries of professionals who responded to advertisements in journals and newsletters and at scholarly gatherings across the globe. Then we sent the personal data of each entrant to him or her to verify the information.

The resulting data fell into three categories:

- Those who responded with corrections to their entries.
- Those who responded without corrections, or who received the letter but did not respond (implying that their entries were correct).
- Those whose letters were returned undeliverable due to incorrect addresses.

Assuming the reliability of the mail system to return undeliverable mail, we treated data as correct in either of the first two categories. Those addresses that proved undeliverable are noted with an asterisk: They are the last known addresses for these professionals, for whom current information is unavailable.

We are confident of the reliability of the resulting information. However, in the rapidly changing world of sport psychology, such a comprehensive list as this is bound to need continual updating. With your cooperation, we can keep your data current in future editions.

Algeria

Bachir-Cherif, Ammar (M.Sc); I.S.T.S.—Alger, Dept. of Social Sciences, Cite des Asphodeles Bat C1 Appt. 13, Ben-Aknoun, Alger, Algeria 16030 (Q132-781583); F,A,E,R; Nervous System, Anxiety, Self-Control, Basketball, Reliability

Argentina

Cabera, Hector C. (B.Sc.) Psychiatrist; Argentine Society of Sport Medicine, Dept. of Social Psychology, Hipolito Irigoyen 1942, Buenos Aires, Argentina 1089; E,S; Stress, Control, Hypnosis, Soccer, Therapy

Escudero, Ernesto (B.Sc.) Psychiatrist; Argentine Society of Sport Medicine, Dept. of Sport Psychology, Jose Luis Cantilo, Buenos Aires, Argentina 3288; E,S; Stress, Control, Top Athletes

Pereiro, Graciela (M.Sc.) Psychologist; Calle Inglaterra 3380-1712 Castelar Pcia, Buenos Aires, Argentina; S,E(S,R); Young, Athletes, Evaluation, Stress, Control

Pondal, Eduardo R. (M.D.) Medical Doctor; Calle Alem 357, Buenos Aires, Argentina; E,S; Sport Injuries, Psychopathology, Athletes

Soslaver, Pedro C. (M.Sc.) Psychologist; Universidad Nacional de Tucuman, Centro de Investigacion Sociologicas, Casilla 164, S. Miguel de Tucuman, Argentina; POR,S,E(S,R); Group Dynamics, Evaluation, Children, Athletes

Australia

*Abernethy, Bruce (Ph.D.) Senior Lecturer; University of Queensland, Dept. of Human Movement Studies, Queensland, Australia 4072 (07-377-3885); E; Vision, Expert Perception, Motor Control, Decision Making, Cognition

*Anderson, Ian J. (M.A., B.Ed., Dip.P.E., T.S.T.C.); Ballarat University College, Dept. of Human Movement and Sport Science, Gear Ave, Mt. Helen, Australia (053-339687); E; Motivation, Arousal, Competition, Personality, Mental Preparation

Anderson, M.B. (Dip.P.E.); Caulfield Grammar School, Dept. Physical Education, 217 Gleneira Rd., East St. Kilda, Australia (528-6544); E; Competition, Motor Skill, Coaching, Psychology, Sociology

*Anshel, Mark H. (Ph.D.) Associate Professor; University of Wollongong, Dept. of Human Movement Science, Wollongong, New South Wales, Australia 2500 (042-270-023, 042-270-486); E; Stress Coping, Warm-Up Decrement

Badenoch, D.C. (Dip.Ed.); Hartley College of Advanced Education, Dept. of Human Movement Studies, Lorne Ave, Adelaide, South Australia, Australia (332-4711); E; Education, Meaning, Recreation, Leisure, Outdoor Education;

*Barras, Neil S. (M.Ed.) Senior Lecturer; Phillip Institute of Technology, Dept. of Human Movement Studies, Plenty Rd., Bundoora, Victoria, Australia (468-2349, 467-3174); E; Eye Movements, Visual Search

Bingham, Ross (Dip.P.E.); University of Queensland, Dept. of Human Movement Studies, Mill Road, Brisbane, Queensland, Australia (07-377-37885); E; Motor Memory, Attention

*Bond, Jeffrey W. (M.A.) Sport Psychologist; Sport Psychology Department, Australian Institute of Sport, P.O. Box 176, Belconnen, Australia, 2616 (06-252-1236, 06-252-1603); E; Applied Sport Psychology, Attention, R.E.S.T., Biofeedback, Hypnosis/Imagery

*Boutcher, Stephen H. (Ph.D.) Professor; Dept. of Human Movement Science, University of Wollongong, P.O. Box 1144, Wollongong, New South Wales 2500, Australia; E,F; Stress, Exercise, Emotion, Mental Health, Attention

Brewer, Robert; P.O. Box 515, South Melbourne, Victoria, Australia 3205

*Couzner, B.N. (M.Ed., B.A., A.U.A, Dip. T., Dip.Ed.); University of South Australia, Dept. of Physical Education, Salisbury Campus, Smith Road, Salisbury East, Australia (259-2213); E; Learning, Motor Skill, Information Processing

*Crampton, John (B.Sc.) Consultant, Performance Enhancement Systems, P.O. Box 3142, Parramatta, NSW, 2124, Australia (02-630-8394); E; Preparation, Management, Control, Cognitions, Golf

*Davey, Colin P. (Ph.D.) Head, Dept. of Physical Education; Victoria College, Rusden Campus, 662 Blackburn Road, Clayton, 3168, Victoria, Australia (542-7372, 544-7413); E; Arousal, Anxiety, Personality, Motivation, Self Hypnosis, Elite Athletes

Davis, Ken H. (Ph.D.) Lecturer; Deakin University, School of Education, Geelong, Victoria, Australia; E; Post Performance Stress, Mental Preparation, Nonverbal Behavior, Control, Tennis

*Dillon, John M. (B.A. (Hons.)) Psychologist; Private Practice, 46 Armstrong St., Hermit Park, Townsville, Queensland, 4812, Australia (077-213967); E; Goal Setting, Motivation, Group Cohesion, Basketball, Imagery/Hypnosis

Douglas, D.R. (Ed.D.); Flinders University, Dept. of Education, Sturt Road, Bedford Park, South Australia, Australia (275-2446); E; Physical Activity, Young Children, Development, Cognitive Psychology

Evans, J.R. (Dip.P.E.); Deakin University, School of Education, Geelong, Victoria, Australia (789966); E; Youth Sport, Motivation, Competition

Fitz-Gerald, R.J. (Dip.P.E.); Dept. of Health and Physical Education, P.O. Box 179, Coburg, Victoria, Australia (350-4222); E,F(R); Competition, Motivation, Aggression, Social Facilitation, Top Athletes

*Glencross, Denis J. (Ph.D.) Professor; Curtin University, School of Psychology, P.O. Box U1987, Perth, West Australia, Australia 6015 (09-351-7279, 09-351-2464); E; Skill, Performance, Cognition, Coaching

*Gordon, Sandy (Ph.D.) Lecturer; University of Western Australia, Dept. of Human Movement Studies, Nedlands, Western Australia, Australia 6009 (380-2361, 380-1039); E; Performance Enhancement, Group Dynamics, Stress, Sport Injuries

*Grove, J. Robert (Ph.D.) Senior Lecturer; University of Western Australia, Dept. of Human Movement and Recreation, Nedlands, Western Australia, Australia 6009 (619-380-2361); E; Motivation, Emotion, Attributions, Exercise, Baseball

*Halbert, John, A. (M.A., B.A., Dip. P.E., Dip. T., MBE) Head, School of Physical Education; University of South Australia, School of Physical Education, 2 Ingrid Street, Clapham, South Australia, Australia (223-8911); E; Skill Acquisition, Children's Sport, Motivation

Hickman, D.C. (Ph.D.); La Trobe University, Dept. of Sociology, Bundoora, Australia (479-2120); E; Self-Concept, Organization, Competition, Ideology, Commitment

Highland, P.D. (Dip.P.E.); Kelvin Grove College of Advanced Education, Dept. of Physical Education, Victoria Park Road, Brisbane, Queensland, Australia (356-9311); E,F(R,W); Motor Skill, Motivation, Competition, Teaching, Coaching

Horsley, Christopher S. (B.Ec., B.Sc.) Sport Psychologist; Australian Institute of Sport, P.O. Box 176, Belconnen Act, Australia 2600 (521253); E; Performance Enhancement, Clinical Sport Psychology, Attention

Kapelis, Lia (Ph.D.) Senior Lecturer; Flinders University, Dept. of Psychology, Bedford Park, Adelaide, Australia 5042 (08-275-2377); E,G,L; Hypnosis, Mental Training

*King, Ronald C. (Ph.D.) Professor; University of Wollongong, School of Learning Studies, P.O. Box 1144, Wollongong, NSW, 2500 Australia (042-270-733, 042-270-089); E,S; Cognition, Expectations, Role, Learning

Lally, J. (Ph.D.); Australian National University, Dept. of Sociology, Box 4, G.P.O., Canberra, New South Wales, Australia (062-494521); E,F(R),S(R); Competition, Motivation, Goal Setting, Peaking

Lee, Christina (Ph.D.) Lecturer; University of Newcastle, Dept. of Psychology, Newcastle, NSW, Australia 2308 (049-685479); E,G,F(R),I(R); Recreation, Health, Psyching Up, Gymnastics, Maintenance

Lockwood, Richard J. (Ph.D.); University of Western Australia, Dept. of Human Movement and Recreation Studies, Nedlands, Western Australia, Australia (380-2366); E; Skill Acquisition, Motor Control, Handicapped

*Martin, Catherine Registered Psychologist; South Australian Sports Institute, Sport Psychology Unit, P.O. Box 219, Brooklyn Pk., South Australia, Australia 5032 (08-352-8877, 08-354-0595); E; Applied, Elite, Enhancement, Hypnosis, Coach

*Martin, Michael B. (M.A.) Consultant; Science Works International, 219 President Ave., Miranda, New South Wales, Australia 2228 (02-524-9568); E; Applied, Intensification, Control Strategies, Pedagogy

Maschette, W.E. (Ph.D.); Rusden College of Advanced Education, Dept. of Physical Education, 662 Blackburn Road, Clayton, Victoria, Australia (544-8544); E; Attention, Visual Perception, Sport, Performance, Motor Learning

*McKenna, James G. (B.A.) Psychologist; Institute of Child Guidance, Queensland Health Department, P.O. Box 68, Spring Hill, Brisbane, Queensland, Australia, 4006 (07-831-9161); E; Anxiety, Concentration, Mental Rehearsal, Athletics, Swimming

McLean, N.J. (M.A.) University of Western Australia, Dept. of Psychology, Nedlands, Western Australia, Australia 6009 (380-2644); E,F(R); Attitudes, Motivation, Counseling, Relaxation, Imagery

Middleton, M.R. (M.A.); Narrabri High School, Dept. of Physical Education, Gibbons Street, Narrabri, Narrabri, Australia (067-921633); E,F(R); Competition, Organization, Coaching, Fitness, Participation

Napier, Sue D. (M.A.) Lecturer; Tasmanian State Institute of Technology, Center for Physical Education, P.O. Box 1214, Launceston, Tasmania, Australia (003-260512, 263-664003); E; Motivation, Cognitions, Emotions, Attentional, Styles

Bruce Abernethy   **Denis J. Glencross**

Nettleton, Brian (Dip.P.E.); Melbourne University, Dept. of Human Movement Studies, Parkville, Victoria, Australia (341-5413); F,E; Research Methods, Sociology, Ball Skill, Tracking, Individual Differences

O'Donohue, Terrence M. (B.Sc.) Consultant Psychologist; 43 Janet Street, Merewether, New South Wales, Australia 2291 (631759); E; Assessment Evaluation, Skills Training, Stress Management, Motivation Attitude Change, Rehabilitation

Owen, Neville (Ph.D.) Senior Lecturer; University of Adelaide, Community Medicine, P.O. Box 498, Adelaide, Australia 5001 (61-8224-5135); E; Exercise, Prevention, Self-Management, Adherence

Parker, Helen E. (Ph.D.) University of Western Australia, Dept. of Human Movement and Recreation Studies, Stirling Highway, Nedlands, Western Australia, Australia (380-2361); E; Skilled Behavior, Learning, Perception, Information Processing, Perceptual Motor Development

Parsons, D.R. (Ed.D.); Newcastle College of Advanced Education, Dept. of Physical Education, P.O. Box 84, Waratah, New South Wales, Australia (671-388354); E,R; Learning, Performance, Coaching, History, Administration

Raine, C.A. (M.Sc.); Kelvin Grove College of Advanced Education, Dept. of Physical Education, Victoria Park Road, Brisbane, Queensland, Australia (356-9311); E,F(R); Women's Sport, Aggression, Arousal, Attitudes, Anxiety

*Robertson, Ian D. (M.Sc.) Lecturer; University of South Australia, Magill Campus, Dept. of Physical Education, Magill, South Australia, Australia 5072 (08-333-9411); E; Youth Sport, Elite Athletes, Socialization, Mental Skills, Peak Performance

Rose, B.A.; University of Western Australia, Dept. of Human Movement Studies, Stirling Highway, Nedlands, Western Australia, Australia; E; Play, Children, Creativity, Interaction, Dance

Saunders, John (D.L.C.); University of Queensland, Dept. of Human Movement Studies, Brisbane, Queensland, Australia 4061 (377-3958); E,F; Skill, Teaching, Learning, Pedagogy

Schembri, H.D. (B.A.); MacQuarie University, Dept. of Education, North-Ryde, New South Wales, Australia 2113 (888-8000); E; Pre-Adolescent, Competition, Culture, Families, Females

Seedsman, T.A. (Dr.); State College Frankston, Dept. of Education, McManons Road, Frankston, Australia (781-1777); E; Anxiety, Competition, Personality

*Sheedy, Jim. D. (M.A. (Hons.)); P.O. Box 301, Willoughby, New South Wales, Australia 2068 (02-412-4560); E; Imagery, Skill, Coaching, Judo, Sports Medicine

Shirling, George (B.A.(Hons.)) Private Consultant; 5 Curlew Camp Rd., Sirius Cove, Mosman, NSW, 2088, Australia (02-969-6286, 02-968-1666); E,G(S); Sports, Performance, Hypnosis, Motivation

Smith, R.G. (Dip.P.E.); Rusden State College, Dept. of Physical Education, Blackburn Road, Clayton, Australia 3168 (544-8544); E; Motor Skill, Performance, Coaching

*Spinks, W.L. (Ph.D.); University of Technology, Sydney (Kuring-Gai Campus), P.O. Box 123, Broadway, NSW 2007, Australia (413-8110, 416-5533); E; Evaluation, Leadership Behavior, Cohesion, Youth Sport

*Summers, Jeff (Ph.D.); University of Melbourne, Dept. of Psychology, Parkville, Victoria, Australia (03-344-6349, 03-347-6618); E,F(R); Motor Control, Timing, Skill, Attention, Top Athletes

*Thomas, Patrick R. (Ph.D.) Senior Lecturer; Griffith University, Brisbane, Queensland 4111, Australia (07-892-2027); E; Learning, Strategies, Performance, Enhancement, Metacognition

*Tremayne, Patsy A. (Ph.D.) Lecturer; University of Western Sydney, Macarthur, P.O. Box 555, Campbelltown, New South Wales, Australia 2560 (569-5479, 02-774-3649); E; Anxiety, Performance Enhancement, Psychophysiology, Cognitions

*White, Jack (Ph.D.) Clinical Psychologist; Hillcrest Hospital, Dept. of Psychology, Box 233, Greenacres, 5086, South Australia, Australia, (08-266-9211, 08-2614092); E; Imagery, Confidence, Athletic Coaching, Performance Measures

*Wilks, Robert L. (M.A.) Psychologist; Sports and Preventive Medical Centre, P.O. Box 160, South Yarra, Victoria, Australia 3141 (3-866-5897); E; Strength, Performance, Cognition, Coaching, Competition

Willie, A.W. (Ph.D.); University of Melbourne, Dept. of Human Movement Studies, Parkville, Victoria, Australia (341-5407); E,F; Methodology, Fitness, Comparative Physical Education, Skill

*Winter, Graham J. Senior Psychologist; South Australian Sports Institute, Sport Psychology Unit, P.O. Box 219, Brooklyn Park, South Australia, Australia 5032 (08-352-8877, 08-354-0595); E; Applied, Peaking, Hypnosis, Elite, Performance

*Wood, Graeme A. (Ph.D.); The University of Western Australia, Dept. of Human Movement Studies, Nedlands, Western Australia, Australia 6009 (09-380-2360); E,G(R); Timing, Fatigue, Reflexes, Motor Control

Austria

*Bachleitner, R. (Dr.) Professor; Universitaet Salzburg, Institut fuer Sportwissenschaften, Addamiestr. 26, Salzburg, Austria 5020 (8049-4851); G,E(S,R); Attitudes, Personality, Sponsoring

*Etlinger, Susan C. (Ph.D.) Assistant Professor; University of Vienna/Institute of Psychology, Dept. of Neuropsychology, Liebiggasse 5, A-1010 Vienna, Austria (0222-40103-2987); E,G,F(R),R(S,R); Psychophysiology of Erroneous Behavior, Emotions, Visual Perception, Subcortical Cognition, Bilingualism

*Fenk, A. (Dr.Phil.Doz.); UBW, Universitaetsstrasse 67, Klagenfurt, Austria A-9022 (04222-23730); E,G; Coaching, Information Processing, Skiing

Guttmann, Gisheler (Prof.Dr.) Professor; Universitut Wein, Institut fuer Psychologie, Liebiggasse 5, Wein, Austria A-1010 (0222-40103-2983); E,G,L,SAN; Angre; DC-Potentials, Ergopsychometry, Stress, Hypnosis, Information Theory

*Lackner, Karin B. (Ph.D.) University Assistant; University of Klagenfurt, Dept. of Psychological Basic Research, Universitatsstr. 65-67, A-9010, Klagenfurt, Austria (0463-5317-532); E,F,G; Motivation, Group Dynamics, Organization, Counseling

Preisinger, J. (Dr.); Floriangasse 521J, Wein, Austria 1080 (422351); E,G; Coaching, Relaxation, Teaching

Weingarten, Paul (Ph.D.); Universitaet Wein, Psychologisches Institut, Liebiggasse 5, Wein, Austria 1010 (431364); G,E; Clinical, Coaching, Top Athletes, Psychmetrics, Concentration

Belgium

*Bardaxoglou, Nicole (Licence psych., Licence Physical Education); Clos banken 4, 1080 Bruxelles, Belgium (2-468-0853); E,F; Psychomotricity, Orthopedagogy, Development, Children Ball Plays and Ball Games

*Barroo, Ignace V.C. (Licenciat) Clinical psychologist; Prinsenlaan 31, Ostend, Belgium 8400 (059-805920); G,E,D,F; Football, Self-Control, Visualization, Management

*Beunen, G.P.C. (Ph.D.); K.U. Leuven, Instituut Lichamelijke Opleiding, Tervuurse Vest 101, Heverlee, Belgium B-3030 (16-201431, 16-201460, FLAAAZO6@BLEKUL11); E,F,G,D; Motor Development, Biological Age, Fitness, Kinanthropometry

Boutmans, J.J.; K.U. Leuven, Tervuurse Vest 101, Heverlee, Belgium B-3030 ; E,F,G,D; Motor Learning, Coaching, Learning Strategies, Methodology

*Buekers, Martinus J.A. Associate Professor; Dept. of Kinanthropology, Tervuursevest 101, Heverlee, Belgium B-3030 (016-201431); FL,E,F, G,D; Motor Learning, Volleyball, Coaching

De Loof, M.M.; Tulpenlaan 59/Deelyk, Ver. Bew. Psychologie, Wagnerstraat 31, Brugge, Belgium 8320 (050-357177); E,F,G,D; Stress, Anxiety, Group Dynamics, Piaget, Outward Bound

Dirix, A. (Dr.); Universiteit Leuven, Instituut Lichamelyke, Tervuusevest 101, Leuven, Belgium B-3030 (031-761179); E,F,G(S,R),D; Sport Medicine, Toxology

Lefebvre, Luc (Ph.D.); Belgische Veirinigung/ Bewegungspsych., School Straet 13, Deerlik, Belgium B-8740 (056-719214); E,F,D,G(R); Stress, Interaction, Aggression, Extraversion, Outward Bound

Meuris, G. (Dr.); Universite Catholique de Louvain, Faculte de Psych. Etudes Sci. de l'Ed., Voie du Roman Pays, 20, Leuven, Belgium B-3030 (010-418181); E(R,W),F,D; Pedagogy

*Pauwels, Jan-Maria (Dr.) Professor; Leuven, Instituut Lichamelijke Opleiding, Tervuurse Vest 101, Belgium 3030 (016-222310, 016-201460); E,F,G,D; Learning, Training, Perceptual Motor Skills

*Swinnen, Stephan P. (Dr.) Professor; K.U. Leuven, Instituut Voor Lichamelyjke Opleiding, Tervuure Vest 101, Heverlee, Belgium B-3030 (016-222310, 016-201460, FLAAA15@BLEKUL11); F,FL,D,E(S,W), G(R); Motor Learning, Motor Control, Interlimb Coordination

Van Coppenolle, H. (Ph.D.); Berkstraat 22, Kortenberg, Belgium B-3070 (016-222370); E,F,D, G(S,R); Coaching, Anxiety, Relaxation, Personality, Psychomotor

*Van Dam, Francis I. (Lic. Psych.) Test Editor, Professor; Institut Libre Maries, Haps (Universite Catholique de Louvai), ATM, 15 Sentier Castiaux, Braine le Chateau, Belgium 1440 (02-3669768); E,F,N,L; Stress, Impairment, Cognition, Interaction, Tests

*Vanden Auweele, Y.M.E. Lecturer; K.U. Leuven, Tervuurse Vest 101, Leuven (Heverlee), Belgium B-3001 (222310); F,G,D,E(W); Body Image, Anxiety, Personality, Mental Training, Motivation

Vanden Eynde, Eric (Ph.D.); K.U. Leuven, Tervuurse Vest 101, Heverlee, Belgium B-3030 (016-222310); E,F,G,D; Coaching, Stress, Motivation, Training, Athletics

Vanfraechem-Raway, Renee (Dr.) Professor; Universite Libre de Bruxelles, CP 168, Laboratoire de l'Effort, Ave. Paul-Heger 28, Bruxelles, Belgium B-1050

Vanhille, L. Assistant; K.U. Leuven, Tervuurse Vest 101, Heverlee, Belgium B-3030 (016-222310); E,F,G,D; Coaching, Basketball, Decision Making, Uncertainty, Behavior Observation

Wielke, C. Professor; Universite Catholique de Louvain, Faculte de Medecine, Pl., de Coubertin 1, Louvain-La-Neuve, Belgium 1348 (010-418181); E,F,P,R(S); Personality, Training, Competition, Autogenic Training, Volleyball

*Wylleman, Paul R.F. (M.Sc.) Assistant Professor; Vrije Universiteit Brussel, H.J.L.O.K., Pleinlaan 2, Brussels, Belgium 1050 (02-641-2744, 02-641-2899, Z27801@BBRBFU01); D,F,E,G; Top Athlete, Psychological Guidance, Youth Sports, Judo, Stress Management

Brazil

Bagatini, Vilson (B.Sc.) University Teacher; FAERS, Dept. of Physical Education, Av. Parana 1950 Apt. 21, Porto Alegre, RS, Brazil; E,POR; Special Child, Physical Activity Programs

Barbanti, Eliane J. (Ph.D.) Psychologist; Sao Paulo University, Dept. of Physical Education, Rua Joao Della Manna 381, Sao Paulo, Spaulo1, Brazil 05535; E,POR; Athlete, Elevation, Children, Training, Mental

Barreto, Joao A. (M.Sc.) Psychologist; VERJ University, Dept. of Psychology, Av. Epitacio Pessoa 3744, Lagoa, Rio de Janeiro, Brazil; E,POR; Judo, Mental, Training, Counseling, Group

Baum, Vera B. (B.Sc.) Psychologist; Feevale, Dept. of Physical Education, Av. Maueico Cardo, Novo Hamburgo, RS, Brazil 50510; E,POR; Young, Athletes, Evaluation, Counseling, Therapy

Becker, Benno (M.Sc.) Psychologist; UFRGS State University RGS, Dept. of Psychology, Protasio Asbes, P. Alegre, RS, Brazil 279/20 (0512-310754, 90.610@RS); E,POR; Stress, Control, Therapy, Counseling, Aggression

Becker, Sergio (M.D.) Medical Doctor; Feevale University, Dept. of Physical Education, Rua Casemiro de Abreu 755, Porto Alegre, RS, Brazil 90410 (0512-315146); G,E(S,R),POR; Recreational Programs, Children, Rehabilitation

Becker, Terezinha (M.Sc.) University Teacher; Feevale University, Dept. of Psychology, Rua Casemiro de Abreu 755, Porto Alegre, RS, Brazil 90410; E(S,R), POR; Children, Sport, Training, Pedagogy, Programs

Brandao, Regina F. (B.Sc.); Celafics, Sports Psychology, Caixa Pastal 268, S. Caetano Do Sul, Brazil (011-852-5214); E, S(S,R); Exertion, Stress, Cognition, Volley, Self-Concept

Castro, Odair P. (M.Sc.) Psychologist; VFRGS, Dept. of Psychology, Rua Felizardo 750, Porto Algre, RS, Brazil (360988); E,POR; Evaluation, Tests, Group Dynamics, Counseling

Castro, Vanderlei (M.Sc.) Psychologist; Catholic University, Dept. of Psychology, Goiania, Goias, Brazil 74.000; POR, E(S,R); Stress, Control, Program, Youth Sport, Athletes

Cauduro, Maria T. (M.Sc.); Feevale University, Dept. of Physical Education, Av. Mauricio Cardoro 510, Novo Hamburgo, RS, Brazil 50510; POR, F(S,R); Dance, Corporal, Language, Education, Rhythmic

Cavasini, Sandra M. (M.Sc.) Psychologist; University S. Caetano Sul, Dept. of Physical Education, Rua Rafael Correa Sampaio 1034, S. Caetano Do Sul, Sao Paulo, Brazil (09500); E,POR; Children, Group Dynamics, Counseling, Therapy

Durante, Rosa Maria (B.Sc.) Psychologist; Centro de Estudos da Crianca, Dept. of Psychology, Rio de Janeiro, Brazil (200.000@RJ); E,S,POR; Physical Therapy Programs, Special Child

Enck, Luis C. (B.Sc.) Physical Education Teacher; Tenni Center P. Alegre, Rva Mal. Simeao 25 Sao Joao, Porto Alegre, RS, Brazil (0512-427050); E,S,POR; Stress, Control, Tennis, Top Athletes, Athlete

Gesatsky, Rolf E. (M.Sc.) Psychologist; Catholic University of Goias, Dept. of Psychology, Pca Setor Universitario, Goiania, Goais, Brazil 74.000; G,POR,E(S,R); Young Athletes, Stress, Control, Evaluation

Leal, Joao P. (B.Sc.) Psychologist; Porto Alegre Institute, Dept. of Psychology, Rua Mal. Floriano, Porto Alegre, RS, Brazil 91/504; POR,E(S,R), S(S,R); Sport, Evaluation, Tests, Group Dynamics

Leal, Pedro A. (Ph.D.) Psychologist; Catholic University, Dept. of Psychology, Rua Mai. Floriano, Porto Alegre, RS, Brazil 91/502; POR,E(S,R); Social Psychology, Group Dynamics, Soccer

Lopes, Fernando (B.Sc.) Psychologist; UFRGS, Dept. of Psychology, Rua Felizardo 750, Porto Alegre, RS, Brazil 90610 (0512-360988); E,POR; Group Dynamics, Mental Preparation, Soccer

Moraes, Luis L.C. (M.A.) Assistant Professor; Federal University of Minas Gerais, Dept. of Physical Education, Campus Universitario, Pampulha-BH, 31310-MG-Brazil (031-4410409); E,POR,S(R); Anxiety, Stress Reduction, Motivation, Attention Control, Concentration

Moura, Santana (B.Sc.) Psychologist; Dept. of Psychology, Rua Cladio Brotherhood 332, Cordeiro-Recife, PE, Brazil; Por, E(R); Group Dynamics, Counseling, Therapy, Child

Negrine, Airton (M.Sc.) University Teacher; State University, Dept. of Physical Education, Rua Felizardo, Porto Alegre, RS, Brazil 750 (0512-360988, 90610@RS); POR, E(S,R); Children, Motor Learning, Disabilities, Programs

Oliveira, Ivan B. (B.Sc.) Psychologist; SEED-MEC, Dept. of Psychology, SDS Edif. Venancio, VI Sala 514, Brasilia, DF, Brazil; POR,E(S,R); Physical Education, Administration, Child Development

Peterson, Ricardo D. (Ph.D.) University Teacher; UFRGS University, Dept. of Physical Education, Rua Felizardo 750, Porto Alegre, RS, Brazil (0512-360988 90610); POR,E; Motor Learning, Child Development

Philippi, Eliane A. (M.Sc.) Psychologist; E. Clube Pinheiros, Dept. of Psychology, Rua Das Camelias, Sao Paulo, SP, Brazil (04048); POR,E; Athlete, Evaluation, Counseling, Therapy, Training

Queiroga, Joao G. (M.Sc.) Physical Education Teacher; Ramiro d'Avila 83 Ap. 01, Porto Alegre, RS, Brazil; POR,E,SP; Young, Athletes, Stress, Control, Programs

Ribeiro Da Silva, Athayde (M.Sc.) Psychologist; ISOP/ Fundacao Getulio Vargas, Dept. of Psychology, Rua Humaita 60 Apt. 201, Rio de Janeiro, RJ, Brazil; POR,E; Group Dynamics, Tests, Evaluation, Counseling

Rosa, Joao A. (M.Sc.) Professor; G. Nautilo Uniao, Dept. of Fencing, Rua Casemiro De Abrew, Porto Alegre, RS, Brazil 90410; E,POR; Fencing, Training, Mental Preparation, Youth Sport

Sa, Carlos A. (B.Sc.) Psychologist; Av. Luis Viana Fo. 436 Bolandeira, Salvador, BA, Brazil Bl 02; POR,E(R); Group Dynamics, Counseling, Therapy

Saldanha, Arthur M. (Ph.D.) Psychologist; Universidade Federal do Rio Grande doSul, Cent. Orientacao e Selecao Psicotecnica, Protasio Alves 297, Porto Alegre, RS, Brazil (0512-323827 90410); POR,S,E(S,R),F(S,R),I(R); Group Dynamics, Counseling, Sport Psychology, Organizational Psychology, Vocational Guidance

Salgado, Ana Lucia (M.Sc.) Psychologist; Av. Protasio Alves #297, Porto Alegre, RS, Brazil 90410; POR,E(S,R); Young Athletes, Counseling, Therapy, Evaluation

*Samulski, Dietmar (Ph.D.) Visitant Professor; Campus Universitario, Dept. of Physical Education, Pampulha-Belo Horizonte, P.O. Box 2102, 31310 Belo Horizonte Brazil (031-4410409); E,G,S,POR; Motivation, Stress, Action Theory, Control, Motor Learning

Santos, Jorge L. (B.Sc.) Psychologist; Rua Roque Barreto 67/202, Rio de Janeiro, RJ, Brazil 21620; POR,E; Top Athletes, Soccer, Mental Training

Silva, Luis A.F. (M.Sc.) Psychiatrist; Av. Mal. Fontenelle, Rio de Janeiro, RJ, Brazil 1200; POR,E; Special, Children, Physical, Programs, Therapy

Silva, Telmo J. Psychologist; Av. Mauricio Cardoso, Novo Hamburgo, RS, Brazil 510 (93-300); POR; Group Dynamics, Social, Research, Education

Targa, Jacinto (B.Sc.) University Teacher; UFRGS, Dept. of Physical Education, Rua Cel Andre Belo 603, Porto Alegre, RS, Brazil; POR,E(R); Physical Education, Administration

Teixeira, Cecilio S. (M.D.) Psychiatrist; Rio Grande Society of Medicine, Edificio Galeria Sao Pedro 40 Andar, Rio Grande, RS, Brazil; POR,E,S; Stress, Control, Top Athletes, Injuries

Veiga Da Silva, Antonio (M.Sc.) Psychologist; Av. Mauricio Cardoso 510, Novo Hamburgo, RS, Brazil (0512-933865 93300); POR,E(S,R); Group Dynamics, Counseling, Therapy, Underwater Sports

*Versari, Christina Bortoni (Ph.D.) Sport Psychologist; Universidade Gama Filho, Rio de Janeiro, Brazil; E,POR,S; NLP, Performance Enhancement, Crisis Intervention, Career and Life Planning, Elite Athletes

Wanner, Marco A. (B.Sc.) Physical Education Teacher; Tennis Center, Dept. of Tennis, Rua Mal. Simeao 25 S. Joao, Porto Alegre, RS, Brazil (0512-427050); E,S,POR; Stress, Control, Tennis, Top Athletes

Bulgaria

Bahtchevanov, D.; Lazo Voyvoula 128, Plovdiv, Bulgaria 4000 (032-76388); B,F(S,R),R(S,R); Stress, Relaxation, Conflict,Competition

Boriskova, Lily; Higher Institute of Physical Culture, 1 Tina Kirkova St., Sofia, Bulgaria 1000

Christova-Kosturkova, Maria; Hochschule fuer Koerperkultur, Rakovskistrasse 148b, Sofia, Bulgaria 1000

Dimitrov, K. (Docent) L. Koschut 10A, Sofia, Bulgaria 1606 (526311); B,G,R; Imagery, Personality, Emotion, Love, Conflict

Dimitrova, S.S. (Dr.) Assistant Professor; L. Koschut 10A, Sofia, 1606 Bulgaria (52-63-11-68-36-62); B,R,G(S,R),E(R); Motor Learning, Personality, Intelligence, Development

Gamanski, U.D.; Boriss 1 121, Sofia, Bulgaria (89-11-24); B,R,F(S,R); Aptitudes, Thinking, Humor, Conflict, Mental Training

*Genov, Filip Filev Professor D-2; Oboriste 99, Sofia, Bulgaria 1505 (44-07-52); B,R,F(S,R); Energy Mobilization, Personality, Attention, Volition, Political

Luc Lefebvre

Renee Vanfraecham-Raway

Benno Becker

Genova, Elizabeta (Docent); Oborite 99, Sofia, Bulgaria 1505 (62-91-21); B,R,F(S,R); Relaxation, Attention, Personality, Thinking

Georgiehe, Y. Assistant; Boul Lenin 35, Sofia, Bulgaria (62-11-82); B,G,R,S,POL; Social Psychology, Personality, Thinking, Mental Training

Givkova, R.; "Orilza," 41, Pleven, Bulgaria 5800 (27435); B,R,E(S,R); Psychodiagnosis, Personality, Relaxation, Sport, Conditioning

Ivanov, T.T. Assistant; Academy of Civil Administration, Pionerski Pat 27, Sofia, Bulgaria (56811); B,R,G(S,R),E(S,R); Self-Evaluation, Personality, Collectivity, Political

*Janev, Venchilav Ch. (Ph.D.) Associate Professor; Ul. Tina Kirkova 1, Sofia, Bulgaria 1000 (51-31-84); B,R; Sport Intellect, Anxiety, Reaction Time, Psychological Training, Personality

Kassabov, T. (Dipl.Psych.); Kvartel Darveniza Blok 18, Sofia, Bulgaria (62-88-81); R,B,F(S,R), E(S,R); Personality, Concentration, Mental States

*Kaltsheva, Anelia V. Post-Graduate Student; Sofia University, Osamska Str. 6, bl. Kaloian, Fl. 39, Lovetch 5500, Bulgaria; G; Motivation, Stress, Psychological Influence, Psychotherapy

*Kaykov, D.T. (Ph.D.) Professor in Psychology; Boul. Bakstov 205, Sofia, Bulgaria (62-91-21); B,R(S,R); Extremal Situation, Situational Psychical Readiness, Psychical Regulation (Self-Regulation), Psycho-Physical Training, Psychical Resources

Kovachev, I.; Bul. "Ch.Botev," N5, Sofia, Bulgaria (62-10-91); B,R,E(S); Psychodiagnosis, Personality, Relaxation, Conditioning

Krastev, B.B. (Dipl.Psych.); Complex Diana Bad (KNPD) Du Sport, Sofia, Bulgaria (62-10-91); B,R,E(R,S); Reaction Time, Attention, Personality, Mental States, Psychological Preparation

Lekova, Diliana Specialist; Zenter za Naucoprilojna dejnost v sporta, Blvd. Wolgograd 16a, Sofia, Bulgaria 1527; R,E; Mental Programs, Fencing, Control, Stress, Motivation

Mutafova, Julia; Higher Institute of Physical Culture, 1 Tina Kirkova, Sofia, Bulgaria 1000

Parraiotova, L. (Docent); Boul Patriarch 15 A, Sofia, Bulgaria (62-91-21); B,R(S,R),F(S,R); Personality, Teams, Interaction, Pedagogy, Education

*Parvanov, B.M. Professor; General Parensov 16, Sofia, Bulgaria (88-21-66); B,R(S,R),F(S,R); Attention, Thinking, Reaction Time, Collectivity, Psychodiagnostics, Mental Preparation

Pavlova, V.; Urvitch 14, Sofia, Bulgaria; B,R; Psychodiagnosis, Personality, Conditioning, Relaxation, Sport

Pironski, V.; V. Dimitrov 245B, Sofia, Bulgaria (58-84-90); B,R,F(S,R); Attention, Mental States, Coaches, Psychological Preparation

*Piseva-Stoyanova, Drozda (Dr.Med.Sci., M.D.) Chief; National Centre of Sport Psychology and Psychopathology, Sport Complex DIANA 2, 402/2, Sofia 1172, Bulgaria (62-10-91); B,R,F,E(R); Sport Psychology, Sport Medical Psychology, Sport Psychopathology, Psycho-Electronics and Cybernetics, Eastern Medicine

*Popov, Nickola S. (Dr.Sc.) Professor; Complex Mladost 100 Apt. 15, Sofia, Bulgaria (71-83-88/68-36-62); R,B,F(R); Personality, Selection, Spatial Orientation, Volleyball, Sensation

Popova, E.; Complex Tztok Bl. 40, Sofia, Bulgaria (72-18-11); B,R,F; Attention, Music, Memory, Gymnastics, Physical Education

Shumanova, Penka; Higher Institute of Physical Culture, 1 Tina Kirkova Strasse, Sofia, Bulgaria 1000

*Takev, A.T. (Dipl.Psych.); Complex Svoboda Bl. 35 B, Sofia, 1231, Bulgaria (37-58-56); B,R(S,R),

G(S,R); Personality, Collectivity, Aptitudes, Physical Activity, Traditions

Todorov, A.G. (Docent); Tina Kirkova 1, Sofia, Bulgaria (629127); B,R,F(R); Personality, Education, Aesthetics, Coaches, Top Athletes

Tohobenov, Michail; Higher Institute of Physical Culture, 1 Tina Kirkova Strasse, Sofia, Bulgaria 1000

Valitshkova-Stojanova, Zwetanka; Rat fuer Hochschulbildung, Zen. f. Anwendungwissenschafteler/Sport, Krasna Poljana, Bloc 43, Eingang A, Sofia, Bulgaria

*Vassilev, Vesselin K., Associate Professor (Reader); University P. Hilendarski, Dept. of Psychology, Plovdiv, Bulgaria 4000 (032-23-86-61,2,3,4); B,R,F(S,R); Stress, Mental States, Praxis Reflection, Conflict, Psychological Preparation

Canada

*Alain, Claude (Ph.D.); Director, Universite de Montreal, Dept. of Education Physique, C.P. Succursale "A," Montreal H3C 357 (514-343-6166); E,F; Decision Making, Reaction Time, Sport, Prediction, Performance

*Albinson, John G. (Ph.D.) Professor; Queen's University, School of Physical and Health Education, Kingston, Ontario, Canada K7L 3N6 (613-545-2666, 613-545-6478, ALBINSON@QUCDN. QUEENSU.CA); E; Anxiety, Stress, Adherence, Motivation

*Alderman, Rikk B. (Ed.D.); University of Alberta, Dept. of Physical Education and Sport Studies, Edmonton, Alberta, Canada (492-3838); E,F(R),G(S),S(S,R); Interpersonal Skills for Coaching, Enhanced Athletic Performance

Allain, Carol (B.Ed.) Owner; 166 Rue Leduc, Hull, Quebec, Canada J8X 3B4 (819-778-3584); F,E; Stress, Anxiety, Confidence, Motivation, Attention

*Bailey, Donald A. (P.ED.) Professor; University of Saskatchewan, College of Physical Education, Saskatoon, Saskatchewan, Canada S7N 0W0 (306-966-6524); E; Growth, Children, Exercise, Bone Density

Bard, Chantal (Ph.D.); Universite Laval, Dept. Education Physique, Quebec, Quebec, Canada; E,F; Visual Perception, Performance Analysis, Neuromotor Function, Motor Learning

*Belisle, Marc (Ph.D.) Professor; University of Sherbrooke, Faculty of Physical Education, Sherbrooke, Quebec, Canada J1K 2R1 (819-821-7735, 819-821-7970); F,E; Stress, Mental Training, Psychotherapy, Behavior Modification, Adherence

*Bell, Robert D. (Ph.D.); University of Victoria, School of Physical Education, Victoria, B.C., Canada (721-8379); E; Competition, Learning, Injuries, Pedagogy, Aging

Bender, Peter R. (Ph.D.); John Abbott College, Dept. of Psychology, Box 2000, St Anne de Bellevue, Quebec, Canada (457-6610); E,F(S,R); Children, Competition, Aggression, Coaching, Political

Birch, J.S. (B.Sc.); University of Waterloo, Dept. of Kinesiology, University Ave., Waterloo, Ontario, Canada (885-1211); E; Aggression, Centrality, Collective Behavior, Violence

*Bird, Evelyn (Ph.D.); University of Guelph, Dept. of Student Affairs, Guelph, Ontario, Canada (824-4120 ext. 2662); E; Stress, Relaxation, Biofeedback, Mental Rehearsal

Birrell, Susan (Ph.D.); McMaster University, School of Physical Education and Athletics, Hamilton, Ontario, Canada (416-525-9140); E; Achievement Motivation, Women, Interaction

Blais, Christine L. (Ph.D.); Lecturer, School of Human Kinetics, University of Ottawa, Ottawa, Ontario, Canada K1N 6N5 (613-564-9134); E,F; Learning, Cognition, Adaptives, Psychomotor, Developmental

Blais, Marc R. (Ph.D.); University de Montreal, Dept. Education Physique, Montreal, Quebec, Canada (343-6151); E,F; Anxiety, Competition, Self-Regulation, Motivation, Counseling

*Booth, Bernard F. (Ph.D.) Associate Professor; University of Ottawa, School of Human Kinetics, Ottawa, Ontario, Canada K1N 6N5 (613-564-9110); E,F,G(R); Autonomy, Attitudes, Lifestyle, Play, Exercise

*Botterill, Cal (Ph.D.) Professor; University of Winnipeg, Physical Activity and Sport Studies, 515 Portage Ave., Winnipeg, Manitoba, Canada R3B 2E9 (204-786-9820, 204-786-1824); E; Goal Setting, Coach Education, Youth Sport, Mental Training, Counseling

*Boucher, Jean-Louis (Ph.D.) Associate Professor; University of Ottawa, School of Human Kinetics, 125 University, Ottawa, Ontario, Canada K1N 6N5 (613-564-9133, 613-564-7689, JLBRE@UOTTAWA); E,F,G(R); Cognition, Motor Control, Feedback, Motor Learning, Neurological

*Boucher, R.L. (Ph.D.) Head, Dept. of Athletics and Recreational Services; University of Windsor, Faculty of Human Kinetics, College Ave., Windsor, Ontario, Canada (519-253-4232); E,F(R); Leadership, Conflict, Management, Group Dynamics, Top Athletes

Brawley, Lawrence W. (Ph.D.) Associate Professor; University of Waterloo, Dept of Kinesiology, Waterloo, Ontario, Canada N2L 3G1

Brunelle, Jean (D.E.P.); Universite Laval, Dept. Education Physique, Quebec, Quebec, Canada G1K 7P4 (656-7240); E,F; Observation, Intervention, Preparation, Analysis, Counseling

Buckolz, Eric (Ph.D.); University of Western Ontario, Dept. of Physical Education, London, Ontario, Canada (679-3230); E,F(S,R); Training, Prediction, Interference, Models, Reaction Time

*Butt, Susan D. (Ph.D., C.Psych.) Clinical Psychologist; University of British Columbia, Dept. of Psychology, #3517 - 2136 West Mall, Vancouver, B.C., Canada V6T 1Y7 (604-228-3269); E,F(R,W); Personality, Measurement, Values, Socialization, Clinical

Canic, Michael J. (Ph.D.) Post Doctoral Fellow; University of Calgary, Dept. of Physical Education, 2500 University Dr. N.W., Calgary, Alberta, Canada (403-220-7014); E,SC; Rhythm, Programming, Attention, Perception, Philosophy

*Carron, Albert V. (Ed.D.) Professor; University of Western Ontario, Faculty of Kinesiology, London, Ontario, Canada N6A 3K7 (519-679-2111, 519-661-3292); E; Cohesion, Leadership, Social Interaction, Group Dynamics

*Chelladurai, P. (Ph.D.); University of Western Ontario, Dept. of Physical Education, London, Ontario, Canada (519-679-2111 ext. 8393, 519-661-3292); E,T; Motivation, Leadership, Sport Management

Chevalier, Nicole (Ph.D.) Professor; Universite du Quebec a Montreal, Departement de Kinanthropologie, C.P. 8888, Succ. A, Montreal, Quebec, Canada H3C 3P8 (514-282-7342); E,F; Imagery, Mental Rehearsal, Mental Preparation, Athletes, Cross-Country Skiing

Cote, Jean (M.Sc.) Student; Human Kinetics, University of Ottawa, 125 University, Ottawa, Ontario, Canada, K1N 6N5 (613-564-9119); F,E; Knowledge, Qualitative Stress, Hockey, Observation

Covey, F.P. (B.P.E.,M.Sc.); Chebucto Heights School, Dept. of Physical Education, Cowie Hill

Drive, Halifax, Nova Scotia, Canada (426-4640); E; Learning, Teaching Methods, Anxiety, Motor Memory, Retention

*Cox, David N. (Ph.D.) Associate Professor; Simon Fraser University, Dept. of Psychology, Burnaby, B.C., Canada V5A 1S6 (604-291-4141); E; Clinical, High Performance, Stress, Behavioral Medicine, Behavioral Therapy

*Crocker, Peter R.E. (Ph.D.) Associate Professor; University of Saskatchewan, College of Physical Education, Saskatoon, Saskatchewan, Canada S7N 0W0 (306-966-6510); E; Stress, Motivation, Confidence, Emotion

*Crossman, Jane (Ph.D.) Chair; Lakehead University, School of Physical Education and Athletics, Thunder Bay, Ontario, Canada P7B 5E1 (807-343-8642); E; Psychosocial Aspects of Athletic Injury, Politics and Sport

*Daniel, J.V. (Ph.D.); University of Toronto, School of Physical and Health Education, 320 Huron St., Toronto, Ontario, Canada M5S 1A1 (978-4384), ESTONIAN,E,G,R; Psychogenic Stress, Leadership, Attitudes, Motivation, Morale, Interaction

Danielson, Richard (Ph.D.); Laurentian University, Dept. of Physical Education, Ramsey Lake Road, Sudbury, Ontario, Canada (705-675-1151); E,J(S); Leadership, Personality, Augmentation, Reduction, Fitness

*Davis, Henry (Ph.D.) Calgary Family Service, Suite #200, 707 10th Avenue SW, Calgary, Alberta, Canada T2R 0B3; Performance Enhancement, Research

Descarreaux, Daniel (M.PS.) Psychologist; Psycho-Sports Enr., 915 Boul. St-Cyrille Ouest, Sillery, Quebec, Canada Quebec 759; E,F; Mental Skills, Stress, Peak Performance, Humanism

Deshaies, Paul (Ph.D.) Professor; Universite de Sherbrooke, Dept. of Kinanthropology, Sherbrooke, Canada Q819-8 (21-7730); E,F; Performance, Psychobiology, Participation, Stress, Sportspersonship

Desharnais, Raymond (Ph.D.); Universite Laval, Dept. Education Physique, Ste. Foy Blv., Laurier, Quebec, Canada (418-656-7108); E,F; Attribution, Competition, Success, Failure, Motivation

Dickinson, John (Ph.D.); Simon Fraser University, Dept. of Kinesiology, Burnaby, B.C., Canada (604-291-3572); E,F(R),G(S,R); Memory, Motor Learning, Motivation, Development, Training Systems

Drouin, Denis (Ph.D.); Universite Laval, Dept. Education Physique, Campus Universitaire, Ste. Foy, Quebec, Canada (656-5563); E,F; Competition, Cooperation, Academic Success, Interests, Stress

Duthie, James H.; University of Windsor, Faculty Human Kinetics, College Ave., Windsor, Ontario, Canada (253-4232); E,F(S,W); Competition, Personality, Athletes, Risk Taking, Play

*Early, J.M. (Med.); University of New Brunswick, Dept. of Athletics, Fredericton, New Brunswick, Canada E3B 5A3 (506-453-4579); E,F(S); Athletics, Psychology

Egan, Sean (Ph.D.); University of Ottawa, School Human Kinetics, 38 McDougall, Ottawa, Ontario, Canada (231-5915); E,F,GAELIC; Stress, Anxiety, Pain, Fear, Psychology

Ferchor, A.D. (B.Ph.E.); Red Deer College, Dept. of Physical Education, Box 5005, Red Deer, Alberta, Canada (346-3376); E; Learning, Self-Concept, Competition, Growth, Physiology

*Fouts, G.T. (Ph.D.) Professor; University of Calgary, Dept. of Psychology, 2500 University Drive N.W., Calgary, Alberta, Canada T2N 1N4 (403-220-5573, 403-282-8249); E; Sport Socialization, TV and Sports, Stereotypes, Sports and Identity Development

Garnier, Catherine (Ph.D.); University of Montreal, Dept. de Kinanthropologie, Case Pastale 8888, Montreal, Quebec, Canada (282-7021); F,E(S,R); Competition, Cooperation, Teams, Interaction, Observation

Gauvin, Lise (Ph.D.) Assistant Professor; Concordia University, Dept. of Exercise Science, 7141 Sherbrooke Street West, Montreal, Quebec, Canada H4B 1R6 (514-848-3321); E,F; Motivation, Health, Well-Being, Children, Self-Concept

Gavin, James (Ph.D.) Professor; Concordia University, Dept. of Applied Social Science, 1455 de Maisonneuve West, Montreal, Quebec, Canada H3G 1M8 (514-848-2272); E,F(R)

Gendron, Stanley C. (M.A.) Chairman; John Abbott College, Dept. of Physical Education, P.O. Box 2000, St. Anne de Bellevue, Quebec, Canada (514-457-6610, 514-457-4730); E; Knowledge Base, Imagery, Racquet Sports, Skiing, Control

Gilbert, Marc-Andre (Ph.D.); Universite de Quebec, Dept. des Sciences de l'Activite Physique, C.P. 500, Trois-Rivieres, Quebec, Canada (819-376-5760); E,F; Leadership, Anxiety, Communication, Social Psychology, Social Facilitation

*Gomez, Ninoska (Ph.D.); Universite de Montreal, Dept. d'Education Physique, 2100 Bl. Ed., Montreal, Quebec, Canada (514-343-7782); E,F,S; Perceptual Motor Development, Learning, Somatic Education, Dance

Gravelle, Luc H. (Ph.D.) Assistant Professor; School of Human Kinetics, University of Ottawa, Ottawa, Ontario, Canada, K1N 6N5 (613-564-9121); E,F; Coaching, Behavior, Mental Preparation, Epistemic Orientation

*Guay, Michel (Ph.D.) Professeur agrege; Universite Laurentienne, Ecole de l'Activite Physiques, Sudbury, Ontario, Canada P3E 2C6; E,F; Perception, Learning, Feedback, Memory, Time

Guilmette, Anne Marie (B.P.H.E.); University of Windsor, Dept. of Psychology, Sunset Ave., Windsor, Ontario, Canada (253-4232); E,F(R,W); Humor, Play, Social Norms, Conflict, Theory Construction

*Hall, Craig R. (Ph.D.); University of Western Ontario, Faculty of Kinesiology, London, Ontario, Canada N6A 3K7; Memory, Learning, Imagery

*Halle, Madeleine (Ph.D.); 2594 Ombrette, Laval, Quebec, Canada (514-628-0956); F,E; Intervention, Education, Elite Athlete, Emotional Control, Cognitive

*Halliwell, W.R. (Ph.D.) Associate Professor; University of Montreal, Dept. of Physical Education, 2100 Edouard Montpetit, Montreal, Quebec, Canada (514-343-7792); E,F; Cross-Cultural Differences, Mental Preparation of Elite Athletes, Youth Sport, Motivation

Hanrahan, Christine (Ph.D.) Assistant Professor, University of Alberta, Faculty of Physical Education and Sport Studies, Edmonton, Alberta, Canada (403-492-1039); E,F; Dance, Imagery, Stage Fright, Stress, Mental Training

Herzog, Walter; University of Calgary/PE, 2500 N.W. University Drive, Calgary, Alberta, Canada T2N 1N4

Hogan, Timothy V. (Ph.D.); Canadian Psychological Institute, 558 King Edouard, Ottawa, Ontario, Canada (238-4409); E,F; Psychotherapy, Marital Counseling, Family, Abnormal, Sport Psychology

Horvath, E.M. (B.A.); Acadia University, Dept. of Recreation and Physical Education, Wolfville, Nova Scotia, Canada (542-2201); E,F(S); Social Psychology, Cooperation, Relaxation, Counseling, Goal Setting

*Howe, Bruce L. (Ph.D.); University of Victoria, School of Physical Education, P.O. Box 3015, Victoria, B.C., Canada V8W 3P1 (721-8383); E,G(R); Competition, Motivation, Personality, Play, Visualization

*Hrycaiko, Dennis W. (Ph.D.) Professor; University of Manitoba, Faculty of Physical Education and Recreation Studies, Winnipeg, Manitoba, Canada (474-8764); E; Social Facilitation, Anxiety, Competition, Top Athletes

Hume, Michelle (M.A.) Student/Coach; P.O. Box 3166, Winnipeg, Manitoba, Canada R3C 4E6 (204-255-2909); E; Behavior Modification, Figure Skating, Organizational Behavior, Swimming

*Jensen, Peter K. (Ph.D.); The Centre for High Performance, 70 Ontario Street, Collingwood, Ontario, Canada L9Y 1M3 (705-444-1234); E,F(S); Mental Fitness, Motivation, Imagery, Psycho-neuroimmunology, Thinking Patterns

*Jerome, Wendy C. (Ph.D.); Laurentian University, Dept. Division of Physical Education, Ramsey Lake Road, Sudbury, Ontario, Canada (705-675-1151); E,F(R); Personality, Stress Management, Growth and Development, Counseling

Kamal, Fouad (B.P.E.); University of Ottawa, Dept. of Physical Education, Ottawa, Ontario, Canada (613-231-5915); E,F,G(R),I,A; Coaching, Top Athletes, Competition, Motivation, Human Performance

Kerr, Barry A. (Ph.D.); University of Calgary, Dept. of Physical Education, Calgary, Alberta, Canada (284-6471); E; Learning, Performance, Control

*Kerr, Gretchen A. (Ph.D.) Assistant Professor; University of Toronto, Dept. of Physical and Health Education, 320 Huron Street, Toronto, Ontario, Canada M5S 1A1 (416-978-3448); E; Stress, Competition, Injuries, Psychological Preparation

Kerr, Robert (Ph.D.) Professor; School of Human Kinetics, University of Ottawa, Ottawa, Ontario, Canada K1N 6N5 (613-564-9136); E,F(S,R); Knowledge, Psychomotor, Learning, Complex Skills

Kingston, George E. (Ph.D.); University of Calgary, Dept. of Physical Education, 2500 University Drive, Calgary, Alberta, Canada (403-284-6548); E,F(S,R),G(S,R); Coaching, Comparative Physical Education, Sport, Top Athletes, Youth Sport

Cal Botterill   Lise Gauvin   W.R. Halliwell

Klavora, Peter (Ph.D.) Associate Professor; University of Toronto, School Physical and Health Education, 320 Huron Street, Toronto, Ontario, Canada (987-6096); E,G,SLOVENE; Competition, Anxiety, Top Sport, Learning, Children

Koroluk, G.A. (B.P.E.); Mount Royal College, Dept. of Physical Education, 4825 Richard Road, Calgary, Alberta, Canada (246-6485); E,F(S,R); Competition, Motivation, Personality, Counseling, Relating

Krasnow, Donna H. (B.A.) Assistant Professor; York University, Dept. of Dance, 4700 Keele St., North York, Ontario, Canada (416-737-5137); E; Dance, Choreography, Alignment Work, Injury Prevention

*Kreiner-Phillips, Kathy M. (M.Sc.); 1618 Ralph Street, North Vancouver, British Columbia, Canada V7K 1V7 (604-980-2756, 604-980-2431); E; Success, Alpine Skiing, Peak Performance, Stress Management

*Lacoste, Pierre (Ph.D.) Professor; Universite du Quebec a Trois-Rivieres, D.S.A.P., C.P. 500, Trois-Rivieres, Quebec, Canada G9A 5H7; F,E,POR(S); Behavior, Leadership, Teams, Coaching, Sport

Lafleur, Johane (M.Sc.) Graduate Student; 228 5th Avenue LDR, Laval, Quebec, Canada H7N 4M6 (514-667-7968); E,F; Motor Learning, Motivation, Swimming, Cohesion

Lariviere, Georges (Ph.D.) Professor; Universite de Montreal, Dept. of Physical Education, C.P. 6128, Montreal, Quebec, Canada H3C 3J7 (514-343-7658); F,E; Measurement, Talent Identification, Conceptual Model Development, Task Analysis, Growth

Leavitt, Jack L. (D.ED.) Professor; University of Windsor, Dept. of Kinesiology, Windsor, Ontario, Canada N9C 1H2 (519-253-4232, BJ2@WINDSOR1); E; Movement, Control, Kinematics, Aging

Levy, J. (Ph.D.); University of Waterloo, Dept. of Recreation, Waterloo, Ontario, Canada (885-1211); E; Children, Leisure, Mental Health, Aging, Retirement

Lewko, John H. (Ph.D.); Laurentian University, Dept. of Child and Developmental Studies, Ramsey Lake Road, Sudbury, Ontario, Canada (675-1151); E; Social Development, Handicapped, Friendship, Peer Group

*Lindner, Koenraad J. (Ph.D.); University of Manitoba, Faculty of Physical Education and Recreation Studies, Winnipeg, Manitoba, Canada R3T 2N2 (204-474-8627, 275-5122); E,F(R,W),G,D; Motor Learning, Growth and Development, Youth Sports, Research Methods

Lonetto, Richard (Ph.D.); University of Guelph, Dept. of Psychology, Guelph, Ontario, Canada (519-824-4120); E,F(R,W); Competition, Personality, Perception, Training, Counseling

MacGillivary, William (Ph.D.); University of New Brunswick, Dept. of Physical Education, Fredericton, New Brunswick, Canada (453-4581); E,F(R,W); Personality, Perception, Perceptual Motor Development, Top Athletes, Competition

MacKenzie, Christine (Ph.D.); University of Waterloo, Dept. of Kinesiology, Waterloo, Ontario, Canada (885-1211); E,F(R,W); Programming, Handedness, Functional Asymmetry, Performance, Statistics

*Mannell, Roger C. (Ph.D.); University of Waterloo, Dept. of Recreation and Leisure Studies, Waterloo, Ontario, Canada (888-4782); E,F(R); Leisure, Cognition, Choice, Attitudes, Humor

Marchand, Pierre; Universite Laval, Ecole de Psychologie, P.O. G1K 7P4, Quebec, Quebec, Canada; E,F; Anxiety, Social Psychology, Competition, Coaction, Social Facilitation

*Marisi, Dan Q. (Ph.D.) Associate Professor; McGill University, Dept. of Physical Education,

475 Pine Avenue West, Montreal, Quebec, Canada H2W 1S4 (514-398-4189, 514-398-4901, INI1@MU-SICB.MCGILL.CA); E,F(R),I(R); Stress, Concentration, Vision, Performance Enhancement, Information Processing

Marteniuk, Ron (Ed.D.); University of Waterloo, Dept. of Kinesiology, Waterloo, Ontario, Canada (885-1211); E; Information Processing, Motor Skill, Motor Control, Memory, Organization

*Martin, Garry L. (Ph.D.) Professor; University of Manitoba, Dept. of Psychology, 129 St. Paul's College, Winnipeg, Manitoba, Canada (204-474-8589); E,S(S),POR(S); Behavior Modification, Figure Skating, Golf, Swimming, Field Hockey

*McClements, Jim (Ph.D.) Professor; University of Saskatchewan, College of Physical Education, Saskatoon, Saskatchewan, Canada S7N 0W0 (306-966-6472, McCLEMENTS@SASK); E; Feedback, Goal Setting, Reinforcement, Adapted

McGuire, E.J.; University of Waterloo, Dept. of Kinesiology, Waterloo, Ontario, Canada N2L 3G1

*McKelvey, Gregg M. (Ph.D.); University of Ottawa, School of Human Kinetics, Ottawa, Ontario, Canada (613-564-9119, 613-564-7689); E,F(R,W); Learning, Children, Play, Games, Interaction

*Meichenbaum, Donald (Ph.D.) Professor; University of Waterloo, Dept. of Psychology, Waterloo, Ontario, Canada N2L 3G1

*Miller, Merry L. (Ph.D.) Sport Psychologist; 90 Eagle Ridge Drive S.W., Calgary, Alberta, Canada T2V 2V4 (403-259-6663); E,F; Confidence, Communication, Concentration, Motivation, Coaching

Minden, Harold (Ph.D.) Dean; York University Toronto, Dept. of Physical Education and Psychology, 4700 Keele Street, Toronto, Ontario, Canada (667-2444); E,F(R); Stress Management, Top Athletes, Motivation

Moody, Gilles (M.Sc.) Student; Universite de Montreal, Dept d'Education Physique, C.P. 6128, Succ "A," Montreal, Quebec, Canada H3C 3J7 (514-343-6151); E,F; Stress, Running, Anxiety, Top Athletes, Psycho-Sociology

Moriarty, D.J. (Ph.D.); University of Windsor, Faculty of Human Kinetics, College Ave., Windsor, Ontario, Canada (519-253-4232); E,F(R,W); Conflict, Analysis of Change, Sport, Organization, Research

Morrison, C.S. (B.P.E.); University of Victoria, Dept. of Physical Education, P.O. Box 1700, Victoria, B.C., Canada (477-6911); E,F; Sensory

Nadeau, Claude-H. (Ph.D.); University de Quebec a Montreal, Dept. de Kinanthropologie, Montreal, Quebec, Canada; E,F,G(R),S(R); Cognition, Motor Control, Ballistic Movements, Learning, Performance

Nault, Louis-P.; Universite de Sherbrooke, Dept. de Kinanthropologie, Sherbrooke, Quebec, Canada (819-565-2203); E,F; Attribution, Competition, Personality, Stress

*O'Halloran, Ann-Merie (M.Sc.) Graduate Student; 1200 Woodland, Verdun, Quebec, Canada H4H 1V9; E,F; Individual Differences, Imagery, Cognitive Styles, Figure Skating, Applied Sport Psychology

*O'Hara, Thomas J. (Ph.D.) Psychologist; Tom O'Hara and Associates, 190 Lisgar Ave., 2nd Floor, Ottawa, Ontario, Canada K2P 0C4 (613-233-0855, 613-563-3850); E,F; High Performance Training, Organization Development, Alpine Skiing, Business, Multisport

*Orlick, Terry (Ph.D.); University of Ottawa, School of Human Kinetics, Ottawa, K1N 6N5, Ontario, Canada (613-564-5920, 613-564-7689); E,F(S,R); Cooperative Games, Children, Excellence, Mental Training, Stress Control

Ouellet, J. (M.A.) Psychologist; Psycho-Sports Enr., 915 Coul. St.-Cyrille Ouest, Sillery, Quebec, Canada G1S 1T8 (418-682-5957); E,F; Achievement Motivation, Stress Management, Mental Preparation, Communication, Applied Sport Psychology

Paoletti, Rene F. (Ph.D.); Universite du Quebec, Dept. de Kinanthropologie, Montreal, Quebec, Canada (282-3710); E,F; Proprioception, Research, Learning, Perceptual Motor Development

*Partington, John T. (Ph.D.) Professor; Carleton University, Dept. of Psychology, Ottawa, Ontario, Canada J0X 3G0 (613-788-2695); E; Performance, Evaluation, Team, Music, Military

Pelletier, Luc (M.Sc.); Universite de Quebec at Montreal, Dept. of Psychology, CP500, Montreal, Quebec, Canada

*Petrie, Brian M. (Ph.D.); Concordia University, Dept. Sociology/Anthropology, 7141 Sherbrooke St. West, Montreal, Quebec, Canada (848-2155, 848-3492); E,F; Athletes, Non-Athletes, Achievement Motivation, Sex, Social Class

Pezer, Vera (Ph.D.); University of Saskatchewan, College of Arts and Science, Saskatoon, Saskatchewan, Canada (343-3788); E; Arousal, Personality, Counseling, Research Design, Test Construction

*Powell, John T. (Ph.D.) Exercise Specialist; University of Guelph, School of Human Biology, Dept. of Human Kinetics, Guelph, Ontario, Canada (519-824-4120); E,F(S,R)AFR(R); Teaching, Aesthetics, Human Movement, Activity, Rehabilitation

*Proteau, Luc (Ph.D.), Associate Professor; University of Montreal, Physical Education, 2100 Edouard, Moutpetit, Quebec, Canada, (514-343-6111); F,E; Motor Control, Decision Strategy

*Regnier, Guy (Ph.D.) Research Director; Regie de la Securite dans les Sports, Service de la Recherche, 100 Laviolette, Trois-Rivieres, Quebec, Canada (819-371-6033, 819-371-6992); F,E; Safety, Risk Factors, Epidemiology, Children

Reid, Greg D. (Ph.D.); McGill University Montreal, Dept. of Physical Education, 475 Pine Ave., Montreal, Quebec, Canada (514-392-8891); E,F(R); Mental Health, Memory, Teaching Strategies, Learning Disabilities, Clumsy Children

*Ringrose, Douglas (M.D., Frcsc.) Director; Ringrose Institute, 8702 Meadowlark Road, # 380, Edmonton, Alberta, Canada T5R 5W4 (403-484-8401); E; Power, Hypnosis, Autogenics, Behavior Modification, Stress Control, Biofeedback, Acupressure

Rodney, Melanie L. (B.P.E.); University of Waterloo, Dept. of Psychology, University Ave., Waterloo, Ontario, Canada (519-885-1211); E,F(S,R), G(S,R); Skilled Behavior, Cerebral Organization, Loss of Function, Attention, Learning

Romanow, Sue K.E (B.Hk.); University of Waterloo, Dept. of Kinesiology, University Ave., Waterloo, Ontario, Canada; E,F,G; Memory, Learning, Organization, Imagery, Knowledge of Results

*Russell, Storm J. (Ph.D.) Research Officer; Canadian Fitness and Lifestyle Research Institute, 200-47 Clarence St., Ottawa, Ontario, Canada, K1N 9K1 (613-236-0173, 236-8857); E,F; Knowledge Representation, Cognitive Skill Development, Multivariate Methods

*Salmela, John H. (Ph.D) Professor; University of Ottawa, Department of Human Kinetics, 125 University St., Ottawa, Ontario, Canada K1N 6N5 (613-564-9119, 564-7689); E,F,G(R); Talent Identification, Gymnastics, Psychological Preparation, Cognitive Processes, Knowledge Structure

*Salmoni, Alan W. (Ph.D.); Laurentian University, Division of Physical Education, Sudbury, Ontario, Canada (675-1151); E; Development, Motor Control, Learning, Children, Skill, Gerontology

Salvail, Jean A. (Ph.D.); Universite de Sherbrooke, Dept. des Sciences de l'Education, Sherbrooke, Quebec, Canada (819-565-5015); E,F; Self-Concept, Attitudes, Learning, Deviance, Competition

*Sarrazin, Claude (Ph.D.) Psychologue, Professeua Agrege; Universite de Montreal, Dept. d'education Physique, 2100 Edouard Montpetit, Montreal, Quebec, Canada H3C 3J7 (514-343-6165); E,F; Psychotherapy, Behavior Modification, Sport, Performance Enhancement, Stress Management

Savage, M.V. (B.A.); Simon Fraser University, Dept. of Kinesiology, 301-1280 Madison Ave., Burnaby, B.C., Canada (604-291-3576); E; Competition, Top Athletes, Anxiety, Motivation, Personality

Scholten, P.M. (M.A.); College Cape Breton, Dept. of Physical Education, Box 3500, Sydney, Nova Scotia, Canada (539-7291); E; Coaching, Competition, Athletes, Motivation, Leadership

*Schutz, R.W. (Ph.D.); University of British Columbia, Dept. of Sport Science, 212 Memorial Gym., Vancouver, British Columbia, Canada (604-228-2767); E; Statistics, Mathematics and Sport, Analysis of Change, Attitudes, Measurement

*Searle, Robert Q. (Ed.D.) Associate Professor; University of Ottawa, School of Human Kinetics, Ottawa, Ontario, Canada (613-564-5916); E,F(R); Learning, Control, Stress

Sheedy, Arthur. (M.Sc.); Universite de Montreal, Dept. d'Education Physique, 2100 Edouard Montpetit, Montreal, Quebec, Canada (343-7847); E,F,G(R,W); Philosophy, Science, Theory, History, Professionalization

*Smith, Garry J. (Ph.D.); University of Alberta, Dept. of Physical Education, 114 St. 87 Ave., Edmonton, Alberta, Canada T6G 2H9; E,F(R); Mass Media, Addiction, Heroes, Alienation, Gambling

Souliere, Danielle (M.Sc.); 5230 Parthenais Apt. 1, Montreal, Quebec, Canada (424243); E(S,R),F; Information Processing, Top Athletes, Decision Making, Anticipation, Prediction

*Spink, Kevin S. (Ph.D.) Associate Professor; University of Saskatchewan, College of Physical Education, Saskatoon, Saskatchewan, Canada S7N 0W0 (306-966-6474, 306-966-6502); E,F(R); Cognitive Strategies, Group Processes, Modified Sport, Children, Coaching

Starkes, Janet L. (Hon. B.A.); McMaster University, School of Physical Education, Main St., Hamilton, Ontario, Canada (525-9140); E,F(R),S; Perception, Arousal, Attention Demands, Development, Signal Detection

Stevenson, Chris L. (Ph.D.); University of New Brunswick, Dept. of Physical Education, Fredricton, New Brunswick, Canada (506-453-4575); E,F(R); Socialization, Sport, Competition, Identity, Symbolic

*Struthers, Georges (M.Sc.) Sport Psychology Consultant; Universite de Montreal, Dept. of Physical Education, 130 Grand Moulin, Deux-Montagnes, Quebec, Canada, J7R 3C9 (514-473-2562); F,E; Mental Training, Relaxation, Individual Sports, Idiographic Approaches

Talbot, S.T. (M.Sc.); Universite Laval, Dept. de l'Activite Physique, Sainte-Foy, Quebec, Canada (418-656-7834); E,F; Teaching, Teacher Training, Teacher Analysis, Learning Styles, Teacher Behavior

*Theroux, Benoit (M.Sc.); 17 Lavigne, Boisbriand, Quebec, Canada (514-435-5080); E,F,S; Respect, Imagery, Football, Pain Tolerance, Concentration

Trudel, Pierre (Ph.D.) Assistant Professor; School of Human Kinetics, University of Ottawa, Ottawa, Ontario, Canada (613-564-9111); E,F; Pedagogy, Coaches, Hockey, Violence, Self-Supervision

Tucker, D.F. (B.P.E.); Boys and Girls Club Calgary, 1318 Regal Cres.,N.E., Calgary, Alberta, Canada (403-276-9045); E; Motivation, Achievement, Recreation, Adaptives

Turchan, W.J. (B.A.); South Caleton High School, Dept. of Physical and Health Education, McBean St., Richmond, Ontario, Canada (613-838-2212); E,SLOVAK(R,S); Competition, Counseling, Personality, Aggression, Anxiety

*Vachon, Lucien V. (Ph.D.); Universite du Quebec, Dept. de l'Activite Physique, Trois-Rivieres, Quebec, Canada G9A 5H7 (376-5633); E,F; Learning, Youth Sport, Teaching, Computer Assisted Learning

*Vallerand, Robert J. (Ph.D.); Universite du Quebec a Montreal, Laboratore du Comportement Social, Dept. de Psychologie, Montreal, Quebec, Canada (514-987-4836, 514-987-7953); E,F; Motivation, Personality, Attribution, Health, Aging

*Van Gyn, Geraldine H. (Ph.D.) Associate Professor; University of Victoria, School of Physical Education, Box 1700, Victoria, B.C., Canada (604-721-8380); E,F(R,W); Memory, Imagery, Development, Children, Learning, Skill

Vaz, E.W. (Ph.D.); University of Waterloo, Dept. of Sociology, Waterloo, Ontario, Canada; E,F; Norms, Theory, Deviance, Sociology

Wagner, B.G. (B.P.E.); Adelaide-W.G. MacDonald School, Strathroy, Ontario, Canada (247-3369); E,F; Learning, Skill, Performance, Memory, Development

*Wall, A.E. (Ph.D.); Dean McGill University, Faculty of Physical Education, 475 Pine Ave., W., Montreal, Quebec, Canada H2W 1S4 (514-398-4190); E,F(S,R); Motor Development, Motor Evaluation, Instruction, Knowledge-Based Research, Adaptives

*Wankel, Leonard M. (Ph.D.) Professor; University of Alberta, Faculty of Physical Education and Recreation, Edmonton, Alberta, Canada (403-492-1002, 403-492-2364); E,F(R); Motivation, Mass Participation, Social Psychology of Leisure and Recreation, Exercise Adherence, Enjoyment and Satisfaction

Whittaker-Bleuler, Sharon A. (Ph.D.) Professor; University of British Columbia, School of Physical Education and Recreation, Vancouver, B.C., Canada (604-228-4267); E; Competition, Stress, Communication, Motivation, Play

Widdop, Valerie A. (M.A.); Lakehead University, Dept. of Physical Education, Oliver Rd., Thunder Bay, Ontario, Canada P7B 5E1 (345-1212); E; Motor Learning, Atypical, Movement Education, Theory of Coaching

Widmeyer, Neil W. (Ph.D.); University of Waterloo, Dept. of Kinesiology, University Ave., Waterloo, Ontario, Canada; E,F(R); Cohesion, Group Dynamics, Aggression, Anxiety, Competition

*Wilberg, Robert B. (Ph.D.) Professor; University of Alberta, Dept. of Physical Education and Sport Studies, Edmonton, Alberta, Canada (403-492-1039, USERWFNO@UALTAM); E; Memory, Learning, Performance, Motor, Skill

*Williams, Ian D. (Ph.D.); University of Waterloo, Dept. of Kinesiology, Waterloo, Ontario, Canada (885-1211); E,F; Learning, Feedback, Performance, Reflexes, Memory

*Wilson, V.J. (Ed.D.); Brock University, Dept. of Physical Education, St. Catharines, Ontario, Canada (684-7201); E; Anxiety, Movement Analysis, Cooperation, Competition, Women

*Worrell, Gary L. (B.P.E., M.S., Ph.D.) Associate Professor; University of New Brunswick, Division of Social Science, P.O. Box 5050, Saint John, New Brunswick, Canada E2L 4L5 (506-648-5522, 506-832-3744, 506-648-5528); E,F(R); Efficacy, Work Values, Job Satisfaction, Motivation

Chile

Chaves, Enrique A. (M.Sc.) Psychologist; Alcalde Alberto, Jenschke 7260, La Reina, Santiago, Chile; E,S; Mental Training, Stress, Control, Child

China

*Chai, Wen-Xiu Professor; Tianjin Institute of Physical Education, Psychology Teaching Group, Tianjin, China; CHI,J(R),E(R); Personality, Control, Parachute, Ancient Sport, Development

L,JiR, Shen-Nian Professor; Development Harbin Teacher's University, Dept. of Education, Harbin, P.R. China; CHI,E(R); Sport Psychology History, Psychological Training, Teaching Psychology

Liu, Xianming (B.A.) Associate Professor; Wuhan Physical Education Institute, Dept. of Sport Psychology, Wuhan, Hubei, P.R. China (716491-354, 5040); CHI,R(R); Motor Learning, Personality, Travel

Ma, Qi-Wei (Ph.D.) Professor; Beijing Institute of Physical Education, Beijing, China 100084 (Cable 7555); E,CHI; Top Athletes, Mental Preparation

*Qiu, Yi-Jun Professor, Dean of Dept. and Director of Research Division; Sport Psychology Dept., Wuhan Institute of Physical Education, Wuhan, P.R. China 430070 (703391-354); CHI,R(R),E(R,W); Psychological Selection, Personality, Counseling, Psychological Diagnosis, Psychological Training

Jim McClements

Terry Orlick

John T. Partington

Robert J. Vallerand

Ma Qi-Wei

Yi-Jun Qiu

*Si, Gang-Yan (M.Sc.) Lecturer; Wuhan Institute of Physical Education, Wuhan, China; E,CHI, G(S); Personality, Anxiety, Stress, Motor Learning, Arousal

*Xianmin, Liu Vice-Professor; Sport Psychology Dept., Wuhan Institute of Physical Education, Wuhan, P.R. China 430070 (703391-354); E(R,W), R(R),CHI; Sports Interest, Psychological Tendency, Personality, Motor Learning, Practice

*Xie, San-Cai Professor; Shenyang Institute of Physical Education, No. 11 Taishan Road, Shenyang, China 110032 (692211); CHI,J(R); Personality, Psychological Training, Winter Events, Shooting

*Ye, Ping (M.Ed.) Assistant Lecturer; Chengdu Institute of Physical Culture, Dept. of Physical Education, Chengdu, China; CHI,J,E; Attribution, Anxiety, Motivation, Cross-Cultural Research

Chinese Taipei

*Chen, Hung (M.Ed.) Associate Professor; National Taiwan Normal University, Dept. of Physical Education, P.O. Box 22-82, Taipei, Taiwan, Chinese Taipei (02-362-5621); E; Personality, Need, Motivation, Aggression, Anxiety

Cheng, Hu (Ph.D.) Head, Professor; National College of Physical Education and Sports, Dept. of Sports Training Science, Kweishan, Taoyuan, Taiwan, Chinese Taipei (03-3283-205); CHI,E; Relaxation, Anxiety, Hypnosis, Tennis, Gymnastics

Chien, Jan Hori (Ph.D.) Professor; Taiwan Normal University, Dept. of Physical Education, P.O. Box 97-32, Taipei, Taiwan, Chinese Taipei (02-931-8123); E; Personality, Learning, Hypnosis, Baseball, Stress

Chien, Lau-Hoei (Ph.D.) President; Taiwan College of Physical Education, Taichung, Taiwan, Chinese Taipei (02-732-8123); E,CHI; Meditation, Stress, Relaxation, Mental, Baseball

*Jwo, Hank J.L. (M.Ed.) Lecturer; Taiwan Normal University, Dept. of Physical Education, P.O. Box 97-32, Taipei, Taiwan, Chinese Taipei (02-931-2901); E; Imagery, Development, Learning, Control, Swimming

Lin, Der-Lung (M.Sc.) Instructor; National Taiwan Normal Univeristy, Dept. of Physical Education, 88 Sec. 5 Roosevelt Road, Taipei, Taiwan, Chinese Taipei (02-931-2901); CHI,E(S,R); Stress, Therapy, Baseball

Lu, Frank J.H. (M.D.) Instructor; National Tsin Hua University, Dept. of Physical Education and Sports, Chinese Taipei; CHI,MA,E; Test, Learning, Control, Hypnosis, Sex

Wu, Wan Fu (B.Sc.) Professor; Taiwan Provincial Teachers' College, Dept. of Physical Education; 134 Sec. 2 Ho-Ping E. Road, Taipei, Taiwan, Chinese Taipei (02-733-5310); J,E(R); Personality, Running, Learning

Colombia

Aguirra, Alvaro A. (B.Sc.) Psychologist; Cra. 45 #56-19, Jundeportes, Barranquilla, Colombia (95-317721); S; Control, Aggression, Hypnosis, Confidence, Stress

Ayala, Luz Estell (Lic. Psych.) Psychologist; Universidad del Valle, Psychology Dept., 49N, #2EN-10, Calle, Colombia (923-652805); S; Motivation, Group Dynamics, Self-Concept, Communication

Camero, Fernando (B.Sc.) Psychologist; Centro Clinico del Deporte, Dept. of Psychology, Calle 118 No. 15A 18 AP. Aereo, Bogota, Colombia 9389; S,E(S,R); Mental Preparation, Soccer, Group Dynamics

Cardinal, Consuelo M. (Lic. Psych.) Psychomotricitist; Cra 22, #P6A-59, Apto 201, Bogota, Colombia (2574687); S; Cognitive Development, Psychomotricity, Play, Movement, Children

Clavijo, O. Jairo (B.Sc.) Psychologist; Av. 0 #10-78 Cons. 402, Cucuta, N. de S., Colombia (970-30771); S; Stress, Fears, Relaxation, Control, Hypnosis

Fuenmayor de la Pena, Maritza (M.Ed.Psy.) Psychologist; Cra. 5, #26-57, Bogata, Colombia (2327678); S; Psychomotricity, Corporal Communication, Special Education

Guzmann, Emilio C. (M.D.) Medical Doctor; Coldeporte, Dept. of Sport Sciences, CRA 72A no.45 E-3, Medellin, Colombia; E,S; Child Development, Sport Injuries, Rehabilitation

Hoyas de Ochoa, Maria V. (M.Sc.) Psychologist; Coldepotes Antiioquia, Division Med. Deportiva, Calle 48 No. 70-180, Medellin, Colombia (230-57-11); S,E(R); Stress Control, Competition, Group Work, Participation

Monsalve, Ruben D. (B.Sc.) Psychologist; Colдеported Antiogeria, Division Jecnica, CU 48 #70-180, Medellin, Colombia (2305711); S,E(R); Motor Learning, Motor Development, Motivation, Youth Sport, Creativity

Orjuela, Margarta P. (B.Sc.) Psychologist; Coldeportes, Medicina des Deporte, Cra 11 #6195, Tunja, Boyaca, Bogota, Colombia (91-2489854); S,E; Anxiety, Concentration, Goal Setting, Physiology, Group Training

*Palacio, Jorge A. (M.Sc.) Professor, Director of Cultural and Physical Activities; Universite de Valle, Dept. of Psychology, Universidad Javeriana, Medio Universitario, Apartado Aereo 26239 Cali, Valle, Colombia (396716, 396785); S,E,F; Psychological Preparation, Cognitive Abilities, Team Building, Coaches Education, Youth Sport

Sanchez, Omar S. (B.Sc.) Psychologist; Jundeportes-Meta, Villavicencio, Colombia; S,E(R)

Zamora Aranda, Uriel E. (M.Sc.) Professor; U. Javeriana, Coldeportes, Carrera 34 No.4-D 70 Barrio san Fernando, Valle Apartadi Aero, S.A., Colombia 20434 (572279 Cali); S,E(R); Clinical Psychology, Organizational Psychology, Sport Psychology, Dance Psychology

Costa Rica

Picado, M.E. (D.P.E.); University of Costa Rica, School of Education, Apt, DO 7-06-70, San Jose, Costa Rica (250749); E,S,F(R); Learning, Motor Skill, Personality, Performance

Cuba

Alzugaray, Josefa (Lic.); Imd, Dept. of Psychology, Sta Catalina 12453, C. de La Habana, Cuba (41-1542); E,S; Control, Fatigue, Recovery, Volition, Motivation

Berm Dez, Angeolina (Ph.D.); Imd, Dept. of Psychology, Sta Catalina 12453, C. de La Habana, Cuba (41-1542); R,S,E(R); Self-Control, Stress, Fatigue, Recovery, Motor Learning

Crusellas, Jorge (Lic.); Imd, Dept. of Psychology, Sta Catalina 12453, C. de La Habana, Cuba (41-1542); E,S; Attention, Stress, Motor Learning, Arousal, Constitution

Cruz, Leonardo (Lic.); Imd, Dept. of Psychology, Sta Catalina Y Boyeros, C. de La Habana, Cuba (41-1542); E,S; Psychophysiology, Experimental Psychology, Attention, Reaction Time, Skill

Del Pino, Marta (Lic.); Imd, Dept. of Psychology, Sta Catalina Y Boyeros, C. de La Habana, Cuba (41-1542); E,S; Leadership, Motivation, Social Psychology, Personality, Stress

Feranandez, Antonio (Lic.); Imd, Dept. of Psychology, Sta Catalina Y Boyeros, C. de La Habana, Cuba (41-1542); E,S; Group, Social Psychology, Motivation, Self Control, Thinking

Fernandez, Estrella (Lic.); Inder, Cinid, Ciudad Deportiva Via Blanca Y Boyeros, Cerro. C. Habana, Cuba (40-3302); S,R,F(R); Trainer Psychology, Social Research Test, Social Psychology, Motivation, Attitude

Garcia, Manuel (Lic.); Imd, Dept. of Psychology, Sta Catalina Y Boyeros, C. de La Habana, Cuba (41-1542); E,S; Relaxation, Children, Talent, Attention, Stress

Garcia Bravo, Marta (Lic.); Cinid-Inder, Mediciones Deportivas, Via Blanca Y Boyeros, Cuidad Habana, Cuba (7-3511); E,S; Cultural Differences, Social Psychology, Stress, Personal Attitudes

Garcia Ucha, Francisco (Ph.D.) Dept. Head; Imd, Dept. of Psychology, Sta Catalina 12543, C. de La Habana, Cuba (41-9680); E,S; Motivation, Stress, Self-Control, Psychological Training, Volleyball

Gonzalez, German (Lic.); Imd, Dept. of Psychology, Sta Catalina 12543, C. de La Habana, Cuba (41-1542); E,S; Stress, Hypnosis, Relaxation, Acupuncture, Attention

Gonzalez, Luis G. (Ph.D.); Imd, Dept. of Psychology, Sta Catalina y Boyeros, C. de La Habana, Cuba (419582); E,S; Stress, Personality, Motivation, Emotion, Set

Gonzalez, Matilde (Lic.); Imd, Dept. of Psychology, Sta Catalina Y Boyeros, C. de La Habana, Cuba (41-1310); E,S; Motivation, Set, Children, Thinking, Attention

Gutierrez, Pablo (Lic.); Imd, Dept. of Psychology, Sta Catalina Y Boyeros, C. de La Habana, Cuba (41-1542); E,S; Relaxation, Attention, Social Psychology, Group, High Altitude

Loiz Morales, Jorge Luis (Lic.); Cinid Inder, Dept. of Sports Measurements, Via Blanca Y Boyeros, Cuidad Habana, Cuba (40-3302); S,E; Social Research, Psychological Diagnosis, Sport Psychology, Computation in Psychology, Application

Martinez, Antoniio (Ph.D.); Imd, Dept. of Psychology, Sta Catalina Y Boyeros, C. de La Habana, Cuba (41-1542); E,S; Motor Learning, Relaxation, Self-Control, Attention, Stress

Martinez, Osmel (Ph.D.); Isfc, Dept. of Psychology, Sta Catalina Y Boyeros, C. de La Habana, Cuba (41-1310); R,S; Skill, Attention, Mental Representation, Motor Learning

Menendez, Raquel (Lic.); IMD, Dept. of Psychology, Sta Catalina Y Boyeros, C. de La Habana, Cuba (41-1542); B,E,S; Motor Learning, Skill, Stress, Attention, Experimental Psychology

Perez, Rosendo (Lic.); Imd, Dept. of Psychology, Sta Catalina Y Boyeros, C. de La Habana, Cuba (41-1542); E,S; Social Psychology, Group Cohesion, Tactics, Thinking

Peron, Raul (Lic.); Isfc M. Fajardo, Dept. of Psychology, Sta Catalina Y Boyeros, C. de La Habana, Cuba (41-1310); E,S; Motivation, Set, Self, Thinking, Emotion

Rivero, Sonia (Lic.); Imd, Dept. of Psychology, Sta Catalina Y Boyeros, C. de La Habana, Cuba (41-1542); E,S; Coordination, Attention, Skill, Self-Control, Balance

Rogriguuez, Ivonne (Lic.); Imd, Dept. of Psychology, Sta Catalina 12453, C. de La Habana, Cuba (41-1542); E,F,I,S; Coordination, Stress, Attention, Motor Learning, Track and Field

Russel, Lionel (Lic.); Isfc M. Fajardo, Dept. of Psychology, Sta Catalina Y Boyeros, C. de La Habana, Cuba (41-1310); R,E,S; Tactics, Cohesion, Stress, Psychological Preperation, Attention

Sabas, Gustavo (Lic.); Imd, Dept. of Psychology, Sta Catalina Y Boyeros, C. de La Habana, Cuba (40-

4506); E,R,S; Motivation, Attention, Relaxation, Stress, Emotion

Sanchez, Maria (Lic.); Isfc M. Fajardo, Dept. of Psychology, Sta Catalina Y Boyeros, C. de La Habana, Cuba (41-1310); E,S; Personality, Attention, State Psyche, Psychophysiology, Preparation

Suarez, Silvia (Lic.); Isfc M. Fajardo, Dept. of Psychology, Sta Catalina Y Boyeros, C. de La Habana, Cuba (41-1310); E,S; Motor Learning, Children, Skill, Attention, Representation

Sus, Cristina (Lic.); Imd, Dept. of Psychology, Sta Catalina 12453, C. de La Habana, Cuba (41-1542); E,S; Skill, Self-Control, Talent, Hypnosis, Adolescent

Vidaurreta, Luisa (Lic.); Imd, Dept. of Psychology, Sta Catalina 12453, C. de La Habana, Cuba (41-1543); E,S; Motivation, Tactics, Talent, Personality, Stress

Czechoslovakia

Badurova, M. (Ph.D.); Fakulta Telesnej Vychojv A Sportu, Bratislava, Czechoslovakia 88621; C,E, G(R),R(S,R); Relaxation, Personality, Top Athletes, Clinical

Bezak, Jozef (Ph.D.); Ftvs Uk, Dept. of Psychology, Nabr. L. Svobodu 9, Bratislava, Czechoslovakia (517-51); C,R; Selection, Perception, Resistance, Top Athletes, Methodology

Frantisek, Man (Ph.D.), Associate Professor of Psychology; Dept. of Psychology, Jeronymova 10, 371 15 Ceske Budejovice, Czechoslovakia; C,E,R,G(R); Achievement Motivation, Test Anxiety, Personality, Top Athletes, Hockey

*Hosek, Vaclav (Ph.D.) Dean, Professor; FTVS UK, Dept. of Psychology, J. Martiho 31, 16252 Prague, Czechoslovakia (362-002, 337-2021); C,E,R; Motivation, Psychodiagnosis, Resistance, Stress, Diving

*Janak, Vladimir (Ph.D.); Charles University, Faculty of Physical Education and Sport, Prague, Czechoslovakia (252656); C,E,R; Personality, Social and Group Training, Sport Talents

*Kabele, Josef (Ph.D.); Physical Education, Charles University, Martiho 31, 160 00 Prague 6, Czechoslovakia Ministry of Education, Youth, and Physical Education, Karmelitska 5, 110 00 Prague 1, Czechoslovakia; C,E,R,SLOVAK,G(R,W),POL(R); Motor and Psychic Development, Sport for All, Participation, Motivation, Psychology of Sport for Disabled People

Kodym, M. (Prof.C.Sc.); Psychologicky Ustav Csav, Pod Vodarenskov Vezi 4, Post 18200, Prague, Czechoslovakia; C,R,F; Selection, Personality, Mental Training, Psychological Preparation

Kodym, Miloslav (Ph.D.) Director; Cas, Institute of Psychology, Husova 4, Prague 1, Czechoslovakia (2314436); R,G,C,F,E(R); Personality, Abilities, Selection of Talents, Learning, Teacher

*Komarik, E. (Ph.Dr.); Karpatske nam. 15, 831 06 Bratislava, Czechoslovakia (+42-7-282-751); E,R, F,SLOVAK,POL; Group Dynamics, Selection, Personality, Team Sports, Social Background

*Kopecka, Tamara (Ph.D.); Charles University, Institute of Physical Education, Rakovsheho 3145, Prague 4, Czechoslovakia, 143 00; C,E,G,R; Top Athletes, Relaxations, Social Psychology, Sport Talents

*Krejci, Milada Assistant, Senior Lecturer; Lehrstuhl fuer Koerperkultur, Pedagogiche Fakultat Ceske Budejovice, Borsov n. Vlt. 244, Ceske Budejovice, Czechoslovakia 37115 (40501); C,G,R,SLOVAK, E(R,W),POL(S,R),UK(S,R); Social Psychology of Sport, Rules of the Game—Socialization, Sport and Education

Macak, Ivan (Ph.D.) Dean; Ftvs-Uk, Dept. of Psychology, Nabr. L. Svobodu 9, Bratislava, Czechoslovakia (53613); C,G,R; Motivation, Consciousness, Coaches, Psychological Preparation, Personality

*Man, F. (Ph.D.) Associate Professor; Dept. of Psychology, Jeronymova 10, 371 15 Ceste Budejovice, Czechoslovakia; C,E,R,G(R); Achievement Motivation, Test Anxiety, Personality, Top Athletes, Hockey

Miksik, O. (Prof.Dr.); Om, 8 Bohinice, Prague 1800, Czechoslovakia; C,R,E; Personality, Top Athletes, Stress, Assessment, Self-Control

*Palkovic, V.; Research Institute of Child Psychology and Patopsychology, Dept. of Gifted Children, Legionarska 4, Bratislava, Czechoslovakia 80100 (07-672-49); SLOVAK,E(S,R),R; Anxiety, Gifted Children, Mental Training, Before Start State

Pokorny, Miroslav; Karlsuniversitaet, Forschungsinstitut fuer Koerperkultur, Ujezd 450, Prague 1, Czechoslovakia 11807

*Polisensky, Miroslav (Ph.D.); SVS MS CR, Dept. of Psychology, Strahov, Blok 12, Praha 6, Czechoslovakia; C,E,R; Top Athletes, Mental States, Regulation, Social Psychology

*Ruisel, Imrich (Ph.D.); Institute of Experimental Psychology, Kocelova 15, Bratislava, Czechoslovakia (66219); E,R,POL; Personality, Laterality, Anxiety, Referees, Cognitive Processes

*Rychtecky, Antonin (Ph.D.) Professor; Charles University, FTVS UK, Jose Martiho 31, Prague 6, 162 52 Czechoslovakia (369941); E,R,G(R); Psychological Preparation of Sportsmen, Motor Learning, Volitional Effort, Need for Achievement, Psychology of Physical Education at School

*Slepicka, Pavel (Ph.D.); Fakulta Telesne Vychovy, Jose Martiho 31, 162 52 Prague 6, Czechoslovakia (369941); E,R,C; Social Psychology, Counseling, Volleyball

*Svoboda, Bohumil (Ph.D.) Professor; Faculty of Physical Education and Sport, Dept. of Pedagogy and Psychology, Jose Martiho 31, Prague, Czechoslovakia (369941-9); E,G,C,F(S,R),R(S,R); Personality, Coach Behavior, Top Athletes, Counseling

Vacko, A.; Faculta Telesnej Vychovoy A Sportu, Bratislava, Czechoslovakia 88621 (51751); C,E(R), G,R; Aggression, Anxiety, Personality, Relaxation, Rowing

*Valkova, Hana (Ph.D.); University Palacky, Dept. of Physical Culture, Sportovni hala UP, Olomouc, Czechoslovakia, 772 (00/68-27761); E,R,C; Teaching, Physical Education, Development, Sport of Disabled

*Vanek, Miroslav (Prof.); University of Charles, Faculty of Physical Education and Sport, Jose Martiho 31, 162 52 Prague 6, Czechoslovakia (369941); E,F,G,R,C; Top Athletes, Personality, Counseling, Competition, Fear, Ice Hockey

Denmark

Gleisner, Freddy Advisor; Sonkt Anna Gymnasium, Dept. of Physical Education, Norrebred 53, Valensbak, Denmark 2625 (2640956); E,G; Mental Training

*Groenlykke, Per (Cand. Psych.) Clinical Psychologist; Esplanaden 46/3, Copenhagen, Denmark DK-1246 (33-12-00-39); E,G; Somato-Psychics, Stress, Agoraphobia, Social Phobia

Hansen, J.-H. (Cand. Psych.); Gladsaxe Seminarium, Dept. of Sport, Tehgialvej 5, Ballerup, Denmark 2750 (02-651555); DAN,E,G; Anxiety, Competition, Personality, Stress Management, Relaxation

Hansen, S.; Dansk Boldspil-Union, Educational Dept., P.H. Lings Alle 4, Copenhagen, Denmark 2100 (01-424540); DAN,E,F(R),G(R); Personality, Counseling

*Jvan, Nickolaj (Ph.D.); Gunlogsgade 22-2-2, Kopenhagen, Denmark 2300 (01-575875); B,DAN, N, R, E(S,R), G(S,R), SC(S,R), SE(S,R), SLOVAK (S,R), SLOVENE(S,R), SW(S,R), UK(S,R), C(S), I(S), POL(S); Anxiety, Alcohol, Sports Medicine, Physical Fitness

Norske, Arno (Ph.D.) Psychologist; Radhuset, Skolepsykologisk Kontor, Fredericksverk, Israels Plads, Romersgade 5, Copenhagen, Denmark DK-1362 (02-1210022); E,F,G,DAN,I,R(S,R); Anxiety, Competition, Top Athletes, Personality, Counseling

Petersen, Jorn Ravnholt (M.S.) Consultant; Thorsgade 11 St.Tv., DK-2200 Copenhagen N., Denmark (4531 85-75-51); E,G(S,R),D; Goal Setting, Stress Management, Mental Training, Sport Psychology for Children, Rehabilitation, Counseling

*Richter, Joern (M.A.) Psychologist; Den Jyske Idratsskole, Dept. of Physical Education, Oernebjerg Vej 22, DK-7100 Vejle, Denmark (75831062); DAN,E,F(S,R),G; Stress, Anxiety, Motivation, Burn-Out, Injuries

*Skovmand, Lars (Ph.D.) Psychologist; Dansk Idraets Forbund, Idraettens Hus., Amundsensvej 35b, Copenhagen, Lyngby, Denmark DK2800; E,DAN,G(S,R),F(R); Anxiety, Competition, Conflict, Soccer, Counseling

*Stelter, Reinhard, Lecturer; Danmarks Hojskole for Legemsovelser, The Danisch State Institute of Physical Education, Norre Alle 51, Copenhagen N, Denmark DK-2200, (+45-31392555, +45-35362414); G,DAN,E; Identity Development in Sport and Movement, Teaching Behavior, Coach Consultation, Movement Therapy (Gestalt Oriented)

*Worm, O., Director; Den jyske ldraetsskole, DK 7100 Vejle, Denmark (75820811, 7582-0680); G; Top Athletes, Counseling

Ye Ping

Chien Lau-Hoei

Vaclav Hosek

Bohumil Svoboda

Ecuador

Delgado, Bolivar A.G. (M.D.) Medical Doctor; Health Ministry, Sport Sciences, Dept. of Medicine, Amazonas F11Y Ramirez Davalol, Quito, Ecuador; S,E(S,R); Sport, Injuries, Rehabilitation, Psychopathology

Farias, Orlando B. (M.D.) Medical Doctor; Health Ministry, Sport Sciences, Dept. of Medicine, Apartado Postal 378, Portoviejo, Manabi, Ecuador; S,E(S,R); Sport, Injuries, Psychopathology, Rehabilitation

Egypt

Allawy, Mohamed (Ph.D.); 62 Abasia Street, Cairo, Egypt (827249); E,G,A,F(S,R); Anxiety, Aggression, Personality, Self-Concept, Attitudes

El-Arabi, Shomoun (Ph.D.) Professor; Faculty of Physical Education, Gymnastics, Giza Pyramids Street, Cairo, Egypt (850776); E,A; Mental Training, Gymnastics, Peak Perfromance, Self-Concept

El-Helaly, E. (Ph.D.); Helwan University, Faculty of Physical Education, Cairo, Egypt (986276); E,A; Sociometric, Attitudes, Group Dynamics, Personality, Sociology

El-Naggar, Abdelwahab (Ph.D.) Professor; King Saud University, Dept. of Physical Education, c/o 30 Shallaby Street, Hadayk El-Kubah, Cairo, Egypt (202-283-1095); E,A; Cognition, Development, Fitness, Coaching, Statistics

El-Swaffy, A. (M.Sc.); Helwan University, Faculty of Physical Education, Cairo, Egypt (986276); E,A; Relaxation, Autogenic Training, Swimming, Emotion, Anxiety

Enan, M. (Ph.D.); Helwan University, Faculty of Physical Education, Cairo, Egypt (986276); E,A; Aspiration, Swimming, Coaching, Success, Failure

Ez-Eldin, H. (Ph.D.); Helwan University, Faculty of Physical Education, Cairo, Egypt (986276); E,A; Morale Relationships, Coaching, Field Hockey, Motor Learning

Ibrahim, S. (Ph.D.); Helwan University, Faculty of Physical Education, Cairo, Egypt (986276); E,G,A; Aggression, Personality, Wrestling, Anxiety, Emotion

Ismail, Magda M. (Ph.D.) Professor; Faculty of Physical Education for Girls, Gymnastics, Gizera, Cairo, Egypt (829596); E,A; Motivation, Gymnastics, Personality

Rizalla, A. (Ph.D.); Helwan University, Faculty of Physical Education, Alexandria, Egypt; E,A; Attitudes, Swimming, Personality, Motivation, Motor Learning

Shamon, M. (Ph.D.); Helwan University, Faculty of Physical Education, Cairo, Egypt; E,A; Self-Concept, Emotion, Gymnastics, Personality, Anxiety

England

Alderson, G.J.K. (Ph.D.); Sheffield City Polytechnic, Dept. Physical Education and Human Movement Studies, Wentworth, Yorkshire, England (0226-742161); E,F(R); Motor Skill, Information Processing, Motion Prediction, Development

*Biddle, Stuart J.H. (Ph.D.) Lecturer; University of Exeter, Physical Education Association Research Centre, Heavitree Road, Exeter, England EX1 2LU (0392-264751, EET260@UK.AC.EXETER); E; Health, Attributions, Achievement, Fitness, Motivation

Bond, Clive E. (M.A.); Leeds Polytechnic, Lsz 9JT, Carnegie College of Physical Education, Leeds,

England (0532-31751); E; Cricket, Teacher Training, Selection, Motor Skill

*Bull, Stephen J. (Ph.D.) Senior Lecturer; Brighton Polytechnic, Chelsea School of Human Movement, Gaudick Road, Eastbourne, East Sussex, England (273-600900, 273-643704); E; Mental Training, Coach Education, Stress, Team Building

*Burwitz, Les (Ph.D.) Head of Sport Science; Crewe and Alsager College, Division of Sport Science, Alsager, Stoke-on-Trent, Staffordshire, England ST7 2HL (0270-500661); E; Learning, Control, Observational Learning, Anticipation, Soccer

Byrne, A.T.J. (M.Sc.) Technical Officer; Coaching Promotions, 4 College Close, Beckett Park, Leeds, England LS6 3QH (0532-744802); E; Motivation, Goal Setting, Service Issues, Education, Future Directions

Cockerill, Ian M. (Ph.D.); University of Birmingham, Dept. of Physical Education, P.O. Box 363, Birmingham, England (021-7421301); E; Anxiety, Competition, Personality, Perception, Motor Control

Cocup, Derek (M.A.); Sheffield City Polytechnic, Dept. Physical Education and Human Movement Studies, Sheffield City, England (0226-742161); E,F(R); Motor Skill, Information Processing, Learning

*Collins, David J. (Ph.D.) Senior Lecturer; St. Mary's College, Movement Studies Dept., Waldegrave Road, Twickenham, Middlesex, England (01-892-0051); E,F; Psychophysiology, Stress, Mental Preparation, Adventure Education, Coach Education

Crisfield, Penny M. (M.Sc.); St. Mary's College, Movement Studies, Strawberry Hill, Twickenham, England (01-8920051); E,G(R); Arousal, Attention, Personality, Top Athletes, Anxiety

Davids, Keith W. (Ph.D.) Senior Lecturer; Liverpool Polytechnic, School of Health Sciences, Byrom Street, Liverpool, England L33AF (051-207-3581); E,F(R); Vision, Motor Control, Soccer, Anxiety, Mental Training

*Fox, K.R. (Ph.D.), Lecturer/Researcher; Physical Education Association Research Centre, University of Exeter, Exeter, England EX1 2LU (0392-264890, 0392-411274); E; Exercise, Health, Self-Perception, Attitudes, Obesity Treatment

*Jones, J. Graham (Ph.D.) Lecturer; Loughborough University, Dept. Physical Education and Sport Science, Loughborough, England LE11 3TU (0509-223287, 0509-231776, JGJONES@MULTICS.LUT.AC.UK); E; Stress, Control, Performance, Models, Mental Training

Kane, John E. (Ph.D.) Principal; West London Institute of Higher Education, Borough Road, Isleworth, Middlesex, England (01-568-8741); E,F; Personality, Stress, Self-Esteem, Cognition, Motivation

Lee, Martin J. (Ph.D.) Director; Institute for the Study of Children in Sport, 37 Lansdowne Road, Bedford, England MK40-2B2 (0234-51966); E; Children, Sportsmanship, Leadership, Stress, Control

McLeod, Peter D. (Ph.D.) Lecturer; Oxford University, Dept. of Psychology, South Parks Road, Oxford, England (0865-271389); E; Vision, Reaction Time, Cricket, Attention

*Miller, Brian P. (M.A.) Private Practice; 10 The Swallows, Harlow, Essex, England (0279 29243); E; Performance, Enhancement, Elite, Injury, Imagery

*Morris, Peter R. (M.Ed., M.Sc., C.Psychol.) Principal Lecturer; Leeds Polytechnic, Carnegie Centre of Physical Education, Recreation and Sport, Leeds, England (759061); E; Skill, Learning, Sports Coaching, Therapeutic Recreation

Morris, Tony (A.M., Ph.D.) Senior Lecturer; West Sussex Ihe, Dept. of Human Movement Studies,

College Lane, Chichester, West Sussex, England (0243-787911); E; Relaxation, Imagery, Attention, Table Tennis, Perception

Roach, Neil K. (B.Sc.) (Hons.) Research Assistant; Crewe and Alsager College of H.L., Dept. of Sport and Human Science, Alsagel, Stoke-on-Trent, Staffordshire, England ST7 2HL (0206-562177); E; Observational Learning, Coaching, Soccer, Cricket, Movement Analysis

Sanderson, Frank H. (Ph.D.) Director; Liverpool Polytechnic, School of Health Sciences, Byrom Street, Liverpool, England L33AF (051-207-3581); E,F(R); Stress Control, Squash, Golf, Attitudes

*Seheult, Carole, L., (M.Sc.), Consultant Clinical Sport Psychologist; Richmond House, High Shincliffe, Durham, England DH1-2PF (091-386-9581); E,F,POR; Mental Skills Training, Elite Athletes, Clinical Problems in Sport, Personality, Cognitive-Behavioral Strategies

*Smith, Nickolas C. (M.Sc.) Principal Lecturer; Crewe & Alsager College, Division of Sport Science, Alsager, Stoke-on-Trent, England ST7 2LN (0270-882500 ext. 3148, 0270-583433); E,F; Stress, Control, Coronary-Prone Behavior, Volleyball, Hypnosis

*Smyth, Mary M. (Ph.D.) Senior Lecturer; University of Lancaster, Dept. of Psychology, Lancaster, England LA14YF (0524-65201, 0524-841710); E; Memory, Skill, Dance, Catching

*Sugden, David A. (Ph.D.); Leeds University, School of Education, Leeds, England (0532-334533); E,F(R); Development, Learning, Control, Handicapped, Education

*Syer, John D. (M.A., M.Litt., M.Ed.) Director and Consultant; Sporting Bodymind Ltd., 18 Kemplay Road, London, England NW3 1SY (071-794-4066, 071-794-6700); E,F,I; Team Building, Individual Mental Training

*Taylor, Adrian H. (Ph.D.) Senior Lecturer; Brighton Polytechnic, Chelsea School of Human Movement, Gaudick Road, Eastbourne, E. Sussex, England BNZO-7SP; (273-600900, 273-643704); E; Stress, Well-Being, Adherence, Attention, Officiating

*Terry, Peter C. (M.A.) Sport Studies Head; West London Institute of Higher Education, School of Physical Education and Sport, Borough Rd., Isleworth, Middlesex, England TW7 5DU (081-568-8741); E,F; Performance Enhancement, Tennis, Coaching Behavior, Youth Sport

*Thorpe, Rod D. (M.Sc.); Loughborough University of Technology, Dept. Physical Education and Sport Science, Leicestershire, England (0509-263171, 0509-231776); E,F(R); Tennis, Information Processing, Psychology of Teaching and Coaching, Leadership

Walton, Andrew P. (B.A.) Psychologist; Blenheim Keep, 279 Leamington Road, Styvechale, Coventry, England (0203-410001); E,F; Confidence, Hypnosis, Top Athletes, Competitive, Emotion

*Whitehead, Jean (Ph.D.) Principal Lecturer; Bedford College of Higher Education, Institute for the Study of Children in Sport, 37 Lansdowne Road, Bedford, Bedfordshire, England MK40 2BZ (0234-51966); E; Motivation, Youth Sport, Motor Learning, Psychological Skills, Cognitive Development

Whiting, H.T.A. (Ph.D.) Professor Emeritus; York University, Department of Psychology, Heslington, York, YO1 5DD, England; E,D; Motor Learning, Motor Control, Skill Acquisition

Wing, Alan M. (Ph.D.); MRC Applied Psychology Unit, 15 Chaucer Road, Cambridge CB2 2EF, England (55294); E,F,G(R); Psychology, Motor Skill, Timing, Handicapped

*Wolfson, Sandy L. (Ph.D.) Senior Lecturer; Newcastle Polytechnic, Dept. of Applied Social Science, Newcastle-Upon-Tyne, England NE1 8ST

(091-232-6002); E; Anxiety, Attribution, Aggression, Stress Management, Sex Roles

Yaffe, Maurice; York Clinic, Guy's Hospital, 117 Borough High St., London SEI 1NR, England (01-4077600); E,F(S,R); Top Athletes, Competition, Behavior Modification, Anxiety, Cognition

Finland

Bjorkman, Anja (Dr.); Tikasniityntie 10, Espoo, Finland 02200

Blantz, Friederich (Dr.) Consultant; Sandelsinkatu 4, 00420 Helsinki, Finland (358-0492504) FIN,E,G,SW; Training, Golf, Stress, Personal Management

Frantsi, Pivi (M.A.) Psychologist; Finnish Sport Institute, 19120 Vierumki, Finland (224622); E,G,SW; Mental Training, Motivation, Young Athletes, Tennis, Team Sports

*Kalliopuska, Mirja A. (Ph.D.) Ph.D. Docent; University of Helsinki, Dept. of Psychology, Box 54, 00131 Helsinki, Finland (358-0833457, MKALLI-OPUSKA@FINUH.BITNET); FIN,SW,E,G(R,W); Top Athletes, Personality Tactics, Self-Esteem, Narcissism, Empathy, Women's Sport, Coaches

*Kirjonen, Juhani (Ph.D.) Professor; University of Jyvaskyla, Faculty of Sport and Health Sciences, Jyvaskyla, Finland SF 40100 (358-41602125, 358-41602011, JKIRJONEN@FINJYU.BITNET); FIN,E, SW(R),G(R); Way of Life, Work, Physical Activity, Mental Well-Being, Motivation

*Laakso, Lauri H.T. (Ph.D.) Associate Professor; University of Jyvaskyla, Dept. of Physical Education, Jyvaskyla, Finland (941-602116); E,G,SW, FIN,S(R); Social Psychology, Socialization, Sociometry, Participation, Motivation

Lappalainen, R. (Filo.Cand.); Sarkatie 4, Kuopio 70, Finland; E,SW,FIN; Coaches, Counseling, Learning, Group Dynamics, Anxiety

*Lintunen, Taru, Research Assistant; Jyvaskyla University, Seminaarinkatu 15, 40100 Jyvaskyla, Finland, (358-41-602-113, 358-41-602-001); FIN, E,SW,G(R,W); Self Perceptions, Body Image, Growth and Development

*Liukkonen, Jarmo Manager; Psychological Training Centre, Sports and Health Centre Kisakeskus, 10420 Pehjankuru, Finland (911-54420, 911-56576); E,SW,G,R; Mental Training, Stress Management, Coaching Behavior, Sportsmanship

Lyytinen, Heikki (Ph.D.) Senior Scientist; University of Jyvaskyla, Dept. of Psychology, Jyvaskyla, Finland SF-40100 (358-41292130, HLYYTINEN@-FINJYO.BITNET); E,FIN,SW(R,W),G(R,W); Psychophysiology, Anticipation, Stress, Preparation, Shooting, ERP

Mutanen, Jouko (Dr.); Finnish Psychology Union, Ylankotie 49-51 C 22, Jarvenpaa, Finland 04400

Naatanen, Risto (Ph.D.) Professor; Helsinki University, Dept. of Psychology, Ritarik. 5, Helsinki, Finland 00170 (358-01913445-3441); E, G(S,R),SW; Attention, Orienting Response, Event-Related Potentials, Sensory Memory, Activation

Numminen, Pirkko (M.Sc.) Associate Professor; University of Jyvaskyla, Dept. of Physical Education, Jyvaskyla, Finland 40100 (358-41291870); E,SW,G; Motor Learning, Motor Control, Pre-School

Pietilainen, Rauno; TUL and Olympic Committee, Dept. of Sport Psychology; Siikakankaankuja, 4 Bio, Kesi 70, Finland 94700

Puhaka, P.O. (M.D.); North Karelian County Administration, Box 116 Joensuum, Joensuu 11, Finland (97327251); E(S,R),G(S,R),SW,FIN; Anxiety, Top Athletes, Ski Jumpers, Relaxation

Salmimies, Pekka (Dr.Med.) Psychiatrist; Vuorikatu 24, Kuopio, Finland 70100

Salminen, Simo T. (Lic.Soc.Sc.) Research Fellow; University of Helsinki, Dept. of Social Psychology, Fabianinkatu 28 A, Helsinki, Finland (358-0890022) E,FIN,SW(S,R),G(S,R); Group Dynamics, Social Psychology, Ice Hockey

Salokangas, S. (Fil.Mag.Psych.); Suuniistajantie 5G18, Kuopio 20, Finland 70200 (971-126001); E,G,FIN; Anxiety, Personality, Health

Silvennoinen, Martti (Ph.D.) Head Assistant; University of Jyvaskyla, Dept. of Physical Education, Jyvasskyla, Finland 40100 (941-217711); E,S,FL,G(R); Motivation, School Children, Leisure Time, Physical Activity, School Physical Education

Telama, Risto (Ph.D.) Professor; University of Jyvaskyla, Dept. of Physical Education, Jyvaskyla, Finland SF 40100 (41-641413); FIN,E,SW,F(R), G(R); Pedagogy, Motivation, Youth Sport, Teacher Training, Nature

Tuominen, Kalevi Training Manager; Finnish Olympic Committee, Radiokatu 12, Helsinki, Finland 00240

Vilpas, Ahti; Kiertomauntie 4, Vantaa, Finland 01260

France

Arnaud, Pierre (Ph.D.); Uereps Universite Lyon, Dep. 69621, 15 Bd. Du 11 Novembre, Villeurbanne, France (891753); F,E(R); Learning, Development, Adaptives, Didactics

Azemar, Georges (M.D.); I.N.S.E.P., Dep. de Formation Superieure, 11 Ave. du Tremblay, Paris, France 75012 (328-1278); F,S; Ontogeny, Motor Learning, Personality, Motivation, Risk Taking

Bayer, C.; 14, Rue du Bout Corneret, Faverolles, France 28210 (336-0734); F,G,E(R); Competition, Top Athletes, Personality

Berjaud, P.; U.E.R. Ireps, 40 Rue S.B. Clement, Villeurbanne, France 69100; F,E(S,R),S; Top Athletes, Personality, Competition, Training, Social Psychology

*Bertsch, Jean C. (Ph.D.) Pr.Dr.; Universite de Caen, Motor Learning and Psychology Laboratory, 14032 Caen, France (31-06-03-66); F,E,G; Motor Learning, Task Analysis, Psychology of Expertise, Coaching

Bilard, Jean (Ph.D.) Professeur; Universite de Montpelier 1, STAPS, 700 Avenue Pic St. Loup, Montpelier, France 34000 (67-654594); E,F,S; Aggression, Stress, Self-Image, Body Image, Physical Activity

Bosc, G.G.; I.N.S.E.P., Haut-Niveau, 11, Ave., du Tremblay, Paris, France 75012 (1808-4120); E(R,S),F,S,I(R,S); Competition, Top Athletes, Coaching, Pedagogy, Learning

*Bouet, Michel A. (Dr.) Emeritus; Les Bouexieres, 35580 Guichen, France (99-57-47-91); E,F,G(R);

Motivation, Decision Making, Gliding, Outdoor Education, Social Psychology

Bregiroux, F.B. (Dipl.); 1 Alle Traversiere, Fresnes, France 94260 (2374525); F,E(R); Selection, Deviance, Personality, Subcultures

*Bricco, Jean Jacques (D.E.A.); Sciences de l'Education, Faculte lettaer et Sciences Humaines, 34 bis Rue du, Grand Pzadet, 34430, Saint Jean de Vedas, Lyon, France (67-47-31-23); F,S(S,R,W); Mental Preparation, Motivation, Stress, Emotional Control, Handball

Caviglioli, B.C. (Prof.Eph.) Direct; Regionale Jeunesse Sport Loisins; 7 Ave., General Leclerc, Marseille, France (91-50-22-23); E,F,I(S); Education, Administration, Pedagogy

Crevoisier, Jacques C. (Ph.D.) Professor; 25 Chemin des Bisquey, 25000 Besancon, France (81-67-37-93); F,E(S,R); Coaching, Soccer, Psychology, Communication, Leadership

Durny, Annick (Maitrise STAPS) Etudiant-Chercheur; Universite de Dijon, UFR-STAPS, Campuo Montmuzard BP138-21004 Dijon, Cedex, France (80-39-67-29); F,E,G; Gymnastics, Handedness in Sports, Mental and Physical Rehearsal in Sports, Reaction Time

Famose, Jean-P. (Ph.D.) Researcher; INSEP, 11 Avenue du Tremblay, Paris, France 75012 (43-74-11-21); E,F,S(R); Motor Learning, Motivation, Task Analysis, Sports Psychology, Sport Pedagogy

Finet-Guevel, Catherine (DEA STAPS) Etudiant-Chercheur; Universite de Dijon, UFR-STAPS, Campus Montmuzard BP138-21004 Dijon, Cedex, France (80-39-67-29); F,E; Judo, Space Representation, Mental and Physical Rehearsal

Garassino, R.; Academie de Lyon, Dir. Region. de la Jeunesse et Des Sports, 38 Rue Leon Lenhoux, Lyon, France 69422 (78-60-63-33); E,F,R(R),I(S,R); Psychology, Pedagogy

*Gillot, Gerard (Ph.D.) Maitre de Conferences; Universite de Dijon, UFR-STAPS, Campus Montmuzard BP138 21004 Dijon, France (80-39-67-29, 80-39-67-02); F,E; Handedness, Information Processing, Decision Making, Mental and Physical Rehearsal, Aviation Psychology

Groslambert, Alain (Professeur EPS, Maitre STAPS) Studiant-chercheur; Universite de Dijon, UFR-STAPS, Campus Montmuzard BP138 - 21004 Dijon, France (80-39-67-29); F,E; Biathlon, Mental and Physical Rehearsal in Sports

Jeu, Bernard (Doct.); Universite Lille, 3, Villeneuve d'Asc., Villeneuve, France 59650 (911300); F,R,E(R); Culture, Society, Sport, Organization

Kane-Toure, Ndeye D. (DEA-STAPS) Etudiant-Chercheur; Universite de Dijon, UFR-STAPS, Campus Montmuzard BP 138 - 21004 Dijon, Cedex, France (80-39-67-29); F,E, Several African; Mental and Physical Rehearsal, Traditional Physical Activities, Judo

*Lecocq, Gilles P. (Docteur) Psychologue; 23 Rue Massenet, Cormeilles-en-Paris, France 95240

Stuart J.H. Biddle

John E. Kane

Juhani Kirjonen

Martti Silvennoinen

(39783724); E,F; Sport Success, School Success, Adolescence, Mental Preparation, Systemic Analysis

*Lefebvre, J.F.; 12 Rue du G.G. Eboue, Hauts de Seine, France 92130; F; Pedagogy, Development, Creativity

Leveque, Marc (Ph.D.), Professor; Physical Education, UFR-STAPS, University of Burgundy, BP138, 21004, Dijon, Cedex., France, (80-39-67-99); E; Clinical Method, Mental Training, Personality, Sailing, Soccer

Louveau, C. (Dec. Sociol.); INSEP, 11 Ave., du Tremblay, Paris, France 75012 (8084120); F,E(R); Family, Outdoor Education, Competition, Psychological Preparation

Lucas, Dominique (DESS) Psychologist; 1 Rue des Cerisiers, Abbeville, France 80100 (22-24-91-55); F,E(R); Personality, Evaluation, Psychological Support, Autonomy, Coach-Athlete Relationship

Macario, B.M. (Ph.D.); D.D.J.S.L., 66, Rue St. Sebastian, Marseille, France (91-37-41-00); E,F; Evaluation, Pedagogy, Learning, Adolesence

Mameletzi, Dimitra (Professeur Sport) Etudiant-Chercheur; Universite de Dijon, UFR-STAPS, Campus Montmuzard BP 138 - 21004 Dijon, Cedex, France (80-39-67-29); F,E,G; Psychomotor Aptitudes, Disabled, Blindness, Mental and Physical Rehearsal

Marcoux, S.; 112 Route de Melon, Saintry, France 91101; E,F; Dance, Athletics

*Missoum, Guy (Ph.D.) Professor; Universite Paris X, Nanterre, UFR.APS, Batiment COSOM, 200 Avenue de la Republique, 92001, Nanterre Cedex, France (40977690); E,F,S(R); Hypnosis, Mental Training, Evaluation, Modeling

Mouret, C. (Prof.Eps.); Centre Regionale Jeunesse Et Sport, Antibes, France (34-95-46-93); F,S(S,R); Competition, Administration, Development

Nougier, Vincent N. (Ph.D.) Professor; UFRAPS, U. Joseph Fourier, BP S3X, 38 041, Grenoble, Cedex, France (76-51-46-94); F,E; Information Processing, Attention, Motor Control

Parlebas, Pierre; INSEP, 11 Ave., du Tremblay, Paris, France 75012; F; Motor Performance, Top Athletes, Sport Games, Communication, Outdoor Education

Pinon, B. (Prof. D'Eps.); UER D'Eps de Paris, 1 Rue Tacretelle, Paris, France 75012 (8285562); E,F; Pedagogy, Learning, Transfer, Tennis

Poncet, Marc (Professeur EPS, DEA STAPS) Etudiant-Chercheur; Universite de Dijon, UFR-STAPS, Campus Montmuzard BP 138 - 21004 Dijon, France (80-39-67-29); F,E; Information Processing, Decision Making, Tennis, Mental and Physical Rehearsal

*Rauch, Andre Professor; Universite de Strasbourg II, 16 Rue Schwendi, Strasbourg, France 67000 (88-35-31-26); G,F,E(R,S); Aggression, Violence, Training, Health, Hobby

Revenu, Daniel (Ph.D.); 92 Fue Haies Fleuries, Vert-St.-Denis, France (8084120); E,F,S; Desire, Anticipation, Adaptives, Relaxation, Self-Control

*Ripoll, Hubert (Ph.D.) Director; I.N.S.E.P., Research Laboratory, 11, Ave Tremblay, Paris, France 75012 (43-74-11-21, 43-74-54-11); E,F; Visual Behavior, Motor Behavior, Attention, Laterality

*Rivolier, J. (Prof.); Rue de l'Universite, 195, Paris, France 75007 (1-47-05-45-32); E,F; Small Groups, Social Psychology, Top Athletes, Stress, Selection, Psychological Preparation

Roche, D. Professeur; Domaine Universitaire, EUR Education Physique et Sport, B.P. 68, St Martin d'Heres, France 38402; F; Pedagogy, Personality, Communication, Competition, Judo

Roget, Jacqueline (Certificat) Physiotherapist; 27 Rue Doyen-Gosse, La Tronche, France 38700 (76-44-19-54); E,F,I(R); Self-Hypnosis, Mental Training

Sivadon, Paul (Dr.); 8 Rue Alboni, Paris, France F-75016

*Temprado, Jean J. (M.Sc.); Membre associe au laboratoire de Psychologie du Sport, INSEP, 11 Ave du Tremblay, Paris, France 75012 (43-74-11-21); E,F; Decision, Information Processing, Motor Control, Task Analysis

Therme, P.; U.E.R. E.P.S., Case Postale 910, Roquevaire, France 13360 (91-41-24-76); F; Therapy, Clinical, Subconscious, Judo

Thill, Edgar E. (Ph.D.) Professor; Universit de Clermont Ferrand, U.F.R. de Psychologie, 34 Blvd. Carnot, Clermont, France F-63.000 (73-92-97-32); F,E,G(S); Motivation, Imagery, Personality Tests

*Thomas, Raymond (Ph.D.) Professor; Universite de Paris X, 200 Ave. de la Republique, Nanterre, France 92000 Nanterre (43-39-68-31); F,E(R); Social Psychology, Winning Factors

Vayer, Pierre (Prof.Ep.); Universite de Rennes II, UER d'Eps, Ave., Gaston-Berger, Rennes, France (99-59-04-82); F,I,E(R); Children, Sociology, Students, Research

*Vom Hofe, Alain (Ph.D.) Maitre de Conference; UER de Psychologie de Paris V, Lab. de Psychologie Differentielle, 28 Rue Serpente, Paris, France 75006 (16-1-40-51-98-99); E,F; Cognitive Processes, Team Sports, Differential Psychology

Germany

Albrecht, Dirk (Ph.D.); Hamburger Sport-Verein, Rotenbaumchaussee 125, Hamburg 13, Germany 2000; G,E; Top Athletes, Personality

*Alfermann, Dorothee (Ph.D.), Professor; University of Giessen, Dept. of Sport Science, Kugelberg 62, Giessen, D-6300, Germany; G,E,F; Women's Sport and Sex Roles, Life-Span Development of Top Athletes, Interaction in Sport Groups, Sport With Psychiatric Patients, Career Development of Athletes

Allmer, H. (Prof.Dr.); Psych. Inst. der Deutschen Sporthochschule, Koln, Germany D-5000 (49821550); E,G; Motivation, Stress, Teacher Behavior

Amesberger, Gnter (Ph.D.); Universitaet Wien, Institute fuer Sportwissenschaften, Auf Dem Schmelz 6, Wien, Germany A-1150; G

Artus, Hans-Gert (Ph.D.); Universitaet Bremen, Sportwissenschaft, Fachbereich 11, Badgaseteiner Straa, Bremen 33, Germany 2800; G

Baedke, Dirkwalter (Ph.D.); Altstadtschule Rendsburg, An der Bleiche, Rendsburd, Germany 2730; G

*Baeumler, Guenther (Dr.Phil.Habil.) Professor (Ordinarius); Technische Universitaet Muenchen, Lehrstuhl fuer Sportpsychologie, Connollystrasse 32, D-8000 Muenchen 40, Germany (089-35491-341); G,E; Ability, Competition, History, Personality, Therapy

Bartels, Ludwig; Am Brink 7, Bederkesa-Ankelohe, Germany 2852; G

*Bartmann, Ulrich (Ph.D.); West. Klinik fuer Psychiatrie, Postfach 1347, 4788 Warstein, Germany (02902-822206); G,E

Baumann, Sigurd (Ph.D.) Professor; Universitaet Wurtzburg, Institut fuer Sportwissenschaft, Spitztannenweg 9, Wurtzburg, Germany D-8700;

*Beckmann, Juergen (Ph.D.); Max-Planck-Institut fuer Psychologische Forschung, Leopoldstr. 24, 800 Muenchen 40, Germany 8000, (089-38602-1, 089-342473); G

Bergmann, Wolfgang; Gemeindehohl 4, Mainz 33, Germany 6500; G

Berndt, Inge (Ph.D.); Universitaet Bielfeld, Fakultt fuer Psychologie und Sportwissenschaft, Abt Sportwissenschaft Universittsstr. 25, Bielefeld, Germany 4800; G

*Besslich, Axel (Dipl.Psych., Dipl.Kaufmann); Pfalzelersh 34, Trier, Germany 5500; G,E,F,S; Endurance Sports, Personal Development and Sport, Management Training and Sport

Bielefeld, Juergen (Ph.D.); Universitaet Dortmund, Sondererziehung und Rehabilitation, Fachbereich 13 Motopdagogik, Emil-Figge-Straae, Dortmund 1, Germany 4600; G

Blanke-Malmberg, Beate; Universitaet Hamburg, Olendorp 33, Hamburg, Germany D-2000

*Blischke, Klaus (Dr.); Universitaet des Saarlandes, Sportwissenschaftliches Institut, Lehrstuhl Sportwissenschaft, Saarbrucken, Germany D-6600 (0681-302-4091); E,G

Borger, Maritta; Im Hippel 17, Postfach 82, Tuettendorf, Germany 6535; G

Bosch, H. (Dipl.); University of Konstanz, Sporthochschule, Am Giessberg, Konstanz, Germany (07531-882590); E,F(S); Personality, Motivation

Brazina, Ivan (Ph.D.); Pfinztalstr. 74, Karlsruhe, Germany 7500; G

Brehm, Walter (Ph.D.); Universitaet Bielefeld, Fakultt fuer Psychologie und Sportwissenschaft, Abt Sportwissenschaft, Universittsstr. 25, Bielefeld 1, Germany 4800; G

Buchmeier, W. (Dipl.Psych.); Universitaet Bayreuth, Institut fuer Sportwissenschaft, Opernstrasse 22, Bayreuth, Germany (608201); E(S,R),F(R),G; Mental Training, Top Athletes, Emotion, Counseling, Pre-Game Preparation

Callies, Peter; Escheweg 3, Tbingen, Germany 7400; G

Christen, J. (Dipl.Psych.); Deutsche Sporthochschule, Psychologisches Institute, Carl Diem Weg, Koln 41, Germany 5000 (0221-4982552); E,F,G; Psychophysiology, Group Dynamics, Learning Theory, Behavior Control, Therapy

Christmann, Erich; Universitaet des Saarlandes Sportwissenschaftliches Institute, Im Stadtwald, Saarbrucken, Germany 6600; G

Classen, Wolfgang; Bergische Universitaet, Gesamthoschule Wuppertal, Grunwalderburg 21, Gauastr. 20, Wuppertal 1, Germany D-5600

*Damm, Albert Teacher, Psychologist; Psychology Institute, Deutsche Sporthochschule, Carl-Diem-Weg 6, D-5000, Koln 41, Germany (0221-4982572) G,E; Group Dynamics, Group Intervention, Movement Therapy, Body Therapy, Social Interaction

Daugs, Reinhard; Universitaet des Saarlandes, Sportwissenschaftliches Institut, Lehrstuhl Sportwissenschaft, Saarbrucken, Germany D-8600

Dohring, Gerhard; EV. Beratungsstelle, Bergstr. 16, Rotenburg, Germany 2720; G

Dombrowski, Oda (Ph.D) Professor; Universitaet Dusseldorf, Institut fuer Sportwissenschaft, Universittsstr. 1 Geb. 28.01, Dusseldorf-1, Germany D-4000

Drexel, Gunner (Ph.D.); Universitaet Tubingen, Institute fuer Sportwissenschaft, Wilhelmsstr. 124, Tubingen 1, Germany 7400; G

Dolle, Reinhard; Fallesleber-Tor-Wall 14, Braunschweig, Germany 3300; G

*Eberspaecher, Hans (Prof.Dr.); Universitaet Heidelberg, Institut fuer Sport and Sportwissenschaft, Im Neuenheimer Feld 710, Heidelberg 1, Germany 6901 (06221-564644, 564645, 564346); E,F(S,R),S(R); Psychoregulation, Group Dynam-

ics, Instruction,Cognition, Applied Sport Psychology in High Performance

Egert, Klaus; Deutscher Verband fuer modernen Funfkampf, Julius-Reiber-Str. 5, Darmstadt, Germany 6100; G

*Ennenbach, Wilfrid (Ph.D.); Universitaet der Bundeswehr Muenchen, Institut fuer Psychologie und Paedagogik, Werner-Heisenberg-Weg 39, 8014 Neubiberg, Germany

*Erdmann, Ralf (Prof., Dr., Dipl.Psych.); Deutsche Sporthochschule, Institut fuer Sport Didaktik II, Carl-Diem-Weg, Koeln 41, Germany 5000 (0221-4982456); E,G; Motivation, Social Psychology, Observation, Statistics, Research Design

*Essing, Willi (Prof., Ph.D., Dipl.Psych.) Professor; Universitaet Muenster, Institut fuer Sportwissenschaft, Horstmarer Landweg 62B, Muenster, Germany 4400; E(S),G; Group Dynamics, Development, Psychology

Feige, Karl (Dr.) Prof.Dr.; Universitaet Kiel, Dept. of Sportwissenschaft, Hohenbergstrasse 18, Kiel, Germany 2300 (0431-568341); G,E(S,R),F(R,W); Development, Motivation, Motor Learning, Top Sport, Children

Frester, Rolf; DHfK, Forschung Institut fuer Koerperkultur, Friedrich-Ludwig-Jahn-Allee 59, Leipzig, Germany 7010

Gabler, Hartmut (Prof.Dr.); Universitaet Tubingen, Institute fuer Sportwissenschaft, Wilhelmsstr. 124, Tubingen 1, Germany 7400 (07071-61457); E,F,G; Motivation, Development, Competition, Top Athletes, Group Dynamics

Gerards, Andreas; AM Trimmelter Hof 87, Trier, Germany 5500; G

*Giess-Stuber, Petra; Deutsche Sporthochschule Koeln, Institut fuer Sportdidaktik; Carl-Diem-Weg 4, Koeln 41, Germany D-5000 (0221-49827, 0221-4971782); G,E, F(R); Motivation, Stress/Coping, Feminist Theory

Goehner, U. (Prof.Dr.); Institute fuer Sportwissenschaft, Wilhelmsstr. 124, 74 Tubingen, Germany (07071-61457); E(R),F(S,R),G; Biomechanics, Motor Learning

Golz, Norbert; Freie Universitaet Berlin, Institute fuer Sportwissenschaft, Rheinbabanallee 14, Berlin 33, Germany D-1000

Grau, Uwe (Ph.D.) Professor; Christian Albrechts-Universitaet, Insitute fuer Psychologie, Olshausenstrasse 40, Olshausenstr. 40, Kiel 1, Germany D-2300

Grosser, Manfred (Ph.D.); TU Muenchen, Lehrstuhl fuer Trainings/Bewegungslehre, Connollystr 32, Muenchen 40, Germany 8000; G

Grupe, Ommo (Prof.Dr.) Professor; Universitaet Tubingen, Institute fuer Sportwissenschaft, Wilhelmsstr. 124, Tubingen 1, Germany 7400 (2912628); E,F(R),G; Movement, Body, Achievement, Sport, Play

Gunz, Detlev; DHfK, Forschung Institute fuer Koerperkultur, Friedrich-Ludwig-Jahn-Allee 59, Leipzig, Germany 7010

Haag, Herbert (Ph.D., M.S.) Professor; Christian Albrechts-University, Institute fuer Sport and Sportwissenschaft; Olshausenstr. 40, Kiel, Germany 2300; E,F; Curriculum, Instruction, Teaching-Learning Processes and Their Evaluation, Research Methodology for Sport Science

Haase, Hermann (Dipl.Psych., Prof.Dr.); Universitaet Frankfurt/M., Institute fuer Sport and Sportwissenschaft; Ginnheimer Landstr. 39, Frankfurt, Germany (7984511); E,G,I(R); Diagnosis, Psychomotricity, Mass Media, Marketing, Psychology

*Hackfort, Dieter (Ph.D.) Professor; Universitaet Heidelberg, Institute fuer Sport and Sportwissenschaft, Im Neuenheimer Feld 700, 6900 Heidelberg 1, Germany (06221-564211); E,G,F; Psychoregulation, Recreation, Pleasure, Gymnastics, Emotional Anxiety, Self Presentation, Action Theory, Methodology

Hagerdorn, Gnter (Ph.D.); Universitaet-Gesamthochschule Paderborn, Fachbereich 2/Sportwissenschaft; Warbuger Str. 10, Paderborn, Germany 4790; G

Hahmann, Heinz (Ph.D.) Professor; Johannes Gutenberg Universitaet, FB 26 Leibeserzienhung/ Sport; Christian-Lechleiner Strasse 24, Mainz, Germany D-6500

*Hahn, Erwin (Dipl.Psych.); Bundesinstitut fuer Sportwissenschaft, Carl-Diem-Weg 4, 5000 Koeln, Germany 5000 (0221-4979161, 8881178); E,F,G; Coaching, Top Sport, Stress, Youth Sport, Creativity

Hamsen, Gerhard; Institute fuer Sport and Sportwissenschaft, Im Neuenheimer Feld 710, Heidelberg, Germany 6900 (06221-564646); E,F(R),G; Human Performance, Motor Learning, Kinesthesis, Perception, Soccer

*Hanke, Udo (Prof. Dr.); University of Erlangen-Neurnberg, Institut fuer Sportwissenschaft, Regensburger Str. 160, 8500 Neurnberg; G

*Hardt, Manfred (Dipl. Psych., Dipl. Soz.-Paed.); Wall 11, Warngau, Germany 8151, (08025-1567, 08025-1418); G,E,F,GRE(S); Team and Organizational Development, Individual Efficiency Disorders, Psychosomatic Disorders

Hecker, Gerhard (Prof.Dr.) Professor; Deutsche Sporthochschule Koln, Institute fuer Sportdidaktik, Carl-Diem-Weg 6, Koeln 41, Germany 5000 (0221-4982454); E,G; Motivation, Achievement, Competition, Pedagogy, Primary School

Hecker, Hartmut (Ph.D.); Bergische Universitaet, Gesamthochschule Wuppertal, Gauadtr. 20, Gebude S 12, Wuppertal 1, Germany 5600; G

*Hermann, Hans-Dieter (Dipl.Psych.); Heiliggeistr. 11, Heidelberg, Germany 6900; G,E

Hindel, Christoph; Johannes-Gutenberg-Universitaet, Psychologices Institute; Saarstr. 21, Mainz 1, Germany 6500; G

Hoertdoerfer, B.; Universitaet Goettingen, Institut fuer Leibesuebungen, Sprangerweg 2, Goettingen, Germany 3400 (0551-395652); E(S,R),G; Movement Theory, Motor Learning, Learning Variables, Diagnosis, Leisure

*Hoff, Heinz -G. Scientific Assistant; Deutsche Sporthochschule Koeln, Psychologisches Institute, Carl-Diem-Weg 6, 5000 Koeln 41, Germany (0221-4982553); G,E,F,S(R); Motivation, Attention, Health, Relaxation, Mental Training

Hoffmeyer, Martin; Christian Albrechts-Universitaet, Institute fuer Sport und Sportwissenschaft, Olshausenstr. 40-60, Haus N 40a, Kiel 1, Germany 2300; G

Hohensee, Torsten; Markstr., Langenhorn, Germany 2255; G

Ilg, Hubert (Prof.Dr.) Professor; Ernst-Moritz-Arndt-Universitat, Sektion Sportwissenschaft, Hansfallada Strasse 2, Greifswald, Germany 2200; G,R(R); Children, Youth Sports, Motivation, Mental Load

Irmscher, Jutta; SC Dynamo Hoppengarten, Sektion Fallschirmsport, Postfach 69, Eilenburg, Germany 7280

Jackschath, Brigit (Ph.D.); Institute fuer Autogenes Training, Dellbrcker Haupstr. 8, Kol 80, Germany 5000; G

Janssen, Jan Peters (Dipl.Psych., Prof.Dr.) Professor; Christian Albrechts-Universitaet, Institute fuer Sportwissenschaft, Olshausenstrasse 40-60, Kiel, Haus N 40a, Germany 2300; E(R,W),F(R),G; Motor Learning, Cognition, Top Athletes, Diagnosis

Jonas, Bertold (Ph.D.); Studeingang Sportwissenschaft, Universitaet Bremen, Fachbereich 11, Bagasteiner Straae, Bremen 33, Germany 2800; G

Kaake, Stephen; Karl-Marx Universitaet, Sektion Psychologie, Tieckstrasse 2, Leipzig, Germany 7030

Kaminski, G. (Ph.D.); Universitaet Tuebingen, Dept. of Psychology, Friedrichstr. 21, Tuebingen, Germany 7400 (07071-292410); E,F(R),G; Cognition, Action, Ecopsychology, Top Athletes, Clinical

Kellmann, Michael; Frankfurter Str. 32a, Wrzburg, Germany 8700; G

Kemmler, Reiner (Dipl.Psych.); Arbeitsgruppe Flugpsychologie, Flugmedizinisches Institute, Postfach 172/KFL, Fuerstenfeldbruek, Germany 8080 (9621); E,G; Clinical, Stress, Mental Training, Top Athletes, Counseling

*Kirkcaldy, Bruce D. (Ph.D.) Psychologist; Dept. of Sport Psychology, Faculty of Sport Sciences, Ruhr University Bochum, 4630 Bochum, Germany (0234-700-2445, 0234-700-2000); E,G,F(R); Human Movement, Motor Skill, Personality, Individual Differences, Psychosomatics

*Kleine, Dietmar (Ph.D.); Freie Universitaet Berlin, Institute fuer Psychologie, Habelschwerdterallee 45, Berlin 33, Germany D-1000 (0049-30-8385640, 0049-30-8385634); E,F,POR,G; Sport Anxiety, Stress, Mood and Physical Activity

Klockner, Wolfgang; Universitaet Konstanz, Fachgruppe Sportwissenschaft, Postfach 7733, Konstanz, Germany 7750; G

Knab, Eckart; St. Josphshaus, Klein-Zimmern, Germany 6111; G

Knobloch, Jrg (Dr.); Deutsche Sporthochschule Kln., Psychologisches Institute, Carl Diem Weg, Koln 41, Germany 5000 (0221-4982553); G,F(S,R), E(R); Personality, Stress, Aggression, Therapy, Psychotherapy

*Kohl, Kurt (Prof.Dr.); Universitaet Bielefeld, Institute fuer Sportwissenschaft, Universitaetsstra, Bielefeld, Germany 4800 (0521-1066109); E,F,G; Motor Learning, Group Dynamics, Competition, Sport Games, Movement Theory

*Konzag, Gerd (Prof.Dr.) Professor; Martin-Luther-Universitat, Sektion Sportwissenschaft, Gimritzer Damm 299/F, Halle, 4090, Germany; G,E; Attention, Cognition, Mental Loads, Action Control

*Korndle, Hermann (Ph.D.); Universitaet Regensburg, Institute fuer Angewandte Psychologie, Universitaetstrasse 31, Regenburg, Germany D-8400

Koslowski, Manfred; Henri-Spaak Str., Alfter-Oedekoven, Germany 5305; G

Kottmann, Lutz (Ph.D.); Bergische Universitaet, Gesamthoschule Wuppertal, FB 3 - Sportwissenschaft, Gauastr. 20, Wuppertal 1, Germany 5600; G

Kramer, Helmut; WLK Stillenberg, Franz-Hegemann-Str. 34, Warstein, Germany 4788; G

Hubert Ripoll   **Erwin Hahn**

*Kratzer, Hannes (Dipl.Dr.Dr.); DHfK, Friedrich-Ludwig-Jahn Allee 59, Leipzig, Germany 7010, 49740; G,E(S,R),R(R); Psychological Training, Shooting, Diagnosis, Stress

*Kraus, Michael (Dr., Dipl.Psych.); Sozialpadaogisches Institute, Stresemannstr. 30, Berlin 61, Germany D-1000 (030-2592-313); G,E,L(R), DAN(R); Physical Activity and Mental Health, Psychoimmunology

Krempel, Rolf (Ph.D); Schulstr. 1, Clausthal-Zellerfel, Germany 3392; G

Kromichal, Vaclav; Westenstr. 25, Eichsttt, Germany 8078; G

*Kuhn, Werner (Ph.D.) Professor; Free University of Berlin, Institute of Sport Science, Hagenstr. 56, Berlin 33, Germany 1000 (030-8265995); G,E,F; Perception, Decision Making, Processing, Control, Games

Kunath, Paul (Prof.Dr.) Professor; Deutsche fuer Koerperkultur, WB Sportpsychologie, Freidrich Jahn Allee 59, Leipzig, Germany 7030 (0947-4974488); E,G,R(S,R); Personality, Social Psychology, Motivation, Theory, Action Regulation

Lange, Walter; Bergstr. 23, Aumhle, Germany 2055; G

Langenkamp, Henrich; Ruhr-Universitaet Bochum, Falkultt fuer Sportwissenschaft, Steipeler Str. 129, Bochum 1, Germany 4630; G

Leibbrand, Gabriele; Knigstrale 103, Reutlingen, Germany 7410; G

*Leist, Karl-Heinz (Prof.Dr.); TU Muenchen 40, Lehrstuhl fuer Sportpdagogik, Connollystr. 32, Muenchen 40, Germany 8000 (089-35491320); E(R,W),F,G; Motor Learning, Anxiety, Aggression, Motor Behavior, Tests

Ludwig, Konrad; Aussenstelle Magdeburg, Deutsche Hochschule fuer Koerperkultur, Wilhelm-Kopeltstrasse, Magdeburg, Germany 3060

Lutter, Heinz (Prof.Dr.); University of Regensburg, Institut fuer Sportwissenschaft, Universitaetsstr. 31, Regensburg, Germany 8400 (0941-9432517); E,G; Anxiety, Personality, Motor Learning, Competition, Children

*Macsenaere, Michael (Dipl.Psych.); Johannes-Gutenberg-Universitaet, Fachbereich Sport, Mainz, Germany 6500; G,E; Triathlon, Freeclimbing, Regeneration

*Mathesius, Renate, (Ph.D.), Head of Sport Psychology; DHfK, Forschung Institute fuer Koerperkultur, Friedrich-Ludwig-Jahn Allee 59, Leipzig, Germany 7010; G,E,R(R); Motivation, Stress, Movement Regulation, Action Control

*Maxeiner, Jurgen Professor, Dr.; Universitaet des Saarlandes—Sportwissenschaftliches Institut —Im Stadtwald, Bau 39.1, 6600 Saarbruecken, Germany

*Mayer, Reinhardt; Amselstr. 2, Balingen-Streichen, Germany 7460, 07433-5389; G,E,F; Youth Sport, Drop-Out, Psychological Counseling

Mechling, Hans (Dr.); Bundesinstitut fuer Sportwissenschaft, Hertzstr. 1, Koeln 40, Germany 5000 (02234-76011); E,F,G; Motor Behavior, Coordination, Children, Diagnosis, Learning

Meischner, Inge; Karl-Marx-Universitaet, Sektion Psychologie, Tieckstrasse 2, Leipzig, Germany 7030

Meyer, Reinhard; Universitaet Tuebingen, Psychologisches Institut, Friedrichstrasse 21, Tuebingen, Germany D-7400;

*Mickler, Werner Scientific Assistant; Deutsche Sporthochschule Koeln, Psychologisches Institute, Carl-Diem-Weg 6, Koeln 41, Germany D-5000 (0221-4982552); Psychological Training, Motivation, Computer Simulation, Communication

Moller, Jens; Christian Albrechts-Universitaet, Institut fuer Psychologie, Olshausenstr. 40, Kiel 1, Germany 2300; G

*Mrazek, Joachim (Ph.D.); Deutsche Sporthochschule Koeln, Institut fuer Sportsoziologie, Carl-Diem-Weg 6, D 5000 Koeln 41, Germany; G,E

Mueller, Siegfried (Prof.Dr.) Professor; Forschung Institut fuer Koerperkultur Sport, Friedrich-Jahn Allee 59, Leipzig, Germany 7010; G,R(R); Motivation, Personality, High Performance, Sport

Muller-Kaler, Michael; Universitaet Wrzburg, Sportzentrum, Judenbhlweg 11, Wrzburg, Germany 8700; G

*Munzert, Jorn (Ph.D.) Wiss. Assistant; Psychologisches Institut, Deutsche Sporthochschule Koeln, Carl-Diem-Weg 6, 5000 Koeln 41, Germany (0221-4982552); G,E(S,R); Motor Learning, Motor Control, Verbal Instructions, Augmented Feedback

*Munzert, Reinhard (Ph.D.) Lecturer; Deutsche Sporthochschule, Institute of Psychology, Carl-Diem-Weg, 5000 Koeln 41, Germany (221-4982-572); G,E,F; Chess, Introspection, Action, Cognition, Grand Unification Perspective of Psychology

Naretz, Wolfgang; Universitaet Kiel, Institut fuer Sport und Sportwissenschaft, Johan Fleckstrasse 32, Kiel, Germany D-2300

*Neumann, Petra (Dipl.Psych.) Psychologist; Rieslingweg 5, Ruedesheim, Germany 6220; G,E,F

*Nitsch, Juergen R. (Prof.Dr.); Deutsche Sporthochschule Koeln, Psychologisches Institut, Carl-Diem-Weg 6, Koeln 41, Germany 5000 (0221-4982550, 0221-4971782); E,F(R),G; Action Theory, Stress, Motivation, Psychological Training

*Olivier, Norbert P.L. (Dr.) Wiss. Mitarb.; Universitaet des Saarlandes, Sportwissenschaftliches Institut, Bau 56, Saarbruecken, Germany D-6600 (0681-3024172, 0681-3024091); E,G,F(S,R); Motor Learning/Control, Eye Movements, Fatigue and Motor Learning/Performance

Peper, Dieter (Ph.D.); Universitaet des Saarlandes, Sportwissenschaftliches Institut, Im Stadwald, Beau 39.1, Saarbruecken, Germany 6600; G

Peterson, Usrel (Usr); Us t Olderburg, FB 5/Sportwissenschaft Ammerlnder-Heerstr. 165-197, Olde 97, Olde 2 900 Germany; G

*Poehlmann, Rilo (Prof.Dr.Sc.Phil.) Dean; Faculty for Pedagogic Psychology and Sports Sciences, Friedrich-Schiller-Universitaet, Institut fuer Sportwissenschaft, Seidelstrasse 20, Jena, Germany 6900

Polenz, Wolfgang; Klinik am Park, Westkorso 14, Bad Oeynhausen, Germany 4970; G

Priemer, Werner (Ph.D.); Eschenweg 27, Obersursel 4, Germany 6370; G

*Quinten, Susanne; Deutsche Sporthochschule Koeln, Psychologisches Institut, Koeln 500041, Carl-Diem-Weg 6, Germany (49-221-4982550, 0221-4971782); G,F,E; Motor Control, Motor Learning, Self Concept, Dance, Movement Rhythm

Ramme, Uwe; Universitaet Hamburg, Lehmweg 38, Hamburg 20, Germany D-2000

*Reulecke, Wolfram (Ph.D.) Professor; Ruhr-University Bochum, Institute for Sport Psychology, P.O. Box 102148, D-463 Bochum, Germany; G,E

*Richter, Klaus Dr.; Padagogische Hochschule Zwickau, Sektion Sportwissenschaft, Am Scheffelberg, Zwickau, Germany 9560 (748-334)

Ricken, Hans J.; JVA Iserlohn, Heidestr. 41, Iserlohn 9, Germany 5860; G

Rieder, Hermann (Prof.Dr.); Universitaet Heidelberg, Institut fuer Sport and Sportwissenschaft,

Im Neuenheimer Feld 710, Heidelberg 1, Germany 6900 (06221-564642); E,G; Motor Behavior, Handicapped, Competition Education, Athletics, Training

Rieke, K. (Dipl.Psych.); Deutsche Sporthochschule, Psychologisches Institut, Karl-Diem-Weg, Koln 41, Germany 5000 (0221-4982575); E,G; Motivation, Stress, Anxiety, Behavior Control, Therapy

Rosenfeldt, Horst (Ph.D.); Abt. Mensch und Technik, TOV Bayern e.v., Oskar-von-Miller Str. 17, Augsburg 22, Germany 8900; G

Rossman, Ernest D.; Alter Markt 16, Elmshorn, Germany 2200; G

Rothig, Peter (Ph.D.); Johann-Wolfgang-Goethe Universitaet, Institut fuer Sport und Sportwissenschaft, Ginnheimer Landstr. 39, Frankfurt/M 90, Germany 6000; G

Rummele, Edgar (Ph.D.); Universitaet Augsburg, Lehrstuhl fuer Sportpadagogik, Schillstr 100, Augsburg 1, Germany 8900; G

Ruoff, Bern A. (Ph.D.); Faschule fuer Sozialpdagogik, Fachrichtung Jugend und Heimerziehung, Hgnach 3, Tningen 1, Germany 7400; G

*Sack, Hans-G. (Prof.Dr.); FU Berlin, Institut fuer Sportwissenschaft, Rheinbabenalle 14, 1000 Berlin 33, Germany (030-8235057); E,F,G,SW; Motivation, Personality, Development, Health Psychology

Schafer, Ortwin; Richtsberg 13, Marburg, Germany 3550; G

Schaller, Ludwig (Ph.D.); A-6465 Nassereith 130, Tirol/Osterwich, Germany; G

*Schedlowski, Manfred (Dipl.Psych); Abt. Med. Psychologie, Medizinische Hochschule Hannover, Postfach 610180, Hannover 61, Germany 3000; G

*Schellenberger, Brigitte (Prof.Dr.); Deutsche Hochschule fuer Koerperkultur, Jahn Allee 59, Leipzig, Germany 7010 (4974170); E(S,R),G,R(R); Self-Direction, Social Interaction, Diagnosis, Sport for All

*Schellenberger, Hans (Dipl.Dr.); Deutsche Hochschule fuer Koerperkultur, Friedrich Ludwig Jahn Allee 59, Leipzig, Germany 7010 (4974488); G,E(S,R),R(R); Theory, Soccer, Mental Training, Diagnosis

Schlicht, Wolfgang (Ph.D.); Christian Albrechts-Universitaet, Institut fuer Sport und Sportwissenschaft, Olshausenstr. 40-60, Haus N 40a, Kiel 1, Germany 2300; G

Schmid, Peter; Sddeutscher Rundfunk, Fernsehen Sport, Postfach 106040, Stuttgart 1, Germany 7000; G

Schmidt, Dieter; Friedrich-Wilhelms-Universitaet Bonn, Institut fuer Sportwissenschaft und Sport, Nachtigallenweg 86, Bonn 1, Germany 5300; G

Schmidt, Werner (Ph.D.); Universitaet Osnabrck., Abt. Vechta, Sportwissenschaft, Postfach 1349, Vechta, Germany 2848; G

Schmole, Matthias (Ph.D.); Sprangerveg 2, Gottingen, Germany 3400 (0551-395652); E,F,G,S(R); Biofeedback, Motivation, Perception, Gender, Track and Field

Schock, Kurt (Ph.D.); Universitaet Bielefeld, Fakultt fuer Psychologie, Postfach 8640, Bielefeld, Germany D-4800

*Schubert, Frank (Dr.) Deutsche Hochschule fuer Koerperkultur, Friedrich-Ludwig-Jahn Allee 59, Leipzig, Germany 7010 (4974488); G,E,R; Theory, Cognition, Motivation, Emotion, Combat and Team Sports

*Schuck, Helga (Dr.Paed., Dipl.Psych.); Forschung Institut fuer Koerperkultur und Sport, Friedrich-Ludwig-Jahn Allee 59, Leipzig, Germany 7010 (4974-447, 4974-540); G,R,E(R); Psychomotor Methods, Psychomotor Theory, Psychoregulation Mental Tr., Temporal Patterns

Schwanbeck, Andreas; Ritterstr. 19, Braunschweig, Germany 3300; G

Schwebel, Hildegard; Heidelberger Landstr. 89, Darmstadt 13, Germany 6100; G

*Schwenkmezger, Peter (Dipl.Psych.,Dr.) Professor, Editor-in-Chief of *German Journal of Sport Psychology*; Universitaet Trier, FB I-Psychologie, Postfach 3825, Trier, Germany D-5500; E,F,G; Anxiety, Personality, Motivation, Psychology

*Seiler, Roland (Ph.D.) Assistant; Deutsche Sporthochschule Koeln, Dept. of Psychology, Carl-Diem-Weg 6, Koeln 41, Germany 5000 (+49-221-4982550, +49-221-4971782); D,E,F,SW(S,R), N(S); Cognition, Action Theory, Motor Control, Orienteering

*Seitz, Willi (Prof.Dr.); Johannes Gutenberg-Universitaet, Institut fuer Sonderpaedagogik, Hegelstr. 59, Mainz, Germany 6500 (06131-392921, 06131-393528); E,G; Personality, Parental Behavior, Delinquency, Stress and Self-Concept, Rehabilitation

Simons, Heribert (Ph.D.); Universitaet Freiburg, Institut fuer Sportwissenschaft, Schwarzwalsdtr. 177, Freiburg, Germany 7800; G

*Singer, Roland (Dipl.Psych.,Prof.Dr.); Technische Hochschule Darmstadt, Institut fuer Sportwissenschaft, Hochschulstr. 1, Darmstadt, Germany 6100 (06151-163161); E(S,R),F(R),G; Peronality, Attitudes, Evaluation, Motor Learning

*Sonnenschein, Inge (Dr.Habil.); Privat-Dozentin der Deutsche Sporthochschule Koeln Lessingstr. 70, Koeln 40, Germany D-5000 (02234-70570); E,F,G; Mental Training

Steiner, Hans (Dr.); Universitaet Heidelberg, Institut fuer Sport und Sportwissenschaft, Im Neuenheimer Feld 710, Heidelberg, Germany 6900 (06221-564648); E,G; Counseling, Attitudes, Motivation, Pre-Start State, Bowling

*Stollenwerk, Hans J. (Ph.D.) Dozent; Deutsche Sporthochschule, Institut fuer Sportsoziologie, Carl-Diem-Weg 6, Koeln 41, Germany 5000 (0221-4982580, 0221-4971782); G,E; Sport Spectators, Leisure Time, Mass Media, Sociometry, Tennis

*Strang, Hanno (Ph.D.); FU Berlin, Institut fuer Sportwissenschaft, Hagenstr. 56, 1000 Berlin 33, Germany

*Stuetzle-Hebel, Monika (Dipl.Psych.) Trainer for Group Dynamics, Psychotherapist; Seilerbruecklstr. 22, Freising, Germany 8050 (08161-7678); G,E; Group Dynamics, Organization, Gestalt Therapy, Aggression, Motivation

*Teipel, Dieter (Dr. Sport Science) Professor; Deutsche Sporthochschule Koeln, Psychologisches Institut, Carl-Diem-Weg 6, 5000 Koeln 41, Germany (0221-4982573); G,E,S; Motor Learning, Performance Analysis, Diagnosis, Motor Development, Stress

Thiel, Gnther; Messhorn 38, Barmstedt, Germany 2022; G

Thimm, Norbert (Dipl.Psych.); Psychologischer Dienst, Bayer Ag, Moskaur Str. 4., Leverkusen 1, Germany 5090 (0214-3071752); E,F,G,S; Counseling, Motivation, Tests

Tholey, Paul (Ph.D.); TU Braunschweig, Institut fuer Sportwissenschaft, Franz-Liszt Str. 4, Braunschweig, Germany 3300; G

*Thomas, Alexander (Prof., Ph.D., Dipl.Psych.); Universitaet Regensburg, Psychologisches Institut, Universitaetsstr. 31, 8400 Regensburg, Germany (0941-9433777); E,G; Psychomotor Education, Social Psychology, Action Psychology, Applied Psychology, Organizational Psychology

*Tschakert, Rainer (Dr.); Hohler Weg 2, 5928 Bad Laaspe 2, Germany (02754-8585); E,G; Social Psychology, Stress Management, Personality, Attitudes, Social Interaction

Tsombatzoudis, Haralambos; Maarweg 13, Kln. 41, Germany 5000; G

Uhlig, Thomas; Franz-Stadekmayer-Str. 38, Wrzburg, Germany 8700; G

Ungerer, Dieter; Universitaet Brehem, Fachbereich 11, Sportwissenschaft; Badgasteiner Straae/Sportturm, Bremen 33, Germany 2800; G

Ungerer-Rhrich, Ulrike (Ph.D.); Hauptstr. 147 d, Karlsdorf-Neuthard, Germany 7528; G

Van Bronswijk, Raymond; Hainbuschenberg 12, Hanstedt, Germany 2116; G

Veit, Hans (Ph.D.); Mankestr. 49, Lehrte, Germany 3160; G

Vogt, Marga; Wilhelm-Pieck-Universitaet, Sektion Sportwissenschaft, Schwaanschestrasse 3, Rostock, Germany 2500

*Vogt, Stefan R. (Dr.) Research Assistant; Lehrstuhl fuer Sportpsychologie du TU, Max-Planck-Institute for Psychological Research, Leopold Str. 24, 8000 Muenchen 40, Germany (0049-89-38602-267, 0049-89-342473); G,E; Motor Learning, Mental Practice, Movement Imitation, Augmented Information, Rhythmic Movement

*Volkamer, Meinhart (Prof.Dr.); Universitaet Osnabrueck, Sportzentrum, Jahnstr. 41, Osnabrueck, Germany 4500 (0541-608-4297); E,F,G; Aggression, Anxiety, Mental Training

*Volpert, Walter (Ph.D.) Professor; TU Berlin, Institut fuer Humanwissenschaft, Ernst-Reuter-Platz 7, Berlin 10, Germany 1000; G

Warwitz, S. (Dipl.,Prof.Dr.); Paed. Hochschule Karlsruhe, Bismarckstr. 10, Kahrlsruhe, Germany (0721-23991); E,F; Learning, Tests, Experimental, Statistics

*Wegner, Manfred G. (M.S.); Christian Albrechts-Universitaet, Institut fuer Sport und Sportwissenschaft; Olshausenstr. 40-60, Kiel 1, Germany 2300 (0431-8803759, 0431-8803783); G,E, F(S,R); Cognition, Concentration, Performance Analysis, Action Psychology, Top Athletes

Weil, Peter; IMT-Zentrum; Leopoldstr. 54/IV, Muenchen 40, Germany 8000; G

*Weinberg, Peter (Dr.) Professor; Universitaet Hamburg, Fachbereich Sportwissenschaft, Mollerstrasse 10, Hamburg 13, Germany D-2000 (040-4123-2781); E,F(S,R)

Wenzlswek, Hans-J.; Armeesportvereinigung, Postfach 68656, Berlin, Germany 1180

Wessling-Lnnemann, Gerburgis (Ph.D.); TH Darmstadt, Institut fuer Sportwissenschaft, Hochschulstr. 1, Darmstadt, Germany 6100; G

Wilken, Thomas; Universitaet Hamburg, Hans-Much-Weg 14, Hamburg 20, Germany D-2000

Willimczik, Klaus (Ph.D., Prof.Dr.); Universitaet Bielefeld, Fak. fuer Psychologie und Sportwissenschaft, Postfach 8640, Bielefeld, Germany D-4800

*Wiskow, Matthias; Borksarkeu 21, Lohmar 1, Germany 5204; G,E,F; Creativity, Health Education (Gesundheitsbilduug)

*Wursthorn, Herbert (Diplom.Psychologe); OSP Stuttgart; Mercedesstr. 85, Stuttgart 50, Germany 7000 (0711-562821); G,E,F(S,R)

*Zieschang, Klaus (Prof.Dr.); Universitaet Bayreuth, Institut fuer Sportwissenschaft, Universitaetsstr. 30, Bayreuth, Germany 8580 (0921-553461); E,G; Anxiety, Competition, Motor Learning, Motor Behavior

*Zimmer, A. (Prof.Dr.); University of Regensburg, Dept. of Psychology, Universitaetsstr. 31, Regensburg, Germany (0941-943-3817, 943-2305, Zimmer@VAX1. RZ. UNI-REGENSBURG. DBP. DE);G,E,F(R),I(R),L(R); Cognition, Motor Control, Motor Learning, Performance Modeling

Zimmer, Renate (Ph.D.); Universitaet Osnabrck, Sportzentrum, Jahnstr. 41, Osnabrck, Germany 4500; G

Greece

*Doganis, George (Ph.D.) Lecturer; Aristotle University of Thessaloniki, Dept. of Physical Education and Sport Sciences (T.E.F.A.A.), Thessaloniki, Greece 54006 (031-213300); GRE,E; Soccer, Dropout, Youth, Attitudes, Preperation

Ioannis, Z. (Dipl.P.E.); Sport Research Institute, Kifisias 37, Marousi, Greece; E,GRE; Sport, Top Athletes, Competition

*Kakkos, Vassilis Scientific Collaborator; University of Athens, Dept. of Physical Education, 41 Olgas Street, Athens, Greece 17237 (01-9752576, 01-9702125); GRE,E; Anxiety Research, Psychological Preparation of Athletes

Kranidiotis, Pantelis (Ph.D.); Asclepeion At Voula, Neuropsychiatry, Omirou St., 27, Athens, Greece 10672 (3626608); E,F(S,R),GRE; Anxiety, Relaxation, Personality, Selection, Social Psychology

Stalikas, Anastasios (Dr.Psych.) Clin. Psychologist; Hellenic Sports Research Inst., Psychology

Gerd Konzag

Paul Kunath

Juergen R. Nitsch

Hermann Rieder

Hans Schellenberger

Anastasios Stalikas

Section, 37 Kifissias, Maroussi, Athens, Greece 15153 (6834060); GRE,G,E(R); Psychodiagnostics, Personality, Stress, Psychological Preparation, Top Athletes

Stamatios, S. (Prof.); Academy of Physical Education, Athens, Greece; E,GRE; Physical Education, Sport, Top Athletes, Competition

*Zervas, Yannis (Ph.D.) Professor; Athens University, Dept. of Physical Education, 43 Lazaraki Street, Glyfada Attiki, Greece 16674 (01-8943078, 9752576); E,SW,GRE; Mental Practice, Learning, Motor Control, Relaxation, Stress

Hong Kong

*Chan, Roy C. (Ph.D.) Lecturer; Chinese University of Hong Kong, Dept. of Physical Education, Shatin, N.T., Hong Kong (6952991); E,CHI, M(S),CAN(S); Psyching, Transactional Analysis, Tennis, Relaxation, Hypnosis

*Cheung, Siu-Yin (M.Sc.) Instructor; The Chinese University of Hong Kong, P.E. Unit, New Asia College, Shatin, N.T., Hong Kong (6952695); CHI,E; Pre-Competitiion Anxiety, Relaxation, Gymnastics, Motivation

Fu, Frank H. Director; Chinese University of Hong Kong, Dept. of Physical Education, Shatin, Hong Kong (0-6952115); E,CHI; Personality, Attitudes, Sport Sciences, Racquet Sports, Cross-Cultural Competition

*Fung, Mary Lena (Ph.D.) Lecturer; Chinese University, Sports Center, Shatin, Hong Kong (0-6952689); CAN,E; Attitudes, Motivation, Adaptives, Cross-Comparison

Hungary

Buechler, R.; Research Instit. for Physical Education, Dept. of Psychology, Alkotas Str. 44, Budapest, Hungary (155-623-96); G,H; Personality, Counseling

*Csider, T. (Ph.D.); Alkotas Str. 44, Budapest, Hungary (1-564-444); E,G,H; Anxiety, Competition, Top Athletes, Personality, Counseling

Hepp, F. (Prof.Dr.); Tartsay Vilmos Utca 3., Budapest, Hungary 1126 (357-880); E,F,G,R,S,H; Motor, Perception, Kinesthesis

Kudar, Katalin (Ph.Dr.) Researcher; Hungarian University of Physical Education, Dept. of Psychology, Budapest, Hungary 1139 (564-444-116); E,H; Egropsychometric Testing, Psychodiagnosis, Personality, Physical Conditioning, Individual Therapy

Nadori, Laszlo (Ph.D.) Professor; Testnevelest Foiskola, Alkotas u. 44, Budapest, Hungary H-ll23 (564-327); G,E,F(R); Perception, Selection, Development, Personality, Instruction

Nagy, George; University of Physical Education, Alkotas 44, Budapest, Hungary 1123 (155-099); E,H; Motor Learning, Children, Top Athletes

*Nagykaldi, Csaba (Ph.D.) Senior Researcher; Hungarian University of Physical Education, Dept. of Psychology, Alkotas Str. 44, Budapest, Hungary H-1123 (1564-444); H,G,E; Group Dynamics, Perception, Anxiety, Personality, Control

Pilvein, Marton; College of Physical Education, Dept. of Sport Psychology, Alkotas 44, Budapest, Hungary 1123 (158-809); F(R,W),R(R,W),H; Top Athletes, Competition, Youth Sport, Preparation, Perception

Rokusfalvy, Pal J. (Ph.D.) Professor; Hungarian University of Physical Culture, Dept. of Psychology, Bartok Belo u. 13, Budapest, Hungary H-1114;

G,E,R,F(S,R),I(R); Personality, Psychodiagnostics, Motivation, Mental Hygiene, Judo

Sipos, Kornel (M.D., Ph.D.) Senior Lecturer; Hungarian University of Physical Education, Dept. of Psychology, Alkotas 44, Budapest, Hungary 1525 (564-444-141); E,R,H; Anxiety, Running, Athletics, Biofeedback, Running Therapy

*Stuller, Gyula (Ph.D.) Dept. Head; Hungarian University of Physical Education, Dept. of Psychology, Bartok Bela ut 55, Hungary H-1114 (0031-156-6337); E,H; Personality, Motivation, Interests

*Szmodis, I. (Dr.); Koezponti Sportiskola, Tudomanyos Csoport, Istvanmezei 3, 1146-Budapest, Hungary (02-511-222/430); E,G(S,W),F,R(R),H; Anthropometry, Child Athletes, Motor Development, Psychology, Biometry

Vura, Marta (Dr.) Psychologist; Sport Club "Spartacus", Dept. of Methodolog., 26, Street Szentkiralyi, Budapest, Hungary (335-547); E(R), R(R,W),H; Anxiety, Personality, Counseling

India

Akhtar, S. Sultan (Ph.D.); Aligarh Muslim University, Dept. of Psychology Aligarh-202 002;

*Bhattacharya, Barid B. (M.D., Ph.D.) Consultant; Sports Authority of India, Dept. of Sport Sciences, JN Stadium, New Delhi, India 110 003 (11-69-9320, NIL); E,BE,HI; Psychiatry, Fitness, Hypnosis, Soccer, Health

Bose, Sukumar (Ph.D.) Professor; Calcutta University College of Science, Dept. of Applied Psychology, 92 A.P.C. Road, Calcutta, India 700003 (55-9429); E,BE,HI; Teaching, Research

*Fortgalland, G.D. (Ph.D.); National Institute of Sports, Patiala - 147001, India; E,G,IND; Cognitive Processes, Personality

*Indramani, Lai Singh (Ph.D.) Research Scientist "B" (Reader); Banaras Hindu University, Dept. of Psychology, Varanasi, Uttar Pradesh, India (54291-385); E,HI; Attention, Personality, Stress, Anxiety, Counseling

Jain, Sangeeta Lecturer; 18 Anand Chowk, Dehra Durv, India (28138); E,HI; Motivation, Performance, Table Tennis, Badminton, Women Sports

*Kamlesh, M.L. (Ph.D.) Principal; Lakshmibai National College of Physical Education, Kariavattom, Trivandrum, Kerala, India (8712); E,HI, PU,UR; Personality, Mind, Football, Research, Management

*Khan, Hussain Ahmed (M.A., D.M., S.P., NIS, Cert., Ph.D.) Scientific Officer and Head; Dept. of Sports Psychology, Faculty of Sports Sciences, Sports Authority of India, Netaji Subhas National Institute of Sports, Motibagh, Patiala 147001 India (0175-74919, 0394-204-NIS-IN); E,HI, IND(S); Mental Training of National Athletes, Psychoregulation Programs, Psychology of Peak Performance, Physical Activity and Mental Well-Being, Development of Sports Specific Psychological Tests

*Khan, Manoranjini (M.A., M.Phil.), Junior Scientific Assistant; Dept. of Sports Psychology, Faculty of Sports Sciences, Netaji Subhas National Institute of Sports, Motibagh, Patiala 147001, India (0175-74919, 0394-204-NIS-IN);E,HI,IND,(S)PU(S); Cognitive Characteristics of Athletes, Psychological Problems of Female Athletes, Psychodiagnostics, Mental Training, Teaching

Kumar, Anand (Ph.D.) Sport Psychologist; Kashi Vidyapith University, Psychology Dept., Varanasi, India (52566); E,HI; Personality, Aggression, Yoga, Hockey, Stress

Mann, N.S.; Punjabi University, Dept. of Physical Education, Chandigarh - 160 014, India

Mohan, Jitendra (Ph.D.) Professor; Panjab University, Dept. of Psychology, Chandigalu, India 160014 (22739); E,HI,PA; Personality, Psychomotor Perfrmance, Motivation, Stress, Effectiveness

Nangia, Suman (Ph.D.) Associate Professor; MKP Post Graduate College, Psychology Dept., New Road, Dehra Dun, India (24531); E,HI,F; Personality, Stress, Androgeny, Attitude, Mental Health

Naruka, J.S. (Ph.D.); 2, Ludlow Castle, Sports Complex, Sham Nath Marg, Delhi - 110 054, India

*Patial, Om, Kumari (M.P. Ed.) Lecturer; 49, New Colony, Beat No-28, Jalandhar-1, India; E,HI,PU; Personality Research, Motivation, Anxiety, Extraversion and Introversion

*Rao, V.V.B.N. (Ph.D., M.A., M.P.E.,M.Sports); University of Hyderabad, Director of Physical Education, Hyderabad 500 134 India (253901 ext.263); E,G,HI,TELUGU, SAN(R,W),UR(S); Mental Practice, Hypnosis, Training Methodology, Yoga, Sports Philosophy

Sandhu, G.S. (M.A.); Panjab University, Dept. of Physical Education, Sector 14, Chandigarh 160 - 014, India E,R,HI; Competition, Training, Psychology, Processes, Attention

Sidhu, Avinash (Ph.D.) Reader; Lakshmibai National College of Physical Education, Shakti Nager, Gwalior, India 25077; HI,E,G; Motivation, Social Intervention, Children, Women, Hockey

*Singh, Agyajit (M.A., M.Ed., M.Litt., Ph.D.) Head; Dept. of Psychology, Punjabi University, Patiala (Punjab), India 147002; E,F,G,HI; Attitudes, Anxiety, Motivation, Adjustment, Learning

Singh, Rajinder (Ph.D.) Lecturer; LNCPE, Shakti Nager, Gwalior - 474 002, India

Singh, Usha (Ph.D.); 2670, Subzi Mandi, Delhi - 110 007 India

*Thakker, L.A. (M.Ed.), Director; Gujarat University, Physical Education, Ahmedabad - 380009 India (440341-42-43); E,HI,SAN; Sports Psychology, Sports Physiology, Sports Sociology

*Thakur, G.P. (Ph.D.) Professor of Psychology; Kashi Vidyapith, Varanasi - 221 002 India (66294); E,HI,SAN; Sport Psychology, Clinical, Psychometrics

Yannis Zervas   **Roy C. Chan**   **Pal J. Rokusfalvy**   **M.L. Kamlesh**

Indonesia

*Rahantoknam, Edward B. (Ph.D.) Lecturer; Ikip Jakarta, F.P.O.K., Jalan Pemuda 10, Jakarta, Indonesia 13220 (4893534); E,IN,D; Learning, Control, Stress, Soccer, Archery

*Setyobroto, Sudibyo (Prof.Dr.) Lecturer; I.K.I.P., F.P.O.K., Jl.-Pemuda No. 11, Jakarta, Indonesia (4893534); E,IN,D(R); Motivation, Stress, Aggression, Mental Training, Team Games

Iraq

Al-Masrif, Luay. (M.Y.) Assistant Professor; University of Baghdad, College of Sport Education, Jadiriya, Baghdad, Iraq (964(1)7764430); E,A; Personality, Stress, Behavior, Socialization

Al-Talib, N.M. (Ph.D.); University of Mosul, College of Sport Education, Mosul, Iraq (813416); E,A; Attitudes, Personality, Achievement, Motivation, Top Athletes

Ireland

*O'Dwyer, Sean (Ph.D.) Dept. Head; CI College of Education, Dept. of Physical Education, University of Dublin, Rathmines, Dublin, 6, Ireland (970033); E,IRISH; Integrated Development, Coordination, Elementary Teaching, Competing

Israel

*Bar-Eli, Michael (Ph.D.) Head; Wingate Institute, Behavioral Sciences Section, Post 42902 Netanya, Israel 42902 (53-29405); HEB,E,G,F; Psychological Crisis, Decision Making, Team Sports, Elite Athletes, Organizational Consultation

*Eldar, D. (Ph.D.); Wingate Institute, The Zinman College of Physical Education, Netanya, Israel 42902 (53-55344/29205, 53-650960); E,G,HEB; Teaching, Personality, Motivation, Movement Education

*Gal-Or, Yaakov (Ph.D.) Clinical and Sport Psychology Consultant; Wingate Institute, Zinman College for Physical Education, Netanya, Israel 42902 (053-29222); HEB,E; Stress Coping Strategies

Geron, Ema (Ph.D.); Wingate Institute, Dept. of Research and Sports Medicine, Netanya, Israel (053-92958); E,F,G,R,I(R),HEB,S(R); Assessment, Youth Sport, Gifted Children, Personality, Motivation

Hermon, S. (M.A.); Ministry of Education and Culture, Office of Chief Superintendant of Physical Education, 32 Ben-Jehuda Street, Tel-Aviv, Israel (03-291031); E,G,HEB; School Sports, Physical Education, Competition, Motor Learning, Philosophy

*Raviv, Shulamit (Ph.D.) Head of Psychomotor Behavior Dept.; Zinman College of Physical Education, Wingate Institute, Netanya, Israel 42902 (53-29216, 53-659960, EM 05 GLU850); HEB,E, G(S); Personality, Cognition, Motor Development, MotorLearning/Control

*Ruskin, H. (Ph.D.), Professor, Chairperson; The Hebrew University, Cosell Center for Physical Education, Leisure and Health Promotion, Jerusalem, Israel (972-2-584430); E,HEB; Recreation, Motivation, Mass Participation, Socialization, Patterns of Behavior, Health Promotion, Industrial Recreation

Sade, Sharga; Wingate Institute, Research Dept., Netanya, Israel 42902

*Tennenbaum, Gershon (Ph.D.) Director; Wingate Institute, Research Dept., Netanya, Israel 42902 (53-29400-1-7, 972-53-54374, J20@TAUNOS. BITNET); HEB,E,POL(S)

*Weingarten, Gilad (Ph.D.) Director; Wingate Institute, Netanya, Israel (053-29543); E,G(S),HEB; Stress, Coaching, Top Athletes, Personality, Intelligence

*Yazdy-Ugav, Orly; Doctor; Wingate Institute, Zinman College for Physical Education, Netanya, Israel 42902 (053-29222-272, 972-53-29265)

*Yuval, Raya (Ed.D.) Sport Psychologist; Israel Tennis Center and the Tennis Academy, P.O. Box 051, Ramat-Hasharon, Israel (03-5447222, 9723-5447997); HEB,E,F; Performance Enhancement, Support Groups

Italy

Agosti, E. (Doctor) Researcher; Rome Psychology University, Instituto di Medicina Dello Sport, 46 Via dei Campi Sportivi, Rome, Italy 00197 (06-3685-9105); I; Psychodiagnosis, Motor Learning, Stress, Anxiety

*Aguglia, Eugenio Chairman; Dept. of Psychiatry, School of Medicine, University of Trieste, Via San Cilino n.16, Trieste, Italy (040-51156); I,E; Mental Imagery, Personality

*Antonelli, Ferruccio (Prof.); Camilluccia 195, Roma, Italy 00135 (3420230); E,F(R,W),I; Psychosomatic Medicine, Psychopathology, Psychotherapy

Avanzi, U.; V.A. Casello 27, Sesto Calende (VA), Italy (0331-924324); E(S,R),F,I; Top Athletes

Baldo Sakara, E.; Instituto Medicina Dello Sport, N. 67 Viale Trastevere, Roma, Italy (8392447); E,F(R),I,S(R); Psychosomatic, Top Athletes, Competition, Family

Bartoletti, B. (Dr.Med.); Via Genova 36, Marmate (VA), Italy (0331-600280); F,I,S(W); Psychology, Competition, Personality, Anxiety, Motor Control

*Benzi, Manuela Psychologist; Associazione Italiana Psicologia Sport, Via Emilio Faa di Bruno 67, Roma, Italy 00195 (06-3722859); I,E(R),S(R); Men-

tal Preperation, Relaxation, Communication, Group Dynamics

Biondo, Radames (Ph.D.) Chairman; University of Padua, Dept. of Psychology and Personality, Via C.Golodoni, n.67/e, Mestre, Venezia, Italy 30174 (13097-612097); E,F,I; Self Presentation, Basketball, Cycling, Biofeedback, Hypnosis

Caldirono, B. (Dr.Med.); Via P. Costa 43, Ravenna, Italy (37161); E(R),F(S,R),G(S,R),I; Counseling, Didactics, Competition

Calserado, G. (Dr.Med.); Scuola Centrale Sport Sce. C.O.N.I., Campi Sportivi, Roma, Italy; G(S),I; Therapy, Counseling

Casteillo, Umberto (Ph.D.); Iniversit di Parma, Institute di Fisiologia Umana, Via Gramsci 14, Parma, Italy 43100 (0521-290380, FISIOM1@IPRUNIV); E,F,I; Attention, Compatibility Effect, Motor Control

Castelli, Paolo (Ph.D.); V. Berto Barbarani 28, Verona, Veneto, Italy 37123 (045-590177); I,E,F(S,R); Hypnosis, Autogenic Training, Tennis, Canoe, Stress

*Cei, Alberto (Doctor Psych.) Psychologist; Scuola dello Sport, Italian Olympic Committee, 48, Via dei Campi Sportivi, 00197 Roma Italy (6-36859171, 6-36859236); E,F,I; Attention, Mental Training, Team Sports, Coaches, Referees

Conio, S. (Dr.Med.); Via Monginero 194, Torino, Italy (011-706953); E(S,R),F,I; Anxiety, Counseling, Personality, Competition

Corpaci, A. (Dr.); Fims Centro Toscano Medicina Bello, Via Del Fosso Nacinante, Firenze, Italy (055-486282); E,F(R),I; Motivation, Anxiety, Competition, Personality, Autogenic Training

*Costa, Antonina, Teacher; I.S.E.F., Via Cesare Vivante N.48, Catania, Italy CP95123 (095-438848); I,E,F; Anxiety, Aggression, Attention, Stress, Arousal

D'Andrea, Tiziana (M.Sc.) Consultant; Via dei Campi Sportivi L8, Roma, Italy (36859172); I,E(R,S); Psychotherapy, Psychodiagnostic, Top Athletes

*De Moja, Carmelo A. (Ph.D.) Psychologist; Via Vespucci N. 11 A, I 89123 Reggio, Calabria, Italy (0965-26885); E,I,F,S; Psychological Training, Methodology of Research, Control of Anxiety, Motocross Performance, Diving

Di Mauro, S. (Dr.); Fasoli, Settare Culturale, Via Republica 10, Biello, Italy (611058); E,F,I; Anxiety, Personality, Self-Control

Dionisio, A (Dr.) Researcher; Rome Psychology University, Instituto di Medicina Dello Sport, 46 Via dei Campi Sportiva, Rome, Italy 00197 (06-3685-9105); I,E(R); Psychodiagnosis, Autogenic Training, Basketball

Falorni, M.L.; Instituto Psicologia, Fac. Magistero Universita, Via Della Pergola 48, Firenza, Italy (298148); E,F,I; Communication, Didactics, Observation

Hussain Ahmed Kahn

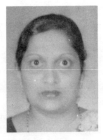

Manoranjini Khan

Shulamit Raviv

Gershon Tennenbaum

Ferruccio Antonelli

Alberto Cei

Federici, Stefano (Laurea psychologia) Psychologist; Istituto Scienza Dello Sport, Psychology, V.D. Campi Sportivi 48, Roma, Italy (06-3685-9129); E,I,F(R),S(R); Top Athletes, Psychodiagnostics, Computers, Research

Fulli, A. (Dr.Med.); Ambulatorio Medicina Sportivi, Palazzetto Della Sport, Caserta, Italy (0823-808382); F,I; Personality, Counseling, Clinical, Anxiety, Top Athletes

Gandini, G. (Dr.Med.); 7 Nizzeli-Buscelle (Re), Roma, Italy; E(R,W),F(S,R),I; Anxiety, Competition, Counseling

Gatti, Mauro; Dept. of Psychology, Via Silvio Benco 8, Roma, Italy (273061); E(S,R),F(S,R); Anxiety, Competition, Personality

Gelo, Carlo (Ph.D.) Psychotherapist; Virtus Gallatre, Piazza Europa 2, Gallarte, Italy 21013 (0331-784255); I,E,F,S(S,R); Hypnosis, Football, Stress, Handicap, Handball

Gelo, Galegero (B.Sc.) Coach; Center D. Guanella, Via Manzoni, 181, Agregento, Italy 92100 (0922-24950); I,F,E(S,R); Relaxation, Physical Training, Handball, Group Encounter, Basketball

Gius, E.; Piazza Capitamiato, Dept. of Psychology, Padoua, Italy (049-35552); E,F,I; Personality, Competition, Behavior, Stress

Guicciardi, Marco (M.Sc.) Psychologist; V. Monte San Marco 40, Udine, Italy (0432-42319); I,F,E(R,W); Motivation, Gender-Schemas, Identity, Motor Learning, Personality

Landucci, G.; Studio Professionale "P.S.R.," Via Porta D'Archi 10, Genova, Italy (010-581718); F,I; Social Psychology, Small Groups

Lanza, L.; Instituto Superiore di Educzione Fi, Mostra D'Oltre Mare, Napoli, Italy (615241); E(R),F(R),I; Personality, Top Athletes, Stress

Lazzari, Renato M. (Doctor) Psychiatrist; Rome Psychology University, Instituto di Medicina Dello Sport, 46 Via dei Campi Sportiva, Roma, Italy 00197 (06-3685-9105); I,F,E(S,R),POR(R); Psychotherapy, Autogenic Training, Psychosomatic, Swimming, Cognition

*Manili, Umberto (Dipl. Psych.) Sport Psychologist; CONI, Dept. Psychologia dello Sport, Istituto di Scienza Dello Sport, Piazza Jan Palach, 41, Roma, Italy 00196 (06-8587417); E,I; Autogenic Training, Counseling, Psychodiagnosis, Top Athletes, Psychosomatic

Maugeri, S. (Dr.Med.); Medicina Del Lavoro, Universita Degil Studi di Pavia, Pavia, Italy (302763); E(R),F(S,R),S(S,R),I; Anxiety, Personality, Competition, Top Athletes

*Mayer, Oskar (Dipl.Psych., Dipl.Sportlehrer;) InForm-Institut fuer Angewandte Psychol., Romstr. 102, Meran, Italy I-39012 (0473-210785); G,I,E,S; Imagination and Relaxation as Methods to Improve Performance

Migliorni, G. (Dr.Med.); 7-Mosadella, Bologna, Italy (233488); E(R,W),F(R,W),I; Personality

*Modenese, Michele (Ph.D.); V.Lo Riva, S. Lorenzo 8, 37138, Verona Veneto, Italy (045-8005425); I,E; Hypnosis, Anxiety, Motivation, Athletics, Scuba Diving

Molina, Iris (Dipl.Psych.) Psychologist; CONI, Psychology, V.D. Campi Sportivi 48, Roma, Italy; I,F,E(S,R); Psychodiagnostics, Relaxation, Clinical

*Nigro, A. (Dr.Med.); Universita, N. Panorama 1300, Messina, Italy (090-650531); E(R,W),F(R,W), I; Rehabilitation, Counseling, Ergonomy, Anxiety, Biology

Orlando, G.; 20 Stalingrado, Parma, Italy (0521-96054); E,F,I; Anxiety

Ossicini, Luca Consultant; Istituto di Scienze Dello Sport, Via dei Campi Sportivi, Roma, Italy (36859172); I,E(S,R); Psychotherapy, Psychodiagnostics, Top Athlete, Research, Didactic

Pase, D. (Doctor) Researcher; Rome Psychology University, Instituto di Medicina Dello Sport, 46 Via dei Campi Sportivi, Rome, Italy 00197 (06-3685-9105); I,E(R,W); Psychodiagnosis, Autogenic Training, Psychotherapy, Psychosomatic, Motivation

Picarelli, A.M. (Doctor) Researcher; Rome Psychology University, Instituto di Medicina Dello Sport, 46 Via dei Campi Sportivi, Rome, Italy 00197 (06-3685-9105); I,E(R,W); Autogenic Training, Psychotherapy, Relaxation, Group Dynamics

*Pirritano, Mirella (Dipl.Psych.) Psychologist; Italian Olympic Committee, Dept. of Sport Psychology, Via dei Campi Sportivi 48, Roma, Italy (06-36859172); I,E,S; Athletics, Mental Training, Psychodiagnostics, Top Athletes, Attention

Plata, Paola (Dipl.Psych.) Consultant; CONI, Dept. of Sport Psychology, Via dei Campi Sportivi 48, Roma, Italy (06-36859172); I,E(R,W); Athletics, Psychotherapy, Psychodiagnostics, Top Athletes

Pocoroba, L.; Via N. Torriani, 1, Milano, Italy 20124 (662534); E(W),F,I; Aspiration, Motivation, Personality, Therapy

*Polani, Diego (Ph.D.) Psychologist; Italian Swimming Federation, Via Cassia 1280, Rome, Italy 00189 (06-3767939); E,I; Cognition, Stress, Dive, Swim, Synchronized Swimming

Pozzi, Luigi; Isef, Universita Catt., 17, Via Trieste, Brescia, Italy; E(R),F,I; Medicine, Psycholoy, Psychosomatic, Movement Education

Ricca, G.C.; Via Marradi 175, Livorno, Italy 57100 (809570); E,F,I; Medicine, Psychosomatic, Top Athletes

*Ripetti-Pacchini, Daniela (Dipl. Psych.) Consultant; CONI, Dept. of Sport Psychology, Vione Vannini Tirrenia, 56018 Pisa, Italy (050-37751, 050-37752, 050-32332); E,I,F,R(R); Teaching, Diagnosis, Hypnotherapy, Self-Regulation Strategies

*Rossi, Gianpietro (Dr.) Psychologist; Via M. Grappa 17, Lumezzane S.S., Italy 25065 (030-826409); I,E,F; Peak Performance, Coach Education, Skiing, Neurolinguistic Programming, Biofeedback

Rota, S.; Instituto di Medicina Dello Sport, 46, Via dei Campi Sportivi, Roma, Italy (3685-9107); E,F,I,S(R); Personality, Psychosomatic, Medicine, Top Athletes

Rottini, E. (Dr.Med.); Medicine Sportive, C. Vammucci 30, Perugia, Italy (65373-21724); F,I; Fatigue, Competition, Top Athletes, Anxiety

Salvini, A.; Universita Delli Studi, Instituto di Psicologia, 5 Piazza Capitaniato, Padova, Italy (049-35552); E(R,W),F(R),I; Personality, Deviance, Top Sport

*Sapienza, Salvatore (Dr.Psych.) Psychologist; U.S.L. 34 Catania, Via Roma, 120, Mascalucia (CT), Italy 95030 (39-95-7274862); I,E,F; Sport

Silvaggi, E. (Doctor) Researcher; Rome Psychology University, Instituto di Medicina Dello Sport, 46 Via dei Campi Sportivi, Roma, Italy 00197 (06-3685-9105); I,F(R,W); Relaxation, Psychotherapy, Autogenic Training

*Tamorri, Stefano (M.D.) Psychiatrist; Associazione Italiana Psicologia Sport, Via Emilio Faa di Bruno 67, Roma, Italy 00195 (06-3722859); I,E; Mental Preparation, Communication, Group Dynamics, Perception, Attention

Tarantini, Francesca (M.Sc.) Psychologist; V. Monte San Markogo, Udike, Italy (0632-62319); I,E(S,W); Motor Learning, Self-Appraisal, Child Development

Tiberi, G. (Doctor) Researcher; Rome Psychology University, Instituto di Medicina dello Sport, 46 Via dei Campi Sportivi, Rome, Italy 00197 (06-3685-9105); I,E(S,R); Autogenic Training, Psychotherapy, Psychodiagnostics

*Tiburzio, Marco (M.A.); Centro di Psicilogia Comportamentale, Via Aquileia 117, Udine, Italy 33100 (0432-299381); I,E; Anxiety, Mental Skills, Coaching Skills

Tonini, A.M. (Doctor) Researcher; Rome Psychology University, 45 Via Rinchiosa, Marina di Carrara, Italy (0585-60001); I,E(S,R),F(R); Psychodiagnosis, Psychosomatic, Autogenic Training, Counseling

Tosi, R. (Dipl.); Isef, 15 S. Vitale, Bologna, Italy (239493); F,I,S; Top Athletes, Alienation, Team Sports, Competition

Veccia, S.; Sinergi-Private Psycho-soc. Res. In., 4, Piazza del Carmine, Milano, Italy; E(R),F(R),I; Social Psychology, Sociology, Group Dynamics, Groups, Personality

Zegretti, Stefana (Dipl.Psych.) Psychologist; CONI, Dept. of Psychology, Via dei Campi Sportivi 48, Roma, Italy (06-3685-9129); I,F,E(S,R); Psychodiagnostics, Clinical, Relaxation, Groups

Zirbetto, R.; Clinica Psichiatrica, Medicina, 54 Via Montanini, Siena, Italy (0577-8340); E,F(R,S),G,I; Personality, Anxiety, Group Dynamics, Psychology

Ivory Coast

Dagrou, Ernest (M.Sc.) Professor; INJS, Ol Bp V.54, Abidjan, Ivory Coast 01 (43-27-28); F,E(R); Motivation, Personality, Anxiety, Control, Social Facilitation

Kouablan, Francois (M.Sc.) Professor; Institut National Jeunesse et Sports, Abidjan, Ivory Coast (43-27-28); F,E(S,R); Superstition, Anxiety, Motivation, Control, Promotion of Sport Psychology

Japan

*Ae, Mieko (M.Sc.) Instructor; Tokyo Women's College of Physical Education, 620 Aoyanagi Kunitati, Tokyo, Japan (0425-72-4131); J,E(R,W),G(R); Group Cohesion, Sport Avoidance, Burnout, Social Identity

Araki, Masanobu (M.Sc.) Associate Professor; Osaka College of Physical Education, Dept. of Sport Psychology, 1588-1 Ooaza Noda Kumatori-Cho, Sennan-Gun, Osaka, Japan 590-04 (0724-53-7000); J,E,G(R); Feedback, Control, Motor Learning, Cognition

Chosi, K. (M.A.); Hiroshima University, 1-1-89 Higashisenda-Cho, Hiroshima, Naka-Ku, Japan 730 (0822-41-1221); J,E(R,W),G(R); Motor Program, Timing, Anticipation, Adaptive Systems, Organization

Doenen, Jerry N. (M.A.) Executive Vice President; Nautilus Group Japan Inc., Landic 2nd Akasaka Bldg. 2f, Akasaka, Minato-Ku, Tokyo, Japan 2-10-9 (03-505-0151); J,S,I; Climbing, Fitness, Video, Adventure, Meditation

Eio-lida, I. (Prof.); Inten N.S. Psyco., 2-20-23 Komachi, Kamakura, Japan (37-1111); E(W,R),J; Personality, Anxiety, Top Athletes, Competition, Counseling

Endo, Toshiro E. (M.P.E.) Lecturer; Yamanashi University, Faculty of Education, 404037, Takeda, Kofu-Shi, Yamanashi, Japan 400 (0552-52-1111); J,E; Anxiety, Psychological Aptitude, Mental Management, Power Resources, Volleyball

Fujimaki, K. (M.P.E.); Saitama University, 255 Shimoomhkubo, Urawa 338 Saitama, Japan (0488-52-2111); E,J; Personality, Obesity, Development, Measurement, Evaluation

Fujita, Atsushi H. (Ed.D.) Professor; Nihon University, Dept. of Physical Education, 3-25-40 Sakurajosui Setagaya, Tokyo, Japan (03-329-1151);

J,E,G(S,R); Mental Training, Physiological Psychology, Eye-Hand Coordination, Reaction Time, Motor Coordination

Fujiyoshi, Hisanori (B.E.,B.P.E.) Dean, Professor; Tenri University, Faculty of Physical Education, 80 Tainosho, Tenri Nara, Japan (07436-2-3076); E,J; Personality, Tennis, Learning, Counseling, Strategy

Fukami, K. (B.A.); #501, Shiroyama First Mansion, 1-9-15,Shiroyama, Odawara, Japan (0559-86-5500); E,J; Coaching, Learning, Skiing, Development, Personality

Fumoto, Nobyoshi (M.Sc.) Associate Professor; Hirosaki University, Dept. of Physical Education, Runkyoh-cho 1, Hirosaki Aomori, Japan (0172-36-2111); J,E,G(R); Soccer, Concentration, Motor Learning, Subjective Evaluation, Judgement

Funakoshi, M.; Osaka Educational College, Ikeda, Johnan 3-1-1, Osaka, Japan (0727-51-8331); E,J; Teams, Cooperation, Sport

Hirahara, T. (Prof.); 3-3-35 Yamate-cho, Suita-Shi, Japan (06-3881121); E,G(R),J; Coaching, Counseling, Peaking, Athletics, Relaxation

Hisao, Ishictaki Assistant Professor; Aichi Institute of Technology, Dept. of Physical Education, 1247 Yachigusa, Toyota City, Aichiken, Japan (0565-48-8121); J,E; Visual Acuity, Visual Field, Peripheral Vision, Visual Perception, Sport Vision

Hoshino, Kimio H. (B.Sc.) Professor; Juntendo University, Dept. of Physical Education, 5-4-54 Fuzisaki, Narashino-Shi, Japan (0484-77-2181); J,E(S,R); Motor Action, Self-Control, Awareness, Training of Motor Action, Motor Action Training

Ichimura, Soichi (Ph.D); University of Tsukuba, Institute for Health and Sport Sciences, J-Sakura, Niihari, Ibararaki, Japan 305; J;

Ikeda, Namiko (Ph.D.) Professor; University of Tsukuba, Dept. of Health and Physical Education, L1-1 Tennodai, Tsukuba City, Ibaragi, Japan; J,E,F(R); Motor Learning, Hockey

Inomata, Kimihiro (Ph.D.) Director; Joetsu University, School of Education, 1-33-16 Minamimagome,Ota-ku, Tokyo, Japan (03-777-7674); J,E; Imagery, Learning, Stress, Motivation

*Ito, Toyohiko (M.P.E.) Assistant Professor; Shimane University, Dept. of Health and Physical Education, Matsue Shimane, Japan (0852-21-7100); J,E(R,W); Attribution, Intrinsic Motivation, Coaching, Social Psychology

Kaga, H. (M.A.); The University of Tsukuba, Institut of Health and Sport Sciences, Ibaraki-Ken, Japan (0298-53-2686); E,F(R),G(R),R(R),J; Perception, Cognition, Intelligence, Motivation, Learning

Kashwabara, K. (Prof.); Osaka Educational College, Ikeda, Johnan 3-1-1, Osaka, Japan (0727-51-8331); E(R),J; Personality, Skill

Kato, Tadashi K. (B.A.) Graduate Student; 3-19-R211 Kotesashi-Cho, Tokorozawa City, Saitama, Japan (0429-49-8793); J,E,G(R); Conditioning, Imagery Training, Relaxation, Stress Evaluation, Mental Stability

Kishi, N.; Tenri University, Professor of Physical Education, Tainosho-Cho 80, Tenri, Japan (0743-42-3076); E,J; Learning, Motor Skill, Teaching

Kobashigawa, Hisamitsu Professor; University of the Ryukyus, Dept. of Education, Senbaru 1 Nishihara-Cho, Okinawa, Japan 903-01 (09889-5-2221); J,E; Learning, Motivation, Personality

Kobayashi, K. (M.A.); Nihon University, Dept. of Psychology, 3-25-40 Setagaya Sakur., Tokyo, Japan (03-3291151); E,J; Attitudes, Personality, Coping, Adjustment, Competition

*Kozuma, Yoichi (M.P.E.) Assistant Professor; Kinki University, Dept. of Health and Physical Education, 3-4-1 Kowakae, Higashiosaka City, Osaka, Japan 577 (06-721-2332, 06-721-2353); J,E;

Mental Training, Anxiety, Motivation, Martial Arts

Masanubo, Araki (M.E., M.P.E.) Associate Professor; Osaka College of Physical Education, Dept. of Sport Psychology; 1-1 Gakuen-Cho, Ibaraki City, Osaka, Japan 567 (0762-43-3141); J,E; Motor Control, Feedback, Motor Learning

Matsuda, Iwao President; Chukyo University, 101-2 Yagoto-Honmachi, Showa-ku, Nagoya, Japan (052-832-2151); J,E; Learning, Development, Stress, Control, Motivation

Matsui, M. (M.A.M); Sendai College, Dept. of Physical Education, Sibata-Chiyo, Miyagi Pref, Fukuaoka, Japan (02245-5-1121); E(R,W),G(R),J; Development, Motivation, Learning, Personality, Adjustment

*Mikio, Tokunaga (M.D.) Professor; Kyushu University, Institute of Health Science, 6-1 Kasugakoen, Kasuga City, Fukuoka, Japan 816 (092-573-9611, 092-592-2866); J,E(R); Mental Training, Biofeedback, Anxiety, Tennis, Psychological Skill

Moriwaki, T. (Prof.); Kinki University, School of Medicine, Physical Education Dept., 3-4-1 Kowakae-Higashiohs, Osaka-Fu, Japan (06-732-2332); E,J; Physical Education, Teacher Training, Learning

*Nakagawa, Akira (M.Ed.) Lecturer; Osaka University of Education, 3-1-1 Johnan, Ikeda-Shi, Osaka-fu, Japan (0727-51-8331); J,E,G(R); Decision Making, Judgement, Ball Games, Rugby, Coaching

Nakamura, Makoto (M.Sc.) Dean; Tokyo Kasei University, Dept. of General Education; 1-18-1 Kaga, Itabashi-ku, Tokyo, Japan 173 (03-961-5226); J,E; Neuro-Muscular Control, Reaction Time, Tennis, Golf, Character Test

*Nishida, Tamotsu (M.P.E.) Associate Professor; Nagoya University, Research Center of Health, Physical Fitness and Sports, Furo-Cho, Chikusa-ku, Nagoya, 464-01 Japan (052-781-5111, 052-783-0653); E,J; Achievement, Motivation, Anxiety, Golf, Imagery Training

Niwa, Takaaki T. Professor; Nara Women's University, Dept. of Physical Education, Nara, Japan 630 (0742-23-1131); J,E,G(R); Personality, Sport, Culture, Stage Fright

Okano, T. (B.A.); University of Niigata, Kyoyo-Bu (General Education), 2 No-Cho Igarashi, Nigata, Japan (0252-6324); J; Coaching, Physical Education, Learning, Competition

Omura, T. (Prof.); 979-3 Taradanawa, Hiratsuka-Shi, Japan (0463-58-1211); E,J; Coaching, Personality, Athletics

Suetoshi, Hirohito (M.A.); The Kansai University of Foreign St., Ogura-333 Hirakata, Osaka Prefecture, Japan (0720-56-1721); E,J; Physical Education, Learning, Teaching, Rugby

Sugihara, Takashi (M.A.) Professor; Tokyo Grakugei University, Dept. of Health and Physical Education, Nukui Kitamachi,Koganei, Tokyo, Japan (0423-25-2111); E,J; Motor Control, Learning, Development, Personality

Takano, K.; Osaka College of Physical Education, 1-1 Gakuen-Cho, Ibaraki, Japan (0726-34-3141); E,G(R),F(R),J; Skill, Development, Learning, Sensory, Reaction Time

Takemura, A. (Prof.); Nara University of Education, Teachers Training College, Nara, Japan; E,J; Learning, Teacher Training, Physical Education

*Taki, Seiji (M.E.) Lecturer; Koshein University, Dept. of Human Movement Studies, Momijgaoka 10-10, Takarzuka, Hyogo, Japan 665 (0797-87-5111, 0797-87-5666); J,E; Learning, Practice, Asthma, Personality, Running and Jogging

Tokunago, Mikio (M.D.) Professor; Kyushu University, Health Institute, 6-1 Kasugakoen, Kasuga City, Fukuoka, Japan (092-573-9611); J.E.; Biofeedback, Imagery, Training, Anxiety, Tennis

Toyohiro, Hirahara Professor; Kansai University, Dept. of Health and Physical Education, 3-3-35 Yanatecho, Suita City, Osaka, Japan (06-388-1121); E,J; Counseling, Peaking, Coaching, Mental Training, Self-Counseling

*Yamaguchi, Yuzo (M.D., Ph.D.) Professor; University of Osaka Pref., Health Sciences, Sakai, Osaka, Japan (0722-52-1161, 0722-55-2981); J,E,F, R,G(R); Sensation, Stress, Biofeedback, Electroencephalography, ERP

Yamamoto, Akio (B.P.E.) Associate Professor; Osaka Woman's University, Dept. of Physical Education, Daisen, Sakai, Osaka, Japan (0772-22-4811); E,J; Volleyball, Learning, Attention, Interest, Attitudes

Yasuda, A.; Tenri University, Physical Education, 1-22-1 Chome, Nada, Kobe, Japan (078-8713400); E,J; Basketball, Learning, Motor Skill, Team Sports

Yonekawa, N. (M.A.); Yamaguchi Women's University, Course of General Education, Saburasbatake 3-2-1, Yamaguchi, Japan (08392-8-0211); E(R,W),J; Competition, Attitudes, Cooperation

Yoshimatsu, S. (Dr.); Sarashinagun Nagana Pref., Yamiyamada, Japan 3166 (02627-5-1581); E,J,G(R,W); Baseball, Orthopedics, Training, Personality

Yoshimoto, Toshiaki (M.A.) Professor; Nihon University, Dept. of Physical Education, 3-25-40 Sakurajosui, Setagaya-ku, Tokyo, Japan; J,E; Development, Learning, Anxiety, Imagery Training, Conditioning

Korea

Chang, K.J. (Ph.D.) Assistant Professor; Korea Yudo College, Dept. of Physical Education, Samkari, Yonginkun, Kyeungki-Do, Korea (02-743-2110); K; Control, Learning, Anxiety, Motivation, Transfer

*Choi, Young-Ock (Ed.D.) Professor; Korean National College of Physical Education, Dept. of Physical Education, Olympic Park, Songpa Ku, Seoul, Korea (418-1001); K,E,G(R),J(R); Confidence, Aggression, Social Facilitation, Stress, Self-Control

Kim, Chong-Sun (Ed.D.) Professor; Ewha Woman's University, Dept. of Physical Education, Soeul, Korea (362-6151); K,E; Motivation, Learning, Personality, T and F Coaching

*Kim, Kee-Woong (Ph.D.) Professor; Ewha Women's University, Dept. of Physical Education, Seoul, Korea (82-2-362-6252, 82-2-393-5903); K,E; Attention, Mental Training, Motivation, Motor Control, Motor Learning

Park, Jao Ho (Ph.D.); Yeugnam-University, Dept. of Psychology, ROK 632, Gyongsan, Korea; K;

Pyun, Young Shin (M.A.) Doctoral Student; 155-205 Namgajua I Dong, Seodaemungy, Seoul, Korea 120-121 (02-307-5088); K,E; Learning, Motivation, Anxiety, Memory, Rhythmic Gymnastics

Ernest Dagrou   **Fujita Atsushi H.**

Yoo, Jin, (Ph.D.), Professor; Physical Education, Chung-Ang University, Seoul, Korea (02-815-5031); K,E; Arousal, Attention, Stress, Adherence, Motivation

Lebanon

Abyad, Abdurazzak (M.D., M.P.H.); American University of Beirut, Dept. of Family Medicine, Beirut, Lebanon; E,F,A,S(S,R),G(S,R); Depression, Tennis, Jogging, Control, Relaxation

Liechtenstein

*Ospelt, R. (Ph.D.); Egerta 26, Vaduz, Liechtenstein Fl-9490 (075-27128); E(R),F(R),G; Physical Education, Personality, Motivation, Mental Training, Soccer

Lithuania

*Palaima, Jurgis J., Professor; Institute of Physical Culture, Sporto g., 6, Kaunas, Lithuania 233000 (757051); R,LITHUANIAN,G(S,R),E(S,R); Coaching, Motives, Personality

Luxembourg

*Steffgen, Georg (Dipl.Psych.); 49 Haaptstrooss, Biwer, Luxembourg L-6833; G,E,F,LUXEMBURGISH; Stress, Emotions

Malaysia

Ismail, Yusoff (Ed.D.) Lecturer; University of Kebangsaan Malaysia, Faculty of Education 43600 Bangi, Selangor, Malaysia (03-8250001); E,MA; Motivation, Fitness, Golf, Teaching, Learning

Vasudevan, Thiru (Ph.D.) Associate Professor; University Malaya, Faculty of Education, Physical Education, Kuala Lumpur, Malaysia (03-7572433); E,MA,T; Motor Learning, Social Psychology, Mental Training, Racquet Sports, Healthy Lifestyles

Mexico

Balboa, Rocio Psychologist; University Autonoma de Nuero Leon, Dept. of Sports Medicine, Gonzalitos Ave., 235 Nte. Monterrey N.C., Mexico (48-00-01); S,E(R),G(R); Motivation, Stress, Control, Mental Training

Dellamary, Guillermo (Ph.D.) Sport Advisor; Club Deportivo Atlas de Guadalahara, Apartado Postal 6-122, Guadalahara, Jalisco, Mexico 44260 (423666); S,E,I,F(R),G(R),POR(R); Development, Human Potential, Personality, Sport

Morocco

*Baria, Abderrahim (M.Sc.) Professor; 364 Rue Mustapha Maani #10, Casablanca, Morocco; A,E,F; Gymnastics, Anxiety, Behavior Analysis, Individual and Transcultural Differences

*El Ouartassi, Abdelhafid (M.Sc.) Professor; Ministry of National Education, Division de l'Education Physique, B.P. 104RP, Rabat 07, Morocco (772605); A,F,E; Motor Learning, Track and Field, Traditional Games, Psycho-Sociology, Psychology of Development

Nabli, El Hassane (M.Sc.) Professor; Ecole Normale Supieure d'Education Physique, Casablanca, Morocco; A,F,E; Cognition, Motor Control, Motivation, Stress, Track and Field

Netherlands

*Adam, J.J. (Ph.D.) Professor; University of Limburg, Dept. of Movement Sciences, Postbus 616, Maastricht, Netherlands 6200 MD (43-437788, 43-478989, AFBEWHHW@HMARL5); D,E; Motor Programming Control, Information Processing, Anxiety, Visual Perception, Individual Differences

Avis, F.J. (M.A.) Professor; University of Leiden, Center of Social Science Research, Hooigrtcht 15, Leiden, Netherlands 2312 KM (071-273796); E,G,F,D; Human Performance, Mental Training, Attention, Fitness, Strength

Baardman, Iman (M.A.) Professor; Free University/ Human Movement Sciences, Dept. of Educational Sciences, P.O. Box 7161, Amsterdam, Netherlands 1007 MC (020-548-6259); D,E,G; Physical Attractiveness, Physical Competence, Psychiatry

Bakker, Frank C. (Ph.D.) Professor; Free University/ Human Movement Sciences, Dept. of Psychology, P.O. Box 7161, Amsterdam, Netherlands 1007 MC (020-548-7249); D,E; Anxiety, Personality, Motor Learning, Mental Training

Beek, Peter J. (M.A.) Professor; Free University/ Human Movement Sciences, Dept. of Psychology, P.O. Box 7161, Amsterdam, Netherlands 1007 MC (020-548-7223); D,E; Motor Control, Motor Learning

Beuse, M.J. (M.A.); Overzicht 14, Kamerik, Netherlands 3471 EE (03481-1882); D,E; Mental Counseling, Mental Training, Athletes

Blitz, Peter S. (M.A.) Professor; Institute for Performance Promotion, Willemsparkweg 21411, Amsterdam, Netherlands 1071 HX (3120-753787); D,F,G,E; Applied Sport Psychology, Mental Training

Bootsma, Reinoud J. (M.A.) Professor; Free University/ Human Movement Sciences, Dept. of Psychology, P.O. Box 7161, Amsterdam, Netherlands 1007 MC (020-548-7228); D,E,G,F; Motor Control, Motor Learning, Visual Information

Bosscher, Rudolf J. (M.Ed.) Professor; Free University/ Human Movement Sciences, Dept. of Educational Sciences, P.O. Box 7161, Amsterdam, Netherlands 1007 MC (020-548-6259); D,E,G,F; Movement, Psychiatry, Depression, Running Therapy, Sport Therapy

Crum, Bart J. (Ph.D.) Professor; Free University/ Human Movement Sciences, Dept. of Educational Sciences, P.O. Box 7161, Amsterdam, Netherlands 1007 MC (020-548-6252); D,E,G; Teaching, Educational Sports Psychology, Physical Education

Den Brinker, Berry P.L. (Ph.D.) Professor; Free University/ Human Movement Sciences, Dept. of Psychology, P.O. Box 7161, Amsterdam, Netherlands 1007 MC (020-548-6297); D,E,N; Software Development, Motor Programming, Learning Strategies

Hopkins, J.B. (Ph.D.) Professor; Free University/ Human Movement Sciences, Dept. of Educational Sciences, P.O. Box 7161, Amsterdam, Netherlands 1007 MC (020-548-6251); E,D; Motor Development, Mother-Infant Interaction

*Kerr, J.H. (Ph.D.) Associate Professor; Netherlands School of Business, Dept. of Physical Education, Steaatweg 25, Breukelen, Netherlands 3621 BG (03462-91236, 31-3462-64204); E,D; Arousal, Anxiety, Stress, Reversal Theory

*Moormann, Peter Paul (DRS.) Lecturer; Dept. of Clinical, Health, and Personality Psychology,

Wassenaarseweg 52, 2300 RB Leiden, Netherlands (071-273694); D,E,F,G

*Oyen, F.G.P.H. (M.D.) Psychiatrist; Slotlaan 2, 3634 AP, Loenersloot, Netherlands (02949-3385); D,E,G; Mental Coaching, Psychotherapy, Mental Training

Pijning, H.F. (Ph.D.) Professor; Utrecht State University, Dept. of Psychology, Heidelberglaan 2, Utrecht, Netherlands 3508 TC (030-533657); D,E,G; Activity Psychology, Learning, Motor Development

Savelsbergh, Geert J.P. (M.A.) Professor; Free University/ Human Movement Sciences, Dept. of Psychology, P.O. Box 7161, Amsterdam, Netherlands 1007 MC (020-548-7222); D,E,G; Visual Perception, Spatial Orientation, Deaf Children, Motor Development

Splinter, Paul G. (M.A.) Professor; College of Dietics, Naaldwijkstraat 45, Amsterdam, Netherlands 1059 GJ (020-171550); D,E,G,F; Nutritional, Stress Management, Mental Training, Ergonomic Aids

Tyldesley, David A. (Ph.D.); Vakgroep Psychologie,Vrije Universi, Interfakulteit L.O., de Boelelaan 1081, Amsterdam, Netherlands (020-548-5771); E,D; Skilled Behavior, Visual Perception, Information Processing, Motor Control, Movement Analysis

*Van der Brug, H.H. (Ph.D.) Professor; University of Amsterdam, Dept. of Communication Sciences, Oude Hoogstraat 24, Amsterdam, Netherlands 1012 CE (020-525-3909, 020-5252086); D,E,G,F; Soccer, Aggression, Hooliganism

Van Essen, Sandra; Heiligenberger Weg 20, Am Amersfoort, Netherlands NL-3816; D

*Van der Knoop, Arjen Sport Psychologist; Post Office Box 11121, Leiden, Netherlands, 2301 EC; D,E,F,G,S,SW; Controlling Psychological Stress Responses, Mental Preparation, Attention, Judging Sports Performance, Speed Skating

*Van Rossum, Jacques H. (Ph.D.) Professor; Free University/ Human Movement Sciences, Dept. of Psychology, V.D. Boechorststr. 9, Amsterdam, Netherlands 1081 BT (020-548-7226, 020-462228); D,E,G; Attribution, Motor Development, Skill in Sport, Play, Referees

Vergeer, Ineke; Ryks Universitaet Leiden, Klikspaanweg 51, Leiden, Netherlands 2312 L2

*Vermeer, Adri (Ph.D.) Professor; Free University/ Faculty of Human Movement Sciences, Dept. of Educational Sciences, Van der Boechorststraatg, 1081 BT, Amsterdam, Netherlands (020-548-6264, 020-462228) and State University of Utrecht, Faculty of Social Sciences, Dept. of Child Studies, Heidelberglaan 1, 3504 CS Utrecht, Netherlands (030-532826);D,E,G,F; Motor Development, Social Development, Disabled Children

*Wieringen, Piet C.W. (Ph.D.) Associate Professor; Free University/ Human Movement Sciences, Dept. of Psychology, Van au Boerhorsl Street 9, Amsterdam, Netherlands 1001 13T (020-548-7227); D,E,G,F; Behavioral Medicine, Motor Control, Motor Learning, Dance

Kim Kee-Woong

New Zealand

*Carpinter, Paul J. (Dip.P.E., M.H.K., B.A.); University of Canterbury, Dept. of Physical Education, Private Bag, Christchurch, New Zealand (667001); E(S,W); Athletes, Assessment, Athletics, Training, Performance Enhancement,

Clarke, G.S. (M.A.) Coordinator; Christchurch Hospital, Dept. of Psychological Medicare, Christchurch, New Zealand (558833); E; Group Cohesion, Liason, Hypnosis, Psychological Medicine

Gross, John B. (Ph.D.) Professor; Aukland College of Education, Dept. of Physical Education, Auckland, New Zealand (09-687-009); E; Coaching Behavior, Social Influence, Children, Basketball, Rugby

*Hodge, Ken P. (Ph.D.) Lecturer; University of Otago, School of Physical Education, P.O. Box 56, Dunedin, New Zealand, 024-798-991, 024-778-811, PSEDKP@OTAGEO); E; Character, Self-Concept, Elderly, Performance Enhancement, Psychological Well Being

*Purdon, Donald, A. (M.A.Hons) Business Psychologist; 9 Tahora Avenue, Remuera, Auckland, New Zealand (529-0486); E,J; Youth, Business, Relaxation, Imagery, Peak Performance

*Russell, David G. (Ph.D.); University of Otago, School of Physical Education, P.O. Box 56, Dunedin, New Zealand (64-24-479-8995); E,F(R); Motor Skill, Motor Control, Youth Sport

Shirley, Goeffrey M (M.A.) Managing Partner; Wellington Psychological Associates, P.O. Box 28067, Wellington, New Zealand (04-758915); E; Anxiety, Anger, Mood, Visualization, Cognitive

*Thomson, R.W. (Ph.D.) Sub-Dean; University of Otago, School of Physical Education, P.O. Box 56, Dunedin, New Zealand (03-479-8941, 03-477-8811); E,F(R),G(R); Deviance, Subcultures, Team Sports, Ideology, Hegemony

*Williams, L.R.T. (Ph.D.); University of Otago, Dept. of Physical Education, P.O. Box 56, Dunedin, New Zealand (64-3-479-1100, 64-3-477-8811); E,F(R); Personality, Top Athletes, Competition, Psychobiology, Motor Behavior

Nicaragua

*Sanchez, Angel (Dr.) Research Chief; Box 4981, IND, Managua, Nicaragua (71760); S,G,E(R,W); Mental Training, Motivation, Cognition, Motor Skills, Stress

Nigeria

Adedoja, Taoheed A. (Ed.D.) Lecturer; Bayero University, Dept. of Physical and Health Education, Kano, Nigeria; E; Disabled Sports, Motivation, Anxiety, Children, Basketball

Amasiatu, Nwanetbo A. (M.Ed.) Lecturer; University of Port-Hancourt, Dept. of Physical Health, Port-Hancourt, Rivers State, Nigeria; E; Motivation, Stress, Biofeedback, Badminton, Tennis

Ikulayo, Philomena (Ph.D.) Senior Lecturer; University of Lagos, Dept. of Physical and Health Education, Akoka-Yaba, Lagos, Nigeria (01-820544); E,Y; Stress, Intervention, Performance Enhancement, Motivation, Perfection

Makanju, Olatunde O.A. (Ph.D.) Senior Lecturer; University of Lagos, Dept. of Psychology Yaba, Lagos, Nigeria (01-821180); E; Motivation, Stress, Agression, Psyching, Soccer

*Oguntuashe, Kayode A. (Ph.D.) Senior Lecturer; University of Lagos, Psychology Dept., Yaba, Lagos, Nigeria (01-821180); Y,E; Mental Preparedness, Audience, Control, Squash

*Omoluabi, Peter F. (Ph.D.) Senior Lecturer; University of Lagos, Dept. of Psychology, Yaba, Lagos, Nigeria; E,Y(S),U(S); Stress, Biofeedback, Motivation, Relaxation, Psychophysiology

*Omotayo, Seun O. (Ph.D.) Lecturer; Ogun State University, P.H.E. Dept., Ago-Iwoye, Ogun State, Nigeria (037-390149); E,Y(S,R); Anxiety, Stress, Aspiration, Personality, Control

*Sohi, Amarjit S. Associate Professor; University of Ibadan, Dept. of Physical and Health Education, Ibadan, Nigeria; E,G,PU; Anxiety, Motivation, Track and Field, Attention, Learning

Northern Ireland

*Mahoney, C. (M.A.) Lecturer; Queen's University of Belfast, Physical Education, Botanic Park, Belfast, North. Ireland (0232-681126, 0232-681129); E; Biofeedback, Personality, Mood, Skill Acquisition, Psychology of Injuries

McKeever, J.J. (D.Lc.,M.A.); St. Joseph's College of Education, Dept. of Physical Education, Stewarts Town Road, Belfast, North. Ireland (617631); E; Curriculum, Motor Learning, Motor Control

Norway

*Moser, Thomas (Mag.rer.nat), Lektor; Tonsberg Idrettsmedisinske Laboratorium, Ramdal, Tonsberg, Norway, N-3100 (0047-33-20721/99137, 0047-33-67146); G,N,E(S,R); Mental Training, Motivation, Psycho-Regulation, Education in Sports Psychology

Nokling, O. (Dr.); Norges Indretshogskole, Postboks, 40 Krinsja, Oslo 8, Norway (047-02234685); E,N; Sport, Sport Psychology, Psychoregulation

*Olsen, A. Morgan (Prof.Dr.); Norges Indretshogskole, Postboks, 40 Krinsja, Oslo 8, Norway (047-02234685, 047-02234220); E,N; Sport Psychology, Sport Theory, Physical Education, Teacher Training

Patriksson, Goran (Ph.D.) Professor; The Norwegian University of Sport, Box 40, Krinsja, 0807 Oslo 8, Norway (472234685); SW,E,G; Stress, Relaxation, Drop-Outs, Sport Career

Railo, Willi S. (Dr.); Norges Indretshogskole, Postboks, 40 Krinsja, Oslo 8, Norway (047-02234685); E,N; Mental Training, Psychoregulation, Relaxation, Top Sport

Sisjord, Mari-Krist Professor; Norges Indretshogskole, Postboks, 40 Krinsja, Oslo 8, Norway N-0807

Skirstad, Berit Professor; Norges Indretshogskole, Postboks, 40 Krinsja, Oslo 8, Norway N-0807

*Sorensen, Marit (Masters) Assistant Professor; The Norwegian University of Sport and Physical Education, Sognsv.220, 0807 Oslo, Norway (02-23-4685, 23-42-20); E,G,F,SCANDINAVIAN; Health, Therapeutic Exercise, Psychological Effects, Motivation, Psychiatry

Peru

Flores, Jorge Alva (B.Sc.) Psychologist; Van Dick 189, San Borja-Surqui, Lima, Peru 110; S,E(S,R); Top Athletes, Stress, Control, Soccer

Poland

Czajkowski, Zbigniew Professor; Academy of Physical Education, Fencing Dept., Ulica Mikolowska 72 a, Katowice, Poland 40-065; POL,E,F, R,U,G; Motor Learning, Motivation, Stress, Fencing

*Dabrowska, Helena (Ph.D.); Institute for Sport, Trylogii 2/16, Warsaw, Poland 01-892; POL,E,R(S); Motivation of Achievement, Causal Attribution

Dolowicz, D.B.; Akademia Wychowania Fizycznego, Zakl. Psychologii Sportu, Marchlewskiego 27/39, Poznan, Poland (330081); E,F(R),R,POL; Personality, Self-Concept, Psychotherapy, Diagnosis, Social Interaction

*Dracz, Barbara (Ph.D.) Psychology Adiunct Akademia Wychowania Fizycznego, Krakow, os. Sienkiewicza 4/11, 32-020, Wieliczka, Krakow, Poland (78-18-04); POL,R,E(R); Tennis Psychology, Motor Learning, Personality Players

*Goracy-Tyborowska, Alicja; Academy of Physical Education, Dept. of Psychology, Marymoncka 34, 01-813 Warsaw, Poland (340431-453); F(R,W), R,POL; Personality, Stress, Anxiety, Top Athletes, Counseling

Gracz, J.G. (Ph.D.) Professor; Academy of Physical Education, Dept. of Psychology, Poznan, Marchlewskiego, Poland 27/39 (204-668); POL,G,R,E(R); Stress, Control, Emotions, Skiing, Tennis

*Graczyk, Marek; Academy of Physical Education, Dept. of Psychology, Marymoncka 34, 01-813 Warsaw, Poland (340431-248); E,POL; Personality, Stress, Anxiety, Psychotherapy, Top Athletes

Guillermo Dellamary

Frank C. Bakker

Adri Vermeer

L.R.T. Williams

Philomena Ikulayo

A. Morgan Olsen

*Juraszczyk Stolecka A. (Dr.); Academy of Physical Education, Dept. of Psychology, Mikolowska 72, Katowice, Poland (514-066442); F,R,POL; Personality, Selection, Anxiety

*Karolczak-Biernacka, B., Associate Professor, Manager; Instytut Badan Edukacyjnych, 00-180 Gorczewska 8, Warsaw, Poland (320221); R,E(R); Motivation, Competition, Stress, Morale and Attitudes, Theory and Methodology

*Klodecka-Rozalska, Jadwiga Head of Laboratory; Institute of Sport, Laboratory of Psychoregulation, Trylogii 2/16, Warsaw, Poland 01-892 (33-95-10); E,R,POL; Psychoregulation, Child in Sport, Soccer, Psychomotorics, Mental Health

Korzeniowska, E. (M.Ps.); Sport Instytut, Dept. of Psycho-Social Problems in Sport, Ceglowska 68, Warsaw, Poland (350981); E(R),R,POL; Clinical, Personality, Temperament, Top Athletes, Shooting

Kosinska, H.; Institute of Sport, Psychological and Social Department, 68/70 Ceglowska St., Warsaw, Poland (350981); E(R),G(R,W),R,POL; Fear, Clinical, Psychology, Personality, Counseling

Koziara, R. (M.A.); Academy of Physical Education, Dept. of Psychology, Marymoncka 34, Warsaw, Poland (340431-453); E,R,POL; Personality, Volleyball, Psychology

Lipska-Blomgren, K. (M.A.); Instytut Sportu, Zaklad Psychologii, Ceglowska 68/70, Warsaw, Poland (350981); E,R,POL; Counseling, Top Athletes, Personality, Self-Regulation

*Mikolajczyk, Maria (Ph.D.); Academy of Physical Education, Dept. of Psychology, Marymoncka 34, 01-813 Warsaw, Poland (340431-248); E,F(S,R), R,POL; Competition, Moral Development, Cognitive Processes, Locus of Control, Alpinism

Nawrocka, W. (Dr.) Professor; Academy of Physical Culture, Marymoncka 34/10, Warsaw, Poland; F,R,POL; Personality, Counseling, Resistance, Human Relations, Consciousness

Nowicki, Dariusz; Institute of Sport, Ceglowska 68/70, Warsaw, Poland 01-809

Pietrzyk, W. (M.A.); Sportsclub "Slask," Worclaw, Oporowska 62, Wroclaw, Poland (611611); G(R,W),R,POL; Counseling, Personality, Competition, Perception, Motivation

Raczkowska-Bekiesinska, Teresa; Academy of Physical Training, Institute of Psychology, Academka 2, Biala Podlaska, Poland (32396); E(R),R,POL; Learning, Shooting, Self-Regulation, Temperament, Top Athletes

*Rychta, Tadeusz (Dr.Hab.); Academy of Physical Education, Dept. of Psychology, Marymoncka 34, 01-813 Warsaw, Poland (340431-466); E,R,POL; Personality, Top Athletes, School Physical Education, Motivation, Youth Sport

Stawowska, L.; Akademia Wychowania Fizycznego, Zaklad Psychologii, Mikolowska 72A, Katowice, Poland (514066); F,R,POL; Personality, Temperament, Individual Differences, Anxiety, Neurosis

Suchozebrska, S. (M.A.); Academy of Physical Training, Institute of Psychology, Akademicka 2, Biala Podlaska, Poland 21-500 (32575); E(R), G(R),R,POL; Personality, Temperament, Self-Control, Students, Top Athletes

Szczepanska, E. (M.A.); Academy of Physical Education, Dept. of Psychology, Nikolowska 72, Katowice, Poland (514066); E,R,POL; Personality, Neurosis, Communication, Human Relations, Psychotherapy

Szkutnik, J. (M.A.); Academy of Physical Education, Institute of Humanistic Sciences, Str. Marymoncka 34, Warsaw, Poland (340431-344); E,R, POL; Child Athletes, Personality, Teams, Small Groups

Trastelaniec, W. (M.A.); Akademia Wychowania Fizycznego, Institut for Humanistic Sciences, Marymoncka 39, Warsaw, Poland (340431-453); E,R,POL; Anxiety, Personality, Aggression, Motivation, Needs

Tymoszvk, D. (M.A.); Akademia Wychowania Fizycznego, Zaklad Mavk Humanist Ycznych, Akademicka 2, Biala Podlaska, Poland; G,POL; R(R,S); Emotion, Interests, Personality, Coaches, Psychological Preparation

Warzynski, F. (Ph.D.); University of Lodz, Dept. of Physiology, 21 Kosciuszki Str., Lodz, Poland (32585); E(S,R),R,POL; Motivation, Competition, Cooperation, Personality, Attitudes

Wasilewski, E. (Dr.); Institut of Sport, Psycho-Social Problems in Sport, Ceglowska 68/70, Warsaw, Poland (350981); E(R),G,R,POL; Concentration, Motivation, Anxiety, Stress, Achievement

Wielochowski, M. (M.A.); Instytut Sportu, Dept. of Psycho-Social Problems in Sport, Ceglowska 68/70, Warsaw, Poland; POL,R; Pathology, Temperament, Personality, Counseling

Wilert-Krajewska, F; Hauptkomitee fuer Korpeerkultur, Litewska 2, Warsaw, Poland P-00581

Zdebski, Janusz (Ph.D.) Dean; Academy of Physical Education, Dept. of Psychology, 31-571 Kirakios, Al Plano 6-Leterego, Poland; POL,E; Mountaineering, Tourism, Psychotherapy, Volleyball

Ziobro, H. (Ph.D.); Academy of Physical Education, Dept. of Physical Education, Witelona 25, Wroclaw, Poland (483071); E,G,R,POL; Mental Ability, Motivation, Personality, School Children

*Zmudzki, Andrzej Z.A. (Dr.) Psychologist; Institute of Sport, Dept. of Psychological Problems of Sport, Trylogii 2/16, 01-892 Warsaw, Poland (34-62-88); E,R,POL; Personality, Stress, Anxiety, Counseling, Competition, Temperament

Zwolinska, D. (Dr.); Central Sports Center, Psychological Room, Br. Czecha S., Zakopane, Poland (5021); E(R),F,POL; Human Relations, Selection, Attitudes, Personality, Counseling

*Zyto-Sitkiewicz, Danuta; Academy of Physical Education, Dept. of Psychology, Marymoncka 34, 01-813 Warsaw, Poland (340431-453); E(R,W),R, POL; Personality, Stress, Anxiety, Top Athletes, Psychotherapy

Portugal

*Alves, Jose A. (Ph.D.), Professor; University Tech.-Lisboa, F.M.H., Dept. of Psychology, Lisbon Codex, Portugal 1499 (1-4196777, 4151248, 62430 UTISEFP); POR,F,E,S; Reaction Time, Cognition, Personality, Stress, Top Athletes

*Cruz, Jose (Ph.D.) Assistant Professor; Universidade do Minho, Instituto de Educacao, Rua Abade da Loureira, 4700 Braga, Portugal (053-27776); POR,F,E,I(S,R),S(S,R); Stress, Anxiety, Cognitive, Handball, Canoeing, Soccer

*Faro Viana, Miguel M. (B.S.) Sport Psychologist; Rua Herculano Nunes LT 7, R/C Dto Areias, S. Pedro Estoril, Portugal 2765 (01-267-1784); POR, E,F,S; Psychological Assessment, Cognitive and Behavioral Interventions, Fencing, Stress Management, Attention Control

Feliz, Joaquim (M.Sc.) Psychologist; Sport Lisboa Benfica, Dept. of Roller Hockey, Estadio da Luz, Lisboa, Portugal (723376); POR,E,F; Roller Skate Hockey, Psychological Testing

*Fernandes, Urbela M. (License) Sport Psychologist; Sport's Medicine Center, Av Bombeiros Voluntarios 37 4E Alges, 1495 Lisbon, Portugal (4100873); POR,F,E,S(S,R),I(R); Psychological Assessment, Emotional Factors, Counseling, Clinical Research, Mental Training

*Freitas, Marta (Dipl.Psych.) Assistant; ISEF/UTL, Dept. of Psychology, Estrada da Costa-Cruz Quebrada, 1499 Lisboa Codex, Portugal (4196777); POR,S; Developmental Psychology

*Paula Brito, Antonio (Ph.D.) Professor; FMH - Technical University of Lisbon, Estrada Costa-Cruz Quebrada, 1499 Lisboa Codex, Portugal (1-4196777); POR,F,E,S,I(S,R); Development, Psychological Profile, Top Athletes, Track and Field, Counseling

Ribeiro, Jose (M.Sc.) Psychologist; Universidade do Porto, Psicilcia-Ciencias da Educacao, Portugal; POR,E,F; Stress, Judo

*Serpa, Sidonio (Ph.D.) Assistant Professor; Universidade Tecnica de Lisboa (F.M.H.), Dept. of Psychology, Estrada da Costa-Cruz Quebrada, 1499 Lisboa Codex, Portugal (4196777, 4151248, 62430 UTISEF P); POR,E,F, S(S,R); Stress, Mental Training, Sophrology, Leadership, Aggression

Wilson, Joseph (Prof.); Institut Superieur d'Education Physique, Estr. Costa-Cruz Quebrada, Lisboa. Cod., Portugal 1499 (2112787); E,F,POR,S; Physical Education, Top Athletes, Learning, Competition

Romania

*Epuran, Mihai I. (Dr.Psy.); Institute d'Education Physique Et du Sport, Dept. de Psychologie-Pedagogie, Str. Stefan Furtuna 140, Bucharest, Romania 76708 (385315); E,ROM,F,I(R); Psychology, Methodology, Top Athletes, Counseling

Eremia, N.; Centrale de Medicina Sportu, Medecine-Neurologiste Et Primaire Phys., Bd. Muncii 37-39-Sect. III, Bucharest, Romania (207040); ROM,F; Psychopathology, Top Sport, Anxiety, Relaxation

Gheorghiu, D. (Dipl.Psych.); Center of Sports Medicine, NR. 37-39 Sector 2, Bucharest, Romania 7000 (207040-100); ROM,F(S,R); Stress, Diagnosis, Self-Regulation, Relaxation, Anxiety

*Holdevici, Irene (Dr.Psy.); Institute of Psychology, Schitu Magureanu 2, Bucharest, Romania; E,ROM,F,G(R),R; Relaxation, Hypnosis, Suggestibility, Anxiety, Yoga

*Horghidan, V. (Dr.Psy.); Institute of Physical Education and Sport, Str. Stefan Furtuna 140, Bucharest, Romania 76708 (385315); ROM,F; Motor Learning, Psychomotricity, Personality, Motivation, Emotion

Kahana-Moscou, Judith; Institut for Pedagogical and Psychological Research, Frumosa 26, Bucharest, Romania; E,ROM,F,G; Anxiety, Competition, Stress Management, Personality, Top Athletes

Niculescu, M. (Dipl.Psych.); C.C.E.F.S., Bdul. Muncii Nr.37-39Sect. II, Bucharest, Romania; E(S,R),ROM,F(S,R); Personality, Psychotherapy, Top Athletes

Samadoiu, O. (Dipl.Psych.); Centruc de Medicina Sportiva, Bdul. Muncii Nr.37-39Sect. II, Bucharest, Romania 7000 (207040-100); E(R),ROM,F(R); Relaxation, Psychotherapy

Smadoiu, Ovidiu; Centrul de Medicina-Bucuresti, Blvd. Muncii Nr.37-39, Sektor III, Bucharest, Romania

Tibara, C. (Dipl.Psych.); C.C.E.F.S., Bdul. Muncii Nr.37-39, Bucharest, Romania (215513); E(S,R),ROM,F; Psychophysiology, Stress, Sport, Competition

Tudos, S. (Dipl. Psych.); Institute of Physical Education and Sports, Str. Maior Ene 12, Bucharest, Romania; G,H,ROM; Personality, Motivation, Decision Making, Social Psychology, Perception

Saudia Arabia

Al-Nakeeb, Yahya K. (Ph.D.) Assistant Professor; King Saud University, Dept. of Physical Education, Riyadh, Saudi Arabia (4674894); A,E,G(R); Stress, Control, Fitness, Athletics, Basketball

Scotland

Carroll, Jean A. (B.Sc.Hon.); Dunfermline College of Physical Education, Cramond Road North, Edinburgh, Scotland EH4 6JD (031-3366001); E; Social Aspects, Sport, Teacher Preparation

*Cox, Richard L. (Ph.D.) Clinical Psychology Lecturer; Moray House College, Cramond Campus, Cramond Rd. North, Edinburgh, Scotland EH4 6JD (031-312-6001, 031-312-6335); E; Competition, Mental Preparation

*Hendry, Leo B. (Ph.D., F.B.P.S.) Professor, Head; Dept. of Education, University of Aberdeen, Kings College, Aberdeen AB92UB, Scotland (0224-272729/272731, 0224-487048); E; Youth Sports, Leisure, Adolescence, Drugs and AIDs, Youth Services

*Lee, David N. (Ph.D.) Reader in Psychology; Edinburgh University, Dept. of Psychology, 7 George Square, Edinburgh, EH8 9JZ, Scotland (031-667-1011, 031-667-7983, D.N.LEE@UK.AC.ED.);E,F(R); Vision, Control, Timing, Rehabilitation, Development

*Mutrie, Nanette (Ph.D.) Assistant Director; University of Glasglow, Dept. of Physical Education and Sport Sciences, Glasgow, Scotland G12 8LT (041-339-8855, 041-330-4808); E,F(S,R); Exercise Therapy, Depression, Drug Abuse, Alcoholism, Exercise Adherence

Reid, R. Malcolm (Ph.D.) Assistant Director; University of Aberdeen, Dept. of Physical Education, University Road, Old Aberdeen, Scotland AB9 2UW (40241); E; Positive Health, Psychophysiology, Fitness, Teaching, Aggression

*Sharp, Robert H. (Ph.D.) Programme Coordinator (Outdoor Education); Jordanhill College, Southbrae Drive, Glasgow, S13 1PP, Scotland; E; Mountaineering, Outdoor Education, Information Processing, Research Methods

Singapore

*Aplin, Nick G. (M.Sc.) Lecturer; College of Physical Education, 21 Evans Rd., Singapore, Singapore 1025 (4605364, 4687506); E; Anticipation, Attitudes, Brain, Hemispheric Dominance, Gender

Chen, Chee-Fong (B.S.) Consultant; Sport and Exercise Consultation Service, 237, Lor.1, Toa Payoh, #04-22, Singapore 1231 (65-2591085); E,CHI; Neuro, Psychology, Attribution, Aggression, Hypnosis

Giam, C.K. (M.D.,M.Sc.) Head; Singapore Sports Council, Sports Medicine and Recearch Center, Singapore, Singapore 1439 (340982); G,E,M(S), CHI(S); Sports Medicine, Stress Management, Relaxation Techniques, Motivation Techniques, Positive Thinking

*Koh, John N.S. (M.Ed.) Deputy Executive Director; Singapore Sports Council, c/o National Stadium, Kallang, Singapore 1439 (3409503); E,MA,IN,M(S); Curriculum, Motivation, Aggression, Behavior, Culture, Sports Administration

*Oon, Desmond S. (Ph.D.) Head of Research; Singapore Sports Council, National Stadium, Kallang, Singapore 1439 (3409640, 3409537); E; Stress, Motivation, Talent, Hypnosis, Tennis

*Quek, Jin-Jong (M.Sc.) Lecturer; College of Physical Education, 21 Evans Road, Singapore, Singapore 1025 (65-4605369, 65-4687506); E,M, MA(S); Coding, Memory, Development, Control, Motivation

*Tan, Harry E.K. (Ms.P.E.) Head; Anglo-Chinese School, Dept. of Physical Education, 60 Barker Road, Singapore, Singapore 1130 (2560747, 2530041); E,MA,CHI(S); Motivation, Attention, Tennis, Stress, Squash

*Wright, Helen C. (M.Sc.) Lecturer; College of Physical Education, 21 Evans Road, Singapore, Singapore 1025 (460-5357); E; Knowledge of Results, Squash, Group Dynamics, Aggression, Personality

South Africa

Coghlan, D. (Dic.); Rhodes University, Dept. of Physical Education, Grahamstown, South Africa (3243); E,D,AFR,F(R); Teaching, Coaching, Motor Learning, Motor Development, Motivation

Dutoit, Percy P. (M.A.) Lecturer; Potchefstroon Univeristy, Dept. of Human Movement Science, Potchefstroon, South Africa (0418-99-1803); E,AFR; Leadership, Cohesion, Rugby, Motivation, Confidence

Erasmus, Hohannes J. (M.A.) Lecturer; University of Pretoria, Dept. of Psychology, Pretoria, South Africa 0002 (012-420-2305); E; Stress, Development, Motivation, Attention Control, Relaxation

Kemp, P.B. (D.Ed.); University of the Orange Freestate, Dept. of Physical Education, Dickie Clarkstr. 28, Bloemfontein, South Africa (70711306); E,G,D,AFR; Anxiety, Personality, Attitudes, Competition, Behavior

Malan, Ewoud E. (Ph.D.) Student Counselor; P.O. Box 904461, Faerie Glen, South Africa 0043 (4202333); E,AFR,SO,D; Rugby, Stress, Motivation, Management, Therapy

*Potgieter, Justus R. (Ph.D.) Professor; University of Stellenbosch, Dept. of Human Movement Studies, Stellenbosch, South Africa (02231-774717); E,AFR,D(R); Stress, Performance Enhancement, Motivation, Attention, Exercise Adherence

*Schomer, Hein Helgo (Ph.D.) Senior Lecturer, Health Psychology Internship Convenor; University of Cape Town, Dept. of Psychology, Private Bag, Rondebosch, South Africa 7700 (021-650-3433, 021-650-3726); E,G,F(R), AFR(R); Cognitive Strategies, Relaxation, Stress, Health, Emotional Stability

*Van Eeden, Cynthia J. (M.A.) Psychologist; 7 Parker Stret, Riviera, Pretoria, Transvaal, South Africa 0084 (012-706431); E,AFR,G(R),D(R)

Soviet Union

Arosiev, D.A. (Dr.); Pr. Marx 20, K8, Moscow, USSR (2028876); R,F(R,W); Coaching, Skill, Rowing, Personality

Avanesian, Grant M. (Ph.D.) Lecturer; ArmGIFK, Dept. of Sport Psychology, 11 Mravian St., Erevan, Armenian I.P.E., USSR 375070 (55-43-20); R,E,ARM; Psychodiagnostics, Psychological Service in Sport

*Belkin, Arnold A. (B.Sc.) Assistant Professor; Obrazcova 15, Miit, Moscow, USSR 2842477 (457-94-52, 200-22-16, 0022394); R; Training, Conditioning, Skill, Gymnastics, Personality, Mental Training

Davli, G; Institute for Physical Culture, Pr. Tchavtchavadze 49, Tbilisi, USSR (223160); R,G(R); Coaching, Mental States, Conditioning, Personality

Filatov, A.T. (Juv.); Ul. Artema 8, Harkov, USSR (456867); R,G(R); Psychotherapy, Relaxation, Emotion, Volition, Personality

*Ganyuskin, Anatoliy D. (Ph.D.) Lecturer; SGIFK, Dept. of Psychology, 23 Gagarin St., Smolensk, USSR 214018 (357203); R,E(R,W); Psychodiagnostics, Personality

Gorbunov, Gennadij D. (Ph.D.) Lecturer; GDOIFK, Dept. of Sport Psychology, Dekabristov 35, Leningrad, USSR 190121 (2166627); R,E; Psychodiagnostics, Psychoregulation

*Hanin, Yuri L. (D.Sc.) Professor; Leningrad Institute of Management/LIMTU/, Gastello Str. 12, Leningrad, USSR 196135 (812-293-2530); E,F,R, G(S,R); Competition, Anxiety, Communication, Organizational Development

Hudadov, Nickolai A.; VNIIFK, Kazakova 18, Moscow, USSR (2618086); R,G,E(S,R); Psychological Preparation, Competition, Diagnosis, Boxing, Personality

Kalinin, E.A.; VNIIFK, Kazakova 18, Moscow, USSR (2618086); R,G(R); Competition, Anxiety, Motives, Gymnastics, Personality

*Kantor, Elena D. (Ph.D.) Scientist; VNIIFK Laboratory of Sport Psychology, 18 Kazakov St., Moscow, USSR 103064 (261-84-05, 261-2553); R,E,F; Personality, Motivation, Psychodiagnostics, Psychoregulation, Expert Systems

Kiselev, Yuri J. (Ph.D.) Lecturer; LNIIFK, Laboratory of Sport Psychology 2 Dinamo St., Leningrad, USSR 197047; R,E; Psychodiagnostics, Personality, Social Psychology

Klimenko, V.V.; Institute of Physical Culture, Ul. Fiskulturnaja 1, Kijev, USSR (275452); R,E(R); Coaching, Skill, Attention, Cycling, Competition

Kolomeitzev, J.A.; Institute of Physical Culture, Leninskij, Pr. 51, Minsk, USSR (327681); R,E(R,W); Social Psychology, Relaxation, Swimming, Personality

*Kolomejtzev, Yurij M. (Ph.D.) Lecturer; BGOIFK, Institute of Physical Culture, Chair Swimming, 105 Masherov St., Minsk, USSR 220005; R,E; Psychodiagnostics, Personality, Social Psychology

Kostanian, Albert O. (Ph.D.) Lecturer; ArmGIFK, Dept. of Sport Psychology, 11 Mravian St., Erevan, Armenian IPE, USSR 375070 (55-43-20); R,E,ARM; Psychodiagnostics, Psychological Service in Sport

**Jadwiga
Klodecka-Rozalska**

Antonio Paula Brito

Giam C.K.

Quek Jin-Jong

Kulakova, Ella A. (Ph.D.) Scientist; GXOLIFK, Dept. of Sport Psychology, 4 Sirenevij Bul., Moscow, USSR; R,E; Psychodiagnostics, Psychoregulation

Medvedev, Vladimir V. (Ph.D.) Scientist; GZOL-IFK, Dept. of Sport Psychology, 4 Sirenevij Bul., Moscow, USSR; R,E; Psychodiagnostics, Personality

*Melnikov, Alexandre V. (Ph.D.) Senior Scientific Researcher; Research Institute for Higher Education, Dept. of Learning, 2Q Podsosensky Per., Moscow, USSR 2735961; R,E; Stress, Performance, Psychodiagnostics

*Melnikov, Vladimir M. (Ph.D.) Head, Professor; GZOLIFK, Dept. of Sport Psychology, 4 Sireneviy Bul., Moscow, USSR (166-49-92); R,E; Psychodiagnostics, Personality

Merlinkin, V.P.; Pedagogical Institute, Ul. Mejlauka 1, Kazan, USSR (24287); R,G(R); Coaching, Acrobatics, Personality

Mirtov, Yuri N. (Ph.D.) Scientist; TzNII "Sport," Laboratory of Sport Psychology, 10 Elisavetinsky St., Moscow, USSR 105007 (261-25-53); R,E; Psychodiagnostics, Motivation, Motivation Training, Interpersonal Perception, Fans' Hooliganism

Nepopalov, Vladimir N., Scientist; GZOLIFK, Dept. of Sport Psychology, 4 Sirenevij Bul., Moscow, USSR; R,E; Psychodiagnostics, Personality

Nilopetz, Michel N. Scientist; VNIIFK, Section of Sport Psychology, 18 Kasakov St., Moscow, USSR 103064 (261-25-53); R,G; Computer's Psychodiagnostics, Personality

*Paly, Vera I. (Ph.D.) Scientist; Central Research Institute of Sport, Laboratory of Sport Psychology, 10 Elisavetinski St., Moscow, USSR 107005 (265-32-44); R,E; Psychodiagnostics, Motivation, Personality, Perception

Plakhtienko, Victor (Dr.) Professor; Sports Psychology Laboratory, Kasakova 18, Moscow, USSR 103064

*Rodionov, Albert V. (Ph.D.) Scientist; Central Research Institute of Sport, Laboratory of Sport Games, 10 Elizavetinski St., Moscow, USSR 107005 (265-35-62, 408-20-21-14); R,E; Psychodiagnostics, Personality, Psychoregulation

Romanin, A.N.; VNIIFK, Kazakova 18, Moscow, USSR (2618086); R,E,G(R); Development, Training, Social Psychology, Shooting, Personality

Romanina, Elena V. (Ph.D.) Scientist; GZOLIFK, Dept. of Sport Psychology, 4 Sirenevij Bul., Moscow, USSR; R,E; Psychodiagnostics, Psychoregulation, Personality

Romanov, Vladimir; USSR Sports Committee, Kazakova 27, Moscow, USSR

Ryzonkin, Yuri J. Scientist; VNIIFK, Section of Sport Psychology, 18 Kasakov St., Moscow, USSR 103064 (261-25-53); R,E; Psychodiagnostics, Social Psychology, Personality

Sirotin, O.A.; Insitute of Physical Culture, Ul. Ordjonikidze 1, Celjabinsk, USSR (337402); R,E(R); Psychological Preparation, Anxiety, Relaxation, Wrestling

Slobunov, Semen M. (Ph.D.) Scientist; VNIIFK, Section of Sport Psychology, 18 Kasakov St., Moscow, USSR 103064 (261-25-53); R,E; Psychodiagnostics, Computer's Psychodiagnostics, Psychomotorics

Solntzeva, Lidia S. (Ph.D.) Scientist; TzNII "Sport," Laboratory of Sport Psychology, 10 Elisavetinski St., Moscow, USSR, 105007 (261-25-53); R,E; Psychodiagnostics, Motivation, Personality, Perception

Sopov, Vladimir N. (Ph.D.) Lecturer; KazGIFK, Dept. of Sport Psychology, 83/85 Abaj St., Alma-Ata, USSR 480072; R,E; Psychodiagnostics, Personality, Social Psychology

Stambulova, Natalia B. (Ph.D.) Lecturer; GDOIFK, Dept. of Sport Psychology, 35 Dekabristov St., Leningrad, USSR 190121 (216-66-27); R,E(S,R); Psychodiagnostics, Personality, Young Sport

Stavitzki, Konstantin R. (Ph.D.) Scientist; TzNII "Sport," Laboratory of Sport Psychology, 10 Elisavetinski St., Moscow, USSR, 105007 (261-25-53); R,F,G; Psychodiagnostics Psychoregulation, Computer's Psychodiagnostics, Psychophysiology, Psychomotoric

Surkov, E.N. (Gdiojk); Decabristov 35, Leningrad, USSR (2168544); R,G(R); Coaching, Anticipation, Gymnastics, Skill

Travina, Albina P. (Ph.D.) Scientist; GZOLIFK, Dept. of Sport Psychology, 4 Sirenevij Bul., Moscow, USSR; R,E; Psychodiagnostics, Personality, Social Psychology

*Viatkin, Bronislav A. (Ph.D.) Lecturer; PGPI Dept. of Psychology, 24 Marx St., Perm, USSR 614000; R,E; Psychodiagnostics, Personality, Psychological Preparation, Anxiety

Vjatkin, B.A.; Pedagogical Institute, Ul. Marx, 24, Perm, USSR (442746); R,G(R,W); Psychological Preparation, Anxiety, Relaxation, Skiing, Personality

Volkov, N.K.; Institute of Physical Culture, Leninskii Br. 51, Minsk, USSR (324681); R,E; Psychological Preparation, Anxiety, Relaxation, Wrestling, Personality

Yermolaeva, Marina V. (Ph.D.) Scientist; TzNII "Sport," Laboratory of Sport Psychology, 10 Elisavetinski St., Moscow, USSR 105007 (261-25-53); R,E; Psychodiagnostics, Psychoregulation, Computer's Psychodiagnostics, Psychomotoric

Zhorov, Peter A. (Ph.D.) Scientist; NII OPP APN USSR, Laboratory of Sport Psychology, 20 Marx St., Moscow, USSR 103009; R,E; Psychodiagnostics, Personality, Social Psychology

Spain

Aguera-Reoyo, Inaki Psychologist; c/Amaya N.7-3c, Pamplona, Spain 31002 (948-262984); S,E(R); Handball, Emotional Control, Top Sport, Performance Monitoring, Anxiety

*Alvarez de Dalmau, Pere (M.Sc) Psychologist; Escola Catalana de l'Esport, Av. Paisos Catalans, 12, 08950 Esplugues de Llobregat, Barcelona, Spain (34-3-371-90-11,34-3-372-01-84); S,CA,F(S,R), I(R); Coaches Formation, Stress, Organization

*Arumi-Ortiz, Marisa (Lic.) Psychologist; Direccio General de l'Esport, S.Docencia-Investigacio, Av. Paisos Catalans 12, 08950 Esplugues de Llobregat, Barcelona, Spain (371-9011, 372-0184); E,S,CA,F,I; Coaches, Tennis, Psychological Preparation, Gymnastics, Organization

Balague, G. (Ph.D.); Institute Nacional d'Educacion Fisica, c/ San Mako S/N, Barcelona, Spain, (3715654); E,F,S,I,POR; Top Athletes, Relaxation, Mental Training

Buceta, Jose; Universidad Nacional d'Education a Dist, Faculty de Psicologia, P.O. Apartado N. 50, Madrid, Spain

Canton Chirivella, Enrique (Ph.D.) Associate Professor; University of Valencia, Dept. of General Psychology, Avenida Blasco Ibanez, No. 21, Valencia, Spain 46010 (96-369-48-50); E,S,F(S,R),I(R); History, Martial Arts, Motivation, Mental Training, Behavior Modification

*Capafons, Antonio (Ph.D.) Professor Titular; University of Valencia, Facultad de Psicologia, Blasco Ibanez, No. 21, 46021 Valencia, Spain (96-3932295); E,F,S,C(S,R); Self-Control, Self-Regulation, Anxiety, Mental Training, Hypnosis

*Cruz, Jaume (Ph.D.) Professor; Universitat Autonoma Barcelona, Psicologia de l'Educacio Apartat de Correus 29, 08193 Bellaterra, Spain (5812187, 5812001); E,S,CA,F(S,R); Behavioral Coaching, Stress, Control, Youth Sports

*DeDiego Escribano, Salome, Psychologist, Co-director; Sport Psychology Serside, Ayala, 150, Madrid 28009, Spain (91-401-7494, 91-401-7243); E,F,S; Cognitive Style, Tests, Stress, Coach, Communication

Fuentes, Francisco (Dr.) Professor; INEF, Martin Fierro S/N, Madrid, Spain

Galilea, Beatriz (M.Sc.) Sport Psychologist; Centre d'Estudes de l'Art Rendiment Esp., Paisos Catalans 12, Esplugues-Llobrega, Barcelona, Spain (93-3712300); S,I,F,E,CA; Mental Training, Preparation for Competition, Stress, Psychological Control Training, Top Athletes

*Gil, Jose (Dr. Psych.) Clinical Psychologist; Invesco, Colon, 4, 4B-46004, Valencia, Spain (96-3515464, 96-1232873); S,E,F; Self-Control, Stress, Relaxation, Handball, Concentration

Menendez-Montanes, Concha (Licendida) Teacher; Universidad de Barcelona, Dept. Psiciliga, Evolutiva y Educacion, c/Urgell,43,1-1a, Barcelona, Spain 08011 (93-2547782); S,F,E(R,W); Teaching, Motor Learning, Motor Handicaps, Motor Therapy, Physical Education

*Munoz-Soler, A.M.S. (Prof.Ph.Ed.) Psychiatrist; Consejo Superior de Desportes, Medicina Deportiva, Ponzano No. 59, Madrid, Spain 28003; E,S,F(S,R); Competition, Top Athletes, Psychopathology, Therapy, Pharmacology

*Pallares Mestre, Jacinto (M.Sc.) Psychologist; Residencia Juvenil Pi-Gros, Generalidad Valenciana, Plaza Dorrainers de Tales, No. S-10-20, Castellon, Spain 12004 (964-229415); S,E,F(S,R); Motivation, Youth Sport, Behavior Modification, Mental Training

Perez Recio, Guillermo (Lic.) Psychologist; Centre d'Alt Rediment, Sport Psychology Dept., 08194 Sant Cugat Del Valls, Barcelona, Spain (675-37-61); S,E,I(R),F(R); Top Athletes, Coping With Stress

Puig, Inma (M.Sc.) Psychologist; High Competition School of Tennis, c/Balmes N-415 4-D, Barcelona, Spain (4183321); CA,F,E,S,I(S,R); Tennis, High Level Competition, Performance, Concentration, Mental Strength

Riera, Joan (D.E.F.); Institute Nacional d'Education Fisica, c/ San Mako, S/N, Barcelona, Spain (3715754); E,F,S; Social Psychology, Top Athletes, Learning

*Roca, Josep (D.E.F.); Institute Nacional d'Education Fisica, c/San Mateo, S/N, Barcelona, Spain (3715754); E,F,S,CA; Reaction Time, Top Athletes, Motor Learning, Selection, Peception

*Sagredo Martinez, Cristina, Psychologist, Co-Director; Sport Psychology Serside, Ayala-150, Madrid, Spain (91-4017494, 91-40172-43); E,S,F; Training Coach, Stress, Self-Confidence, Team

*Segura-Bernal, Jordi (Dr.) Collaborator; Universitat de Barcelona, Dept. of Social Psychology, Lluis Pascual, 77 Sant Boi, Barcelona, Spain 08830 (93-6614378); CA,E,F,S; Group, Social, Leader, Sport Education, Humanistic Psychology

Velasco-Covde, Jose A. (Licence) Psychologist; La Diana 3, Irun Guipuzcoa, Spain 20300 (943-627218); F,S; Handball, Rugby

Sweden

Anderson, Peter N.G.; Bospitalsg 5, Malm Sweden 21133 (46-40-117538); SW,DAN,E,F,S; Relaxation, Tennis, Biofeedback, Positive Thinking, Visualization

*Apitzsch, Erwin (M.Sc.) Lecturer, Registered Psychologist; Lund University, Dept. of Applied Psychology, Paradisgatan 5, Lund, Sweden S-22350 (4646-109115, 4646-104720); SW,E,G,F(R); Personality, Group Dynamics, Soccer, Athletics, Anxiety

Backman, Lars (Ph.D.) Research Scientist; University of Uneo, Dept. of Psychology, Redhusesplanaden 2, Umea, Sweden S-90247 (90-166405, LARSB-@SEUMDC57); E,G(R),SW; Stress, Aging, Motor Perfromance, Automaticity, Cognition

*Borg, Gunnar A.V. (Ph.D.) University Professor; Division of Perception and Psychophysics, Dept. of Psychology, Stockholm, Sweden S-106 91 (08-16-39-40); SW,E,G,F(R); Perception, Exertion, RPE, Exercise Tests, Psychophysiology

*Carlson, Rolf R. (Ph.D.); College of Physical Education, Dept. of Sport Educational Research, P.O. Box 5626, Stockholm, Sweden S-11486 (8-23-37-20); SW,E,G; Socialization, Sport Engagement, Steering Factors, Training, Elite Sport

Henrysson, Sven (Ph.D.); University of Umea, Dept. of Education, Umea, Sweden S-90187 (090-165757); E,F(R),G,SW; Exercise, Ordinary People, Orienteering, Leadership, Women in Sport

Herkel, M. (B.A.); Brahe Basket, Dept. for Coaching, Box 75, Huskuarna, Sweden (036-144010); E,G,R(S,R),SW,C; Personality, Top Athletes, Practice Conditions, Coach Education

Isberg, Leif G. (Ph.D.); University College of Falun, Borlange Box 2004, Falun, Sweden S-79102 (0046-2381959); SW,E,G; Violence, Aggression, Communication, Relation, Methods

Molander, Bo O. (Ph.D.) Senior Lecturer; University of Umea, Dept. of Psychology, Umea, Sweden S-90187 (090-166410, BOM@SEUMDC51); SW,E, G(R),N(R),DAN(R); Motor Behavior, Aging, Cognition, Stress, Development

*Patriksson, Goran (Ph.D.) Professor; Gothenburg University, Dept. of Education, Box 1010, 43126 Molndal, Sweden (4631679481); SW,E,G; Stress, Relaxation, Drop-Outs, Sport Career

Schelin, Bo (B.A.); University of Lund, Dept. of Sociology, Magistratsvaegen 55N, Lund, Sweden 22244 (046-108869); E(R),SW; Stratification, Sport, Preference

Setterlind, Sven V. (M.A.); University of Karistad, Dept. of Education, Box 9501, Karistad, Sweden 65009 (054-130020); E,G,SW; Anxiety, Relaxation, Mental Training, Children, Athletes

*Unestahl, Lars-Eric (Ph.D.); Orebro University, Dept. of Psychology, Box 923, Oerebro, Sweden S-70130 (46-19-332233, 46-19-332235); E,F,G,SW; Mental Training, Hypnosis, Stress Management, Motivation, Top Athletes

Switzerland

Ackermann, Ueli (Cand. Phil.) Teacher; Wallenthalstrasse 6, Erlenbach, Switzerland CH-8703 (01-9104726); G

*Bader, Hans (M.Sc.); Erlenstrasse 92, CH-8832 Wollerau, Switzerland (01-7850447, 01-7850561); G,E; Psychoregulation, Stress, Self-Management, Organizational Development, Team Development

*Baur, Walter (Ph.D.) Manager; Erlenweg 2, Buelach, Switzerland CH-8180 (01-8602137); G,E,F; Group Dynamics, Conflict Analysis, Top Athletes

Bernath, Walter; Kiefernweg 2, Scaffhausen, Switzerland CH-8200 (053-44643); G

Biedermann, Franz (Dipl.Psych.); Landstrasse 128, Zollikon, Switzerland CH-8702 (01-3913730); G

Biedermann, Hildegard (Dipl.Psych.); Landstrasse 128, Zollikon, Switzerland CH-8702 (01-3913730); G

*Bizzini, Lucio (Ph.D.); 7, ich des Tulipiers, Geneva, Switzerland 1208 (022-736-61-86); F,I,G (R,S),E(R,S); Cognitive Therapy, Counseling, Applied Psychology, Elite Athletes

Breitenmoser, Kurt; Ludwigstrasse 128, St. Gallen, Switzerland CH-9010 (071-240299); G

Crittin, Jean-P. (M.Sc.) Psychologist; Eschholzstr. 17, Forch, Switzerland CH-8127 (01-9803345); G,F,E; Stress, Didactic Methodology, Group Dynamics, Management

Despot, Milenko (Lic. Phil.); Ave. de la Plantaud, Monthey, Switzerland CH-1870 (025-717439); F,G

Eberle, Gerda (Ph.D.); Hegibachstrasse 119, Zurich, Switzerland CH-8032 (01-555890); G

Egger, Kurt (Ph.D.) Professor; Bremgartenstrasse 145, Bern, Switzerland CH-3012 (031-658321); G,E,F; Observation, Curriculum, Evaluation, Instruction, Media

*Franklin, Eric (B.F.A.) Trainer; Rebbergstr. 2, Ruschlikon, Switzerland 8803 (01-724-2260, 01-724-2280); E,G,F; Sports Training, Body Therapies, Mental Training, Dance

*Gikalov, Vladimir (Ph.D.) Professor; University of Bern, Bremgartenstrasse 145, Bern, Switzerland CH-3012 (031-658321); F,G,R,C,E; Motor Learning, Mental Practice

*Graf, Heinz (Ph.D.) Managing Director; Verkehrs-Paedagogisches Institute, Habsburgerstrasse 21, Luzern, Switzerland CH-6005 (041-231066); G,E; Traffic, Sport, Stress Management, Aggression

Handloser, Juerg (Lic.Phil.); Eigenheimstrasse 30, Kusnacht, Switzerland CH-8700 (01-9105600); G

Hangii, Reinhard (Dipl.Psych.); Hans Huberstrasse 27, Slothurn, Switzerland CH-4500 (064-225302); E,F,G(S,R); Mass Media, Personality, Conflict, Group Dynamics, Attitudes

Hasler, Hansreudi (Lic.Phil.); Chemin des Noyeres 1, Evilard, Switzerland CH-2533 (032-227421); G,F

Hauert, Claude A. (Ph.D.) Teacher; University of Geneva, F.P.S.E, 24, Rue General-Dufour, Geneva 4, Switzerland 1211 (22-209333, HAUERT@ CGEUGE51.BITNET); F,E; Development, Motricity, Perception, Cognition

Hegg, Jean-Jacqu (Dr.Med.); Usterstrasse 54, Dubendorf, Switzerland CH-8600 (01-8200288); G

Herzog, Walter (Ph.D.) Professor; Scheuchzerstrasse 114, Zurich, Switzerland CH-8006 (01-3633421); G; Physical Education, Body Awareness, Adolescence, Physical Development

Kistler, Peter (Lic.Phil.); Stampfenbrunnenstrasse 30, Zurich, Switzerland CH-8048 (01-643345)

Klauser, Walter (Ph.D.) Professor; Pestalozzidorf, Trogen, Switzerland CH-9043 (071-941431); G

Lechmann, Alex (Lic.Phil.); Kanzlerstrasse 5, Frauenfeld, Switzerland CH-8500

Loetscher, Fredy (Lic.Phil.); Seehof, Stansstad, Switzerland CH-6362 (041-615347); G

Miller, Martin (Lic.Phil.); Pestalozzistrasse 18, Zurich, Switzerland CH-8032 (01-2511806)

*Moor, Ruedi (Ph.D.); Falkenriedweg, Hinterkappclen, Switzerland CH 3032 (031-360230) D,E,F; Psychoregulation, Mental Training, Communication Training, Career Counseling

*Potterat-Reichenbach, Anne (M.Sc.) Assistant; Institut de Psychologie, BFSH 2, Universite de Lausanne, Lausanne, Switzerland, CH-1015 (021-6924684); F,E(S,R),G(R); Mental Imagery, Attention, Stress, Tennis, Ski

*Riesen, Werner (M.Sc.) Psychologist; 30, Rue du 26-Mars, Tramelan, Switzerland, 2720; F,G,E, I(S,R); Sport, Movement, Control, Relaxation, Performance

Ruchti, Hansreudi; Im Stock, Uebeschi, Switzerland CH-3611 (033-455724)

Ruschetti, Paul (Lic.Phil.); Veilchenstrasse 6, Zurich, Switzerland CH-8032 (01-2531706); G

*Schilling, Guido (Ph.D.) Director; ETH Z, Dept. of Physical Education,P.O. Box 8092, Zurich, Switzerland CH 8092 (01-2564225); G,E,F; Coaching, Psychoregulation, Stress, Track and Field, Curriculum

*Schori, Beat (M.Sc.) Psychologist FSP; Fischerweg 51, Thun, Switzerland 3600 (033-229615); G,F,I,E(S,R); Mental Training, Motivation, Youth Sport, Top Sport, Stress Management

Schuetz, H.B. (Ph.D.) Psychologist; Ets Magglingen, Magglingen, Switzerland CH-2532; E,F,G; Soccer, Leadership, Relaxation, Personality, Skating

Schurch, Peter (Dr.Med.); Huebeliweg 7a, Muri, Switzerland CH-3074 (031-5221-50); G

Sebestyn, Erwin M. (Ph.D.) Sport Psychologist; Birseckstr. 33, Munchenstein, Switzerland CH4142 (061-46-41-36); G,H,ROM,E,I(S,R),F(S,R); Psychoregulation, Psycho-Organization

*Stancheris, Vivian (M.Sc.) Psychologist; 20 Ch. Redern, Bienne, Switzerland 2502 (032-42-39-59); F,E,G,S; Neuropsychology, Professional Orientation, Sport

Vladimir M. Melnikov

Joan Riera

Erwin Apitzsch

Goran Patriksson

Guido Schilling

*Von Bidder, Konstantin (Psychologe FSP); Eulerstrasse 1, CH-4051, Basel, Switzerland (061-355908); G,F(S,R),E(S); Organisatiouseutwicklung, Beratung

Wunderli, Rene (Dipl.Psych.); Muhlerain 40, Meilen, Switzerland CH-8706 (01-9233462)

Tunisia

Bahri, M. Adel (M.Sc.) Professor; 11 Ave., Ali Belhouane, Mahdia, Tunisia 5100 (011-21638062); A,F,E; Stressors, Anxiety, Motivation, Team Sport, Youth Sport

Bel Gaid, Mohamed (M.Sc.) Professor; 20 Rue de Rempart, Tunis, Tunisia 1006 (2161-263967); A,F,E; Soccer, Motivation, Incentives, Top Athletes

Taktak, Khaled (M.Sc.) Professor; Ave Habib Bourgiba, Sfax, Ouled, Yahrg, Tunisia; A,F,E; Learning, Handball, Stress, Indivudual Differences, Group Dynamics

Turkey

Cebiroglu, R. (Prof.); Child Psychology Clinic, Capa Topkapi, Istanbul, Turkey (258946); E, Turkish,F(S,R); Personality

United States

*Aberman, Rick (Ph.D.) Psychologist; University of Wisconsin, Athletic Dept., 1440 Monroe Street, Madison, Wisconsin, USA 53711 (608-262-9422, 608-231-2535); E; Family, Stress, Individualism

*Abraham, Larry D. (Ph.D.), Associate Professor; University of Texas, Dept. of Kinesiology and Health Education, Austin, Texas, USA 78712 (512-471-1273, 512-471-4526, PYDV272@UTXVM.BITNET); E,F(R),G(R); Biomechanics, Motor Control, Learning

*Acevedo, Edmund O. (Ph.D.) Assistant Professor, Director; Center for Exercise Research, Dept. of PELS, Manhattan, Kansas, USA 66506 (913-532-6765)

Addersen, Mark; 4364 East 3rd St., Tucson, Arizona, USA 85711

Adderson, Eugene; University of Texas, Dept. of Physical Education, Arlington, Texas, USA 76019

Adler, Jack D. (Ed.D.); University of Oregon, Dept. of Physical Education, Eugene, Oregon, USA 97403 (686-5430); E; Motor Learning, Motor Performance, Golf, Coaching, Teaching

*Aharoni, Hezkiah A. (Ph.D.) Consultant; SPECTRA Assoc., 1001 Eastwind Drive Suite 202, Westerville, Ohio, USA 43081 (614-252-3885); E,HEB, A(S); Assessment, Motor Development, Motor Learning, Playground, Risk Taking

Allen, D.J. (Ph.D.); State University of New York, Dept. of Physical Education, Brockport, New York, USA 14420 (395-2160); E; Personality, Self-Control, Meaning, Control, Anxiety

*Ammons, Robert (Ph.D.) Editor; Box 9229, Missoula, Montana, USA 59807 (406-543-5359); E,G,F(R),S(R); Learning and Performance of Skills, Cultural Effects on Skilled Behavior, Sports as Expressing Cultural Problems

*Anderson, D.F. (Ph.D.), Professor; Iowa State University, Dept. of Physical Education, 250 NPE Bldg., Ames, Iowa, USA 50010 (515-294-8650); E; Meaning, Youth Sport, Aggression, Gender Roles, Exercise Adherence

Anderson, John E. (Ph.D.) President; Center For Sports Psychology, 3208 N. Academy Blvd. Suite

160, Colorado Springs, Colorado, USA 80917 (719-597-5959); E; Performance, Stress, Leadership, Effectiveness, Mental Tools

*Andersen, P. Andrew (Ph.D.), Owner, Sports Adviser Features; The Sport Psychology Adviser, P.O. Box 891, St. Charles, Illinois, USA 60174 (708-377-6676); E; Performance Intervention, Social Psychology, Freelance Journalist, Media Broker

*Anderson, R.E. (C.Phil.); University of California, 405 Hilgard Avenue, Los Angeles, California, USA 90024; E,F(R),L; Personality, Motivation, Individual Differences, Personality and Nervous System Types, Motivation, Addiction

*Arend-Higgins, Susan (Ed.D.); Hunter College, Dept. of Physical Education, 695 Park Ave., New York, New York, USA 10001 (212-570-5021); E,S,P; Motor Learning, Perceptual Training, Kinesiology, Biomechanics, Movement Analysis

Armenti, Nicholas P. (Ph.D.) Sport Psychologist; Psychology Consulting Group, Upper Montclair Plaza, Montclair, New Jersey, USA 07043 (201-744-5353); E,F; Coach-Athlete Relationship, Performance Enhancement

Armstrong, Hubert (Ph.D.); University of Washington, Dept. of Psychiatry RP-10, Seattle, Washington, USA 98105

*Arnold, R.K. (Ed.D.); Montclair State College, Dept. of Physical Education, Upper Montclair, New Jersey, USA 07143 (201-893-7091); E; Motor Learning, Measurement, Research, Biomechanics, Psychology

*Asken, Michael J. (Ph.D.) Psychologist; Dept. of Physical Medicine and Rehabilitation, Polyclinic Medical Center, 2601 North Third Street, Harrisburg, Pennsylvania, USA 17011 (717-782-2411); E; Performance Enhancement, Stress, Physically Disabled Athletes, Drug Abuse, Rehabilitation

Askew, Michael; 1608 Brassfield Road, Raleigh, North Carolina, USA 27614

*Austin, Jeffrey S. (Ph.D.) Professor; USAF Academy, Dept. of Behavioral Sciences, Colorado Springs, Colorado, USA 80914 (719-472-3860); E; Stress, Leadership, Team Performance, Goal Setting

*Avila, Katheleen (M.A.) Licensed Psychologist; 401 Groveland Avenue, Minneapolis, Minnesota, USA 55403 (612-872-9231)

Bahrke, M.S. (Ph.D.); University of Kansas, Dept. of Physical Education, 161 Robinson Gymnasium, Lawrence, Kansas, USA 66644 (913-864-5552); E; Anxiety, Relaxation, Personality, Adherence, Ergogenic Aids

*Ballinger, Debra A. (Ph.D.) Assistant Professor, Chief Dept.al Advisor; Old Dominion University, HPER, Norfolk, Virginia, USA 23508 (804-683-3379); E,G(S,R),S(S,R),D(S,R); Stress, Goal Setting, Time Management, Coaching, Psychotherapy

Ballinger, J.L. (Ed.D.); University of Missouri, Dept. of Health and Physical Education, 102 Rothwell Gymnasium, Columbia, Missouri, USA 65201 (882-8321); E; Motor, Neuropsychology, Motivation, Character

Barthol, Richard P. (Ph.D.) Professor Emeritus; University of California, Dept. of Psychology, Los Angeles, California, USA 90024 (213-825-5723); E; Mental, Stress, Slumps, Training, Therapy

*Baylor, Ann M. (Ph.D.) Associate Professor; University of Texas, Dept. of Kinesiology and Health Education, Bellmont 222, Austin, Texas, USA 78712 (512-471-1273); E; Effects of Exercise and Aging on Neuromuscular System, Parameters of Motor Skill Acquisition

Beale, Charles; University of Delaware, Center for Counseling, Newark, Deleware, USA 19711

*Beitel, Patricia A. Associate Professor; The University of Tenessee, Dept. of Human Performance and Sport Studies, 1914 Andy Holt Avenue, Knoxville, Tenessee, USA 37996-2700 (615-974-5111); E; Attention, Motivation, Feedback, Experience, Task Demands

*Bell, Tom; Florida State University, 108 Montgomery Gym, c/o David Pargman, Tallahassee, Florida, USA 32306

Benison, B.S. (Ph.D.); Texas Christian University, Dept. of Kinesiological Studies, Ricken Building-209, Fort Worth, Texas, USA 76129 (817-921-7665); E,F(R,W),G(R),S; Personality, Competition, Curriculum, Instruction, Counseling

*Bennet, R.S. (Ph.D.); San Francisco State University, Dept. of Physical Education, 1600 Holloway Ave., San Francisco, California, USA 94132 (415-469-2160); E; Women in Sport, Unskilled, Biomechanics, Neuromotor Control and Learning

*Bergel, Richard (Ph.D.); 119 Mitzi Drive, Napa Valley, Calistoga, California, USA 94515 (415-642-5403); E,F,G; Growth, Development, Youth Sport, Psychology

*Berger, Bonnie G. (Ed.D.) Professor; Brooklyn College, Dept. of Physical Education, Brooklyn, New York, USA 11210 (212-532-4014); E; Stress Reduction, Anxiety, Depression, Health Psychology, Mood

*Berkley, Lester T. (Ph.D.) Psychologist, Psychotherapist, Counselor; 799 Broadway, New York City, New York, USA 10003 (212-995-8693); 60 East 9 Street, New York City, New York, USA 10003 (212-995-5618); E,S; Anxiety, Stress, Success, Failure Fears, Motivation

*Billing, John E. (Ph.D.), Professor and Chairman; University of North Carolina, Dept. of Physical Education, Exercise and Sport Science, 209 Fetzer Gym, Chapel Hill, North Carolina, USA 27599

Bird, Anne Marie (Ph.D.); California State University, Dept. of Physical Education, Fullerton, California, USA 93731 (213-773-2620); E,F(R); Cohesion, Modeling, Anxiety, Attention, Attribution

Bischoff, Judith A. (Ph.D.) Associate Professor; Northern Illinois University, Dept. of Physical Education, Anderson Hall, Dekalb, Illinois, USA 60115 (815-753-1407); E

*Blacksmith, W.A. (Ed.D.); Indiana University of Pennsylvania, Dept. of Health and Physical Education, 228 Zink Hall, Indiana, Pennsylvania, USA 15705 (412-357-5656); E,GRE(R); Anxiety, Aggression, Motivation, Counseling, Competition

Blumenthal, James (Ph.D.) Professor; Duke University Medical Center, Dept. of Psychiatry, Durham, North Carolina, USA 27710

Bolan, Shawn; 2117 Castelar, Omaha, Nebraska, USA 68108

*Bowman, John J. (Ph.D.) Director; Mind Plus Muscle Institute, Davis Professional Park, 5225-49 Rte. 347, Port Jefferson Station, New York, USA 11776

*Bredemeier, Brenda J. (Ph.D.) Associate Professor; University of California at Berkeley, Dept. of Physical Education, 200 Hearst Gym, Berkeley, California, USA 94720 (415-624-1704, 415-642-3355); E,G(R); Moral Development, Gender, Aggression

*Brennan, Stephen J. (M.Ed., M.P.E.) Managing Partner; Peak Performance Consultants, 14728 Shirley Street, Omaha, Nebraska, USA 68108 (402-334-1676); E; Basketball, Coaching Education, Mental Training, Motivation, Parent Involvement

Brenner, Richard; 5 High Ridge Drive, Cumberland, Rhode Island, USA 02864

*Brooks, Dana D. (Ed.D.) Associate Dean; West Virginia University, School of Physical Education,

285 Coliseum, Morgantown, West Virginia, USA 26506-6116 (304-293-4812); E; Leadership, Networking, Recruitment, Cohesion, Athletics, Racism

Brown, Robert (Ph.D.); 477 North El Camino Real, A306, Encinitas, California, USA 92024; Golf, Individual and Team Sports

Brustad, Robert J. (Ph.D.) Assistant Professor; Portland State University, School of HPE, Portland, Oregon, USA 97201 (503-274-2703); E,S; Youth Sport, Motivation, Anxiety

Bruya, L.D. (Ph.D.); Physical Education, Sport, and Leisure, Washington State University, Pullman, Washington, USA 99164-1410; E; Perceptual Learning, Behavior, Development, Primary School, Play Environments

Bryan, Anne; University of Minnesota, Dept. of Psychology, Duluth, Minnesota, USA 55812

Buckellew, W.F. (Ed.D.); Eastern Illinois University, College of Education, McAfee Building, Charleston, Illinois, USA 61920 (217-581-2524); E; Vision, Perception, Reaction Time

Bunker, Linda K. (Ph.D.) Professor; University of Virginia, Curry School of Education, Ruffner Hall, Charlottesville, Virginia, USA 22904 (804-924-0740, 804-924-0747, LKB4@VIRGINIA); E; Self-Talk, Visualization, Golf, Tennis, Confidence

Burke, Kevin (Ph.D.) Assistant Professor; Illinois State University, Dept. of Health, Physical Education, Recreation, and Dance, Normal, Illinois, USA 61761 (309-438-8661, KLBURKE@ILSTU); E; Attention, Stress, Youth, Motivation, Referees

Burton, Damon D. (Ph.D.) Associate Professor; University of Idaho, Dept. of HPERD, 107 PEB Moscow, Moscow, Idaho, USA 83843 (208-885-7921, BURTON9@IDUI1); E; Goal Setting, Motivation, Anxiety, Coaches Education, Youth Sport

Byrd, Martin E. (B.A.) Executive Recruiter; 8324 NW 105th Street, Oklahoma City, Oklahoma, USA 73162 (405-720-7669); E; Future, Success, Sport, Personality, Growth

Caird, Jeff (M.Sc.) Research Assistant; University of Colorado, Dept. of Kinesiology, Box 354, Boulder, Colorado, USA 80309 (303-492-7692); E; Modeling, Imagery, Hypnosis, Biofeedback, Biomechanics

Campbell, J.G. (M.S.); University of Maine, Dept. of Physical Education and Athletics, 140 Memorial Gymnasium, Orono, Maine, USA 04473 (207-581-7240); E; Counseling, Top Sport, Sport Medicine

Cancelmo, Lucia; 3618 Marlbrough Way, College Park, Maryland, USA 20740

Candeletti, Glenn; 133 Route 9 South, Forked River, New Jersey, USA 08731

Capka, Donna D. (Ph.D.) Clinical Psychologist; The Psychotherapy and Counseling Center, 15928 Ventura Blvd #221, Encino, California, USA 91436 (818-783-1707); E; Figure Skating, Subliminal Perception, Focusing

Carroll, Richard; 2333 Whitehorse-Mercerville Rd., Trenton, New Jersey, USA 08619

Carter, M.C. (Ph.D.); U.C.L.A., Dept. of Kinesiology, 405 Hilgard, Los Angeles, California, USA 90024 (825-8010); E,F(W); Motor Learning, Motor Performance, Motor Control, Motor Development, Skill Acquisition

Caruso, John L. (Ph.D.) Professor; Southern Massachusetts University, Dept. of Psychology, North Darthmouth, Massachusetts, USA 02747 (508-999-8384); E,S(R,W); Cognitive Processes, Learning, Performance Enhancement

Catalano, J.F. (Ph.D.); SUNY Cortland University, Dept. of Psychology, Cortland, New York, USA 13045 (607-753-4219); E,F(R),I(R); Motor Learning, Performance, Arousal, Human Factors, Ergonomy

Chalip, Laurence H. (Ph.D.) Assistant Professor; University of Maryland, Dept. of Kinesiology, College Park, Maryland, USA 20740 (301-405-2502); E,F,S; Organizations, Motivation, Skill, Hypnosis, Swimming

Chang, Hoeng (M.A.) School Psychologist; S. Gate Junior High School, Psychological Services, 4100 Firestone Blvd., S. Gate, California, USA 90280 (213-625-6171, 213-567-1431); CHI,E; Communication, Stress, Relaxation, Imagery

Chaumeton, Nigel; 4001 Potter #32, Eugene, Oregon, USA 97405 (503-687-1373); Youth Sports, Perceived Ability, Developmental Psychology

Christensen, C. (M.Ed.); University of Vermont, Dept. of Physical Education and Athletics, 202 Patrick Gymnasium, Burlington, Vermont, USA 05401 (802-656-3020); E,F(R),G(R),S; Management, Pedagogy, Competition, Learning, Counseling

Christina, R.W. (Ph.D.); Pennsylvania State University, Dept. of Physical Education, 102 Sports Research Bldg., University Park, Pennsylvania, USA 16802 (814-865-9543); E,G(R); Motor, Learning, Control, Feedback, Performance

Clark, C. (M.Sc.); Dartmouth College, Dept. of Athletics, DCAD-Alumni Gym, Hanover, New Hampshire, USA 03755 (603-646-3494); E,F; Competition, Top Athletes, Personality, Counseling, Coaching

Clark, Jane E. (Ph.D.); University of Pittsburgh, Dept. of Physical Education, 104 Trees Hall, Pittsburg, Pennsylvannia, USA 15261 (412-624-4396); E,F(W); Psychomotor Development, Response Processes, Evaluation, Sex Differences, Children

Cobb, R.B. (Ph.D.); Syracuse University, Dept. of Physical Education, 820 Comstock Ave., Syracuse, New York, USA 13210 (315-423-3732); E; Motor Memory, Motor Control, Motor Development, Success, Statistics

Colby, Marilyn F. (Ph.D.); State University of New York, Dept. of Physical Education, Brockport, New York, USA 14420 (716-395-2601, 716-395-2246, M.COLBY@BROCK1P); E; Attention, Memory, Perception, Locomotion

Colgan, Sharon, M., (Ph.D.); San Diego Sports Medical Center, 6699 Alvarado Rd., San Diego, California, USA 92120 (619-229-3909, 619-582-1497); Performance Enhancement, Fear of Success and Fear of Failure, Female Athletes, Stress Management, Health Psychology

Connelly, Deidre; 526 Reno Street, Iowa City, Iowa, USA 52245

Cook, David L. (Ph.D.) Professor; University of Kansas, HPER, Lawrence, Kansas, USA 66044 (913-864-5552); E; Confidence, Mental Rehearsal, Drugs in Sport, Emotion Management

Cooley, Eric; Western Oregon State, Dept. of Psychology, Monmouth, Oregon, USA 97361

Cooper, C. (Ed.D.); University of Northern Iowa, School HPER, Cedar Falls, Iowa, USA 50613 (319-273-2601); E,F(R); Recreation, Leisure, Reaction Time, Swimming, Perception

Coots, J.H. (Ph.D.); Sport Science Services, 2718 Monogram Ave., Long Beach, California, USA 90815 (213-598-7661); E,F(R),G(R); Competition, Performance, Cognition, Learning Strategies, Cognimechanics

Coppel, David B. (Ph.D.) Clinical/Sport Psychologist; 2200 24th Ave. East, Seattle, Washington, USA 98112 (206-328-0910); E; Performance Enhancement, Athlete-Parent-Coach Interactions, Commitment/Burnout Issues, Mood Management in Athletes, Clinical Disorders/Personality Variables in Athletes

Corbin, Charles B. (Ph.D.) Professor; Arizona State University, Dept. of Exercise Science and Physical Education, Tempe, Arizona, USA 85287

(602-965-3875, 602-965-8108, ATCBC@ASUACAD); E; Fitness, Confidence, Commitment, Development, Motivation

Courtney, James; 204 Sharon Lane, North Aurora, Illinois, USA 60542

Cox, Richard H. (Ph.D.) Professor; Ball State University, Dept. of Physical Education, Muncie, Indiana, USA 47306 (317-285-1748); E; Attention, Anxiety, Intervention, Volleyball

Crabbe, J.M. (Ph.D.); University of Nebraska-Lincoln, School HPER, Coliseum Rm. 18, Lincoln, Nebraska, USA 68588 (402-472-1865); E; Social, Attention, Perception, Competition, Personality

Crace, R. Joseph President; Hickory Specialities, Box 1669, Brentwood, Tennessee, USA 37027

Crace, R. Kelly (M.A.), Co-Editor and Publisher; Sport Psychology Training Bulletin, P.O. Box 52234, Durham, North Carolina, USA 27717-52234 (919-361-4621, 919-361-2391); Career Development Within Athletes, Student-Athlete Role Adjustment, Life/Performance Enhancement Intervention Strategies, Social Influence Processes

Cratty, Bryant J. (Ed.D.); University of California, Dept. of Kinesiology, 405 N. Hilgard Ed., Los Angeles, California, USA 90024 (213-825-3436); E,F(R),R(S),S; Motor Learning, Social Meaning, Sport, Sport Psychology

Crespi, Tony D. (Ed.D.) Counselor, School Psychologist; 420 Swain Ave., Meriden, Connecticut, USA 06450 (203-238-0534); E; Stress, Control, Alpine Skiing

Critchfield, T.S. (B.A.); West Virginia University, 504 Allen Hall, Morgantown, West Virginia, USA 26505 (304-293-3879); E,G(R); Behavior Analysis, Sport

Cylkowski, Greg J. (M.A.) Sports Analyst/Human Performance; Michigan State University, 3036 Ontario Road, Little Canada, Minnesota, USA 55117 (612-484-8299); E; Performance, Competition, Speaker, All Sports, Corporate

Daitzman, Reid J. (Ph.D.) Practice; 1425 Bedford St. Suite 1a, Stamford, Connecticut, USA 06905 (203-359-1779); E; Tennis, Arousal, Concentration, Stress

Danish, Steven J. (Ph.D.) Professor and Chairman; Virginia Commonwealth University, Dept. of Psychology, VCU Box 2018, Richmond, Virginia, USA 23284 (804-367-8089); E; Transitions, Prevention of Substance Use, Goal Setting, Performance Enhancement, Self Talk

Davies, Simon; 3450 Nicholson Drive, Baton Rouge, Louisiana, USA 70802

Davis, Diane; 2711 Allen Road #J-1, Tallahassee, Florida, USA 32312-2655

Dean, Janice; 21144 Fleetwood, Harper Woods, Michigan, USA 48225

De Bease, Celeste F. (Ph.D.) Therapist; Comprehensive Psychological Services, 1100 West Chester Pike, Havertown, Pennsylvania, USA 19083 (215-446-1127); E; Imagery, Cognition, Biofeedback, Electroencephalography, Stress

Bonnie G. Berger

*Del Rey, Pat (Ed.D.) Professor, Director, Women's Studies Program; University of Georgia, Dept. of Physical Education, Athens, Georgia, USA 30602 (404-542-4380, 404-542-2846); E,I; Motor Learning, Women in Sport, Women's Studies

*Diepold, John H. Jr. (Ph.D.) Psychologist; Victoria Medical Arts, East Building, 701 E. Main Street, 2nd Floor, Morestown, New Jersey, USA 08057 (609-778-9300); E; Hypnosis, Imagery, Stress, Pain Management, Wrestling

*DiRico, John; 1035 N. Broome Ave., Lindenhurst, New York, USA 11757; E, I(S),S(S); Performance Enhancement, Sport Group Communication

*Dishman, Rod K. (Ph.D.) Professor; University of Georgia, Dept. of Physical Education, Athens, Georgia, USA 30602 (404-542-9840, 404-542-4377); E; Exercise Adherence, Mental Health, Motivation, Psychometrics, Psychobiological Analysis

*Dobson, Donald (M.Ed.); University of Missouri-Columbia, P.O. Box 677, Columbia, Missouri, USA 65211

*Dodds, P. (Ph.D.); University of Massachusetts, Professional Preparation Physical Education, North Physical Education Building, Amherst, Massachusetts, USA 01002 (413-545-2323); E, G(R),S; Pedagogy, Movement Patterns, Children, Coach Behavior

Donahue, Gerard; 63 Lake Sreet, Upper Saddle River, New Jersey, USA 07458

*Doody, S.G. (Ph.D.); University of Northern Iowa, Schindler Education Center, Cedar Falls, Iowa, USA 50614-0615 (319-273-2719, 319-273-6997); E,F(R); Short-Term Memory, Motor Control, Modeling, Learning, Performance

Dowell, L.I. (Ed.D.); Texas A & M University, Dept. of Health and Education, College Station, Texas, USA 77840 (845-6841); E; Competition, Learning Strategies, Athletes, Self-Control

*Downey, T.J. (Student); Ferrum College, P.O.Box 1949, Ferrum, Virginia, USA 24088 (703-638-7856); R,E

*Drowatzky, J.N. (J.D., Ed.D.); The University of Toledo, Dept. of Exercise, Science and Physical Education, Toledo, Ohio USA 43606 (419-537-2747, 419-537-7719); E; Performance, Learning, Personality, Handicapped, Law

Duane, Maryellyn; 500 West End Ave. Ground Fl. B, New York, New York, USA 10024

*Duda, Joan L. (Ph.D.) Professor; Purdue University, PEHRS, Lambert 113, West Lafayette, Indiana, USA 47907 (317-494-3172, LYNNE@PURCCVM); E; Motivation, Exercise Adherence, Gender, Age, Cultural Differences

*Dulberg, Harvey N. (Ph.D.) Sport Psychologist; 1330 Beacon Street, Suite 248, Brookline, Massachusetts, USA 02146 (617-232-5200); E; Performance Enhancement, Consultation, Eating Disorders, Injuries, Teaching, Writing

*Dunham, P., Jr. (Ed.D.); University of Wyoming, Corbett Gym, Dept. of Physical Education, Laramie, Wyoming, USA 82070 (307-766-3169); E; Originality, Persistence, Aggression, Competition

Duquin, Mary E. (Ph.D.); University of Pittsburgh, HPER, 158 Trees Hall, Pittsburgh, Pennsylvania, USA 15261 (412-624-4383); E; Androgeny, Attribution, Social Comparison, Socialization, Sex Roles

Durrant, Sue M. (Ph.D.) Associate Professor; Washington State University, PESLS, Pullman, Washington, USA 99164 (509-335-8337); E; Consciousness, Gender, Philosophy, East-West, Self

*Durtschi, Shirley K. (Ph.D. Candidate); Sport Psychology, 2230 S.W. Caldew Street, Portland, Oregon, USA 97219 (503-244-9467); G,E; Mental Training, Psychological Intervention

*Dzewaltowski, D.A. (Ph.D.) Assistant Professor; Kansas State University, PELS, Manhattan, Kansas, USA 66502 (913-532-6765, 913-841-5217, DADX@KSUVM.BITNET); E; Motivation, Exercise Adherence

*Edwards, Steven W. (Ph.D.) Professor; Oklahoma State University, Stillwater, Oklahoma, USA 74078 (405-744-5500); E; Performance Enhancement, Learning, Personality, Intelligence, Ergogenic Aids

*Eisen, G. (Ph.D.); California State Polytechnic University, Physical Education Department, 3801 West Temple Ave., Pomona, California, USA 94368 (714-869-2781, 714-869-2814); E,G,H,HEB; Anxiety, Competition, Ethnicity

Ellis, Michael J. (Ph.D.); University of Oregon, Dept. of Physical Education, Esslinger Hall, Eugene, Oregon, USA 97403 (503-686-4106); E,F(R),G(R); Activity, Play, Learning, Social, Administration

Eskridge, V.L.; Ithaca College, Dept. of Physical Education, Muller 102-G, Ithaca, New York, USA 14850 (274-3411); E; Androgeny, Hypnosis, Kinesthesis, Research, Counseling

Estes, B. (Ed.D.); Grand Canyon College, Dept. of Athletics, 3300 W. Camelback, Phoenix, Arizona, USA 85017 (602-249-3300); E; Activation, Counseling, Top Athletes, Stress, Coach

*Ewing, Martha E. (Ph.D.) Assistant Professor; 201 IM Sports Circle, Michigan State University, Dept. of Physical Education, East Lansing, Michigan, USA 48824 (517-353-4652, 517-353-6393); E, S(R); Achievement Motivation, Anxiety, Gender Differences, Cross-Cultural Differences, Performance Enhancement

Ewing, Samuel; Michigan State University, Youth Sports Institute, East Lansing, Michigan, USA 40824

Faria, I.E. (Ph.D.); California State University, Dept. of Physical Education, 6000 J. Street, Sacramento, California, USA 95819 (916-454-6389); E,G(R); Perception, Motivation, Learning, Personality, Competition

*Faulkner, Margaret E. (Ed.D.) Associate Professor; Towson State University, Dept. of Physical Education, Dept. of Psychology, York Rd., Baltimore, Maryland, USA 21204 (301-321-3168); E; Sex Roles, Women, Anxiety, Neuroendocrine Functioning in the Stress Response

Feely, Thomas; 6719 Drifting Sands, Temple Terrace, Florida, USA 33617

*Feigley, David A. (Ph.D.) Professor; Rutgers University, Youth Sports Research Council, New Brunswick, New Jersey, USA 07003 (908-932-6537, 908-932-9151); E,G; Youth Sport, Fear, Development, Psychobiology, Gymnastics

*Feltz, Deborah L. (Ph.D.); Michigan State University, Youth Sport Institute, I.M. Sports Circle, East Lansing, Michigan, USA 48909 (517-355-4732); E,F(R); Anxiety, Modeling, Self-Efficacy, Youth Sports

*Fender, Lisa K. (M.A.); 753 Cliffside Circle, Akron, Ohio, USA 44313 (216-867-3931); E

Fenker, Richard M. (Ph.D.) Professor; Texas Christian University, Dept. of Psychology, Fort Worth, Texas, USA 76129 (817-921-7410); E,G; Imagery, Prediction, Applications, Golf, Gymnastics

*Ferguson, Richard M. (Ph.D.); 105 Minor Road, Charlottesville, Virginia, USA 22903 (804-296-9687); E; Running, Obsessive Compulsion, Addiction, Stress, Hypnosis

Ferrante, A.P. (Ed.D.) Psychologist; East Carolina University, Counseling Center, Greenville, North Carolina, USA 27834 (919-757-6661); E; Human Factors, Shooting, Concentration, Team Cohesion, Yachting

Ferrera, Christine (Ph.D.); 3543 Felton St., San Diego, California, USA 92104 (714-823-8258); E,F(R); Clinical, Interpersonal Communication, Group Dynamics, Female Athletes

*Finch, Laura M.; University of North Carolina at Greensboro, 103 D Yester Oaks Way, Greensboro, North Carolina, USA 27408; E

Fineberg, Michael; 1710 Goodridge Drive, McLean, Virginia, USA 22102

*Fineman, K.R. (Ph.D.); Family and Child Mental Health Center, 17822 Beach Blvd., Huntington Beach, California, USA 92647 (714-842-9377); E,F(R),S; Hypnosis, Biofeedback, Anxiety, Performance Augmentation

Finn, Joan A. (Ed.D.); Southern Connecticut State College, WPED, 501 Cresent Street, New Haven, Connecticut, USA 06015 (203-397-4485); E; Perception, Anxiety, Aggression, Personality, Behavior Modification

*Fisher, A. Craig (Ph.D.); Ithaca College, Exercise and Sport Sciences, Ithaca, New York, USA 14850 (607-274-3112); E,F(R); Anxiety, Personality, Cognition, Arousal, Self-Confidence

*Fisher, John L. (M.Sc.) President; Ultimate Performance Sport Psy. Consult., 7118C Crosscreek Circle, Dublin, California USA 94568 (415-829-7454); E,F(R,W),S(R,W); Applied Sport Psychology, Stress Management, Performance Enhancement, Baseball, Golf

Foster, Judy L. (B.A.) Executive Director; Porter Foster Sports, P.O. Box 5584, Eugene, Oregon, USA 97405 (503-342-6875); E,F(S,R); Stress, Imagery, Golf, Track and Field, Mental Training

Frager, Stanley R. (Ph.D.) Professor; University of Louisville, College of Urban and Public Affairs, Louisville, Kentucky, USA 40292 (502-893-6654); E; Competition, Anxiety, Teamwork, Basketball, Baseball

*Frederick, A. Bruce (Ph.D.) Curator/Historian; International Gymnastics Hall of Fame, 1043 11th Avenue, Wilmington, Delaware, USA 19808 (302-995-2148); E,F(S,R); Progressive Relaxation, Gymnastics, Anxiety, Pedagogy

Freischlag, Jerry (Ph.D.) Professor-Chair; California State University, Dept. of Physical Education, 5500 University Parkway, San Bernadino, California, USA 92409 (714-887-7561); E,S; Arousal, Attribution, Anxiety, Psychodynamics, Stress Management

*Frey, Richard D. (Ph.D.) Director, Human Kinetics Books; Human Kinetics Publishers, Box 5076, Champaign, Illinois, USA 61825-5076 (217-351-5076, 217-351-2674); E, S(S,R); Attention, Learning, Perception, Performance, Team Building

Friedman, Alan (Ph.D.); Kaiser Medical Center, Dept. of Psychiatry, Haward, California, USA 94545

Friedman, Alan W. (Ph.D.) Director of Clinical Training; Pacific Graduate School of Psychology, 935 East Meadow Drive, Stockton, California, USA 94303 (415-494-7477); E; Consultation, Psychotherapy, Intervention, Drugs, Basketball

*Friedrich, J. (Ph.D.); Duke University, HPER, 105 Card Gym, Durham, North Carolina, USA 27707 (684-2202); E,F(S,R),G(R); Administration, Social Psychology, Health, Fitness, Counseling

Friend, Jed (Ph.D.) Assistant Professor; Texas A & M, Dept. of Psychology, College Station, Texas, USA 77843 (409-845-2581); E; Management, Selection, Evaluation, Training, Motivation

*Furst, David M. (Ph.D.) Professor; San Jose State University, Dept. of Human Performance, San Jose, California, USA 95192-0054 (408-924-3039); E, HEB(S); Anxiety, Attribution, Running, Self-Control, Officials

*Gabert, Trent E. (Ph.D.); University of Oklahoma, Dept. of Health, Physical Education, and Recreation, 1401 Asp, Norman, Oklahoma, USA 73069 (405-325-5211); E,F(R),S(R); Motor Performance, Motor Learning, Elite Athletes, Administration, Sport Psychology

*Garaman, Sharene; 430 Nutmeg, San Diego, California, USA 92103

Gardner, Frank L. (Ph.D.) Psychologist; East Hills Professional Building Ste.105, 70 Glen Cove Road, East Hills, New York, USA 11577 (516-621-1446); E; Professional, Basketball, Hockey, Football, Baseball

*Gauron, Eugene F. (Ph.D.) Professor; University of Iowa, Dept. of Psychiatry, 500 Newton Road, Iowa City, Iowa, USA 52242 (319-356-1541); E,F(S,R), L(R); Coping Skills Training, Stress Management, Team Building, Counseling, Pain Management

Gayton, William F. (Ph.D.) Professor; University of Southern Maine, Dept. of Psychology, Portland, Maine, USA 04103 (207-780-4251); E; Self-Efficacy, Home Advantage, Arousal Control, Goal Setting, Ice Hockey

*Gentile, Antoinette M. (Ph.D.); Teachers College, Columbia University, Movement Sciences, Psychology and Neurosciences and Education, New York, New York, USA 10021 (212-878-3329); E,F(R); Learning, Task Taxonomy, Coordinative Processes,Brain Mechanisms, Motor Recovery

*Georgiadis, Nikos N.G. (Ph.D.) Lecturer; Physical Education, University of Illinois at Chicago, 1508 W. Harrison #1A, Chicago, Illinois, USA, 60607, (312-996-6363); E,GRE; Emotionally and Socially Handicapped, Empowerment, Basketball, Aggression

*Geraty, Patrick; University of Utah, College of HPER, Salt Lake City, Utah, USA 84112

Gilbert, Rob; Montclair State University, Dept. of Physical Education, Upper Montclair, New Jersey, USA 07043

*Gill, Diane L. (Ph.D.) Professor; University of North Carolina at Greensboro, Dept. of Exercise and Sport Science, Greensboro, North Carolina, USA 27412 (919-334-3303, GILLDL@UNCG); E; Social Psychology, Women in Sport, Achievement, Exercise Motivation, Cognitive Motivation

Gilliland, K. (Ph.D.); University of Oklahoma, Dept. of Psychology, 455 West Lindsey, Norman, Oklahoma, USA 73069 (405-325-4511); E; Personality, Motivation, Parent-Child Relationships, Psychobiology

*Gold, Ginger L. (Ed.D.) Physical Education Chairperson; 810 South Main Street, Salisbury, North Carolina, USA 28144 (708-638-5587); S,E; Sport Psychology

Goldberg, Alan S. (Ed.D.) Psychologist; Competitive Advantage, 8 High Meadow Rd., Northampton, Massachusetts, USA 01060 (413-586-6823); E; Performance Blocks, Hypnosis, Concentration, Pregame Preperation, Motivation

*Goldberg, Howard B. (Ph.D.) Psychologist; 41 Timberlane, South Burlington, Vermont, USA 05403 (802-864-9040); E; Youth Sport, Stress, Health Psychology, Recreational Athletes, Consultation

*Gombar, Imrich (Ph.D.) Psychologist; Spectrum Professional Group, 6965 Melinski Square, Bethlehem, Pennsylvania, USA 18017 (215-821-6281); E,C,R; Soccer, Basketball, Peak Performance, Gymnastics, Swimming

*Gordin, Richard D. (Ed.D) Associate Professor; Utah State University, Dept. of HPER, Logan, Utah, USA 84332-7000 (801-750-1506); E,F;Hypnosis, Gymnastics, Peak Performance, Autogenics, Stress

Gorman, Brian; United States International University, 10455 Pomerado Road, Box 294, San Diego, California, USA 92131

*Gould, Daniel R. (Ph.D.) Professor; University of North Carolina-Greensboro, Exercise and Sport Science, Greensboro, North Carolina, USA 27412 (919-334-3037); E; Motivation, Stress, Children, Intervention, Coaches

Graetzer, Daniel; University of Utah, Dept. of Physical Education, Salt Lake City, Utah, USA 84112

*Graham, Deborah J. (Ph.D.) Psychotherapist; International Sports Consultants, 2102 Business Center Drive, Irvine, California, USA 92715 (714-253-5713, 714-752-9316); E; Imagery, Concentration, Focus, Personality, Personality Research

*Grant, Polly (D.S.W.) Director; The Boston Psychological Center for Women, Inc., 60 Charlesgate West, Apt 1a, Boston, Massachusetts, USA 02215 (617-267-4068)

*Graybill, Edward E.K.G. (B.S.) Graduate Student; University of Iowa, Exercise Science, 207 Myrtle Ave #12, Iowa City, Iowa, USA 52246 (319-351-5303); E,S(R); Motor Behavior, Stress, Self-Efficacy, Gymnastics, Psychophysiology

Greer, Scott; Indiana University, School of HPER, Bloomington, Indiana, USA 47405

*Griffin, Joy (Ed.D.) Assistant Professor; Sport Psychology/Sport Sociology, Dept. of HPPELP, University of New Mexico, Albuquerque, New Mexico, USA 87131 (505-883-7122); E; Biofeedback, Stress, Peak Performance, Eating Disorders

Gruber, Joseph J. (Ph.D.) Professor; University of Kentucky, HPER, Lexington, Kentucky, USA 40536 (606-257-3293); E; Stress, Counseling, Health Psychology, Personality

*Gundersheim, Julius (Ph.D.) Associate Professor; University of Massachusetts, Dept. of Sport Studies, Curry Hicks Building, Amherst, Massachusetts, USA 01002 (545-5058); E; Motivation, Personality, Adherence, Stress, Performance

Haack, Linda; 3866 Sequoia Street #8, San Diego, California, USA 92109

*Hale, Bruce D. (Ph.D.) Professor; Penn State University, 328 Boucke Building, University Park, Pennsylvannia, USA 16802 (814-865-0407); E; Stress, Imagery, Enhancement, Psychophysiology, Developmental

*Hall, Evelyn G. (Ph.D.) Associate Professor; University of Utah, Dept. of Exercise and Sport Science, Salt Lake City, Utah, USA, 84112 (801-581-7646, 801-581-5580); E,G; Hemispheric Dominance, Stress and Performance, Locus of Control, Imagery, Gender Issues

*Hall, Howard K. (Ph.D.) Assistant Professor; Syracuse University, Dept. of Health and Physical Education, 820 Comstock Avenue, Syracuse, New York, USA 13244-5040 (315-443-4413, HKHALL@SUVM.ACS.SYR.EDU); E; Motivation, Goal Setting, Achievement, Perceived Ability, Youth Sport

*Hardy, Charles J. (Ph.D.) Associate Professor; University of North Carolina, Dept. of Physical Education, Exercise and Sport Science, CB #8700 Fetzer, Chapel Hill, North Carolina, USA 27599 (919-962-2260, HDOG@UNC); E; Social Loafing, Social Support, Life Stress, RPE, Affect

*Harris, Wayne C. (Ph.D.) Professor; Mankato State University, Dept. of Psychology, Mankato, Minnesota, USA 56001 (612-431-2552); E; Ice Hockey, Psychological Preparation, Managing Competition Stress

*Hatfield, Brad D. (Ph.D.) Professor; University of Maryland, Dept. of Kinesiology, 2138 Perth Bldg., College Park, Maryland, USA 20742 (301-405-2489, 301-314-9167, BH5@UMAIL.UMD.EDU); E,F(S,R); Stress, Psychophysiology, Electroencephalography, Evoked Potential, B-Endorphin

*Hawkins, Barton K. (B.Sc.), Research Associate; University of South Carolina, Dept. of Chemistry, Columbia, South Carolina, USA 29208 (803-777-5726); E,G,L(R); R(R); Biochemistry and Biophysics of Oxygen Utilization

Hawkins, R. Ray (Ph.D.) Psychologist; College Associates, 7765 Brookview, Indianapolis, Indiana, USA (317-849-5752); E,S; Stress, Concentration, Motivation, Imagery

*Haywood, Kathleen (Ph.D.) Professor; University of Missouri, Dept. of Physical Education, 8001 Natural Bridge, St. Louis, Missouri, USA 63121 (314-553-5223, 314-553-5503, BITNET.C1812@UMSLVMA); E; Motor Learning, Perception, Motor Development, Coincidence Anticipation, Eye Movement

Healey, J. (Ph.D.); University of North Carolina, Dept. of Health and Physical Education, UNCC Station, Charlotte, North Carolina, USA 28223; E,F(R),S(R); Development, Learning, Perception, Handicapped

*Heckel, R. (Ph.D.); University of South Carolina, Dept. of Psychology, Columbia, South Carolina, USA 29208 (777-5125); E,F(R),I(R),S(R); Sport, Nonverbal and Group Behaviors

Hefferan, Mark; 852-B 21st Street, Santa Monica, California, USA 90403

Heffner, Gary; P.O. Box 336, China Springs, Texas, USA 76633

*Heil, John (D.A.) Psychologist; Lewis-Gale Clinic, Dept. of Counseling and Psychology, 4910 Valley View Blvd., Roanoke, Virgina, USA 24012 (703-772-3485, 703-366-7353); E,S; Injury, Mental Training, Imagery, Drugs, Rehabilitation

Heilman, Nancy; Mankato State University, Dept. of Psychology, Mankato, Minnesota, USA 56001

Helmreich, R. (Ph.D.); University of Texas, Dept. of Psychology, 330 Mezis Hall, Austin, Texas, USA 78712 (512-471-4308); E,F; Competition, Personality

Henry, Franklin (Ph.D.); University of California, Dept. of Physical Education, Berkeley, California, USA 94720 (415-642-0372); E,F(R),G(R); Motor Learning, Motor Programming, Individual Differences, Motivation, Neurophysiology

Rod K. Dishman

Deborah L. Feltz

Daniel R. Gould

*Henschen, Keith P. (P.E.D.); University of Utah, Dept. of Exercise and Sport Science, Salt Lake City, Utah, USA 84112 (801-581-7772); E,G(R); Performance Enhancement, Psychology for the Disabled, Elite Athletes, Hypnosis, Anxiety

Herkowitz, Jacqueline (Ph.D.); Ohio State University, School of HPER, 309 Pomenrene Hall, Columbus, Ohio, USA 43210 (614-422-5479); E; Children, Development, Playgrounds, Infancy, Learning

*Heyman, Steven R. (Ph.D.) Professor; University of Wyoming, Dept. of Psychology, Box 3415 University Station, Laramie, Wyoming, USA 82071 (307-766-6303); E,S(R,W),F(R,W); High Risk Sports, Clinical Issues, Hypnosis, Sport Psychology

Higgins, Joseph (Ed.D.); Teacher's College, Columbia University, Dept. of Movement Sciences, 525 W. 120th St., Columbia, New York, USA 10025 (212-678-3326); E,S; Learning, Movement Analysis, Neuropsychology, Teaching, Perception

*Higgins, Susan (Ed.D.) Dept. Chair and Director; Program in Human Movement Studies, Hunter College, Dept. of Physical Education, 695 Park Ave., New York, New York, USA 10021 (212-772-4640); E,S; Motor Learning, Movement Analysis

*Hill, Karen L. (Ph.D.) Assistant Professor; Exercise and Sport Science, Penn State University, 25 Yearsley Mill Road, Media, Pennsylvania, USA 19063, (215-565-3300); E; Imagery, Cognition, Cohesion, Gender, Neurophysiology

*Hisanaga, Bruce M. (Ed.D.); 555 University Avenue #106, Honolulu, Hawaii, USA 96826; E; Anxiety, Competition, Top Athletes, Counseling

Hodge, Kenneth; University of Illinois, Dept. of Physical Education, Urbana, Illinois, USA 61801

*Holding, Dennis H. (Ph.D.) Professor; University of Louisville, Dept. of Psychology, Louisville, Kentucky, USA 40292 (502-588-5952, DHHDLD01@ULUYVM.BITNET); E,I(R),S(R),D(R),F(S); Fatigue, Sensory, Retention, Training, Transfer

Hollandsworth, J.G., Jr. (Ph.D.) Professor; University of Southern Mississippi, Dept. of Counseling Psychology, Box 8272, Southern Station, Mississippi, USA (601-266-7163); E,F(R); Anxiety, Health, Stress, Fitness, Counseling

Horevitz, R.P. (Ph.D.) Professor; University of Illinois-Chicago, Dept. of Psychology, Chicago, Illinois, USA 60612 (312-372-1447); E; Mental Training, Hypnosis, Clinical, Stress

*Horn, Thelma S. (Ph.D.) Associate Professor; Miami University, Dept. Physical Education, Health and Sport Studies, Oxford, Ohio, USA 45056 (513-529-2723); E; Developmental Issues, Self-Perceptions, Anxiety, Arousal

*Houseworth, Steven D. (Ph.D.) Assistant Professor; Illinois State University, HPERD, Horton Fieldhouse, Normal, Illinois, USA 61761 (309-438-8661); E; Performance, Mental Training, Relaxation, Endurance Training, Distance Running

Houston, David R. (Ph.D.) Psychologist; Kennebec Valley Mental Health Center, 66 Stone Street, Auguste, Maine, USA 04330 (207-622-3455); E; Hypnosis, Stress, Performance Enhancement, Football

Howe, M.A. (Ph.D.) Professor; United States International University, Dept. of Sport Psychology, 10455 Pomeranow Road, San Diego, California, USA 92131 (714-271-4300); E; Clinical, Interpersonal, Communication, Group Dynamics, Leadership

*Hu, Edward; Office of Admissions, Brown University, P.O. Box 1876, Providence, Rhode Island, USA 02912

Hubalik, N.E. (Ph.D.) Professor; Western Michigan University, HPER, Kalamazoo, Michigan, USA 49009 (616-383-4987); E; Stress, Baseball, Golf, Mental Toughness, Cognitive

Hubbard, A.W. (Ph.D.) Professor; University of Illinois, Dept. of Physical Education, 211 Huff Gym, Champaign, Illinois, USA 61820 (217-333-3224); E,F,G; Homokinetics, Vision, Research Methods, Experimental Design

*Huddleston, Sharon (Ph.D.) Graduate Coordinator; 122 N. College Street, Cedar Falls, Iowa, USA 50613-2211

Husman, Burris F. (Ph.D) Professor; University of Maryland, Dept. of Physical Education, College Park, Maryland, USA 20740 (301-454-2928); E; Aggression, Emotion, Personality, Motivation, Top Athletes

*Hutton, Robert S. (Ph.D.) Professor; University of Washington, Dept. of Psychology, Guthrie Hall, NI-25, Seattle, Washington, USA 98105 (206-543-4177, 206-685-3157, RSHUTTON@MAX.U.WASHINGTON.EDU); E,G,S(R); Motor Control, Neurophysiology, Reflexes, Neural Control, Exercise

*Ingalls, Joan (Ed.D) Private Practice; 315 Riverside Drive, Apt. 4D, New York, New York, USA 10025 (212-662-1480); E,G(S,W),S(S,W), R(R,W); Performance Enhancement, Neuro-Linguistic Programming, Ericksonian Hypnosis

*Jackson, Charles W. (D.P.E.) Professor; Old Dominion University, Dept. of Health, Physical Education, and Recreation, Norfolk, Virginia, USA 23529-0196 (804-683-4995, 804-683-5155, CWJ100U@ODUVM); E,S(R); Mood, Traits, Assessment, Enhancement, Relaxation

Jackson, Christina (Ed.D.) Professor; College of William and Mary, Dept. of Physical Education, Williamsburg, Virginia, USA 23186; E; Relaxation, Mood, Enhancement, Traits, Assessments

*Jackson, Susan A. (M.S.) Doctoral Student; University of North Carolina at Greensboro, Dept. of Exercise and Sport Science, 250 HPERD Building, Greensboro, North Carolina, USA 27412-5001 (919-334-3275); E; Performance Enhancement, Motivation, Flow, Cognitions, Peak Performance

Jacobs, Andrew A. (Ph.D.) President; The Winning Edge, 6724 Troost Suite 407, Kansas City, Missouri, USA 64131 (816-333-1054); E; Concentration, Attitude, Communication, Tennis, Performance

Jarvis, James M. (Min.D.) Psychologist; 141 N. Meramec Ave. #217, St Louis, Missouri, USA 63105 (314-726-6117); E; Hypnosis, Stress, Control, Motivation, Performance

*Jennett, C.W. (Ph.D.) Professor; San Jose State University, Dept. of Human Performance, San Jose, California, USA 95120 (408-924-3043); E; Competition, Anxiety, Learning, Self-Concept, Neuroscience

Jennings, S.E. (Ph.D.) Professor; Physical Education Dept., Earham College, Richmond, Indiana, USA 42374; E; Sport Psychology, Women, Anxiety, Competition

Jibaja-Rusth, Maria; University of Houston, 3614 Montrose Blvd., Suite 206, Houston, Texas, USA 77006

Johnson, Robert W. (Ph.D.) Professor; University of Minnesota, Dept. of Physical Education, 1900 University Avenue, S.E., Minneapolis, Minnesota, USA 55455 (612-373-4946); E; Learning, Practice Conditions, Feedback, Memory, Control

Johnson, William G. (Ph.D.) Professor; University of Mississippi Medical Center, Dept. of Psychiatry, 2500 North State Street, Jackson, Mississippi, USA 39216 (601-984-5805); E,G(R),F(R),S(R); Coaching, Eating Disorders, Stress, Triathlon

Jones, F.B. (Ed.D.) Professor; California State University, Dept. of Physical Education, Sacramento, California, USA 95819 (916-454-6192); E,S; Competition, Personality, Aggression, Teaching, Counseling

Jowdy, Doug P. (M.Sc.) Mental Health Technology; Penn State University, 251 Clearview Ave., State College, Pennsylvania, USA 16801 (814-234-4290); E,F; Imagery, Concentration, Exercise, Adolescents, Counseling

Juaire, Stephen; Winona State University, 717 Main Street, Winona, Minnesota, USA 55987

Kamen, G.P. (Ph.D.) Professor; St. Louis University, Dept. of Physiology, 1402 S. Grand Blvd., St. Louis, Missouri, USA 63103 (314-664-9800); E; Fatigue, Reflexes, Neural Control, Muscle, Electromyography

*Kang, Lingjiin; 3510 Ivy Commons Drive #302, Raleigh, North Carolina, USA 27606 (919-828-6760); E,M; Sport Psychology, Pedagogy

*Kauss, David R. (Ph.D.); 1100 Glendon Ave, #900, Los Angeles, California, USA 90024 (213-826-9576); E; Performance Enhancement, Imagery, Anxiety Management

*Kazoroski, Ronald W. (M.Sc.) Director; Central Florida Criminal Justice Institute, 2950 West Oak Ridge Rd., Orlando, Florida, USA 32809 (407-859-2512); E; Stress, Aggression, Police, Wellness, Karate

Keele, Stephen W. (Ph.D.) Professor; University of Oregon, Dept. of Psychology, Eugene, Oregon, USA 97403 (686-4931); E; Human Performance, Motor Control, Attention, Skill, Information Processing

Kelly, Kevin; 2815 NE 107th Avenue, Bellevue, Washington, USA 98004

Keogh, Jack F. (Ph.D.) Professor; UCLA, Dept. of Kinesiology, 405 Hilgard, Los Angeles, California, USA 90042 (825-3891); E; Development, Perception, Confidence

*Kerr, Beth (Ph.D.) Professor; University of Washington, Dept. of Psychology, NI-25, Seattle, Washington, USA 98105 (206-453-4159, BKERR@MAX.U.WASHINGTON.EDU); E; Motor Control, Attention, Cognitive Processes

Kessler, David; 3 Dickens Avenue, Dix Hills, New York, USA 11746

Kimiecik, J.C. (M.Sc.) Professor; Miami University, 804 Melinda Drive, Oxford, Ohio, USA 45056 (513-529-2700); E; Exercise, Attitudes, Motivation

King, M.W. (M.Sc.); Bradley University, Dept. of Physical Education, Haussler Hall, Peoria, Illinois, USA 61625 (309-676-7611); E; Competance, Understanding, Achievement, Relating

*Kirschenbaum, Daniel S. (Ph.D.) Professor; Northwestern University, Medical School, Eating Disorders Program, 446 East Ontario, 8th Floor, Chicago, Illinois, USA 60611 (312-908-7850); E; Obesity, Eating Disorders, Self-Control, Performance Enhancement

*Klentz, Bonnie A. (Ph.D.) Associate Professor; Stonehill College, Dept. of Psychology, North Easton, Massachusetts, USA 02357 (508-230-1037); E; Team Cohesion, Gender

*Klonsky, Bruce G. (Ph.D.) Associate Professor; SUNY, College at Fredonia, Psychology Dept., Fredonia, New York, USA 14063, (716-673-3123); E,F(S),G(S); Leadership, Socialization, Sex Differences, Attributions

*Knoppers, A. (Ed.D) Professor; Michigan State University, Dept. of Physical Education, 131 IM Sports Circle, East Lansing, Michigan, USA 48824 (517-355-3775); E,F,D; Gender, Top Athletes, Coaches, Female Athletes, Socialization

Kozar, Bill (Ph.D.) Professor; Texas Technical University, Dept. of Physical Education, Box 4070,

Lubbock, Texas, USA 79409 (806-742-3335); E,R(S); Social Facilitation, Competition, Youth Sport, Personality, Goal-Setting

*Krane, Vikki (Ph.D.); HPER, Bowling Green State University, Bowling Green, Ohio USA 43403 (419-372-7233);

Krems, Sheldon; 27 Collegeview Ave., Poughkeepsie, New York, USA 12603

Krenz, E.W. (Ph.D.) Psychologist; Southeastern Louisiana University, Comprehensive Counseling Center, P.O. Box 310 University Station, Hammond, Louisiana, USA 70402 (504-549-3894); E; Stress, Autogenic Training, Competition, Mental Health, Sport

*Kroll, Walter W. (P.E.D.) Professor; University of Massachusetts, Dept. of Exercise Science, Amherst, Massachusetts, USA 01002 (413-545-0784); E,S; Competition, Personality, Statistics

Kronenberger, Earl J. (Ph.D.) Professor; Xavier University, Dept. of Psychology, 3800 Victory Parkway, Cincinnati, Ohio, USA 45207 (513-745-3531); E; Goals, Performance, Mental Preparation Strategies, Therapy, Anxiety

*Krotee, March L. (Ph.D.) Professor; University of Minnesota, Dept. of Kinesiology, Sociology and American Studies, 218 Cooke Hall, Minneapolis, Minnesota, USA 55455 (612-625-0538, 612-626-7700); E,S; Personality, Anxiety, Cross-Cultural and Social Comparisons of Elite Athletes and Systems

Krueger, Kurt A. (M.S.Ed.) Director; Institute of Sport Psychology, 13120 Bradley #22, Sylmar, California, USA 91342; E; Performance, Holistic, Systems, Spirit, Education

Kubistant, Tom; P.O. Box 13309, University Station, Reno, Nevada, USA 89507

Kuehl, Karl; 8218 Via de Ka Escuela, Scottsdale, Arizona, USA 85256

*Kusick, Becky A. (M.A.) Consultant; 6186 West 75th Place, Arvada, Colorado, USA 80003 (303-421-8107); E; Tennis, Meditation, Imagery, Education, Programs

*Kusick, Bradley R. (M.A.) Consultant; 6186 W. 75th Place, Arvada, Colorado, USA 80003 (303-421-8107); E; Concentration, Balance, Rhythm, Skiing, Education

*Landers, Daniel M. (Ph.D.) Regents Professor; Arizona State University, Dept. of Exercise Science and Physical Education, Pebe 112, Tempe, Arizona, USA 85287 (602-965-7664, 602-965-8109, IACDML@ASUACAD); E,F(R); Attention, Arousal, Performance, Stress, Exercise, Psychophysiology

*Langendorfer, S.J. (Ph.D.); P.E.R.D., Kent State University, Kent, Ohio, USA 44242 (216-672-2117, SLANGEND@KENTVM); E,G(S); Children, Development, Behavior, Neuromuscular, Kinesiology

Lanning, W.L. (Ed.D.) Professor; University of Wyoming, Counselor Education, Box 3374, University Street, Laramie, Wyoming, USA 82071 (307-766-2366); E,G(R); Counseling, Personality, Assessment, Stress, Research

Lannon, M.J. (Ph.D.); Ski-Lan, Dept. of Research, 155 Porter Place, Box 156, Rutland, Vermont, USA 05701 (802-775-5375); E; Early Childhood, Motivation, Nutrition, Development, Motor Learning

*LaPoint, J.D. (Ph.D.) Professor; University of Kansas, Dept. of Physical Education, 104 Robinson Gym, Lawrence, Kansas, USA 66045 (913-864-3371); E,G(S); Competition, Personality, Cooperation, Individuality, Team Sports

Larish, D. (Ph.D) Professor; University of Iowa, Dept. of Physical Education, 3015 Fieldhouse, Iowa City, Iowa, USA 52242 (319-353-4117); E; Atten-

tion, Spatial Orientation, Response Processes, Programming

Larson, Edwin R. (M.D.) Adjunct Assistant Professor; University of Cincinnati, Dept. of Psychiatry, 9200 Montgomery, 8A, Cincinnati, Ohio, USA 45242 (513-793-6500); E; Psychotherapy, Performance, Injuries, Careers, Consultation

*Larson, Glenda J. (M.A.) Physical Education Teacher; 4425 U St., Sacramento, California, USA 95617-1436 (916-731-8381); E

*Latane, Bibb Professor; Florida Atlantic University, Boca Raton, Florida, USA 33431; Social Loafing, Evaluation Apprehension, Group Performance, Social Impact

Lawther, John D. (Ph.D.) Professor; 205 Seapath Tower, Wrightsville Beach, North Carolina, USA 28480; E,F; Methodology, Sport, Coach Education, Motor Learning, Motor Performance

Lee, M.J. (Ph.D.) Professor; University of Oregon, Dept. of Physical Education, Eugene, Oregon, USA 97331 (503-686-5601); E,F; Intergroup Relations, Competition, Group Dynamics, Value, Attention

*Leibowitz, Benji A. (Ph.D.) President; Sports Psychology and Counseling Associates, Inc., P.O. Box 836, Union, New Jersey, USA 07083 (201-686-6888); E; Coaching, Style, Behavior, Motivation, Athletes

Leland, Ted Director; Dartmouth College, Dept. of Athletics, Hanover, New Hampshire, USA 03755

Lender, Jerre L. (Ph.D.) Director; AOCP, Clinical/Sport Psychology Dept., P.O. Box 3129, Newport Beach, California, USA 92663 (714-760-6661); E,G(R); Performance Enhancement, Hypnosis, Individual, Team

Lepley, E. (Ed.D.) Professor; Indiana University, Dept. of Physical Education, Bloomington, Indiana, USA 47405 (412-357-2762); E; Motivation, Achievement, Teacher Preparation

*Lesyk, Jack J. (Ph.D.) Clinical and Sport Psychologist; 3789 South Green Road, Beachwood, Ohio, USA 44122 (216-575-6175); E; Performance Enhancement, Imagery

*LeUnes, Arnold (Ed.D.) Professor; Texas A & M University, Dept. of Psychology, Psychology 266, College Station, Texas, USA 77843 (409-845-2558); E; Teaching, Fitness, Selection, Top Athletes

*Lewthwaite, Rebecca (Ph.D.) Assistant Professor; University of Wisconson-Milwaukee, Dept. of Human Kinetics, P.O. Box 413, Milwaukee, Wisconson, USA 53201 (414-229-4591, 414-229-4666, BECK@CSD4.CSD.UWM.EDU); E; Stress, Children, Motivation, Sport, Exercise

*Libkuman, Terry (Ph.D.) Psychologist; Central Michigan University, Dept. of Psychology, Mt. Pleasant, Michigan, USA 48859; E; Application of Organizational/Industrial Principles to the Evaluation and Selection of Athletes, Prediction of Athletic Performance, Behavior Analysis and Sport

*Lidstone, James E. (Ed.D.) Associate Professor; South Dakota State University, HPER, Brookings, South Dakota, USA 57007-1497 (605-688-5023, 605-688-5999); E,F(R); Anxiety, Self-Esteem, Goal-Setting, Injury Rehabilitation

*Lindquist, E.L. (Ph.D.) Professor; San Jose State University, Dept. of Human Performance, Washington Square, San Jose, California, USA 95192 (294-3034); E,G(R); Cognition, Tennis, Verbal Learning, Non-Verbal Learning, Conditioning

Lipkin, Julie; 244 E. Pearson #1605, Chicago, Illinois, USA 60611

*Lobstein, Dennis (Ph.D) Professor; HPPELP, University of New Mexico, Albuquerque, New Mexico, USA 87131 (505-277-5721); Psychobiology, Fitness, Peaking, Martial Arts, Neuroscience

Lockhart, A.S. (Ph.D.) Professor; Texas Women's University, Dept. of Physical Education and Dance, Box 237177, TWU Station, Denton, Texas, USA 76204; E,F(R),G(R); Reaction Time, Accuracy, Speed, Skill Acquisition

Loeffler, Michael; 23 Old East, Chapel Hill, North Carolina, USA 27514

*Loehr, James E. (Ed.D) Director of Sport Science; USTA, 5500 34th Street, Brandenton, Florida, USA 34210 (813-755-1000, 813-753-1337); E

Lofthus, G.K. (Ph.D.) Professor; University of California at Berkeley, Dept. of Physical Education, Harmon Gym, Berkeley, California, USA 94720 (415-642-5893); E,R(R),S(R,W); Neuromuscular Fatigue, Cordination, Motivation, Aging

Lord, R.H. (Ed.D.) Professor; Northwest Missouri State University, Dept. of Psychology, Maryville, Missouri, USA 64468 (816-582-7141); E; Development, Competition, Personality

Loughlin, W.T. (M.Sc.); York College, Dept. of Physical Education, Jamaica, New York, USA 11451 (212-969-4057); E; Behaviorism, Learning, Motivation, Competition, Personality

Love, Kevin; Central Michigan University, Dept. of Management, Mount Pleasant, Michigan, USA 48859

*Loy, John W. (Ph.D.) Professor; University of Illinois, Dept. of Kinesiology, 213 Freer Hall, Urbana, Illinois, USA 61801 (217-333-6380); E,F(R),S(R); Body Culture, Expressive Behavior, Game Simulation

Lundergen, H.M. (Ph.D.) Professor; Penn State University, Dept. of Physical Education, 267 Recreation Bldg., University Park, Pennsylvania, USA 16802 (814-865-1851); E; Self-Concept, Perceptual Motor Development, Handicapped, Aging, Fitness

*Lutz, David J. (Ph.D.); Southern Missouri State University, Dept. of Psychology, 901 South National, Springfield, Missouri, USA 65804 (417-866-1058, DJL524F@SMSVMA); E; Preparation, Relaxation, Goal Setting, Recovery

Lynch, Gerald; 616 National Street, Santa Cruz, California, USA 95060

Keith P. Henschen

Joan Ingalls

Walter W. Kroll

Daniel M. Landers

*Lyon, Lewis A. (M.Sc.) Director; Mercy Medical Center, Health/Fitness Promotions, 301 St. Paul Pl., Baltimore, Maryland, USA 21202 (301-332-9812, 301-332-9789); E; Exercise Physiology, Stress, Performance Enhancement, Hypnosis, Baseball

*MacCracken, Mary J.W. (Ph.D.) Professor; University of Akron, Physical and Health Education Dept., Akron, Ohio, USA 44325-5103 (216-972-7473); E,F; Social Facilitation, Anxiety, Self-Efficacy, Children, Dynamic Balance

*Mack, Gary (M.Sc.) President; Sports Assist, 11811 N. 56 St., Scottsdale, Arizona, USA 85254 (602-991-6225); E

*Mackenzie, Marlin M. (Ed.D.) Professor; Teachers College, Columbia University, Dept. of Movement Science, Box 100, New York, New York, USA 10027 (212-678-3323); E,F(R); Counseling, Athletes, Motivation, Performance Enhancement

*Maerlander, Art (M.A.); 235 David Street, South Bend, Indiana, USA 46637 (219-271-9272); E,S(R); Performance Enhancement, Research Methodology

*Magill, Richard A. (Ph.D.) Professor; Louisiana State University, Dept. of Kinesiology, Baton Rouge, Louisiana, USA 70803 (504-388-3548, 504-388-6400, HPMGIL@LSUVM.BITNET); E, S(R); Skill Acquisition, Practice Conditions, Feedback, Youth Sport

Mahoney, Michael J. (Ph.D.) Professor; University of California, Santa Barbara, Dept. of Educational Counseling, Santa Barbara, California, USA 93106; E,S; Clinical, Cognition, Competition, Methodology, Top Athletes

*Malina, Robert M. (Ph.D.) Professor; University of Texas, Dept. of Kinesiology and Health Education, Austin, Texas, USA 78712 (512-471-6582); E,S(R),F(R); Growth, Performance, Maturation, Cross-Cultural, Motor Development

Margolies, Michael; University of Wyoming, Physical Education Dept., Laramie, Wyoming, USA 82070

*Markle, A. (Ph.D.) Psychologist; 3819 Medford Circle, Northbrook, Illinois, USA 60062 (708-498-2836); E; Counseling, Motivation, Anxiety Control, Individual Differences, Performance Enhancement

*Marshall, William (Ph.D.) Psychologist; Suite 3, 1317 N. Elm Street, Greensboro, North Carolina, USA 27401 (919-275-6595); E; Performance Enhancement

*Martens, Rainer (Ph.D.) Publisher; Human Kinetics Publishers, Inc., Box 5076, Champaign, Illinois, USA 61825-5076 (217-351-5076, 217-351-2674) E; Anxiety, Competition, Personality, Self-Confidence, Imagery

*Martin, L.A. (D.P.E.) Professor; SUNY at Cortland, Dept. of Physical Education, PER Center, Cortland, New York, USA 13045 (607-753-5701); E; Competition, Personality, Aggression, Motivation, Cohesion

Massimo, Joseph L. (Ph.D.) Psychologist; Newton Public Schools, 100 Walnut St., Newton, Massachusetts, USA 02158 (617-552-7658); E,I; Top Athletes, Personality, Counseling, Evaluation

*Mathes, S.A. (Ph.D.) Professor; Iowa State University, Dept. of Physical Education, Ames, Iowa, USA 50011 (294-8766); E,F(R),S(R); Gender Bias, Role Conflict, Diminishing Role of Women in Sport

*May, Jerry R. (Ph.D.) Clinical Psychologist; University of Nevada, School of Medicine, Reno, Nevada, USA 89557 (702-784-6001, 702-784-6096); E; Performance Enhancement, Teamwork, Organizational Systems, Injury Prevention and Rehabilitation, Psychotherapy

McAllister, Ann Clinical Psychologist; 3115 N.E. Piedmont Road #B200, Atlanta, Georgia, USA 30305-2526

McAllister, Gerald E. (M.Sc.) Counselor; North Pocono Schools, Guidance Dept., Church Street, Moscow, Pennsylvania, USA 18444(717-842-4569); E,F(R); Goals, Relaxation, Visualization, Basketball, Self-Image

*McAuley, E. (Ph.D.) Associate Professor; University of Illinois, Dept. of Kinesiology, 215 Freer Hall, 906 S. Goodwin Ave., Urbana, Illinois, USA 61801 (217-333-6487, BITNET.REMERM@ UIUCVMD); E; Motivation, Self-Efficacy, Attribution, Exercise, Emotion, Health

McCarty, M.G. (Ph.D.) Professor; Southwest Missouri State University, Dept. of HPER, 901 South National, Springfield, Missouri, USA 65804 (417-836-5251); E; Development, Atypical, Perceptual Motor Development, Personality, Coaching

*McCauley, John M. (Ph.D.) Clinical/Sports Psychologist; Box 8829A, Notch Rd., Mendon, Vermont, USA 05701 (802-773-6348); E; Psychotherapy, Hypnosis, Relaxation, Imagery, Sports Consultation

McCausland, W.S. (M.Sc.); 45 Martens Blvd., San Rafael, California, USA 94901 (437-3168); E; Running, Stress, Clinical, Evaluation, Health

*McCracken, Hugh D. (D.L.C.) Professor; Northeastern University, Dept of Physical Education, 360 Huntington Ave, Boston, Massachusetts, USA 02115 (617-437-6138); E,F(S,R); Development, Assessment, Motor Learning, Cognition, Research

*McCullagh, Penny (Ph.D.) Professor; University of Colorado, Dept. of Kinesiology, Boulder, Colorado, USA 80309 (303-492-8021, MCCULLAGH.P @CVBLDR.COLORADO.EDV); E; Modeling, Youth Sport, Imagery, Participation Motives in Exercise and Sport

McDonald, Susan; R#1 Box 119, Morrisville, North Carolina, USA 27560

*McGown, C.M. (Ph.D.) Professor; Brigham Young University, Dept. of Physical Education, 235 SFH, Provo, Utah, USA 84602 (801-378-2276); E,F(S,R); Learning, Teaching, Volleyball, Motor Learning, Psychology

McGuire, Richard; University of Missouri, P.O. Box 667, Columbia, Missouri, USA 65205

*McKelvain, Robert (Ph.D.) Professor; Abilene Christian University, Dept. of Psychology, Box 8167, ACU Station, Abilene Texas, USA 79699-8167 (915-674-2287); E; Consulting, Organization, Gymnastics, Intervention, Clinical

*McKenzie, Thomas L. (Ph.D.) Professor; San Diego State University, Dept. of Physical Education, San Diego, California, USA 92182 (619-594-5541); E; Behavior Analysis, Motivation, Self-Control, Pedagogy, Volleyball

McKinney, E.D. (Ed.D.) Professor; University of North Carolina, Dept. of Physical Education, Greensboro, North Carolina, USA 27412 (334-3033); E; Personality, Stress, Intervention, Motivation, Perceptual Motor Learning

*Melnick, M.J. (Ph.D.) Associate Professor; SUNY at Brockport, Dept. of Physical Education and Sport, Brockport, New York, USA 14420 (716-395-2394); E; Sociology of Sport, Group Dynamics in Sport, Social Psychology of Sport, Sport Spectatorship

*Meyers, Andrew W. (Ph.D.) Professor; Memphis State University, Dept. of Psychology, Memphis, Tennessee, USA 38152 (901-678-2146); E; Anxiety, Self-Regulation, Concentration, Self-Confidence, Imagery

Meyers, Michael C. (Ph.D.) Graduate Student; Texas A & M University, Dept. of Health and Physical Education, College Station, Texas, USA 77844

(409-845-4530); E; Performance, Profiling, Rodeo, Tennis, Exercise

Millhouse, James I. (Ph.D.) Psychologist; Sports Medicine of Atlanta, 118 Summit Creek Drive, Stone Mountain, Georgia, USA 30083 (404-296-4849); E; Hypnosis, Performance, Health, Slumps, Imagery

*Milne, D.C. (Ph.D.); New Mexico State University, Dept. of Physical Education, Recreation and Dance, P.O. Box 3M, Las Cruces, New Mexico, USA 88001 (505-646-4068); E; Children, Growth, Motor Development, Skill

*Miner, M. Jane (Ed.D) Assistant Professor; Dept. of Exercise and Sport Science, University of Utah, Salt Lake City, Utah, USA 84112 (801-581-4729); E; Team Dynamics, Leadership, Individual Performance Enhancement, Female Athletic Performance

Misner, J.C. (Ph.D.) Professor; Central Michigan University, Dept. of Physical Education, Rose 100A, Mt. Pleasant, Michigan, USA 48859 (617-774-3041); E,S(R); Anxiety, Cohesion, Motivation, Personality, Coaching

Morgan, William P. (Ed.D.) Professor; University of Wisconsin-Madison, Dept. of Physical Education and Dance, 2000 Observatory Drive, Madison, Wisconsin, USA 53706 (608-262-1655); E,G(R), I(R); Hypnosis, Motivation, Emotion, Perception, Personality

*Morris, A.F. (Ph.D.) Professor and Director of Health and Fitness Programs; A.F. Staff College, 7800 Hampton Blvd., Norfolk, Virginia, USA 23511-6097 (804-444-5547, 804-444-5120); E; Health Psychology, Long-Distance Road Racing, Life Quality, Locus of Control, Athletics

*Morris, Harold H. (P.E.D.) Professor and Chairperson; Indiana University, Dept. of Kinesiology, Bloomington, Indiana, USA 47405 (812-855-3114, 812-855-6778, MORRIS@IUBACS.BITNET); E; Vision, Proprioception, Reaction Time, Experimental Design

*Murphey, Milledge (Ph.D.) Associate Professor; University of Florida, Dept. of Exercise and Sport Sciences, 309-B FLG, Gainsville, Florida, USA 32611 (904-392-0584, 904-392-5262); E,F(R),SP(R); Risk, Combatives, Attention, Wrestling, Scuba Diving

Murphy, Betty Lou; East Stroudsburg University, School of Health Sciences, East Stroudsburg, Pennsylvania, USA 18301

Murphy, Harvey; University of North Carolina, Dept. of Health and Physical Education, Charlotte, North Carolina, USA 28223

*Murphy, Shane M. (Ph.D.) Head; U.S. Olympic Committee, Sport Psychology Dept., 1750 E. Boulder, Colorado Spings, Colorado, USA 80909 (719-578-4516); E; Elite Athletes, Motivation, Coaching Education, Imagery

Nabors, Laura; Xavier University, 7455 Graves Road, Cincinnati, Ohio, USA 45243

Nesvig, David T. (Ph.D.); San Diego State University, Center for Counseling, San Diego, California, USA 92192; E,S(R),N(R); Stress Management, Small Groups, Communication, Top Athletes

*Newman, Mark (M.Ed.) Student; Dept. of Health and Physical Education, Memorial Gymnasium, University of Virginia, Charlottesville, Virginia, USA 22903; E,F; Self-Confidence, The Gifted, Psychological Rehabilitation From Injury

*Newman, Neal (Ph.D.) Psychologist; Ohio State University, Sport Psychology Clinic (Health Service), 1875 Millikin Rd., Columbus, Ohio, USA 43210 (614-292-5726); E; Neuro-Linguistic Programming, Gestalt, Mental State, Performance Enhancement, Psychotherapy

*Newsham, Sherry L. (Ph.D.) Sport Psychology Consultant; International Institute for the Enhancement of Human Performance, 324 La Mesa, Encinitas, California, USA 92024 (619-753-9014); E,F; Children's Sport, Triathletes, Cognitive Strategies, Ultra-Endurance Athletes

Nichols, T.R. (Ph.D.) Professor; University of Washington, Dept. of Kinesiology, Seattle, Washington, USA 98105 (206-453-7919); E,F(R); Research, Teaching, Neurophysiology, Movement, Muscle

***Noble, M.E. (Ph.D)** Professor; Pennsylvania State University, Dept. of Psychology, 547 Moore Bldg., University Park, Pennsylvania, USA 06802 (814-863-1731); E; Attention, Information Processing, Motor Skill

***O'Block, Frank R. (Ed.D.)** Professor, APA Division 47 Membership Committee Chair; Chicago State University, Dept. of Psychology, 9500 S. King Dr., Chicago, Illinois, USA 60628 (312-995-2175); E; Sport Psychology, Stress Management, Counseling

***O'Connor, Patrick J. (Ph.D.)** Assistant Professor; Arizona State University, Exercise and Sport Research Institute, Tempe, Arizona, USA 85287-0404; E; Mood, Anxiety, Health, Mechanisms, Psychobiology

Ogilvie, Bruce C. (Ph.D.) Emeritus Professor; San Jose State University, Dept. of Psychology-Counseling, Building V, San Jose, California, USA 95192 (408-354-2293); E,F(R,W); Top Athletes, Psychotherapy, Counseling, Coach Education, Competition

***Oglesby, Carole A. (Ph.D.)** Professor; Temple University, Dept. of Physical Education, Pearson Hall, Philadelphia, Pennsylvania, USA 19122 (215-787-1940); E,S; Gender Identity, Personality, Family Systems, Values, Self-Concept

O'Hare, Heather; 2489 Seminde, Detroit, Michigan, USA 48214

***Ostrow, Andrew C. (Ph.D.)** Professor; West Virginia University, Dept. of Sport and Exercise Studies, 265 Coliseum, Morgantown, West Virginia, USA 26506 (304-293-3295); E; Aging, Psychometrics, Anxiety, Tennis

Owens, DeDe; Cog Hill Country Club, 119th and Archer Ave., Lemont, Illinois, USA 60439

***Page, Debra L. (Ph.D.)** Psychologist; 4495 Hale Parkway, Suite 250, Denver, Colorado, USA 80220 (303-777-8884); E; Dancers, Athletes, Depression, Stress, Relationship

***Papanikolaou, Zissis (Ed.M.)** Part-Time Faculty; Dept. of Physical Education, Temple University, 6842 Marshall, Upper Darby, Pennsylvania, USA 19082 (215-352-1464); E,GRE,SWAHILI; Cohesion, Soccer, Active Game Approach, Psychological Skills Training Program, Professional Teams

***Pappas, George P. (Ph.D.)** Sports Psychotherapist/Director; Hartwood Sports Medicine and Wellness Center, 656 Loretta St., Pittsburgh, Pennsylvania, USA 15217; E,GRE; Running, Football, Baseball, Golf, Tennis

***Pargman, David (Ph.D.)** Professor; Florida State University, Dept. of Physical Education, Tallahassee, Florida, USA 32306 (904-644-6058); E, G(S,R), S(S,R); Stress and Performance, Psychology of Sport Injury, Psychological Aspects of Running

Passer, Michael W. (Ph.D.) Professor; University of Washington, Dept. of Psychology, Seattle, Washington, USA 98105; E; Competition, Youth Sport, Self-Esteem, Anxiety, Attribution

Patterson, A.H. (Ph.D.) Professor; Pennsylvania State University, Dept. of Human Movement, University Park, Pennsylvania, USA 06802 (814-865-1467); E; Personality, Aggression, Environment

Paulus, P.B. (Ph.D.) Professor; University of Texas at Arlington, Dept. of Psychology, Arlington, Texas, USA 76019 (817-273-2283); E,D,F(S,R),

G(R); Groups, Crowding, Social Facilitation, Modeling, Stress

***Pease, D.G. (Ph.D.)** Professor; University of Houston, HHP, Houston, Texas, USA 77004 (713-749-7571); E; Youth Sport, Attention, Stress, Emotions, Self-Concept

***Pemberton, Cynthia L. (Ph.D.)** Associate Professor; University of Missouri at Kansas City, Physical Education, 219 Swinney Recreation, Kansas City, Missouri, USA 64110 (816-235-2751, 816-276-1717, CPEMBERTON@UMKCVAXI.BITNET); Motivation, Exercise, Coaching, Children

***Perlstrom, James R. (M.A.);** 701 Boulder Springs Drive #B6, Richmond, Virginia, USA 23225 (804-320-9794); Performance Enhancement, Hypnosis

***Perrin, Thomas A. (Ph.D.)** Assistant Basketball Coach; University of Virginia, Dept. of Athletics, P.O. Box 3785, Charlottesville, Virginia, USA 22903 (804-982-5400); E; Improving the Performance of Top Level Athletes and Coaches, Team or Individual Level, Concentration, Coach-Athlete Communication, Confidence and Team Building

***Petitpas, Albert (Ed.D.)** Chairperson; Springfield College, Dept. of Psychology, Springfield, Massachussets, USA 01109 (413-788-3325, 413-783-8877); E

Petlichkoff, L.M. (Ph.D.) Professor; Boise State University, HPER, Boise, Idaho, USA 83725 (208-385-1231); E; Youth Sport, Achievement Motivation, Percieved Ability, Stress, Sailing

***Petruzzello, Steven J.;** Arizona State University, Dept. of Exercise Science and Physical Education, Tempe, Arizona, USA 85287-0404; E; Psychophysiology of Exercise and Sport, Self-Confidence

Piparo, Anthony J. (M.A.) Graduate Student; 1712 Aftonshire Drive, Greensboro, North Carolina, USA 27410; E; Coping, Anxiety, Performance Enhancement, Golf, Self-Talk

***Pistacchio-Aguiar, Teri (Ph.D.)** Exercise Physiologist; Scottsdale Memorial Hospital, Healthsteps, 9007 E. Shea Blvd., Scottsdale, Arizona, USA 85007 (602-860-3949); E; Exercise, Physiology, Psychology, Nutrition, Stress

***Polvino, Geri (Ph.D.)** Professor; Eastern Kentucky University, Dept. of Physical Education, Lancaster Avenue, Richmond, Kentucky, USA 40475 (606-622-2141, 606-622-1020); E; Performance Enhancement, Stress Management, Stabilizing Performance, Motivation, Volleyball

Ponzo, G. (Ph.D.) Professor; University of Vermont, Dept. of Organizational Counseling, Burlington, Vermont, USA 05405 (802-656-3888); E,F(R),S(R); Counseling, Groups, Personality

***Porter, Kay (Ph.D.)** President; Porter Performance Systems, P.O. Box 5584, Eugene, Oregon, USA 97405 (503-342-6875); E,S; Visualization, Track and Field, Mental Training, Competitive Stress Reduction, Team Building

Powell, Frank M. (Ph.D.) Associate Professor; Furman University, Dept. of Health and Physical

Education, Greenville, South Carolina, USA 29613 (803-294-3418); E; Stress, Fitness

***Prentzel Maurer, Sue (M.S.,A.T.C.)** ATC Coordinator; Chilton Sports Medicine, 21 Struble Lane, West Milford, New Jersey, USA 07480 (201-492-9373); Performance Enhancement, Counseling, Health Psychology

Pressman, Murray D. (M.D.) Psychiatrist; Albert Einstein Medical Center, Dept. of Psychiatry, Old York and Tabor Road, Philadelphia, Pennsylvania, USA 19141 (215-329-0700); E,F; Counseling, Top Athletes, Actualization, Stress Management

Purdy, D.A. (M.A.); Colorado State University, Dept. of Sociology, Fort Collins, Colorado, USA 80521 (303-491-5197); E,G(R); Competition, Children, Anxiety, Failure

Purvis, Jamie W.; 110 Viking Court #5, Athens, Georgia, USA 30605-3565

Quick, Clifford; 48 Longview Drive, Bryan, Texas, USA 77802

***Rainey, David (Ph.D.)** Associate Professor of Psychology; John Carroll University, Dept. of Psychology, Cleveland, Ohio, USA 44118; E; Sport Officiating, Children in Sport, Competition Anxiety

Raiport, G. (M.D.); New York Chiropractic College, P.O. Box 167, Glen Head, New York, USA 11545; E,R,F(S),G(S,R),I(S); Personality, Performance Enhancement

Rarick, G.L. (Ph.D.) Professor; University of California at Berkeley, Dept. of Physical Education, 103 Harmon Gym, Berkeley, California, USA 94720 (415-642-5403); E,F(R); Motor Development, Handicapped, Statistics, Competition, Learning

***Ravizza, Kenneth H. (Ph.D.)** Professor; California State University at Fullerton, Dept. of Health and Physical Education, Fullerton, California, USA 92634 (714-773-3316); E; Stress, Peak Performance, Imagery, Consultation

Rawlins, Robert; 346/6 Pennell Circle, Tallahassee, Florida, USA 32304

Rees, C.R. (Ph.D.) Professor; Adelphi University, Dept. of Physical Education, South Avenue, Garden City, New York, USA 11530 (516-294-8700); E,F(S); Competition, Sex Roles, Interpersonal Attraction, Motivation

Reiter, Henry H. (Ph.D.) Associate Professor; Cupoost College, Dept. of Psychology, Greenvale, New York, USA 11548 (516-499-2006); E,F(S),S(S); Hypnosis, Imagery, Stress, Control, Tennis

Resnkoff, Arthur (Ph.D.) Counseling Psychologist; 11980 San Vicente, Los Angles, California, USA 90049 (213-396-4499); E,S(R); Stress, Anxiety, Track, Basketball, Performance

***Richardson, Peggy A. (Ph.D.)** Professor, Assistant Chair; University of North Texas, Dept. of Kinesiology, Health Promotion, and Recreation, Denton, Texas, USA 76203 (817-565-3427, 817-565-6464); E,F(S,R); Performance Models, Competition, Personality, Female Athletes, Motivation

Rainer Martens   **William P. Morgan**   **Kenneth H. Ravizza**

*Ridenour, Marcella V. (Ph.D.) Professor; Temple University, Biokinetics Research Laboratory, 143 Fernbrook Ave., Wyncole, Pennsylvania, USA 19095 (215-576-0928, 215-576-1669); E; Development, Perception, Learning, Movement Analysis

Riebsame, M.V. (Ed.D.) Professor; Teachers' College, Columbia University, Dept. of Movement Science and Education, New York, New York, USA 10027 (212-678-3325); E; Clinical, Anxiety, Aggression, Motivation, Hypnosis

*Riemer, Brenda (M.S.); 6140 N. Hagadorn #7, East Lansing, Michigan, USA 48823; E; Sport Psychology

Riessinger, Camala; 5023 Amsterdam Avenue, Holt, Minnesota, USA 48842

Rife, F.N. (Ph.D.) Professor; University of Massachusetts, Dept. of Physical Education, Amherst, Massachusetts, USA 01002 (413-545-0541); E; Motivation, Learning, Cooperation, Games, Ethics

Robb, Margaret D. (Ph.D.) Professor; University of Rhode Island, Dept. of Arts and Science, Kingston, Rhode Island, USA 02881 (401-792-2566); E; Motor Skill, Feedback, Skill Acquisition

*Roberton, Mary-Ann (Ph.D.) Associate Professor; University of Wisconsin-Madison, Dept. of Physical Education and Dance, 310 Lathrop Hall, Madison, Wisconsin, USA 53706 (608-262-6576); E; Motor Development, Fundamental Movement, Children, Patterns of Behavior, Cinematography

*Roberts, Glyn C. (Ph.D.) Professor; University of Illinois, Dept. of Kinesiology, 906 South Goodwin, Urbana, Illinois, USA 61801 (217-333-6563); E,W(S,R); Motivation, Children, Competition, Gymnastics, Research

*Rogers, Carolyn A. (Ph.D.) Consultant; Psychological and Family Consultants, Inc., 926 Blackwood Avenue, Tallahassee, Florida, USA 32303 (904-575-8954); E; Sport Psychology, Health Psychology

*Roseman, Jeffrey (Ph.D.) Sports Psychologist/ Clinical Psychologist; 122 Maytime Drive, Jericho, New York, USA 11753 (516-681-3056); E,G, HEB(R),S(R); Behavioral Medicine, Stress Control, Hypnosis, Psychotherapy, Biofeedback and Psychosomatic Medicine

Rosenbaum, D.A. (Ph.D.); Bell Laboratories, Dept. of Human Information Processing, 600 Mountain Ave., Murray Hill, New Jersey, USA (201-582-4369); E,F(R); Motor Programming, Movement, Timing, Body Image

*Ross, Diane (Ph.D.) Professor; California State University, Fullerton, Dept. of Physical Education, Fullerton, California, USA 92634 (714-773-3316/ 2620, 714-773-3314); E; Memory, Observational Learning

*Rotella, Robert J. (Ph.D.) Professor; University of Virginia, Dept. of Health and Physical Education, 201 Memorial Gym, Charlottesville, Virginia, USA 22903 (809-924-6183); E,F(R); Anxiety, Achievement, Top Athletes, Self-Confidence

*Rothstein, Anne L. (Ed.D.) Professor and Associate Dean; Herbert L. Lehman College, Dept. of PERD and Division of Professional Studies, Bedford Bldg. West, Bronx, New York, USA 10468 (212-960-8569); E; Perception, Motor, Prediction, Feedback, Motor Learning

Ruble, Virgil; Ball State University, Dept. of Physical Education, Muncie, Indiana, USA 47368

Rushall, Brent S. (Ph.D.) Professor; San Diego State University, Dept. of Physical Education, San Diego, California, USA 92182 (619-594-4094); E; Assessment, Consulting, Coaching, Behavior, All Sports

Russel, K.R.E. (Ph.D.) Professor; University of Arizona, Dept. of Physical Education, Bldg. #93, #102, Tucson, Arizona, USA 85721 (602-626-4028);

E; Female Athletes, Learning Variables, Competition, Motor Control

Ryan, E. Dean (Ed.D.) Professor; University of California, Davis, Dept. of Physical Education, Davis, California, USA 95616 (916-752-0511); E; Motivation, Competition, Anxiety, Personality

Saccuzzo, Dennis; San Diego State University, Dept. of Psychology, San Diego, California, USA 92182

Sachs, Michael L. (Ph.D.) Associate Professor; Temple University, Dept. of Physical Education, 048-00, Philadelphia, Pennsylvania, USA 19122 (215-787-8718, V5289E@TEMPLEVM); E,F; Mental Health, Addiction, Cognitive Strategies, Peak Experiences, Therapy

*Sacks, Michael H. (M.D.) Professor; New York Hospital/Cornell Medical Center, 525 E. 68th Street, New York, New York, USA 10024; Psychiatry of Sport, Sport and Athletics in Normal Development, Exercise and Mental Health

*Sage, George H. (Ed.D.) Professor; University of Northern Colorado, Dept. of Kinesiology, Greeley, Colorado, USA 80631 (303-351-1737); E; Coaches, Values, Leadership, Top Athletes

*Sandbek, Terence J. (Ph.D.) Director; The California Clinic, Suite C303, 3838 Watt Avenue, Sacramento, California, USA 95821, (916-488-3772); E; Cognitive Restructuring, Stress, Consulting, Skill Training, Habit Control

*Sandvick, Roger W. (Ph.D.) Psychologist; Consulting Services, 14280 Stratford Road, Eden Pairie, Minnesota, USA 55346 (612-937-9107); E; Ice Hockey, Tennis, Mental Training, Leadership, Team Cohesion

San Giovanni, L.F. (Ph.D.) Professor; Seton Hall University, Dept. of Sociology/Anthropology, South Orange Avenue, South Orange, New Jersey, USA 07079 (210-762-9000); E; Sex Roles, Role Theory, Deviance, Bureaucracy, Social Organization

Sayre, B.R. (M.A.); U.S. Coast Guard Academy, Dept. of Physical Education, 31 Nob Hill Road, New London, Connecticut, USA 06320 (203-493-8463); E,G; Competition, Women's Sport, Intercollegiate, Androgeny, Sex Roles

*Scanlan, Tara K. (Ph.D.) Professor; UCLA, Dept. of Kinesiology, 405 Hilgard Ave., Los Angeles, California, USA 90024 (213-825-4210); E; Youth Sport and Elite Athletes, Stress, Motivation, Enjoyment, Competition

*Scarborough, Karen L. (Ph.D.) Professor; California State University, Dept. of Health and Physical Education, Sacramento, California, USA 95819 (916-278-7309); E; Performance Enhancement, Sport, Dance

Schleser, Robert; Illinois Institute of Technology, Dept. of Psychology, Chicago, Illinois, USA 60616

*Schmid-Shapiro, Andrea B. (Ed.D.) Professor; San Francisco State University, Physical Education, San Francisco, California, USA 94132 (415-587-0592); E,G(S),H(S), F(R); Peak Performance, Competition, Concentration, Biofeedback, Stress

*Schmidt, Richard A. (Ph.D.) Professor; UCLA, Dept. of Psychology, 405 Hilgard Ave., Los Angeles, California, USA 90024-1563 (213-206-8084, 213-206-5895, IUY5RAS@UCLAMVS); E, G(R),S(R),F(R); Motor Control, Motor Learning, Memory, Motor Skill, Human Factors

Seabourne, Tom; San Jacinto College South, 13735 Beamer Road, Houston, Texas, USA 77089

*Selder, Dennis J. (Ph.D.) Professor; San Diego State University, Dept. of Physical Education, San Diego, California, USA 92182 (714-265-5540); E,F(R); Motivation, Performance, Top Athletes, Age Groups, Health

Serkin, Bruce A. (Ph.D.) Psychologist; 104 Carmen Road, Dix Hills, New York, USA 11746 (516-673-6128); E,F; Cognition, Behavior, Hypnosis, Running, Health

*Serrano, Alejandro; Florida State University, 215 Hayden Rd., Apt. 131, Tallahassee, Florida, USA 32304 (904-574-6418); E,S

Sgro, Joseph A. (Ph.D.) Professor; Virginia Techical University, Dept. of Psychology, 5088 Derring Hall, Blacksburg, Virginia, USA 24061 (703-961-5628); E,G(R); Personality, Coaches, Performance, Competition, Training

Shapiro, Mickie; 1792 Kinglet Ct., Costa Mesa, California, USA 92626

*Shapiro, Susan (M.A.) Consultant, Personal Trainer; 1147 6th Street, #101, Santa Monica, California, USA 90403 (213-395-0948); E; Performance Enhancement, Organizational Psychology, Health Psychology, Stress Effects, Group Dynamics

*Shaw, Gerard (Ed.D.) Sports Performance Consultant, Psychotherapist; 294 Argyle Road, Brooklyn, New York, USA 11218 (718-941-7201); E,F

*Shea, Charles H. (Ph.D.) Professor; Texas A & M University, Dept. of Health and Kinesiology, College Station, Texas, USA 77843; E; Control, Programming, Statistics, Design, Timing

*Sheehan, Thomas J. (Ph.D.) Professor; University of Connecticut, Dept. of Sport, Leisure and Exercise Sciences, Storrs, Connecticut, USA 06269 (203-486-3564); E

Shelton, T.O. (M.A.); Pennsylvania State University, Dept. of Psychology, Moore Building, University Park, Pennsylvania, USA 06802 (814-863-0225); E; Clinical, Psychotherapy, Counseling, Cognition, Therapy

*Shen, Ju-nie (Ed.D.); 7 Terkwile Rd., Montvale, New Jersey, USA 07645 (201-307-9154, 201-307-8720); E,M

*Sherrard, Peter A.D. (Ed.D.) Assistant Professor, Counselor Education; University of Florida, 1215 Norman Hall, Gainesville, Florida, USA 32611 (904-392-0731); E; Group Dynamics/Team Building, Performance Enhancement, Stress Management, Ethics of Sport, Youth Sport

Sherwood, D.E. (Ph.D.) Professor; University of Southern California, Dept. of Physical Education, University Park, Los Angeles, California, USA 90032 (213-741-8068); E,F(R); Motor Control, Motor Programming, Limb Control, Performance Models, Spatial-Temporal Errors

*Shultz, B. (Ph.D.); The University of Utah, Dept. of Exercise and Sport Science, Salt Lake City, Utah, USA 84112 (801-581-4440); Motor Learning/Control, Memory, Practice, Perceptual Processes, Mood States

*Siedentop, Darryl L. (P.E.D.) Professor; Ohio State University, Dept. of Physical Eucation, 337 W. 17th Avenue, Columbus, Ohio, USA 43210 (614-422-6736); E; Management, Motivation, Behavioral Practice, Systems

Glyn C. Roberts   **Brent S. Rushall**

*Siegel, D.S. (Ed.D.) Professor; Smith College, Dept. of Physical Education, Ainsworth Gym, Northampton, Massachusetts, USA 01063 (584-2700); E; Statistics, Motor Learning, Motivation, Perceived Exertion

*Sifft, Josie M. (Ph.D.) Associate Professor; California State Polytechnic University, Dept. of Physical Education, 3801 W. Temple Avenue, Pomona, California, USA 91768 (714-869-2786); E; Stress, Self-Esteem, Relaxation, Peak Performance, Hemisphericity

*Silva, John M., III (Ph.D.) Associate Professor; University of North Carolina-Chapel Hill, Dept. of Physical Education, Exercise and Sport Science, 203 Fetzer, 8700, Chapel Hill, North Carolina, USA 27599 (919-962-0017, USILVA@UNC); E; Elite Athlete, Performance Enhancement, Psychometrics, Aggression

*Sime, Wesley E. (Ph.D.) Associate Professor; University of Nebraska, 107 MLH, Lincoln, Nebraska, USA 68588-0229 (402-472-2410); Stress Management in Sport, Health Benefits of Exercise, Counseling Athletes, Peak Performance Training

*Simmons, R.W. (Ph.D.) Professor; San Diego State University, Dept. of Physical Education, San Diego, California, USA 92182 (714-886-5543); E; Learning, Performance, Skill, Control, Practice

*Simons, Jeffery P. (Ph.D.) Performance Consultant; 2125-C Ohio Avenue, Long Beach, California, USA 90804 (213-597-5752); E; Psychological Skills, Stress, Elite, Imagery, Physiology

*Simpson, Warren K. (Ed.D.) Vice President/Athletic Counseling, Sport Psychologist; ConnTex International Sports Consultants, 2583 Whitney Avenue, Hamden, Conneticut, USA 06518 (203-248-2182, 203-248-9466); E; Coaching Education, Youth Sports, Hypno-Counseling for Athletic Enhancement, Leadership Role Modeling for Motivation and Team Cohesion, Athletics and Academic Mental Strategies

*Singer, Robert N. (Ph.D.) Chairman; University of Florida, Dept. of Exercise and Sport Sciences, 305 Florida Gym, Gainesville, Florida, USA 32602 (904-392-0584, 904-392-5262); E,F(R); Cognitive Processes, Motivation, Achievement Potential, Learning Strategies

*Skadden, David; 806 S. Maple, Urbana, Illinois, USA 61801

Sleet, David A. (Ph.D.) Professor; San Diego State University, Dept. of Physical Education, San Diego, California, USA 92182 (714-265-6828); E,F(R); Play, Self-concept, Socialization, Fitness, Phenomenology

Smith, Dan (Ph.D.); University of Illinois, Dept. of Athletics, Champaign, Illinois, USA 61820

*Smith, Donald C. (Ph.D.) Professor; Florida International University, Dept. of Educational Psychology, Tamiami Trail, Miami, Florida, USA 33199 (305-348-2094); E,F,S(R,W); Stress Management, Anxiety, Counseling, Psychological Skills Training, Cognitive Behavioral Techniques

Smith, Robert; University of Cincinnati, Dyer Hall, Cincinnati, Ohio, USA 45221-0001

*Smith, Ronald E. (Ph.D.) Professor; University of Washington, Dept. of Psychology, NI-25, Seattle, Washington, USA 98195 (206-543-8817); E; Youth Sport, Top Athletes, Clinical, Mental Training, Coach Behavior

*Smoll, Frank L. (Ph.D.) Professor; University of Washington, Dept. of Psychology, NI-25, Seattle, Washington, USA 98195 (206-543-4612, 206-685-3157); E,S(R); Motor Development, Youth Sport, Coach Behavior, Attitudes, Coach Education

*Solt, Gail P. (M.A.) Director; JFK University, Dept. of Psychology, 370 Camino Pablo, Orinda, California, USA 94563 (415-254-0110); E; Imagery, Goal Setting, Youth Sport, Woman in Sport, Relaxation

Spillman, Stephen; 309 Nicholas, Vincennes, Indiana, USA 47591

Spirduso, Waneen (Ed.D.) Professor; University of Texas, Dept. of Physical and Health Education, Austin, Texas, USA 78712 (512-471-4168); E,S(R); Motor Control, Aging, Laterality, Hemispheric Dominance, Brain Mechanisms

*Stadulis, Robert E. (Ed.D.) Associate Professor; Kent State University, School of Physical Education, Recreation and Dance, 162 MGA, Kent, Ohio, USA 44266 (216-672-2117); E; Motivation, Competition, Learning, Practice Conditions, Coincident Timing

Stainback, R.D. (Ph.D.) Professor; University of Alabama at Birmingham, Dept. of Psychology, Birmingham, Alabama, USA 35294 (205-991-0144); E; Addictions, Exercise, Injury Rehabilitation, Tennis, Golf

*Steel, Don; University of Maryland, Dept. of Physical Education, College Park, Maryland, USA 20742

Stelmach, George E. (Ed.D.) Professor; Arizona State University, Dept. of Exercise Science and Physical Education, Tempe, Arizona, USA, 85287 (602-965-7664; 602-965-8109); E,F(R,W); Learning, Control, Retention, Feedback, Attention

Stenrude, C. (Ph.D.); Sports Performance Associates, 228 N. Cascades, Suite 300, Colorado Springs, Colorado, USA 80901 (303-634-4811); E; Stress Management, Top Athletes, Counseling

Stolberg, D.C. (Ph.D.) Professor; University of Toledo, Dept. of Physical Education, 2801 W. Bancroft St., Toledo, Ohio, USA 43606 (419-537-2764); E,F(R),G(R); Competition, Aggression, Personality, Motivation, Anxiety

*Stone, Marvin A. (M.D.) Professor; University of Texas H.S.C. at Houston, Dept. of Psychiatry, 4550 Post Oak Place #341, Houston, Texas, USA (713-621-2400); E; Peak Performance, Stress Management, Motivation, Burnout, Injury Prevention

*Stratton, Richard K. (Ph.D.) Associate Professor; Virginia Polytechnic Institute, Dept. of Physical Education, War Memorial Gym, Blacksburg, Virginia, USA 24061-0326 (703-231-5617); E; Information Processing, Competition, Children, Stress, Anxiety

*Straub, William F. (Ph.D.) Professor; Ithaca College, School of Health Science and Human Performance, Ithaca, New York, USA 14882 (607-274-3152, 607-274-1137); E; Peak Performance, Motivation, Aggression, Personality, Cohesion

Strickland, Bonnie; University of Massachussetts, Dept. of Psychology, Amherst, Massachussetts, USA 01002

Struzinsky, Alice; State University College, Lee Hall, Oswego, New York, USA 13126

Subala, Vic; 1924 Seventh St., Port Hueneme, California, USA 93041

*Suinn, Richard M. (Ph.D.) Professor; Colorado State University, Dept. of Psychology, Fort Collins, Colorado, USA 80521 (303-491-6364); E; Top Athletes, Behavior Modification, Stress Management, Imagery

Surgent, Frederick C. (Ed.D.) Professor; Frostburg State University, Physical Education Center, Frostburg, Maryland, USA, 21532 (301-689-4461); E; Imagery, Anxiety, Control, Relaxation

Tait, G.T. (Ph.D.) Professor; Pennsylvania State University, Dept. of Physical Education, 261 Recreation Bldg., University Park, Pennsylvania, USA 06802 (814-863-0237); E,G(R),R(R); Hypnosis, Competition, Top Athletes, Confidence, Psychophysiology

*Tammen, V.V (M.Sc.) Graduate Student; University of Illinois, Dept. of Kinesiology, Urbana, Illinois, USA 61801 (217-244-1191); E; Golf, Motivation, Leadership, Football, Baseball

*Taylor, Jim (Ph.D.) Director of Sport Psychology Program; School of Psychology, Nova University, Fort Lauderdale, Florida, USA 32014 (800-541-NOVA); E; Enhancement, Clinical, Hypnosis, Coaches, Slumps, Momentum

*Temple, I.G. (Ph.D.) Professor; Bowling Green State University, School of HPER, Bowling Green, Ohio, USA 43403 (419-372-6902); E; Information Processing, Visual Perception, Balance, Learners

Tennant, L. Keith (Ph.D.) Associate Professor; University of Florida, Dept. of Exercise and Sport Science, FIG 134, Gainesville, Florida, USA 32611 (904-392-0580); E; Motivation, Stress, Anxiety, Rewards, Attention

Thierfelder, William K. (Ed.D.) Sport Psychologist; 725 Hilltop Dr., New Cumberland, Pennsylvania, USA 17070 (717-774-7230); E; Subliminal, Applied, Enhancement, Pedagogy, Sport Medicine

*Thirer, Joel (Ph.D.) Professor and Director; State University of New York, Division of Physical Education and Athletics, P.O. Box 6000, Binghamton, New York, USA 13902-6000 (607-777-4255, 607-777-4597); E; Personality, Aggression, Depression, Anxiety, Health Psychology

*Thomas, Jerry R. (Ed.D.) Professor; Arizona State University, Dept. of Exercise Science and Physical Education, Tempe, Arizona, USA 85287

Darryl L. Siedentop

John M. Silva III

Robert N. Singer

William F. Straub

Richard M. Suinn

Jerry R. Thomas

(602-965-7655, 602-965-8108, BITNET:AGJRT@ ASUACAD); E; Motor Development, Youth Sport, Research Methods, Motor Performance/ Learning/Control

Thompson, Laurance; 960 Disston View Drive, Lititz, Pennsylvania, USA 17543

Thueson, Neil; East Stroudsburg Univeristy, Dept. of PAPE, East Stroudsburg, Pennsylvania, USA 18301

Todor, John I. (Ph.D.) Professor; University of Michigan, Dept. of Physical Education, 401 Washtenaw Ave., Ann Arbor, Michigan, USA 48109 (313-764-4472); E; Development, Learning, Motor, Argumentation

Tonymon, Phyllis; 921 N. Chrysler Drive, Tucson, Arizona, USA 85716

Toth, Joe (Ed.D.) Professor; Montclair State College, Dept. of Physical Education, Upper Montclair, New Jersey, USA 07043 (201-893-4247); E,G,H; Motivation, Mental Training, Competition, Psychomotor Abilities, Top Athletes

Tracanna, Kim; 172 E. Katherine Ave., Washington, Pennsylvania, USA 15301

Tricker, Raymano; 160 Robinson Center, Lawrence, Kansas, USA 66045

*****Tutko, Thomas A. (Ph.D.);** San Jose State University, Dept. of Psychology, San Jose, California, USA 95192; E; Personality, Top Athletes, Self-Control, Competition, Counseling

Tyler, Robert W. (Ph.D.) Professor; University of Maryland, Dept. of Physical Education, College Park, Maryland, USA 20742 (301-454-3284); E; Feedback, Reaction Time, Short-Term Memory

Uhlig, George E. (Ed.D.) Professor; University of South Alabama, College of Education, 124 Instructional Lab Bldg., Mobile, Alabama, USA 36688 (205-460-6205); E; Testing, Measurement, Evaluation, Research, Organizational Development

*****Ungerleider, Steven (Ph.D.)** Licensed Psychologist; Integrated Research, 66 Club Road, Eugene, Oregon, USA 97401 (503-683-9278, 503-683-2621); S,E; Sports, Psychologist, Drug, Alcohol, Imagery

Vander Velden, L.R. (Ph.D.) Professor; University of Maryland, Dept. of Physical Education, College Park, Maryland, USA 20742 (301-454-3262); E; Small Groups, Leadership, Socialization, Quality of Life

*****Vealey, Robin S. (Ph.D.)** Assistant Professor; Dept. of Physical Education, Health, and Sport Studies, Miami University, Oxford, Ohio, USA 45056 (513-529-2700, RSVEALEY@MIAMIU); E; Self-Confidence, Anxiety, Motivation, Intervention, Coaching

*****Vercruyssen, Max (Ph.D.)** Assistant Professor; University of Southern California, Human Factors Dept., ISSM, Los Angeles, California, USA 90089 (213-740-4067); E,J(S,R); Ergonomics, Stressors, Reaction Time, Attention, Aging

*****Vernacchia, Ralph A. (Ph.D.)** Associate Professor; Western Washington University, Dept. of Physical Education, Carver Gym 106, Bellingham, Washington, USA 98225 (206-676-3514); E; Applied, Track, Basketball, Imagery, Confidence Building

Vicory, J.R. (Ed.D.) Director; Gottlieb Hospital Health and Fitness Center, 551 W. North Avenue, Melrose Park, Illinois, USA 60160 E,S; Performance Enhancement, Stress Management

*****Vlahov, Eric (Ph.D.)** Professor; University of Tampa, Dept. of Physical Education, 401 West Kennedy Blvd., Tampa, Florida, USA 33606 (813-253-3333); E,G(R); Sensation, Vision, Performance, Stress, Learning

*****Vojtisek, John E. (Ph.D.)** Psychologist; Marbleworks Professional Building, 2 Maple Street, Suite 202, Middlebury, Vermont, USA 05753 (802-388-

3666); E; Performance Enhancement, Well-Being, Mental Health, Stress Management, Effects of "Home Field" Advantage

Vokes, L.S. (Ph.D.) Professor; Allan Hancock College, Dept. of Physical Education, 800 S. College Drive, Santa Maria, California, USA 93454 (805-922-6966); E; Humanistic, Listening, Groups, Sport, Counseling

*****Wallace, Stephen A. (Ph.D.)** Professor, Chair; University of Colorado, Dept. of Kinesiology, Campus Box 354, Boulder, Colorado, USA 80309; E; Motor Learning, Motor Control, Memory

*****Wandzilak, T.M. (Ph.D.)** Professor; University of Nebraska, School of HPER, Mable Lee Hall, Lincoln, Nebraska, USA 68504 (402-472-1706); E,S(R); Sociology, Comparative Physical Education, Sport, Youth Sport

*****Ware, Michael C. (Ph.D.)** Psychologist, Director; Sports Psychology Service, The Center for Mental Health and Chemical Dependency, 5361 McAuley Drive, P.O. Box 1127, Ann Arbor, Michigan, USA 48106 (313-572-2595); E,F(S,R); Anxiety Reduction, Tennis, Performance Enhancement Training

Warren, Barbara; 41 Park Row, 14th Floor, New York, New York, USA 10038

Watkins, D.L. (Ph.D.) Professor; Dickenson College, Dept. of Physical Education, High Street, Carlisle, Pennsylvania, USA 17013 (717-243-5121); E; Motivation, Competition, Anxiety, Personality, Performance

*****Watterson, G. David (Ph.D.)** Management Consultant; William Lynde and Williams, 33 River St., Chagrin Falls, Ohio, USA 44022 (216-247-8577); E; Personality, Self-Talk, Performance Enhancement

Weiberg, W.T. (Ph.D.) Professor; University of Louisville, Dept. of Physical Education, Belknap Gym, Louisville, Kentucky, USA 40292 (502-588-6641); E,G(R),S(R); Achievement Motivation, Attribution, Anxiety, Competition, Personality

Weinberg, Robert S. (Ph.D.) Regents Professor; University of North Texas, Dept. of Kinesiology, Denton, Texas, USA 76203 (817-565-3430); E; Anxiety, Momentum, Motivation, Goal-Setting, Tennis

*****Weinmann, Carol (Ed.D.)** Professor; California State University, Fullerton, Dept. of Physical Education, 800 State College Bldg., Fullerton, California, USA 92634 (714-773-3140); E; Self-Esteem, Ordinary People, Self-Concept, Top Athletes, Cognitive Restructuring, Biofeedback

Welford, A.T. (Sc.D.); 581 Kamuku St., Apt 506, Honolulu, Hawaii, USA 96826; E,F; Experimental, Aging, Ergonomy, Skill

Wentzell, Spud; Houghton College, 1 Willard Avenue #128, Houghton, New York, USA 14744

*****Wenz, Betty J. (Ph.D.)** Psychologist, Counseling Services Director, Psychology Professor; California State University, Hayward, California, USA 94578 (415-881-3766); E; Performance Enhancement, Multi-Disciplinary Approach, Stress, Coping, Track and Field

Wessel, Douglas; Family Medical Center, 1406 N. Main, Spearfish, South Dakota, USA 57783

Wessell, J.A. (Ph.D.) Professor; Michigan State University, Dept. of HPER, 134 IM Circle Building, East Lansing, Michigan, USA 48823 (517-355-4740); E,S(R); Handicapped, Mental, Curriculum, Design, Assessment

*****Whelan, James P.;** Memphis State University, Dept. of Psychology, Memphis, Tennessee, USA 38152; E; Performance Enhancement, Exercise and Mental Health, Role of Sports in Child Development

*****White, C. Ronald (M.D.)** Psychiatrist; P.O. Box 76010, St. Petersburg, Florida, USA 33734-6010 (813-823-4055); E; Motivation, Stress, Control, Biofeedback, Injuries

*****White, Sally A. (Ph.D.)** Assistant Professor; University of New Hampshire, Dept. of Physical Education, 209 New Hampshire Hall, Durham, New Hampshire, USA 03824 (603-862-2058, 603-862-2030, S_WHITE1@UNHH.); E; Self-Concept, Tennis, Personality, Motivation, Disabled Athletes

Whitt, Frederick (Ed.D.) Professor; Kennesaw State College, HPER, P.O. Box 444, Marietta, Georgia, USA 30061 (404-423-6216); E; Social, Facilitation, Administration, Curriculum

Wiegand, Debra; 5803 Sir Galahad Road, Glen Dale, Maryland, USA 20769

Wiegand, R.L. (Ed.D.) Professor; West Virginia University, Dept. of Physical Education, 264 Coliseum, Morgantown, West Virginia, USA 26506 (304-293-3839); E; Skill Acquisition, Atypical, Physical Education, Motor Development

*****Wiese, Diane M. (Ph.D.)** Assistant Professor; University of Minnesota, Division of Kinesiology, 1900 University Ave. S.E., Minneapolis, Minnesota, USA 55455 (612-625-6580, DWIESE@ UMNACVX); E; Sport Skill Modeling, Psychology of Athletic Injury, Coaching Education, Volleyball

Wildfogel, Jeffrey; Stanford University, Dept. of Psychology, Stanford, California, USA 94304

*****Williams, Jean M. (Ph.D.)** Associate Professor; University of Arizona, Dept. of Exercise and Sport Sciences, Tucson, Arizona, USA 85721 (602-621-6989); E; Stress, Exercise, Gender Roles, Peak Performance, Injuries

*****Williamson, Rodney G. (M.Sc.)** Doctoral Student; University of Maryland, Dept. of Kinesiology, 1612 Mt. Airy Court, Crofton, Maryland, USA 21114 (301-721-8659); E; Intelligence, Cognition, Development, Youth Sports, Soccer

*****Willis, Joe D. (Ph.D.)** Professor; Georgia State University, Dept. of Physical Education, University Plaza, Atlanta, Georgia, USA 30303 (404-658-2536); E,F(R); Competition, Achievement Motivation, Body Image, Personality, Exercise Psychology

Wilson, Robert; Syracuse University, 329 Hall of Languages, Syracuse, New York, USA 13244

Winters, Robert K. (M.A.) Director of Education; Sports Vision Center, P.O. Box 24, Logansport, Indiana, USA 46947 (219-626-3158); E; Hypnosis, Confidence, Golf, Motivation, Relaxation

*****Wittig, A.F. (Ph.D)** Professor; Ball State University, Dept. of Psychological Science, Muncie, Indiana, USA 47304 (317-285-1024); E; Attitudes, Learning, Gender Differences

Wolf, M.D. (Ph.D.) Professor; New York University, Dept. of Curriculum and Instruction, 239 Green Street, New York, New York, USA 10003 (212-598-3457); E; Learning, Neuropsychology, Pharmacology, Design, Measurement

Wood, D.T. (Ed.D.) Professor; University of Toledo, Dept. of Physical Education, Bancroft St., Toledo, Ohio, USA 43606 (419-537-2742); E, F(R,W),S(R); Anxiety, Motivation, Top Sport, Failure, Personality

*****Woods, Ronald B. (Ph.D.)** Director of Player Development; United States Tennis Association, 707 Alexander Road, Princeton, New Jersey, USA 08540 (609-452-2580, 609-452-2265)

Woolfolk, Robert; 14 Lakeview Drive, Box 399, Kingston, New Jersey, USA 08528

Wright, Dianna; 918 Francis Street, Knoxville, Tennessee, USA 37916

Wright, Lilyan; Trenton State College, Dept. of HPER, Trenton, New Jersey, USA 08625

*****Wrisberg, Craig A. (Ph.D.)** Professor; University of Tennessee, Dept. of Human Performance and Sport Studies, Knoxville, Tennessee, USA 37996-

2700 (615-974-5111); E; Attention, Control, Memory, Learning, Timing

Wurzer, David; Wurzer and Associates, 2005 Palo Verde Ave., Long Beach, California, USA 90815

*Yambor, Jodiann (Ph.D.) Director of Student Services; University of Miami, Athletic Dept., #1 Hurricane Drive, Coral Gables, Florida, USA 33124 (305-284-2690); E; Performance Enhancement, Self-Talk, Concentration, Self-Confidence, Cohesiveness

*Yukelson, David (Ph.D.) Sport Psychologist; Penn State University, Academic Support Center for Student Athletes, 328 Bouke, University Park, Pennsylvania, USA 16802 (814-865-0407); E; Self-Esteem, Concentration, Motivation, Group Dynamics, Youth Sport

Zaichkowsky, Leonard D. (Ph.D.) Professor; Boston University, School of Education, 605 Commonwealth Ave., Boston, Massachusetts, USA 02215 (617-353-3300); E,F(R); Anxiety, Stress, Biofeedback, Research Design, Statistics

Zaichkowsky, Linda B. (Ph.D.) Professor; Metropolitan College, Dept. of Physical Education, 704 Commonwealth Ave., Boston, Massachusetts, USA 02215 (617-353-4393); E; Attitudes, Competition, Moral Development, Self-Concept, Socialization

Zaremski, Barbara M. (Ph.D.) Director; Biofeedback and Optimal Performance Center, 9931 Lee Ct., Leawood, Kansas, USA 66206 (913-383-9345); E,F(R); Stress Control, Hypnosis, Swimming, Family Process, Learning Disabilities

*Zechmeister, Kathleen M. (M.Sc.) Psychotherapist; 3020 Old Ranch Parkway, Suite 300, Seal Beach, California, USA 90740 (213-799-5522); E; Stress, Injuries, Motivation, Triathletes, Anxiety

*Zeigler, Susan G. (Ed.D.) Associate Professor, Associate Dean, College of Graduate Studies; Cleveland State University, Dept. of Physical Education 223, Euclid Avenue, Cleveland, Ohio, USA 44115 (216-687-4876); E; Stress, Attention Control, Visualization, Psychological Skills, Cognitive Technology

*Zelaznik, Howard N. (Ph.D.) Professor; Purdue University, Dept. of Physical Education, West Lafayette, Indiana, USA 47907 (317-483-0370); E,F(R); Control, Performance, Memory, Information, Learning

Zientek, C.E. Cates (Ph.D.) Professor; Shippensburg University, Dept. of Physical Education, Shippensburg, Pennsylvania, USA 17257 (717-532-1599); E; Attribution, Cue Utilization, Field Hockey, Causal Schema, Winning Stereotypes

*Zimmerman, M. Nadine (Ph.D.) Professor; Northern Illinois University, Dept. of Physical Education, 214 Knollwood Drive, Dekalb, Illinois, USA 60115 (815-753-0678, 815-753-1314)

Zingraf, S.A. (Ed.D.) Professor; Texas A & M University, Dept. of Physical Education, College Station, Texas, USA 77843 (846-5311); E,F; Measurement, Statistics, Sport Psychology, Motor Learning

Zion, L.C. (Ed.D.) Professor; Humboldt State University, Dept. of Health and Physical Education, Aracta, California, USA 95521 (707-826-4536); E,F(S); Perception, Cognition, Holism, Ordinary People, Learning

Uruguay

Ferres, Carlos (B.Sc.) Teacher; Famailla 3277, Montevideo, Uruguay; E,S; Special, Children, Education, Physical, Therapy

Lodeiro, Pedro (M.Sc.) Psychologist; University of Uruguay, Dept. of Physical Education, Escuela de Ed. Fisica, Estadio Centenario, Montevideo, Uruguay; E,S; Athlete, Evaluation, Training, Group Dynamics

Pilatti, Luis (B.Sc.) Teacher; Ministry of Health, Dept. of Recreation, Cuareim 1680 Apt. 2, Montevideo, Uruguay; S,E(S,R); Special Child, Recreation, Therapy Programs

Venezuela

Calistri, J. (M.D.) Professor; Universidat Los Andes, Faculty of Medicine, Merida, Venezuela; E,S; Exercise, Anxiety, Counseling

Perez, J.G. Professor; Universidad Las Andes, Dept. of Physical Education, Av Tulio Febres, Merida, Venezuela; S,E(R),F(R); Top Athletes, Motor Learning, Amxiety, Personality

Wales

Fazey, John A. (Ph.D.) Lecturer; University of Wales, Bangor, Dept. of Physical Education, Bangor, Wales (248-351151); E,G,F(S,R),W(S); Control, Learning, Children

*Hardy, Lew (Ph.D.) Senior Lecturer; Sport, Health and Physical Education, University of Wales, Ffriddoedd Building, Victoria Drive, Bangor, Gwynedd, Wales LL57 2EN (0248-351151); E,F(R); Stress and Performace, Mental Training, Coping, Imagery, Motor Control, Evaluation of Psychological Skills Training

*Parfitt, C. Gaynor (Ph.D.) Lecturer; Sport, Health and Psychical Education, University College of North Wales, Ffriddoedd Building, Victoria Drive, Bangor, Gwynedd, Wales LL57 2EN; E; Multidimensional Anxiety and Motor Performance, The Relationship Between Psychological Well Being, Physical Fitness, and Physical Health, Development and Evaluation of Mental Training Programs to Enhance Sports Performance

*Power, Sean L.D. (M.A.) Head of School; Cardiff Institute of Higher Education, School of Sport, Physical Education and Leisure, Cyncoed, Cardiff, Wales (0222 551111); E; Anxiety, Competition, Elite Performers, Mental Training, Personality

Yugoslavia

*Arzensek, Srdan (M.Sc.) Consultant; Presernova 9A, Velenje, Yugoslavia 63320 (063-853-847); E,SC,SLOVENE,G(R); Tennis, Athlete Nutrition, Dance, Training Process, Relaxation Techniques

*Bele-Potocnik, Zivana (M.Sc.) Senior Consultant; Zavod R. Slovenije za Produktivnost Dela, Center za Psihodiagnosticna Sredstva, Titova 118/VII, 6100 Ljubljana, Yugoslavia (061-348434, 061-344788); G,E,SC,SE,SLOVENE,R(R); Psychodiagnostics, Rhythmic Gymnastics, Management, Industrial Psychology, Creativity Training

*Blatnik, Uros V. (B.Sc.) Market Researcher; Bilecanska 5, Ljubljana, Yugoslavia 61110 (061-441-155); SLOVENE,SC,E,F,R,G(R); Alpine Skiing, Children, Football, Basketball

*Bosnar, Ksenija (M.A.) Assistant Professor; Faculty of Physical Culture, Dept. of Anthropology, Horvacanski Zavoj 15, Zagreb, R Hrvatska, Yugoslavia (41-336-822); E,R(R); Cognitive Abilities, Motor Abilties, Psychometrics

Lazarevic, Ljubisa L. (Ph.D.) Professor; Faculty of Physich Culture, B. Parovic 156, Belgrad, Yugoslavia (555-000); E,R(S); Personality, Motivation, Anxiety, Psychodiagnostics, Mental Preparation

Milojevic, Aleksander (M.A.) Assistant; Faculty of Philosophical Sciences, Dept. of Physical Culture, Cirila i Metodija 2, Nis, Blagoja, Yugoslavia 18000 (018-320-677); E,R,F; Intelligence, Human Relations, Motivation, Achievement, Stress

*Momirovic, Konstantin (Ph.D.) Professor; Faculty of Physical Culture, Dept. of Anthropology, Horvacanski Zavoj 15, Zagreb, Yugoslavia (3941-336-822); E,R,F; Statistics, Psychometrics, Judo, Personality, Motorics

Sabioncello, Nikola (Ph.D.) Assistant Professor; Faculty of Physical Culture, Dept. of Psychology, Horvacanski Zavoj 15, Zagreb, Yugoslavia (3941-312-433); G(R); Recreation, Personality, Motivation, Ergonomics

Robin S. Vealey

Robert S. Weinberg

Jean M. Williams

Craig A. Wrisberg

Leonard D. Zaichkowsky

Ljubisa L. Lazarevic

Name Index

Subject Index

About the Author

John Salmela is one of the most well-known sport psychologists in the world. His first edition of *The World Sport Psychology Sourcebook* helped to crystallize the international community of sport psychologists.

Dr. Salmela earned a PhD in motor behavior from the University of Alberta in 1972. He was president of the Canadian Psychomotor Learning and Sport Psychology Symposium (SCAPPS) from 1975 to 1977, and served on the Managing Council of the International Society of Sport Psychology (ISSP) from 1977 to 1985 and was vice president of the ISSP from 1985 to 1989. Dr. Salmela has also served as treasurer of ISSP.

He is a former Montreal and Quebec gymnastic champion, member of the 1968 Canadian intercollegiate gymnastic championship team, and president of the Canadian Intercollegiate Gymnastic Coaches Association. He has also served as a sport psychology consultant with the Canadian World and Olympic Gymnastic Teams since 1985.

Dr. Salmela is a prolific writer, editor, publisher, and international speaker on physical education, motor learning/performance, sport psychology, and gymnastics. He is a professor of sport psychology in the Department of Human Kinetics at the University of Ottawa.